Doubtful and dangerous

Manchester University Press

Politics, culture and society in early modern Britain

General Editors

DR ALEXANDRA GAJDA
PROFESSOR ANTHONY MILTON
PROFESSOR PETER LAKE
DR JASON PEACEY

This important series publishes monographs that take a fresh and challenging look at the interactions between politics, culture and society in Britain between 1500 and the mid-eighteenth century. It counteracts the fragmentation of current historiography through encouraging a variety of approaches which attempt to redefine the political, social and cultural worlds, and to explore their interconnection in a flexible and creative fashion. All the volumes in the series question and transcend traditional interdisciplinary boundaries, such as those between political history and literary studies, social history and divinity, urban history and anthropology. They thus contribute to a broader understanding of crucial developments in early modern Britain.

Recently published in the series

Chaplains in early modern England: Patronage, literature and religion
HUGH ADLINGTON, TOM LOCKWOOD and GILLIAN WRIGHT (eds)

The Cooke sisters: Education, piety and patronage in early modern England
GEMMA ALLEN

Black Bartholomew's Day DAVID J. APPLEBY

Insular Christianity ROBERT ARMSTRONG and TADHG Ó HANNRACHAIN (eds)

Reading and politics in early modern England GEOFF BAKER

'No historie so meete' JAN BROADWAY

Republican learning JUSTIN CHAMPION

News and rumour in Jacobean England: Information, court politics and diplomacy, 1618–25 DAVID COAST

This England PATRICK COLLINSON

Sir Robert Filmer (1588–1653) and the patriotic monarch CESARE CUTTICA

Brave community JOHN GURNEY

'Black Tom' ANDREW HOPPER

Impostures in early modern England: Representations and perceptions of fraudulent identities TOBIAS B. HUG

The politics of the public sphere in early modern England
PETER LAKE and STEVEN PINCUS (eds)

Henry Neville and English republican culture GABY MAHLBERG

Royalists and Royalism during the Interregnum JASON MCELLIGOTT and DAVID L. SMITH

Laudian and Royalist polemic in Stuart England ANTHONY MILTON

Full details of the series are available at www.manchesteruniversitypress.com.

Doubtful and dangerous

The question of succession
in late Elizabethan England

Edited by
SUSAN DORAN and PAULINA KEWES

Manchester
University Press

Published by Manchester University Press
Altrincham Street, Manchester M1 7JA, UK
www.manchesteruniversitypress.co.uk

British Library Cataloguing-in-Publication Data is available

Library of Congress Cataloging-in-Publication Data is available

ISBN 978 1 7849 9359 7 *paperback*

First published by Manchester University Press in hardback 2014

This edition first published 2016

Printed by Lightning Source

Queen Elizabeth I by an unknown artist (*ca* 1580).
By permission of Westminster School, London.

To the memory of
Patrick Collinson

Contents

Part V — Britain and beyond

Notes on contributors

Patrick Collinson, the pre-eminent historian of English Puritanism, was Regius Professor of Modern History at the University of Cambridge from 1988 to 1996, a Fellow of Trinity College, Cambridge, and a Fellow of the British Academy. His extensive body of work on the religious and political history of Elizabethan and early Stuart England continues to exert powerful influence. His final book, published posthumously, was *Richard Bancroft and Elizabethan Anti-Puritanism* (2013).

Alexander Courtney is the Head of History at the Haberdashers' Aske's Boys' School, Elstree. He took up the post in 2011, having previously taught at Tonbridge School, Kent, and the Perse School, Cambridge. He studied at Selwyn College, Cambridge, where he gained a double-starred first-class degree in History in 2003. He went on to undertake graduate study into aspects of Jacobean kingship and politics, obtaining degrees of M.Phil. in Early Modern History in 2004 and a Ph.D. in 2008.

Susan Doran is a Senior Research Fellow in History at Jesus College, Oxford. Her books include *Monarchy and Matrimony* (1993), *England and Europe in the Sixteenth Century* (1999), *The Tudor Chronicles* (2008) and *Elizabeth I and her Intimates* (forthcoming). She has also co-edited several volumes of essays and edited three exhibition catalogues.

Richard Dutton is a Humanities Distinguished Professor of English at Ohio State University. He has published widely on early modern drama, especially on censorship and authorship. His books include *Mastering the Revels: the Regulation and Censorship of English Renaissance Drama* (1991), *Licensing, Censorship and Authorship in Early Modern England: Buggeswords* (2000) and the edition of Jonson's *Epicene* (2003). His most recent publications are *The Oxford Handbook of Early Modern Theatre* (2009) and an edition of *Volpone* in the *Cambridge Ben Jonson* (2012). With Steven Galbraith he is preparing an edition of Thomas Drue's *The Duchess of Suffolk* and he is currently completing a monograph, *Shakespeare, Court Dramatist*.

Alexandra Gajda is John Walsh Fellow and Tutor in History at Jesus College, Oxford. She is the author of *The Earl of Essex and Late Elizabethan Political Culture* (2012) and of essays and articles on ideas and politics in late sixteenth- and early seventeenth-century England.

Arnold Hunt is a Curator of Historical Manuscripts at the British Library, and a Senior Research Fellow at King's College London. His book *The Art of Hearing: English Preachers and their Audiences 1590–1640* was published in 2010, and his current research focuses on religion and gesture in early modern England.

Paulina Kewes is a Fellow and Tutor in English Literature at Jesus College, Oxford. Her books include *Authorship and Appropriation: Writing for the Stage in England, 1660-1710* (1998), *This Great Matter of Succession: Politics, History, and Elizabethan Drama* (forthcoming) and, as editor or co-editor, *Plagiarism in Early Modern England* (2003), *The Uses of History in Early Modern England* (2006), and *The Oxford Handbook of Holinshed's* Chronicles (2013). She is a Co-Investigator on the AHRC-funded Stuart Successions project.

Peter Lake holds the position of University Distinguished Professor of Early Modern English History at Vanderbilt University. He taught previously at the universities of London and Princeton. He is currently working on a study of Shakespeare's histories and the politics of the 1590s and on turning his Ford lectures on 'Bad queen Bess? Libelous secret histories in an age of confessional conflict' into a book.

Richard A. McCabe is a Professor of English Language and Literature at Oxford University and a Fellow of Merton College. He was elected a Fellow of the British Academy in 2007. He currently holds a Major Leverhulme Research Fellowship (2011–14). He is author of *Joseph Hall: A Study in Satire and Meditation* (1982), *The Pillars of Eternity: Time and Providence in 'The Faerie Queene'* (1989), *Incest, Drama, and Nature's Law 1550–1700* (1993) and *Spenser's Monstrous Regiment: Elizabethan Ireland and the Poetics of Difference* (2002). He is the editor of the Penguin edition of Spenser's *Shorter Poems* (1999). Most recently he has edited the *Oxford Handbook of Edmund Spenser* (2010), and is currently working on a monograph on literary patronage.

Thomas M. McCoog, SJ, the sometime Director of Publications at the Jesuit Historical Institute (Rome), is currently the Archivist of the British Province of the Society of Jesus (London) and Curator of the Archives of Avery, Cardinal Dulles, at Fordham University (New York). He has published widely on British and Irish Jesuits. His most recent publication is *'And touching our society': Fashioning Jesuit Identity in Elizabethan England* (2013).

Michael Questier is a Professor of Early Modern English History at Queen Mary University of London. He has published widely on various aspects of post-reformation English Catholicism and is currently working on an overview volume on that subject and, in collaboration with Peter Lake, on the accession crisis of King James VI and I.

Rory Rapple is an Assistant Professor in the Department of History at the University of Notre Dame. He is the author of *Martial Power and Elizabethan Political Culture: Military Men in England and Ireland 1558–1594* (2009). He is currently working on a biography of Sir Humphrey Gilbert as well as on other topics to do with English political thinking in the sixteenth century.

R. Malcolm Smuts is a Professor Emeritus of the University of Massachusetts at Boston. His publications include *Court Culture and the Origins of a Royalist Tradition in England* (1987), *Culture and Power in England 1585–1685* (1999) and numerous articles on the political and cultural history of early modern England. He is currently engaged in a study of problems of religious instability in late Elizabethan and early Stuart Britain.

Blair Worden has taught at the universities of Oxford, Cambridge, Sussex, London and Chicago and is an Emeritus Fellow of St Edmund Hall, Oxford. His books include *The Sound of Virtue: Philip Sidney's 'Arcadia' and Elizabethan Politics* (1996), *Literature and Politics in Cromwellian England: John Milton, Andrew Marvell, Marchamont Nedham* (2007) and a series of studies of the political and religious history of the Puritan revolution.

Acknowledgements

Many friends and colleagues have provided encouragement, conversation and advice when this book was in the making. We have benefited from the support of the late Pat Collinson, Paul Hammer, Richard Proudfoot, Alex Walsham and Blair Worden. For comments on earlier drafts of Chapters 1 and 2, we are grateful to Tom Freeman, Norman Jones, Peter Marshall, Tom McCoog, Noel O'Sullivan, Malcolm Smuts and Arthur Williamson, and for research assistance to Tim Wales and Kelsey Jackson Williams, who has also compiled the index.

We wish to thank Jesus College Oxford for the award of a Major Research Grant which helped defray the cost of indexing the volume. Paulina Kewes also wishes to acknowledge the financial support of the Arts and Humanities Research Council, the British Academy, the English Faculty at the University of Oxford, and the Huntington Library, San Marino, California.

We are indebted to Dr Stephen Spurr, the Head Master of Westminster School, for giving us permission to use the school's portrait of Elizabeth I, and to the archivist Elizabeth Wells, for help with reproducing the image.

Our thanks also go to Manchester University Press, the series editors, and especially Emma Brennan for her patience and support.

Patrick Collinson was an inspiration for this study. Although we may on occasion take issue with some of his interpretations, we wish to acknowledge formally our debt to his luminous scholarship, and dedicate this collection to his memory.

Susan Doran and Paulina Kewes
9 March 2014

Abbreviations and conventions

AAW	Archives of the Archdiocese of Westminster
ABSI	Archivum Britannicum Societatis Iesu
APC	*Acts of the Privy Council of England*, ed. John Roche Dasent *et al.*, new series, 46 vols (London, 1890–1964)
ARSI	Archivum Romanum Societatis Iesu
ASV	Archivio Segreto Vaticano
BAV	Biblioteca Apostolica Vaticana
BL	British Library
Bodl	Bodleian Library
CJ	*Journal of the House of Commons 1547–1629* (London, 1802)
CJRC	*Correspondence of King James of Scotland with Sir Robert Cecil and Others in England*, ed. John Bruce, CS 78, first series (1861)
CS	Camden Society
CSPDom	*Calendar of the State Papers Domestic: Edward, Mary and Elizabeth, 1547–80*, ed. Robert Lemon (London, 1856) and *Elizabeth, 1601–3 with Addenda 1547–65*, ed. Mary Anne Everett Green (London, 1870)
CSPScot	*Calendar of the State Papers Relating to Scotland, and Mary, Queen of Scots, 1547–1603*, ed. Joseph Bain *et al.*, 13 vols in 14 parts (London, 1898–1969)
CSPSpan	*Calendar of Letters and Papers … Preserved Principally in the Archives of Simancas*, ed. Martin A. S. Hume, 4 vols (London, 1892–1899)
CSPVen	*Calendar of State Papers, Relating to English Affairs Existing in the Archives of Venice, and in other Libraries of Northern Italy*, ed. G. C. Bentinck *et al.*, 38 vols (London, 1864–1947)
CUL	Cambridge University Library
HMC	*Historical Manuscripts Commission*
HMC Sal	*Historical Manuscripts Commission, Calendar of the Manuscripts of the Most Honourable the Marquess of Salisbury*, 24 vols (London, 1883–1976)
ITL	Inner Temple Library
LPL	Lambeth Palace Library
NLS	National Library of Scotland.
NS	New Style date
ODNB	*Oxford Dictionary of National Biography* (www.oxforddnb.com/)
TLN	through-line numbering
TNA	The National Archives, Kew

NOTE ON DATES AND TEXTS

All dates used are Old Style unless otherwise indicated, but the New Year is taken to begin on 1 January rather than 25 March. Original spelling has been retained throughout except that contractions have been expanded.

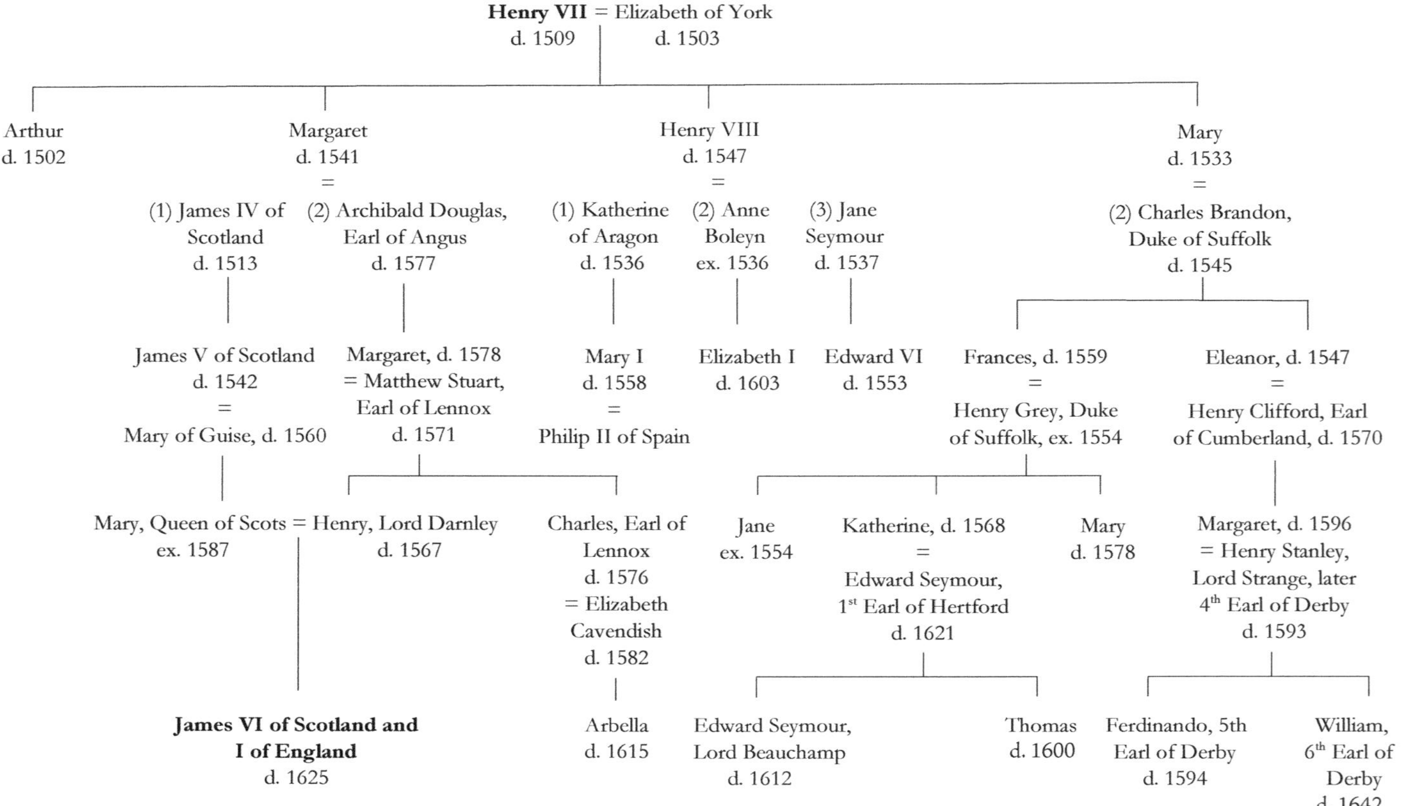

Genealogical chart 1 The Stuart and the Suffolk claims

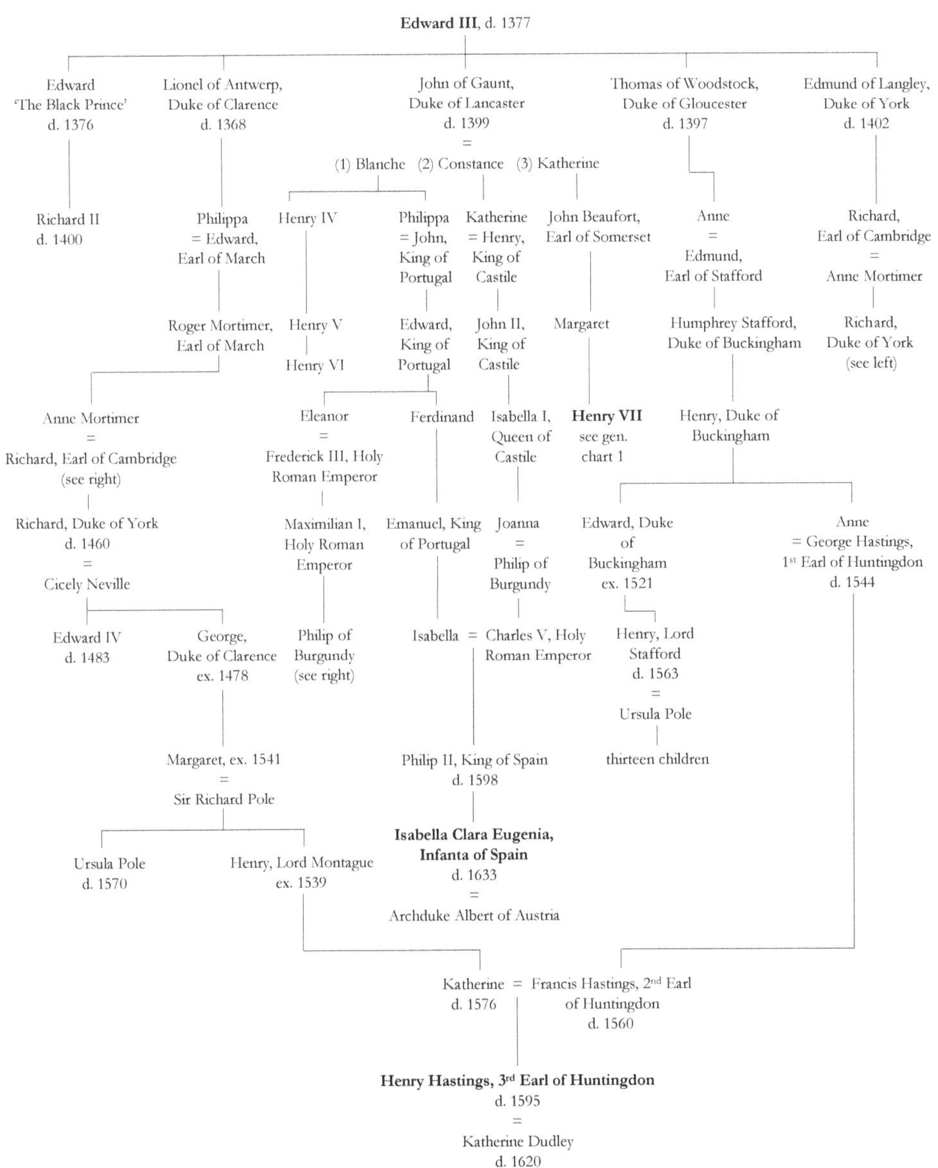

Genealogical chart 2 (*abridged*) The claims of Henry, third Earl of Huntingdon, and the Infanta of Spain

Part I

Contexts and approaches

Chapter 1

Introduction: a historiographical
perspective

Susan Doran and Paulina Kewes

Although the succession controversy during the earlier part of Elizabeth's
reign has long captured the interest of historians and literary scholars, the
period following Mary Stuart's execution has suffered from relative obscurity.
Our main aim in this book is to remedy this situation by examining the dominant part played by the succession issue during the 'long' 1590s from several
closely related perspectives. Individual essays explore the changing perceptions
of the rules of monarchical succession, the impact of confessional divisions,
the international and 'archipelagic' dimensions, the role of key political actors
(Elizabeth, James VI, Essex, Robert Cecil, Richard Bancroft), and the reverberations of the succession debate in pamphlet literature, imaginative writing,
sermons, and other printed and manuscript ephemera. The interdisciplinary
scope of the volume should, we hope, make it of particular interest to students
of both early modern British and Irish history and literature.

Our title, 'doubtful and dangerous', hints at why we consider that this later
period requires closer attention, coming as it does from the Catholic polemical
tract *Newes from Spayne and Holland* (1593). The purpose of its author, the
Jesuit Robert Persons, was to exploit the fears and suspicions about who
should be Queen Elizabeth's heir in order to destabilize the Protestant regime
and improve the chances of international support for a Catholic claimant.[1]
Persons would pursue this aim vigorously in his more ambitious and provocative pamphlet, *A Conference about the Next Succession to the Crowne of Inglande*
(1594/5). At around the same time, the Puritan MP Peter Wentworth used a
near-identical expression, emphasizing 'the doubtfulnesse and ambiguitie of
the title it self', in his tract designed to persuade the Queen to let parliament
come up with a settlement.[2] Persons and Wentworth were not just making

rhetorical points, but reflecting wider contemporary opinion. On both sides of the confessional frontier the succession was being viewed as vexed and divisive after the Catholic Mary Queen of Scots' execution in February 1587, just as it had been before.

Why should this be? Granted, before Mary's beheading Protestants had lived in terror of a Catholic restoration were she to take the throne, and grew ever more exasperated when Elizabeth refused to name a successor, to exclude Mary or to put her on trial for allegedly plotting in England. But with the Scottish Queen out of the picture, we might surely expect that their anxieties about England's future would be over. After all, her son James VI of Scotland, who had inherited the Stuart dynastic claim, was a Protestant. He was also male, an experienced ruler, and a pensioner of the English Queen. Yet, as this book argues, uncertainties and worries about the succession did not disappear with Mary's removal, and the outcome was far from predictable. Many late Elizabethans, not just a few committed Catholics, did not see the Scottish King as the incontrovertible heir or rally to his cause.[3]

First of all, James was not the only potential claimant; on the contrary, he had a disturbingly large number of rivals. By the mid-1590s, Persons named some sixteen possible heirs to Elizabeth.[4] In 1601, the civil lawyer Thomas Wilson identified twelve competitors who 'gape for' the death of the Queen: 'Thus you see', he declared, 'this crown is not like to fall to the ground for want of heads that claim to wear it, but upon whose head it will fall is by many doubted'.[5] Alongside James, the main contenders were Edward and Thomas Seymour, the sons of Katherine Grey of the Suffolk line; Arbella, the English Stuart from a cadet line; and the Infanta Isabella Clara Eugenia of Spain whose claim dated back to her fourteenth-century Lancastrian ancestor. Other plausible candidates were Ferdinando Stanley, briefly fifth Earl of Derby, from the cadet Suffolk line (until his sudden death in 1594) and Henry Hastings, third Earl of Huntingdon (who died childless in 1595), lineally descended from Edward III on both his mother's and his father's side (see genealogical charts 1 and 2). Bringing up the rear were the Duke of Parma and the Earl of Westmorland.

All these rival claims were problematic. Katherine Grey's sons and Huntingdon had the advantage of being English and Protestant, but the former were officially bastards and the latter was not descended from Henry VII. The elder Seymour, Edward Lord Beauchamp, had moreover married beneath him in the early 1580s. Born in 1575, Arbella Stuart was an inexperienced and unmarried young woman; Derby and Westmorland were Catholics; and the Infanta Isabella, also Catholic, had the further disadvantages of being female and a foreigner. Nonetheless, James's own position remained insecure. William Cecil Lord Burghley was rumoured to back Arbella's claim or that of Lord Beauchamp. Equally unsettling, as Thomas M. McCoog, SJ, argues in Chapter 13, there existed a real possibility that, with or without the pope's blessing, Spain or France or English Catholic exiles in cahoots with their co-religionists at home might back an alternative candidate: in 1593, for example, a Catholic plot was hatched in Flanders to assassinate Elizabeth and raise Derby to the throne; and throughout the 1590s English spies warned of conspiracies to seize Arbella and marry her to a foreign Catholic prince. At the same time (as will be seen in Paulina Kewes's Chapter 3), many godly Protestants in England were suspicious about the depth of James's commitment to 'true religion', given his troubled relationship with the Kirk and apparent willingness to tolerate Catholics in Scotland. Some Englishmen also voiced unease about the prospect of a foreign king, especially one from a nation that was the traditional enemy of England (see Susan Doran's Chapter 11). Finally, James faced legal impediments to his title (as discussed by Doran and Kewes in Chapter 2) that could be exploited by those who opposed his succession on other grounds. As a result of all these factors, the Elizabethan *fin de siècle* witnessed growing alarm that an internal power struggle would ensue upon the Queen's death which would attract foreign intervention, as had the recent war of succession in France about which a steady stream of news flowed from English presses.[6] Protestants were obsessively scared of the intrusion of Spain;[7] and during the later 1590s Catholics suspected that James would seek military support from the Protestant royal kin of his wife Anne of Denmark. Once again, we can see symmetry in the anxieties and conspiracy theories of the two rival confessions.

On account of these circumstances, James believed he needed Elizabeth's explicit endorsement of his title, preferably confirmed by parliament, to be sure of the crown. However, although the Queen evidently favoured his candidacy, she refused to recognize him formally as the heir apparent. Her reasons were political. Because she distrusted both the Scottish King and her own subjects, the succession could be employed as bait to keep James in line whenever his policies within Scotland appeared to be moving against English interests, whilst dynastic uncertainty, she hoped, would keep her subjects loyal and prevent them turning towards the rising sun. Nevertheless, Elizabeth carried out some practical measures to aid James's eventual take-over and weaken the position of his leading competitors. She ensured that the illegitimacy of Katherine Grey's sons was not revoked and had their father, the Earl of Hertford, briefly imprisoned in 1595 when he planned to challenge the ruling of a royal commission of enquiry that he had not legally married their mother. Arbella Stuart was left isolated in Derbyshire, unable to build up a following. Moreover, Elizabeth repeatedly told James that his mother's treason would not affect his title to the English throne. These reassurances, though, were insufficient to satisfy the King, and his ongoing efforts to advance his title meant that the succession remained very much a live issue.

All the more surprising, therefore, that a problem of such immediacy during the last sixteen years of the reign was accorded a disproportionately small amount of scholarly attention, at least until quite recently, by comparison with the extensive coverage of the preceding three decades (which, as we'll see, also demands reconsideration).

THE HISTORIOGRAPHY OF THE PRE-1587 SUCCESSION

Almost half a century ago, Mortimer Levine took up the topic in his pioneering study of the 1560s succession tracts, a work that is now seriously dated, not least because of its limited range of sources and mistaken conclusion that the problem was effectively resolved by 1571.[8] Since Levine, the significance of the succession has been acknowledged in wider surveys of Elizabethan history, politics, and literature, while many articles and some monographs have addressed specific aspects of the issue.

There is insufficient space here to mention all these secondary works, but a number are especially noteworthy. Marie Axton's book of 1977 alerted us to the influence of the medieval theory of the 'king's two bodies' on succession polemic and traced how contemporary drama engaged with the prospect of Elizabeth's death without either a child of her own or a proper settlement of the succession. Susan Doran's 1996 interdisciplinary study of Elizabeth's courtships inevitably tackled the succession as part of its analysis of dynastic and confessional politics.[9] Still more momentous were two of Patrick Collinson's essays that introduced the concepts of 'the Elizabethan exclusion crisis' and 'monarchical republic' into our historical lexicon. By coining the first term, Collinson emphasized 'the sustained concern of much of the "political nation"…to forestall the accession to the English throne of Mary Queen of Scots'.[10] This he saw as the predominant feature of Elizabethan politics until Mary's execution. By the second, Collinson meant extensive participation of Englishmen in local government and, more relevant for our purposes, a mindset of the governing elites which, he believed, was formed largely through fears that the Queen might die without a known heir. Dreading a power vacuum and, worse yet, the enthronement of a papist, suggested Collinson, royal councillors had to conceive of a political future without a monarch and, in consequence, devised unprecedented schemes, such as a conciliar interregnum, to prevent the worst happening.[11] Stephen Alford built on Collinson's insights in his account of the political creed and activities of Sir William Cecil – whom Collinson identified as the key architect of the 'monarchical republic' – by analysing Cecil's 1563 interregnum scheme designed to stave off the threat from the popish Mary, and drawing attention to the British dimension of the 1560s succession crisis.[12] More controversially,

Anne McLaren injected a strongly gendered perspective into the topic with her attempt to show that the 'crisis...conflated issues of monarchical authority, gender and confessional conviction'.[13] And, most recently, Peter Lake has deconstructed the rhetorical strategies of Protestant and Catholic polemicists from the 1560s through the 1580s, whose writings directly or indirectly impinged on the succession; and R. Malcolm Smuts has drawn attention to the government's recurrent resort to repression and organized violence against Catholics so as to prevent mobilization on behalf of a Catholic heir.[14]

This diverse body of work, however, tells only part of the story. None of the above studies brings together the different strands of the succession question, and none except Axton's spans the entire period from Elizabeth's accession until the execution of Mary Queen of Scots. In Chapter 2 of this book, therefore, we revisit the earlier Elizabethan succession issue, not only to set the scene for the later debates but also to offer a fresh and more rounded interpretation. We uniquely discuss various and interconnected facets of the problem: how it related to domestic, archipelagic and continental politics; how anxieties and solutions were presented in both parliament and public argument; and how that cross-confessional polemic deployed a wide range of forms and genres. Furthermore, we identify and examine the different phases of the succession crisis from the Queen's accession until the Spanish Armada, an approach that both allows readers to recognize continuities and changes over an extended time-frame and rejects the historiographical division of the reign into two. As far as the succession is concerned, there was no 'second reign of Elizabeth I' as identified by John Guy.[15] Rather, the problem mutated and evolved from 1558 till 1603, responding to shifts in political circumstances in Britain and on the Continent. Finally, in our revised narrative, we contest some other widely accepted interpretations, for example the perception of Cecil's radicalism in his abortive constitutional experiments.

THE HISTORIOGRAPHY OF THE POST-1587 SUCCESSION

The impact of the unsettled succession upon later Elizabethan politics was mostly neglected until the turn of the twenty-first century. The topic, for example, barely warranted a mention in the influential collection of essays, *The Reign of Elizabeth I*, edited in 1995 by John Guy.[16] Like most historians, Guy simply assumed that after Mary's death James VI's path to the English throne was untroubled and his elevation virtually unstoppable. Yet, several older studies had pointed to an alternative interpretation. For instance, Helen Georgia Stafford's 1940 monograph valuably disclosed James's insecurities and his 'frenzy of preparation' to win the eventual prize of the English throne.[17] And Joel Hurstfield's essay (first printed in 1961) discussed the entanglement of the succession with the factional politics of the late 1590s, and demonstrated that Burghley's son, Sir Robert Cecil, had been responsible for steering James towards a peaceful accession.[18] Despite the impeccable scholarship of both historians, the implications of their research were mostly ignored.

Thirty-four years after Hurstfield's article first appeared, a challenge to the conventional wisdom arose when Howard Nenner examined the principles of succession to the English crown throughout the 'long' seventeenth century, from the arrival of the Stuarts in 1603 until that of the Hanoverians in 1714. In his opening chapter, Nenner surveyed later Elizabethan succession tracts, demonstrating the contested nature of what he termed 'the right to be king', and openly questioning the inevitability of the Jacobean succession.[19] Although Nenner's analysis of this material was limited in scope and marred by some factual inaccuracies, it is nonetheless a pity that his monograph went largely unnoticed by students of the sixteenth century.[20] The major stimulus for a reassessment of the subject, therefore, only came with the impending quatercentenary of Elizabeth's death and James I's advent to the throne. To mark this occasion Jean-Christophe Mayer prepared a sourcebook containing abridgements of some of the later Elizabethan succession tracts, and convened at the University of Montpellier a colloquium entitled 'The Succession Struggle in England (1590–1604): Artistic Representations and Polemical Writings'.[21] The papers delivered there were published afterwards and some of them are cited in this volume.[22]

More generally, several methodological innovations within early-modern history have aided the revival of interest in the Elizabethan succession question, both early and late, and influenced the nature of the academic inquiries. The first of these was the New Catholic Historiography spearheaded by Alexandra Walsham, Thomas M. McCoog, SJ, Peter Lake and Michael Questier.[23] Thanks to their influence, the writings of Catholic polemicists – notably Robert Persons – and the activities of the English Catholic community at home and abroad were brought into the mainstream and situated alongside those of their Protestant counterparts. Consequently, we are now aware of how much the succession mattered to Catholics – whether recusants, church-papists, clerics or exiles – and how far they shaped the unfolding debates. We also appreciate that Catholics were in dialogue with Protestant propagandists, addressing many of the same issues and often adopting the same tropes. The essays collected in our volume variously build on this seminal scholarship. Persons's persistent endeavour to secure a Catholic future for England is one of its themes, while his most apposite work, *A Conference about the Next Succession*, is the starting-point of Peter Lake and Michael Questier's chapter and the end-point of Paulina Kewes's. Furthermore, Lake and Questier demonstrate that the dispute within the English Catholic community known as the Appellant or Archpriest controversy reveals a great deal about the confessional politics of incipient regime change. So too, albeit from a different angle, does Patrick Collinson who considers the Appellant controversy in his chapter on the hotly anti-Catholic – and no less hotly anti-Puritan – cleric Richard Bancroft. McCoog, meanwhile, shows that the identity of England's next ruler was of deep concern to English Catholic exiles, European Catholic monarchs and the papacy; and that Spain's eventual refusal to intervene could not be taken for granted.[24]

The second essential development in the discipline was the emergence of the New British History which stemmed from the recognition that England could not be safely studied in isolation from events in the other two realms of the archipelago, something that had been a matter of course for nineteenth-century historians such as Macaulay. Originally an approach associated with new research into seventeenth-century politics and the Civil War (duly renamed the Wars of the Three Kingdoms), the 'British' dimension soon proved fruitful when applied to the long-running problems of the English succession during the previous century. Alford took this on board in his monograph on William Cecil and the 1560s 'British' succession crisis;[25] and, in the 2003 Stenton Lecture, John Morrill – a leading proponent of the New British History – spoke of the interplay between the 'dynastic roulette' in England and state formation within the archipelago from 1500 to the mid-eighteenth century.[26] Doran was another who took up the British theme, when she investigated James's diplomatic and polemical endeavours to further his claim to be Elizabeth's heir and assessed their impact upon Anglo-Scottish relations after 1586.[27] In this volume, she turns to the cultural traffic between the two realms, examining the influence of English prejudices against the Scots on both the polemical exchanges of the 1590s and the union debates once James ascended the throne. And Kewes brings together religious and national priorities in her account of the changing attitudes of English and Scottish reformers and Catholics to the prospect of a Jacobean succession. Ireland is, of course, one of the three kingdoms, and too often ignored in studies of the later Elizabethan succession issue. David Edwards first uncovered James's contacts and manoeuvres in Ireland to advance his claim to the English (and Irish) thrones.[28] Here Rory Rapple takes a fresh look at Ireland in the 1590s to show how the imminent regime change shaped the conduct of both Hugh O'Neill and the Earl of Essex during the so-called Nine Years' War (sometimes called Tyrone's Rebellion) that took place between 1594 and 1603. And R. Malcolm Smuts explains how the British aspect of the succession and ultimate accession of the Scottish King intent on forging a closer union influenced the late Elizabethan and early Jacobean writings of the civil lawyer and historian Sir John Hayward.

Thirdly, the New Political History has also been instrumental in resurrecting the later Elizabethan succession question and facilitating a novel and more wide-ranging assessment. For a time – in the mid- to late-twentieth century

– the study of high politics became unfashionable, as historians turned away from what they saw as narrow political narratives in favour of broader social or cultural processes. However, from the 1990s onwards, scholars led by Patrick Collinson, John Guy, Paul E. J. Hammer, Peter Lake and Blair Worden expanded the study of national politics to encompass ideology (both religious and political) and its manifestations in literary and material culture.[29] In particular, we are now more attuned to the many and varied strategies adopted by the government (above all Burghley), its mouthpieces and freelance supporters, as well as its critics and enemies, in order to win over public opinion, especially at moments of crisis.[30] Public debate about the succession had been banned by act of parliament in 1571, but the wealth of textual evidence marshalled by our contributors highlights its astonishing vitality despite the official constraints.

Our volume has benefited from this broadening of perspective: no longer does the study of kings and queens appear dated. A preoccupation with political ideas that can be extrapolated from a variety of sources rarely used by older historians underpins many of the contributions. Constitutional principles relating to hereditary kingship and elective monarchy are the subject of Chapter 2, where we outline the shift in Protestant thought from elective solutions of a variety of kinds to not-quite-unadulterated legitimism – a process that paralleled the ascendancy among Protestant conformists of authoritarian conceptions of monarchical power since the early 1570s – and the opposite drift in direction by Catholics. In Chapter 6, Alexandra Gajda discusses the political thinking of the Earl of Essex that determined his view of the court politics leading up to the 1601 revolt; while in Chapter 7 Alexander Courtney analyses how the rhetoric of counsel shaped James VI's relationships with Elizabeth's courtiers.[31] And in the last chapter, Smuts charts the evolution of Hayward's thought and the wider intellectual currents of the period.

Meanwhile, the emergence of these historiographical trends – the New Catholic, the New British, and the New Political History – coincided with, and in some respects both shaped and subsequently drew on, a corresponding thematic and methodological shift in literary scholarship. The result has been a healthy burgeoning of interdisciplinary approaches to texts. Under what we might call a Post- or perhaps New-New Historicist dispensation, literature specialists have begun to produce increasingly sophisticated contextual readings of texts. Shakespeare, perhaps inevitably, has been at the forefront of this movement, though even his works are nowadays effectively scrutinized alongside those of his less august contemporaries. Besides, the range of genres garnering critical scrutiny has grown exponentially. Transcending the usual suspects – drama and poetry – it now routinely includes sermons, progress entertainments, Lord Mayor's Shows, historical chronicles, ballads, translations and so on. Students of literature, moreover, have turned their attention to Catholic works (Alison Shell, Molly Murray); national identity and 'archipelagic' writing (Andrew Hadfield, Christopher Highley, Philip Schwyzer, John Kerrigan); and the political implications of literary texts (Curtis Perry, Hadfield, Kewes).[32]

More germane to the theme of our book, literary scholars have long been sensitive to the resonance of anxieties about the succession in imaginative writing. Pioneering studies of Lily B. Campbell, David Bevington, and Marie Axton in the 1940s, 1960s, and 1970s respectively, have been followed in recent years by numerous essays exploring their oblique treatment by Shakespeare, Spenser and others.[33] Here Richard Dutton focuses on the multiple versions of *Hamlet*, and Richard A. McCabe on poems by Spenser, James VI himself and a host of lesser lights, to illuminate how imaginative writers coped with the constraints of censorship and how genre, formal properties and paratextual apparatus shaped the meanings of texts. In reconstructing topical allusions to the succession, Dutton draws on theatre history and textual variation, and McCabe on the presentational aspects of early-modern books such as, for instance, authorial commentary and annotation. There is definitely scope for further work along these lines, and we very much hope that our volume will boost such new research.

With disciplinary boundaries melting around us, however, the distinction between 'literary' and 'historical' types of enquiry, as also between the sorts of evidence used by each constituency, has become increasingly fluid and permeable. Thus, while the majority of contributors to this volume are historians by training, they are aware of the power of rhetorical tropes and generic conventions to inflect the 'message' of any text, and they employ a multitude of popular forms of writing alongside more traditional archival sources preserved in state papers and diplomatic correspondence. In Chapter 8, for example, Arnold Hunt scrutinizes sermons for references to the succession, and demonstrates how the wider public was engaged in matters normally regarded to be *arcana imperii*. In doing so, Hunt analyses closely the language and structure of the homilies. And in Chapter 2, Doran and Kewes, a historian and a literary critic respectively, join forces in traversing all manner of material; while in their solo pieces each ventures to cross over to 'the other side' so to speak. The book as a whole looks at a wide variety of evidence to explain how politicians, pamphleteers, imaginative writers and divines conceived the succession problem, grappled with the objections to James's title and sought to reconcile confessional and political concerns with the claims of blood and statute law. In the process, we trust that the volume corrects a number of myths about James and the succession, allowing us to see England's first Stuart king-in-waiting – and how contemporaries saw him – in a rather new and unexpected light.

SIGNIFICANCES

Our book reinforces the view that political actors and writers across the confessional spectrum did not accept the Jacobean succession as a done deal but on the contrary either advanced or contested it passionately. Furthermore, it confirms Morrill's declaration that the contingency of past events is acutely relevant to the history of political dynasties in the early-modern period. The fertility of monarchs (or their partners) as well as the fragile hold on life of heirs always determined the course of hereditary successions and could have a decisive impact on wider political life. In the 'long' 1590s contingency played a vital role.

James VI of Scotland *did* succeed Elizabeth, and it is incumbent on a book such as this one to explain how and why that came to pass, but at the same time we should not lose sight of alternative possibilities. Hence we need to balance the benefit of hindsight against counterfactual scenarios. What would have happened, for example, had James died before Elizabeth, especially if his death had occurred prior to the birth of his son, Prince Henry, in 1594? Who would have been England's next monarch? And, what if Ferdinando, Earl of Derby, had not died (possibly by poison) in 1594? Would English Catholics and Philip III of Spain have rallied around him in 1603 as the best candidate to back? What might have occurred if Philip II had listened to English Catholic exiles such as Persons and intervened in the English succession after his hopes in France had crumbled? It was only because events such as these did not actually happen and because Sir Robert Cecil changed tack after the Essex rising that England had no war of succession and James took the crown without any opposition in 1603.

Once a disputed succession had been settled, people tended to jump on the bandwagon of the successful candidate, or at least to keep quiet about their misgivings, making the outcome seem more inevitable than it actually was. This is evident in the orchestration of James's proclamation and arrival in England in 1603 and the outpouring of gratulatory addresses and poems. Modern scholars have perhaps been taken in by this showmanship. And they have too readily inferred that everyone believed in James's hereditary title to the English crown, which the King paraded in his first speech to parliament in March 1604 and which was swiftly reaffirmed in the Act of Recognition.[34] Yet a different, far less orthodox construction surfaced in the severely contested 1614 Parliament. Opposed to the royal impositions, some MPs reportedly dared to argue that James was in fact a king not only 'by blood' but also by election 'because in passing from Scotland to England he was called and to some extent chosen'.[35]

Our volume focuses tightly on one historical issue over a relatively short time-scale, but from a variety of viewpoints and perspectives. This enables readers to appreciate how anxieties about individual claimants, and fears that

England might succumb to a civil war, foreign conquest or both, informed much of the writing and culture of the 'long' 1590s. At the same time, we fully recognize that the question of succession had much wider ramifications and demonstrate that it was not a new preoccupation of the *fin de siècle*. Of course, Mary Queen of Scots' execution was a decisive event, but its impact should not be exaggerated. Even after 1587, the politics and polemics of succession underwent different phases, which can be marked out by the watersheds of the Armada, the publication of Persons's *A Conference* and the 1601 Essex rebellion.

What of the longer-term significance of the constitutional issues discussed in our book? Disagreements about the relative merits of hereditary right, royal nomination, election by parliament (with or without the monarch at the helm) or statutory limitations on the succession were confined neither to the Elizabethan era nor even to the 'long' sixteenth century. Such debates had been a feature of earlier periods, but they were revitalized and more fully articulated from the 1530s onward due to Henry VIII's inability to sire a son by his first wife and his failure to produce a male sibling for his heir. Henry created a legal quagmire with his three Succession Acts (1534, 1536 and 1544) and his extraordinary will of 1546 that ignored the progeny of his elder sister. Soon afterwards, Edward VI's attempt to change the succession by letters patent and Mary's toying with the idea of excluding her heretical and bastard half-sister from the crown raised further questions about what was legally and politically possible.

The accession of James I failed to provide a lasting resolution, and controversies over the succession continued into the seventeenth and eighteenth centuries. Notable challenges to the principle of indefeasible hereditary right, so strongly asserted by James, occurred several times during the Stuart period. In 1649, monarchy was overthrown and replaced with a republic after the execution of Charles I, while the restoration of kingly rule in the person of Charles II could not take place until 1660 and even then seemed an astounding development to contemporaries. In the late 1670s and early 1680s some predominantly Whig MPs and Lords attempted to exclude the Catholic James Duke of York from the succession by statute. In 1688, strict hereditary principles were waived when James II's Protestant daughter Mary and her husband William of Orange were jointly given the crown by parliament in preference to James's Catholic infant son or even Mary alone. In 1701 the Act of Settlement successfully excluded all Catholics from inheriting the throne and laid down principles of succession that allowed the accession in 1714 of the first Hanoverian, George I, whose family descended from Charles I's sister, Elizabeth.

During these succession crises, the tracts of Elizabethan polemicists were given an unexpected afterlife when they came into print for the first time: *inter alia* the anonymous 1565 piece *Allegations in behalf of … Mary … Queen of Scots* in 1690; Thomas Craig's 1602 'De Jure Successionis Regni Angliae, Libri Duo' translated into English in 1703; and John Hales's 1565 *A Declaration of the Succession of the Crown Imperial of England* in 1713.[36] An abridged edition of the first part of Persons's *A Conference*, meanwhile, appeared in 1648 during the second Civil War and an abbreviated adaptation of both parts in 1655 under the Cromwellian Protectorate; tellingly, the tract was later reprinted *in toto* in 1681 at the height of the Exclusion Crisis.[37] Indeed, defenders of legitimism in the later Stuart period found themselves repeatedly engaging with the arguments found in that Elizabethan text and its Presbyterian and then Whig appropriations. The AHRC-funded Stuart Successions project is already bringing to light further polemical tracts as well as other writing which demonstrate that the succession remained of crucial importance in the political and literary culture of the 'long' seventeenth century.[38]

These are some of the reasons why Collinson's memorable concept of the Elizabethan exclusion crisis needs some modification. The Protestant justifications and machinations to exclude Mary were not, as he suggests, simply a dress rehearsal for the crisis in Charles II's reign. Exclusion recurred many times during the sixteenth and seventeenth centuries as a political expedient to prevent unwanted successions. Protestants tried unsuccessfully to exclude Henry VIII's elder daughter Mary (and, by default, Elizabeth)[39] as well as Mary Queen of Scots; Catholics would have liked to exclude Elizabeth; some – but far from all – Anglicans turned to the tool again in the later seventeenth century to ensure a Protestant succession.

Early-modern Britain was not unique in its experience of succession crises. Monarchies on the Continent were equally prey to such phenomena and for similar reasons: the break in direct male descent, unclear hereditary laws and, in some places, confessional divisions. Sometimes disputes could be resolved peacefully, but calamitous wars of succession erupted in numerous European countries, including Portugal after the death of the childless king Cardinal Henry in 1580, France on the assassination of Henry III in 1589, Jülich-Cleves-Berg in 1609, Bohemia in 1618, Spain in 1701 and Austria in 1740. However, the British experience was different from the European one. Only in Britain were rules of succession elaborated and changed to reflect the religion of the established Church.[40]

As a final point, this book underlines the centrality of monarchy in the political thought of the early-modern period. It suggests that the first word in Collinson's 'monarchical republic' carries far more weight than the second. In his 1987 essay, Collinson had correctly pointed out that in the sixteenth century commitment to a commonwealth or *res publica* did not necessarily exclude monarchism, and he was disconcerted by some scholars extending the word 'republic' beyond his original, playful meaning.[41] Collinson took a minimalist view of the 'monarchical republic', cautiously suggesting that at moments of succession crisis an inner core of councillors considered constitutional experiments, the full implications of which they would not normally have articulated, that revealed a vision of the English polity as potentially elective and capable of existing in the short term without a monarch. Later on, though, several historians and students of literature, notably Markku Peltonen and Andrew Hadfield, expanded the concept beyond Collinson's carefully circumscribed sense, announcing that they found 'republican' strands in the Elizabethan *mentalité* and political thought that are simply not there.[42] Regarding the succession – Collinson's starting-point – our contributors show that there was not a republican in sight. Elizabethan statesmen, clerics and writers were evidently exercised by the problem of the royal succession, but in seeking ways to protect religion and the state, they sought also to perpetuate monarchical rule. Cecil and his humanist colleagues neither promoted non-monarchical solutions nor countenanced converting 'England from a hereditary monarchy into an elective one like Poland', as Edward Vallance has maintained.[43] All their proposed constitutional remedies were designed to put another monarch on the throne as quickly, painlessly and legitimately as possible in the hope that the new dynasty would endure.

NOTES

1 ([Antwerp,] 1593), fo. 35^r. For the attribution of *Newes* to Persons, see A. F. Allison and D. M. Rogers, *The Contemporary Printed Literature of the English Counter-Reformation between 1558 and 1649*, 2 vols (Aldershot, 1989–1994), vol. 2, p. 124. It has been suggested that Persons may have collaborated with either Henry or Richard Walpole or Richard Verstegan, but this is unproven; we stick with the traditional attribution because of similarities between the views expressed in *Newes* and Persons's views expressed elsewhere. On the Jesuit's likely debt to intelligence supplied by Verstegan, see Peter J. Holmes, 'Robert Persons and an unknown political pamphlet of 1593', *Recusant History*, 17 (1985), 341–7 (esp. pp. 345–6).

2 Peter Wentworth, *A Pithie Exhortation to her Maiestie for Establishing her Successor to the Crowne Whereunto is added a Discourse Containing the Authors Opinion of the True and Lawfull Successor to Her Maiestie* ([Edinburgh,] 1598), p. 48 (1st pag.). The tract was composed in 1587, after Mary's beheading, and circulated in surreptitious scribal copies until its publication in 1598. For further discussion, see Chapter 3 in this volume.

3 Even Puritans were hardly unanimous in their support for James, *pace* Nicholas Tyacke's 'Puritan politicians and King James VI and I, 1587–1604', in Thomas Cogswell, Richard Cust, and Peter Lake (eds), *Politics, Religion and Popularity in Early Stuart Britain: Essays in Honour of Conrad Russell* (Cambridge, 2002), pp. 21–44 (esp. pp. 22–3).

4 R. Doleman [Robert Persons], *A Conference about the Next Succession to the Crowne of Ingland* ([Antwerp], 1594 [1595], esp. pp. 84ff. (2nd pag.); cf. *Newes*, fos 35^v–36^r.

5 *The State of England, Anno Dom. 1600*, ed. F. J. Fisher, Camden Miscellany, 16, 3rd series, no. 52 (London, 1936), pp. 2, 5.

6 Lisa Ferraro Parmelee, *Good Newes from Fraunce: French Anti-League Propaganda in Late Elizabethan England* (Rochester, NY, 1996).

7 As is shown by the policy pursued by Burghley: see Glyn Parry, *The Arch-conjuror of England: John Dee* (New Haven, CT, and London, 2011), esp. ch. 19.

8 Mortimer Levine, *The Early Elizabethan Succession Question, 1558–1568* (Stanford, CA, 1966).

9 Marie Axton, *The Queen's Two Bodies: Drama and the Elizabethan Succession* (London, 1977); Susan Doran, *Monarchy and Matrimony: The Courtships of Elizabeth I* (London, 1996).

10 Patrick Collinson, 'The Elizabethan exclusion crisis and the Elizabethan polity', *Proceedings of the British Academy*, 84 (1994), 51–92, p. 51.

11 Patrick Collinson, 'The monarchical republic of Queen Elizabeth I', *Bulletin of the John Rylands University Library of Manchester*, 69 (1987), 394–424, repr. in Collinson, *Elizabethan Essays* (London, 1994), pp. 31–56, and in John Guy (ed.), *The Tudor Monarchy* (London, 1997), pp. 110–34.

12 *Ibid.*

13 Anne McLaren, 'The quest for a king: gender, marriage, and succession in Elizabethan England', *Journal of British Studies*, 41 (2002), 259–90; Anne McLaren, 'Political ideas: two concepts of the state', in Susan Doran and Norman Jones (eds), *The Elizabethan World* (London, 2011), 92–112. See also Victoria de la Torre, '"We few of an infinite multitude": John Hales, parliament, and the gendered politics of the early Elizabethan succession', *Albion*, 33 (2001), 557–82.

14 Peter Lake, Ford Lectures, University of Oxford, 2011; R. Malcolm Smuts, 'Organized violence in the Elizabethan monarchical republic', *History*, forthcoming, and his book-in-progress on *State Formation, Political Culture and the Problem of Religious War: Britain 1580–1610*. See also Neil Younger, 'Securing the monarchical republic: the remaking of the lord lieutenancies in 1585', *Historical Research*, 84 (2010), 249–65. We are grateful to Peter for sending us copies of two of the Ford Lectures, and to Malcolm for the article and book chapters.

15 John Guy (ed.), *The Reign of Elizabeth I: Court and Culture in the Last Decade* (Cambridge, 1995).

16 *Ibid.*

17 Helen Georgia Stafford, *James VI of Scotland and the Throne of England* (New York and London, 1940), pp. 196–7. Also important was J. E. Neale's 1924 article which chronicled the changing views of the Puritan MP Peter Wentworth ('Peter Wentworth: II', *English Historical Review*, 39 (1924), 175–205), and which informs Neale's discussion of the succession in his study of Elizabeth's parliaments (J. E. Neale, *Elizabeth I and Her Parliaments*, 3 vols (London, 1953–58), vol. 2, pp. 251–66).

18 Joel Hurstfield, 'The succession struggle in late Elizabethan England', in S. T. Bindoff, Joel Hurstfield and C. H. Williams (eds), *Elizabethan Government and Society: Essays Presented to Sir John Neale* (London, 1961), pp. 369–96, reprinted in his *Freedom, Corruption and Government in Elizabethan England* (London, 1973), pp. 104–34.

19 Howard Nenner, *The Right to be King: The Succession to the Crown of England, 1603–1714* (Chapel Hill, NC, 1995), esp. pp. 13–25.

20 For instance, Nenner's work is neglected by McLaren; he did, however, influence

Doran, as can be seen in her 'Revenge her foul and most unnatural murder? The impact of Mary Stewart's execution on Anglo-Scottish relations', *History*, 85 (2000), 589–61.

21 Jean-Christophe Mayer, *Breaking the Silence on the Succession: A Sourcebook of Manuscripts and Rare Texts* (Montpellier, 2003).

22 Jean-Christophe Mayer (ed.), *The Succession Struggle in Late Elizabethan England: Politics, Polemics and Cultural Representations* (Montpellier, 2004).

23 Among others: Alexandra Walsham, *Church Papists: Catholicism, Conformity and Confessional Polemic in Early Modern England* (Woodbridge, 1993); Thomas M. McCoog, SJ, *The Society of Jesus in Ireland, Scotland, and England, 1541–1588:'Our Way of Proceeding?'* (Leiden, 1996); Michael Questier, 'The politics of religious conformity and the accession of James I', *Historical Research*, 71 (1998), 14–30; Peter Lake, 'Anti-popery: the structure of a prejudice', in Richard Cust and Ann Hughes (eds), *Conflict in Early Stuart England: Studies in Religion and Politics 1603–1642* (Harlow, 1989), pp. 72–106; and Peter Lake, 'The King, (the Queen) and the Jesuit: James Stuart's *True Law of Free Monarchies* in context/s', *Transactions of the Royal Historical Society*, 6th series, 14 (2004), 243–60. More recently, see Ethan H. Shagan (ed.), *Catholics and the 'Protestant Nation': Religious Politics and Identity in Early Modern England* (Manchester, 2005); Victor Houliston, *Catholic Resistance in Elizabethan England: Robert Persons's Jesuit Polemic, 1580–1610* (Aldershot, 2007).

24 Paul C. Allen, *Philip III and the Pax Hispanica, 1598–1621: The Failure of Grand Strategy* (New Haven, CT, and London, 2000), pp. 26 *passim*.

25 Stephen Alford, *The Early Elizabethan Polity: William Cecil and the British Succession Crisis* (Cambridge, 1998).

26 John Morrill, *'Uneasy Lies the Head that Wears a Crown': Dynastic Crises in Tudor and Stewart Britain 1504–1746*, The Stenton Lecture 2003 (Reading, 2005), p. 14.

27 Susan Doran, 'Three late-Elizabethan succession tracts', in Mayer, *Succession Struggle*, pp. 100–117; Susan Doran, 'Loving and affectionate cousins? The relationship between Elizabeth I and James VI of Scotland 1586–1603', in Susan Doran and Glenn Richardson (eds), *Tudor England and Its Neighbours* (Basingstoke, 2005), pp. 203–34; Susan Doran, 'James VI and the English succession', in Ralph Houlbrooke (ed.), *James VI and I: Ideas, Authority, and Government* (Aldershot, 2006), pp. 25–42. See also Glenn Burgess, 'Becoming English? Becoming British? The political thought of James VI & I before and after 1603', in Mayer, *Succession Struggle*, pp. 143–75; Jenny Wormald, 'O Brave New World? The union of England and Scotland in 1603', Joint British Academy/Royal Society of Edinburgh Special Lecture, 24 March 2003, British Academy Publications Online.

28 David Edwards, 'Securing the Jacobean succession: the secret career of James Fullerton of Trinity College, Dublin', in S. Duffy (ed.), *The World of the Gallowglass* (Dublin, 2007), pp. 188–219.

29 Among others: Collinson's *De Republica Anglorum: Or, History with the Politics Put Back: Inaugural Lecture delivered 9 November 1989* (Cambridge, 1990); Guy (ed.), *Tudor Monarchy*; Paul E. J. Hammer, *The Polarisation of Elizabethan Politics: The Political Career of Robert Devereux, 2nd Earl of Essex, 1585–1597* (Cambridge, 1999); Blair Worden, *The Sound of Virtue: Philip Sidney's Arcadia and Elizabethan Politics* (New Haven, CT, and London, 1996); Peter Lake with Michael Questier, *The Antichrist's Lewd Hat: Protestants, Papists and Players in Post-Reformation England* (New Haven, CT, and London, 2002).

See also Natalie Mears, 'Court, courtiers, and culture in Tudor England', *Historical Journal*, 46 (2003), 703–22.

30 Alford, *Burghley*; Peter Lake and Michael Questier, 'Puritans, papists, and the "public sphere" in early modern England: The Edmund Campion affair in context', *The Journal of Modern History*, 72 (2000), 587–627; Peter Lake, 'The politics of "popularity" and the public sphere: the "monarchical republic" of Elizabeth I defends itself', in Peter Lake and Steven Pincus (eds), *The Public Sphere in Early Modern England* (Manchester, 2007), pp. 59–94; Lake's forthcoming Ford Lectures; Glyn Parry, 'The monarchical republic and magic: William Cecil and the exclusion of Mary Queen of Scots', *Reformation*, 17 (2012), 29–47.

31 For a broader account of the Earl's mental world, see Alexandra Gajda's *The Earl of Essex and Late Elizabethan Political Culture* (Oxford, 2012); of James's correspondence and its role in smoothing his accession, see Alexander Courtney, 'The Accession of James VI to the English Throne, 1601–1603' (M. Phil., University of Cambridge, 2004).

32 To name but a few, Alison Shell, *Catholicism, Controversy and the English Literary Imagination, 1558–1660* (Cambridge, 1999); Molly Murray, *The Poetics of Conversion in Early Modern English Literature* (Cambridge, 2009); Andrew Hadfield, *Literature, Politics and National Identity: Reformation to Renaissance* (Cambridge, 1994); Christopher Highley, *Catholics Writing the Nation in Early Modern Britain and Ireland* (Oxford, 2008); John Kerrigan, *Archipelagic English: Literature, History, and Politics 1603–1707* (Oxford, 2008); Curtis Perry, *Literature and Favoritism in Early Modern England* (Cambridge, 2006); and Paulina Kewes, '"A fit memoriall for the times to come …": admonition and topical application in Mary Sidney's *Antonius* and Samuel Daniel's *Cleopatra*', *Review of English Studies*, 63 (2012), 243–64.

33 Lily B. Campbell, *Shakespeare's 'Histories': Mirrors of Elizabethan Policy* (San Marino, CA, 1947); David Bevington, *Tudor Drama and Politics: A Critical Approach to Topical Meaning* (Cambridge, MA, 1968); Axton, *Queen's Two Bodies*. Recent studies include: Robert Lane, '"The sequence of posterity": Shakespeare's *King John* and the succession controversy', *Studies in Philology*, 92 (1995), 460–81; Jason Scott-Warren, *Sir John Harington and the Book as Gift* (Oxford, 2001) and 'Harington's gossip', in Susan Doran and Thomas S. Freeman (eds), *The Myth of Elizabeth* (Basingstoke, 2003), pp. 221–41; Andrew Hadfield, 'Spenser and the Stuart succession', *Literature and History*, 13 (2004), 9–24; Stuart M. Kurland, '*Hamlet* and the Scottish succession?', *Studies in English Literature*, 34 (1994), 279–300; Ronald Knowles, 'The political contexts of deposition and election in Edward II', *Medieval and Renaissance Drama in England*, 14 (2001), 105–21; Jean-Christophe Mayer, *Shakespeare's Hybrid Faith: History, Religion, and the Stage* (Basingstoke, 2006); Paulina Kewes, 'History plays and the royal succession', in Paulina Kewes, Ian W. Archer and Felicity Heal (eds), *The Oxford Handbook of Holinshed's Chronicles* (Oxford, 2013), pp. 493–509. Note that Lisa Hopkins's *Drama and the Succession to the Crown, 1561–1633* (Aldershot, 2011) suffers from poor grasp of context and simplistic readings of plays.

34 'A Proclamation, declaring the undoubted Right of our Soveraigne Lord King James, to the Crowne of the Realmes of England, Fraunce and Ireland', 24 March 1603, in James F. Larkin and Paul L. Hughes (eds), *Stuart Royal Proclamations*, 2 vols (Oxford, 1973), vol. 1, pp. 1–4; 'Speech to parliament of 19 March 1604', in Johann P. Sommerville (ed.), *King James VI and I: Political Writings* (Cambridge, 1994), pp. 132–46; 1 Jac. I, c. 1: 'A Moste joyfull and juste Recognition of the immediate lawfull and undoubted Succession Descent and Righte of the Crowne', in *The Statutes of the Realm*, 4, pt. 2, pp. 1017–18.

35 Antonio Foscarini, Venetian Ambassador in England, to the Doge and Senate, 27 June 1614, *CSPVen*, 13, p. 138.

36 *Allegations*, in appendix to William Attwood, *The Fundamental Constitution of the English Government Proving King William and Queen Mary our Lawful and Rightful King and Queen* (London, 1690); Thomas Craig, 'De Jure', transl. and pub. by James Gadderar as *Concerning the Right of Succession to the Kingdom of England, Two Books* (London, 1703); Hales, *Declaration*, in appendix VIII to *A Declaration of the Succession of the Crown Imperial of England*, in George Harbin, *The Hereditary Right of the Crown of England Asserted* (London, 1713).

37 *Severall Speeches Delivered At a Conference concerning the Power of Parliament, to proceed* [sic] *against their King for Misgovernment*, ed. Henry Walker (London, 1648); *A Treatise Concerning the Broken Succession of the Crown of England: Inculcated, about the later end of the Reign of Queen Elisabeth. Not Impertinent for the better Compleating of the General Information Intended* (London, 1655); *A Conference About the Next Succession to the Crown of England: Divided into Two Parts* (n.p. 1681).

38 For further information about this project and the publicly accessible database of Stuart succession literature, see http://stuarts.exeter.ac.uk.

39 See Paulina Kewes, 'The exclusion crisis of 1553 and the Elizabethan succession', in Susan Doran and Thomas S. Freeman (eds), *Mary Tudor: Old and New Perspectives* (Basingstoke, 2011), pp. 49–61.

40 We would like to thank Thomas Freeman for a helpful discussion of this point.

41 See his Afterword in John F. McDiarmid (ed.), *The Monarchical Republic of Early Modern England: Essays in Response to Patrick Collinson* (Aldershot, 2007), pp. 245–60.

42 Markku Peltonen, *Classical Humanism and Republicanism in English Political Thought, 1570–1640* (Cambridge, 1995), and his two essays: 'Citizenship and republicanism in Elizabethan England', in Martin van Gelderen and Quentin Skinner (eds), *Republicanism: A Shared European Heritage*, 1: *Republicanism and Constitutionalism in Early Modern Europe* (Cambridge, 2002), pp. 85–106, and 'Rhetoric and citizenship in the monarchical republic of Queen Elizabeth I', in McDiarmid (ed.), *The Monarchical Republic*, pp. 109–27; Andrew Hadfield, *Shakespeare and Republicanism* (Cambridge, 2005). For Lake's critique, see Peter Lake, 'The monarchical republic of Queen Elizabeth I (and the fall of Archbishop Grindal) revisited', in McDiarmid (ed.), *The Monarchical Republic*, pp. 129–47.

43 Edward Vallance, 'Loyal or rebellious? Protestant associations in England 1584–1696?', *The Seventeenth Century*, 17 (2002), 1–23 (esp. 4), a claim repeated in Vallance's *Revolutionary England and the National Covenant: State Oaths, Protestantism, and the Political Nation, 1553–1682* (Woodbridge, 2005), p. 25.

Chapter 2

The earlier Elizabethan succession question revisited

Susan Doran and Paulina Kewes

The succession issue was subject to many twists and turns during Elizabeth's reign, and it is therefore misleading to treat it as a single crisis or even as two, the first ending with the execution of Mary Queen of Scots in February 1587 and the second with the accession of James I in March 1603. In this chapter, we explain the shifts in the political actions and polemical output of both Protestants and Catholics during the early and middle decades of the reign. Hence, we contextualize the 'long' 1590s – the main subject of this book – when again there were distinctive phases and characteristics.

We do more than that, however. Throughout the chapter, we extend or challenge the current historiography. By using a broader range of archival and printed sources, we bring to the fore neglected arguments about the idea of monarchical election. In situating the succession debates within the wider political environment, we emphasize the impact of Anglo-Scottish relations – especially the various negotiations for the restoration of Mary to the Scottish throne – on parliamentary proceedings and polemical literature. By looking at the whole confessional spectrum, we demonstrate that religious beliefs did not necessarily determine positions taken on the succession during the first decade of the reign, but that the two confessions became politically polarized over the issue during its middle decades, even though at a community and personal level, the boundary between Protestants and Catholics of various stripes remained fluid and permeable. Overall, we show that there was more to the succession question before February 1587 than just the exclusion of the Catholic claimant, Mary Stuart. That is why, after her death, the succession remained disputed. Methodologically, our approach is holistic and interdisciplinary, as we combine the perspectives of political history, confessional history, political thought, and literary studies.

1558–68: POSITIONS IN FLUX

The prevailing narrative of the 1560s tells how Protestant Privy Councillors, MPs and polemicists – with Sir William Cecil at the helm – tried to persuade or browbeat the Queen into either naming a Protestant heir or allowing some statutory settlement that would prevent Mary's accession. Resisting their manoeuvres, Elizabeth is seen as standing alone in her grim determination to keep the succession undecided, her attitude moulded by fears that a named heir would endanger her authority.[1] Yet, for much of the 1560s, the succession was a highly divisive issue that did not always follow predictable confessional lines, while the debates in parliament and the public media focused on legal and constitutional principles rather than on a particular candidate's religion. As for Elizabeth, her approach to the succession question was more flexible than has yet been recognized, and shaped as much by her Anglo-Scottish diplomacy as by concerns about her political power and security.

It is true that the Protestant 'political nation' was united in its fears about an uncertain succession. Equally true, during the first few years of the reign, everyone wanted the Queen to marry and produce an heir of her own body, preferably male. Elizabeth's rejection of some dozen suitors and her near-fatal attack of smallpox in October 1562, however, changed the focus of concerns. Yes, all still agreed that the ideal solution for the future would be for the Queen to marry and deliver healthy sons, but the possibility of her dying childless had to be confronted. To avoid civil war, usurpation or a foreign invasion the 'political nation' accepted that an heir presumptive needed naming, both as an interim measure until Elizabeth bore a child and as a fall-back position in case she never did. But there the unanimity ended. Divisions soon arose over the four most important questions involved in bringing this about: what principles of succession should be followed; who had the best right according to those principles; who should make the decision; and finally, how to implement it.

Much of the debate centred on the principles of succession. English laws and customs on the matter were far from clear-cut. It was uncertain whether or not a foreigner could succeed to the crown, since common law prohibited aliens from inheriting property, and a statute of 1351 (25 Edward III) excluded from the succession those born outside the monarch's allegiance. Even more confusingly, the same statute exempted from its provisions the *'enfants du roi'* but left vague whether the wording referred just to Edward III's children or to the royal family in general.[2] Another problem concerned bastardy. As the fifteenth-century common lawyer John Fortescue had explained, 'to the childe borne out of matrimonye the lawe of Englande alloweth no succession' even though civil law 'geveth unto it succession in ye parents' inheritance'.[3] Yet in 1544, Henry VIII had contravened common law and placed his bastard daughters in the line of succession by statute, and Elizabeth – still legally a bastard – was now sitting on the throne. Given that several potential heirs also had the stain of bastardy in their line (including Katherine Grey and her two sons, born in 1561 and 1563 respectively from a clandestine marriage declared invalid by a royal commission of enquiry), this issue was as relevant to the succession as to Elizabeth's own title. Henry VIII's will (authorized by the 1544 Act of Succession) added to the legal mess. In privileging the line of his younger sister Mary, Duchess of Suffolk, and ignoring that of the elder sister Margaret, once married to the King of Scotland, the will disregarded the principle of primogeniture which usually governed the royal succession.[4]

These legal puzzles dominated the debates. Nonetheless, the question of who would be most desirable as the next monarch actually took precedence over matters of principle, since polemicists and politicians promoted those rules that worked in the interest of their own favoured candidate, while a few men were prepared to discard legal precedent altogether, advocating instead some form of election based on the public good or what we might call Protestant reason of state.[5] Unquestionably, confessional considerations determined the preferences of many early Elizabethans. Cecil's opposition to Mary's claim arose from his fear of popery; and he used rumour and manuscript newsletters to slur her reputation and so damage her claim.[6] Though religion was not mentioned in most tracts, it often explained the positions taken by their authors. The MP John Hales, whose pamphlet supported the Protestant Katherine as 'the right Heyre', was himself an ardent reformer, whilst the writer who most effectively promoted Mary's title was the recusant common lawyer Edmund Plowden.[7] Although during the earlier 1560s Katherine and Mary were the leading contenders, candidates with a weaker claim could also command a confessional following. The Protestant Henry Hastings, Earl of Huntingdon, had strong support on account of his religion and gender. Some Catholics, meanwhile, backed Margaret Lady Strange (a grand-daughter of the Duchess of Suffolk through the cadet line), whereas others favoured Margaret Countess of Lennox (the daughter of Henry VIII's sister Margaret by her second marriage), because of their Roman religion, English birth and male offspring (see genealogical charts 1 and 2).

Nonetheless, confessional beliefs did not always translate into political allegiance. On the international stage, Mary's Protestant councillors – William Maitland of Lethington and James Stewart, Earl of Moray (her half brother) – pushed hard their sovereign's claim to the English succession, while Philip II of Spain was wary of supporting it because he believed Mary to be a pawn of her powerful Guise family in France. At home, the anonymous author of 'Allegations in behalf of … the Lady Mary now Queen of Scots' (1565) expressed both anti-papal and anti-Suffolk sentiments. Despite his denial of Rome's authority in England, he still disputed Katherine's claim on the grounds that she was descended from a bastard line and had herself 'by dalliance' fallen 'to carnall company' with the Earl of Hertford.[8]

Furthermore, this disjunction between religion and politics was not confined to polemicists. At the time of Elizabeth's near-fatal illness, the Spanish ambassador believed that her Protestant council 'was almost as much troubled as she, for out of the 15 or 16 of them…there were nearly as many different opinions about the succession to the Crown'.[9] Outside the council, the prominent Protestant Sir Nicholas Throckmorton was recognized as a 'devoted friend' of Mary and her 'right and title to the succession'. Indeed Throckmorton may have been one of the MPs who spoke in her favour in the 1563 Parliament.[10] Within the Lords, Mary also had Protestant support. Robert Dudley (Earl of Leicester from 1564) was counted as one of her adherents for most of the decade.[11] Thomas Howard, fourth Duke of Norfolk, had backed Katherine for a while, but was persuaded (seemingly by Plowden in 1567) that Mary's title was the stronger.[12] On the Catholic side, Anthony Browne, Viscount Montagu and his father-in-law Baron Dacre were thought to favour the staunchly Protestant Huntingdon in early 1563.[13] The adherents of Katherine and her two sons relied on statute, common law and Henry VIII's will to assert the primacy of their claim and illegality of Mary's. By contrast, Mary and her champions upheld primogeniture within the bloodline as the over-riding maxim according to civil law, and argued that 'manye lawes made for the subiectes [i.e. common law] take no howlde in case of the prynce'.[14] Thus the common law ban on alien inheritance, they insisted, did not affect the transfer of the crown, which was a species of corporation whose succession was governed by descent; besides, they added, Mary was not actually an alien since Scotland was still within England's allegiance.[15]

In addition to matters of principle, polemicists on both sides probed matters of fact. Was Katherine's marriage to Hertford invalid and so her sons bastards, as judged in May 1562 by the Queen's commission of enquiry (tellingly, composed of Protestants and headed by Matthew Parker, Archbishop of Canterbury)? Was Katherine herself descended from a bastard line because her grandfather's first wife had been alive when he married Henry VIII's sister? Had Henry's other sister Margaret been legally divorced from her first husband, which would make her daughter legitimate?[16] Was Henry's will signed by the King, as mandated by the 1544 statute, or merely stamped by a clerk, which would deny it legal standing? And, crucially, did the King have the right to settle the succession as he pleased?

Although the succession was supposed to be among the *arcana imperii*, these principles and questions were debated in a variety of media and genres throughout the 1560s. Pro- and anti-Marian tracts circulated in both print and manuscript.[17] The play *Gorboduc* by Thomas Sackville and Thomas Norton, which glanced favourably at the Suffolk claim while intimating that parliament should *choose* a successor, was performed at the Inner Temple on 27

December 1561 and before the Queen at Whitehall on 18 January 1562, and printed three years afterwards.[18] On 3 September 1566, an academic disputation about the relative merits of hereditary succession versus election was held during Elizabeth's visit to the University of Oxford, and a 'moot' took place at Lincoln's Inn in London later that autumn, where the lawyers concluded that as a foreigner Mary could not succeed to the crown, even if she were the next in bloodline.[19] Just before the 1566 Parliament opened, a scribally circulated pamphlet 'The Common Cry of Englishmen' petitioned the Queen to appoint her heir in this session and urged MPs to take the matter in hand if she proved too timorous to act.[20]

When parliament turned its attention to the succession in 1563 and 1566, the question proved just as controversial. Members disagreed about what kind of succession bill should be passed, and indeed whether parliament had the competence to introduce one without the express sanction of the Queen. In their petition of 28 January 1563 the Commons called upon Elizabeth to publish the 'limitacion of succession' that had been established in Henry's 1544 statute and his will, and 'to provide most gratious remedy' if no such limitation existed.[21] Had Henry's 'limitacion' been published, it would, of course, have worked to Katherine's advantage. The Lords' petition of 1 February, however, requested that 'suche certen limitacion might be made how th'imperiall crowne of this realme shuld remain' if the Queen died childless.[22] This presumably meant that Elizabeth should set down a limitation in a statute of her own. And, if the Spanish ambassador is accurate, the Lords envisaged that the crown should be entailed to some 'four lines or families in the kingdom', leaving Elizabeth to choose her heir presumptive from amongst them.[23] Given the Queen's known hostility to Katherine, this solution would have undermined her interests. Also considered was an exclusionary measure, stating that anyone who in any way claimed (either in the past or in the future) Elizabeth's throne during her lifetime 'shalbe utterlie disabled for ever to have or enioy' the English crown.[24] Had this bill been enacted, it would have effectively disinherited Mary, as she had borne the arms of England when in France.

Not everyone agreed, however, that parliament had the right unilaterally to name a successor or lay down the rules of succession that would exclude some candidates and privilege others. An unnamed nobleman maintained in 1563 that the succession was the preserve of the royal prerogative, but that the Queen should take the advice of her lawyers whose judgement could be kept secret until the time was thought right to publicize it in a forum such as parliament: 'In this wise your Matie shall both preserve the dignitie, prerogative and majestie of your estate royall, and also satisfie the desire of your good subjectes'.[25] A similar line was taken by the one-time Marian exile, Roger Edwardes, in a manuscript tract 'Castra Regia' (1569). Denying parliament's right 'to deale in the matter', Edwardes proposed that the Queen should reach a decision after listening to her nobility.[26] At least two other staunch Protestants – Sir Ralph Sadler and Sir Nicholas Throckmorton – argued in the 1566 Parliament against the body's competence to resolve the succession.[27]

Parliamentary disagreements, together with Elizabeth's known reluctance to tackle the issue, stimulated Cecil in 1563 to consider a constitutional arrangement which, though unusual, was considerably less radical than Stephen Alford has suggested.[28] In order to fill the political void in the event of Elizabeth dying without a known heir, Cecil devised a scheme to establish a conciliar interregnum until a new monarch was 'by parlement declared'.[29] Aside from being adumbrated in the concluding sequence of *Gorboduc*, this role for parliament had historical precedents, as readers of chronicles would appreciate when coming across references to the 'election' of kings such as Edward III or Henry IV.[30] Conciliar rule was also the norm during royal minorities (though admittedly in the name of the child monarch). What is more, the thinking behind the initiative reflected contemporary ideas about the role of the English parliament as both a court and a body to 'consult and shew what is good and necessarie for the common wealth'.[31] In our view, then, Cecil had no plan to usurp monarchical power but simply sought to utilize one of parliament's existing functions in the event of an emergency so as to preserve England from civil war, foreign intrigues and a Catholic monarch. His proposal, moreover, may have been intended as a lever to persuade the Queen to marry so as to obviate the need for any such expedients. Even had the plan come to pass, it would have been a one-off measure, the succession reverting to the hereditary course thereafter until another line died out.

By autumn 1566, the succession caused even greater anxiety within the country, especially amongst Protestants. With the suspension of recent matrimonial negotiations, the prospect of the thirty-three-year-old Queen giving birth to a healthy heir was looking dim. Mary, meanwhile, had strengthened her claim by marrying her English cousin – Henry Stuart, Lord Darnley – and producing a son. Even worse, she was now reportedly far less accommodating towards the Scottish Kirk. Consequently, some MPs initiated a succession debate in the session of that year. Historians have long disagreed about whether the debate was 'managed' by Cecil and other Privy Councillors or whether it was the result of MPs acting independently.[32] We think the latter. All but one of the MPs were godly Protestants who already had (or would soon develop) a history of hostility towards Mary.[33] Cecil thought that a petition on the succession was constitutionally legitimate but probably unwise, since 'to require the succession is hardest to be obteyned'.[34] Privy Councillors in the Commons attempted to forestall further debate by urging MPs to 'see the Sequal' of Elizabeth's promise to marry 'before further Suit touching the Succession'; and it was in this session that Sadler (a Privy Councillor) admitted that the succession was 'matier farre out of our reche and compase'.[35] Only when the Queen ordered the Parliament to cease its suit did Cecil and other councillors weigh in on the Commons' side. They then successfully persuaded her to acknowledge that the succession 'belongeth properly to hir Majesty and the three estates of the realme', even though she still refused 'to enter *at this tyme* into the decision therof' (our italics).[36]

As far as Elizabeth was concerned, the time was not right for any announcement on the succession, as she had then opened up negotiations for a treaty of amity with Mary. If parliament attempted to bar her, Elizabeth's Scottish policy might well collapse; and if Elizabeth named Mary, many of her Protestant subjects would be outraged. Nevertheless, there is some evidence that the Queen planned to consult leading lawyers, in accordance with the anonymous peer's advice in 1563. She said as much to her cousin as well as to the delegation from the Lords who approached her in October 1566.[37] And, since common law held with custom rather than the new-fangled statute and since many prominent common lawyers were Catholic, such a decision might have given Mary the legal edge, the outcome that Elizabeth preferred. The Queen had already permitted an examination of Henry's will so that its authenticity could be determined, though probably no agreement was reached because the fragile state of the document made it impossible to ascertain whether it had been stamped by a clerk or signed by the royal hand.[38] However, even had a full judicial review taken place, it is unlikely that Elizabeth would have allowed the judgement to be immediately publicized, but would have made it available on her death or used it as the basis of her own will.

This possible solution, however, faded away with the outbreak of tremendous upheavals in Scotland. Darnley's murder in February 1567 and Mary's marriage to the Earl of Bothwell in the spring sparked off rebellion which resulted in her deposition. Understandably, Mary ceased to be preoccupied with the English succession, while Scottish Protestant support for her claim pretty much evaporated. As it turned out, the supporters of the Suffolk line could not benefit from this setback to Mary's hopes, for Katherine died on 27 January 1568 and Elizabeth would not reconsider the status of her sons. The confinement of Hales and Hertford (continuing well past Katherine's death) provided a warning that the Queen would not countenance political activity on the boys' behalf. Nonetheless, contrary to Mortimer Levine's view, the way was not now clear for Mary's son James. If Elizabeth died before Katherine's children grew into adults, might not one of them take the throne through the machinations of a Protestant council? Furthermore, even if the councillors chose to support James, would he be strong enough to take precedence over his mother were France or Spain to intervene on her behalf? Given these uncertainties, Elizabeth's first decade as queen concluded with the succession question no nearer resolution.

1568–72: ACCOMMODATION OR POLARIZATION?

As is well known, some English Protestants – including Leicester and Throckmorton – endeavoured to reach an agreement with the deposed Scottish Queen in 1568 shortly after her flight to England. Their surreptitious plan involved her marriage to the Duke of Norfolk, restoration to the Scottish throne with a Protestant husband at her side, and the succession vested in the Stuart line.[39] The ensuing failure of this dynastic solution, however, is generally taken to mark the end of Protestant attempts at accommodation with Mary. Consequently, the historiography has emphasized how the two rival faiths became politically polarized over Mary Stuart and the succession during the crisis years, when England was shaken by the Northern Rebellion (1569), Papal Bull of excommunication (1570), and Ridolfi Plot (1571). But this approach neglects several important points: first that while outright hostility to Mary was the order of the day amongst committed Protestants after 1569, accommodation remained the preferred strategy of Elizabeth who was negotiating for Mary's return to Scotland right until 1571; second, that Protestant polemic, mainly sponsored by Cecil, was directed not only at the public at large but also, crucially, at the Queen, who seemed to be pursuing a perilous course of appeasement; and third, that the Protestant pamphleteers who savaged Mary's reputation also began to shift the arguments against her succession from legal right to reason of state. An appreciation of these points allows us to see the Cecilian agitprop in a new light and gain a more balanced view of these years.

Once Mary's dealings with Norfolk were revealed, her character and religion took centre-stage. From 1567, she had been defamed in a range of media in Scotland, but English presses had initially refrained from following suit, doubtless because Elizabeth would have disapproved. Cecil may have done his best to brand Mary a witch while rumour and ballads blackened her name,[40] but the incendiary 'casket letters' proving her an adulterous murderess had remained in the English government's safe-keeping. Now this semi-official propaganda would serve a covert crusade against the ongoing secret negotiations for Mary's restoration.

Initiated in April 1569, these talks were resumed in the spring of 1570.[41] On the English side they were conducted by Cecil and Sir Walter Mildmay, men who, far from welcoming their Queen's appeasement policy, favoured instead direct support for the 'King's party' in Scotland, under threat from Mary's adherents after the assassination in January of the Anglophile Regent Moray. However tough the demands put to the Scottish Queen in May and again in October, Cecil, Mildmay, and their zealous associates must have been appalled that Elizabeth was ready to pledge in return that she would not bar Mary from the succession.[42] Nor did they deem sufficient the stipulation that the Scottish Queen (though not her offspring) would be *ipso facto* deprived of any title if she violated the agreement. That is why, even as he was making promises on his mistress's behalf, Cecil was simultaneously orchestrating this veiled counter-offensive in print. One imagines that both he and Mildmay must have been thrown by Mary's ostensible tractability – she even agreed for James to be raised in England while only requesting supervised visiting rights! So the flat veto to the plan for her restoration that the new Scottish regime finally issued on 19 February 1571 brought mighty relief.[43]

The first of the anti-Marian pamphlets of these years was *A Discourse touching the pretended match betwene the Duke of Norfolke and the Queene of Scottes* (1569). Printed by Cecil's *protégé* John Day, it denounced Mary as a die-hard papist (or, worse still, an atheist), and unworthy of the English crown. The unnamed author vigorously protested that the marriage would endanger Elizabeth's life, imperil true religion and boost Catholic hopes in both kingdoms. Significantly, he advised against trusting to any deals with the treacherous Mary. Instead, in a transparent exposition of the Cecilian programme, he recommended that the too lenient Elizabeth should capitalize on cordial relations with Moray.[44]

Similarly, in the wake of the Northern Rebellion, the objective of Protestant publicists was as much to scupper Elizabeth's rapprochement with Mary as it was to incite public opinion against Catholics and the Scottish Queen. Linked to Cecil, these pamphleteers wanted Elizabeth to keep Mary in captivity and outlaw her claim to the succession. Furthermore, they insinuated that any decision about the succession should be made not primarily with an eye to legal proprieties but, rather, for reasons of sheer expediency, or, to put it more charitably, the public good. Again printed by Day, Norton's *To the Quenes Maiesties poore deceyued subiectes of the north countrey* (1569) categorically disallowed the Scottish Queen's title both because it was 'fayned and false' and because it could not 'stande with the safetye of the Quéenes Maiestie', two fundamentally different things.[45] Norton's *A warning agaynst the dangerous practises of Papistes* (1570) harped on the same theme. Lamenting Elizabeth's lack of issue, it urged the statutory exclusion of the Catholic Stuart claim, no matter its validity: 'What other title so euer be pretended, be it good or bad, if it shall once threaten danger to the Q. Maiestie whose title and gouernance we know to be true and haue felt to be good, I wish it destroyed and put out of hope'.[46] The violent language here and elsewhere prefigured the emergent drive for Mary's treason trial and execution.

This manifestly prudential line of reasoning gained momentum in the aftermath of Pope Pius V's bull. Now at stake was not just who should succeed Elizabeth but also whether she was in fact the rightful queen. Accordingly, two fresh Norton pamphlets, *A Bull graunted by the Pope to Doctor Harding & other* and *An addition declaratorie to the Bulles*, both 1570, ratcheted up the anti-Catholic pitch, while others mounted painstaking apologias for Elizabeth's title. The survival of Protestant England, Norton was adamant, depended on the survival of the Queen's body natural, which is why the regime had to act fast, firmly and in unison to protect her from an imminent popish onslaught. The second, authorized edition of *Gorboduc*, re-titled *The Tragidie of Ferrex and Porrex* (1570) – a play strident in its anti-foreign bias and fixation with the succession – served a similar purpose. Published singly and in Day's collection of Norton's prose pamphlets, this version omitted the eight-line exhortation to obedience.[47] While the deletion seems primarily motivated by sympathy with the Scottish Protestants who toppled Mary, it may also betray impatience with Elizabeth.

It was not only Norton and his backers who were prepared to dispense with legal arguments in their attempts to exclude Mary. Probably writing in the early months of 1571, the anonymous author of 'An Advertisement of a True and Christian Subiect to Queene Elizabeth: Touching the Declaring of a Successor' suggested that Elizabeth should take advantage of the matter being so uncertain, and 'by Consent of Parlyment' choose James as the 'most fitt to succeede'. This manuscript provides, therefore, the earliest recorded proposal to bypass Mary's hereditary claim and instead elect her son, then not yet five, as Elizabeth's heir presumptive. On a spectrum of constitutional radicalism, this scenario would score high – higher in some respects than Cecil's various interregnum drafts which made provision for the acephalous parliament summoned after the Queen's death to name the person with the best right as successor. Yet it has been ignored in the historiography. Confronting head-on the logical objection that 'the limitation of this Crowne passeth by succession, and not by election', the godly author brazenly admitted that in so fraught a situation 'publique Benefitt' trumped all other considerations.[48] James's candidacy, in his view, provided the optimum guarantee of the Queen's personal security, the country's welfare, and subjects' satisfaction; even so, to be on the safe side he recommended entailing the crown *after* James to twelve noble houses, while inserting a proviso that any successor who tried to alter religion would be immediately debarred and replaced with the next in line.

Support for Mary's exclusion was evident in the Parliament that met in April 1571. Thanks to Norton's interventions, the Treasons Act mandated that anyone challenging the crown in Elizabeth's lifetime would be rendered automatically ineligible to succeed. Mary may have got away with contesting her cousin's title in the past, but from now on she would lose any stake in the succession were she to speak out of turn. Furthermore, the Act deemed it treason both to question whether the common law of the realm, unmodified by statute, was sufficient to determine the succession and to dispute the capacity of the Queen and parliament to devise further statutory provisions. The only clause that satisfied Elizabeth was the prohibition of public discussion on the succession.[49]

The negotiations for Mary's restoration came to an abrupt end that summer, when the Ridolfi Plot implicated the Scottish Queen in an international conspiracy to depose Elizabeth. One of its main architects was John Leslie, Bishop of Ross, who had written an impassioned defence of Mary's honour in 1569 which doubled up as a weighty succession tract supporting her title on legal grounds.[50] Leslie, a key negotiator in the talks for Mary's restoration, had counselled his mistress in early October 1570 to acquiesce in the conditions relayed by Cecil and Mildmay. But in early 1571, as a preparative for a Spanish invasion, Leslie arranged for a new, revised edition of the earlier tract. Taking a cue from the bull of excommunication, this expunged all deferential references to Elizabeth, whom it downgraded from Queen to 'present Governor'.[51]

The Ridolfi Plot gave Cecil (now Burghley) another opportunity to smear Mary. By early autumn 1571 he connived in the publication of George Buchanan's Latin summary of her alleged wrongdoing in Scotland, meant chiefly for foreign consumption, and an augmented English (actually *faux* Scots) translation for the home market.[52] In late 1571, Burghley was also behind *Salutem in Christo* by one R. G., a short pamphlet printed by Day that revealed details of the plot.[53] Unsurprisingly, given all this agitprop, a majority in the Parliament of 8 May to 30 June 1572 bayed for Mary's blood. Yet, despite the onslaught, Elizabeth refused to deliver either trial or exclusion. She acceded only to Norfolk's execution, and while she intimated that a bill of exclusion would be desirable, in the end she vetoed it and prorogued Parliament.[54] By this point, political instincts and religious sympathies shaping attitudes towards the succession were almost exactly in sync. Only two MPs (both Protestants) spoke up for Mary in the 1572 parliamentary session – Arthur Hall and Francis Alford – and both were reprimanded by the House.[55] After that, no Protestant worth his salt would ever again venture to stand up for Mary's title; and few if any Catholics would consider supporting anyone else.[56]

For Catholics, the preceding few years had brought nothing but defeat. All that remained for those at home was to wait for better times. Meanwhile, the activists living abroad and enjoying access to Continental presses riled the regime by purporting to expose its true colours as the quintessential conspiracy of evil counsel and by upholding the supposedly inviolable title of Mary, whom the self-serving creatures had traduced. This radical strain of papist polemic was first evident in the poisonous libel *Treatise of Treasons* (1572) that excoriated the pillars of Elizabethan government, Bacon and Cecil, as baseborn upstarts at once godless and disloyal who were making a traitorous bid to divert the succession from its proper channels.[57] Thenceforth Catholic conspiracy theory would compete with its Protestant counterpart as the rival camps sought to win over public opinion.[58]

1573–81: SUCCESSION UNDER WRAPS

The period from 1573 until 1581 hardly figures in the historiography of the Elizabethan succession. It is easy to see why. The 1571 Treasons Act – reinforced in 1581 by the so-called 'statute of silence' against prophesying Elizabeth's death or speculating about the identity of her successor – had suppressed discussion of the succession; and the subject was not raised in the 1576 Parliament, unlike the sessions of 1563 and 1566. With Mary in secure confinement, a Protestant Regent ruling Scotland, and the Guise family embroiled in renewed civil war in France, there seemed little danger of the Catholic claimant seizing the English throne in the event of Elizabeth's sudden death. Moreover, with James being educated by Calvinist tutors, Protestants could rally behind a future Stuart succession. What was there to fear, or for modern historians to write about, except the Queen's plan to marry a French Catholic, Francis, Duke of Anjou, and its potential bearing on the succession?

Nonetheless, the issue did not entirely disappear from view during this period. One person at least was foolhardy enough to address it directly. As a 1576 New Year's gift to the Earl of Leicester, Roger Edwardes presented a manuscript, 'Cista Pacis Anglie', in which he called for the succession to be determined immediately so that England might avoid the sort of civil unrest destroying France and the Low Countries. When copies were discovered abroad, he was imprisoned for fifteen months in the Tower and fined £500.[59]

Others broached the succession question more obliquely to allow 'plausible deniability'. In his tract on the parliament of England (first published in two different editions in 1572 and reprinted in 1575), John Hooker *alias* Vowell portrayed the institution as a form of Roman senate which ought to be summoned 'for weightie & great causes'. Paramount among these 'causes' was 'the establishing of succession'.[60] An even better example is the sermon of the radical reformer Robert Crowley, delivered before the Lord Mayor and citizens of London in 1574 and printed in a bumper version on 7 January 1576, just before the opening of a new parliamentary session. Ostensibly providing instructions on the proprieties of choosing a mayor, the homily was in reality more directly relevant to the future of England's crown. For instance, drawing upon biblical precedents of God's preference for Jacob over his older twin Esau and for David over his older brothers, Crowley effectively vilified the Catholic Mary Stuart's lineal title: 'If that people [of Israel] might not make them a Ruler of one that were not a brother by bloud and Religion how may we that professe the religion of Christ, chuse one to be our Ruler that is not of one religion with us?'[61]

It is tempting to think that the publication of Crowley's sermon was timed to encourage MPs to exclude the Scottish Queen or elect the next monarch in the February Parliament, since international developments had brought the danger from Mary once more to the fore. In France, a religious peace seemed imminent, which would leave Henry III and the Guises free to take up her cause. Meanwhile, Philip II appeared on the brink of defeating the rebels in the Low Countries, and all feared he would follow up such a victory with advancing 'that bosom serpent the Scottish Queen'.[62] Anticipating trouble in the House, the Speaker took steps to control the subject of debates. And, indeed, it does look as if the Puritan MP Peter Wentworth planned to raise the issue. He was interrupted and detained following his immoderate call for free speech, at precisely the moment when he was criticizing Elizabeth for having disallowed two bills against that Jezebel Mary, which had been introduced in the previous session.[63] After Wentworth's incarceration in the Tower, MPs did not dare revive the subject and confined themselves to humbly petitioning the Queen to marry and give them an heir.[64]

Contemporaries fully appreciated that Elizabeth's projected match with Anjou had implications for the succession. John Stubbes painted alarming scenarios about a future without Elizabeth were the marriage to take place. What would happen, for example, after her death if she and Anjou had a son who would inherit the thrones of both England and France? Would Anjou act as a regent for any infant son or daughter?[65] Stubbes also raised the possibility that if Elizabeth pre-deceased Anjou, the Duke might try to keep the throne by marrying Mary, and suggested that this was the Frenchman's real objective. Stubbes even argued that the chief beneficiaries of the match would be the Scottish Queen and her foreign Catholic allies.[66] Of course, Protestant opposition to the match mainly stemmed from the Duke's demand for a Mass and was further fuelled by the near-simultaneous launch in 1579–80 of the Jesuit mission in England and Hispano-papal expedition in Ireland;[67] nonetheless worries about the succession helped whip up popular opinion against it.

Even before this 'mini-exclusion crisis' (Collinson's phrase[68]) blew over, another Catholic initiative brought the succession centre-stage. This was the proposal – devised by John Leslie, who in January 1574 had withdrawn to the Continent after his release from prison – to revive the negotiations of 1569–71 and have Mary restored to the throne of Scotland in association with her son.[69] The fall of the Regent Morton in 1580 and the adolescent James VI's emerging propensity for Catholic favourites added a new dimension and urgency to the problem. Could he be trusted one day to safeguard the English polity and Church?

1581–87: ASSOCIATIONS AND THE ENTERPRISE

The significance for the succession of the Association scheme, and more generally of Anglo-Scottish relations in the 1580s, has been typically overlooked or misunderstood: indeed, there is no proper scholarly account of either. Yet only by taking these on board can we make sense of the ensuing measures the English government adopted towards both Mary and James.

Mary raised the plan for joint sovereignty with the English in the autumn of 1581, pretending it originated with James, King Henry III of France and his mother Catherine de Médicis.[70] But well before then, Leslie had obtained papal support for the scheme and begun obliquely publicizing it in print. A Latin version of his succession tract, published in 1580, with a genealogy graphically demonstrating the priority of the Stuart title, and dedicated jointly to Mary and James, served as a retort to Buchanan's construal of the Scottish crown as elective in *De jure regni apud Scotos* (1579) and a reminder to the English that they now had to reckon with two Stuart princes, not just the one in captivity.[71] It also subtly reminded James that his own title derived from his mother. Notwithstanding the statutory ban on discussing the succession, the English government's disquiet led them to commission a formal rebuttal, which, however, never saw print.[72]

From Mary's point of view, the timing of the Association initiative seemed propitious because of recent reports that Elizabeth was dying and because James was now nominally in charge in Scotland and under the sway of his French Catholic kinsman Esmé Stuart (soon created Earl and then Duke of Lennox). Whether this diplomatic solution should be pursued exercised the English regime for the next few years, a fact mostly unremarked in the historiography. Potentially, the tripartite deal could be beneficial to all. For Mary, it would spell freedom and possibly a return to Scotland. James, whom at his mother's bidding Catholic potentates refused to recognize as King, would gain full legitimacy albeit at the price of letting Mary partake in the government via intermediaries. And, with the Scottish Queen formally acknowledging Elizabeth's present title, the English Queen would at long last neutralize the Stuart threat and arrive at an efficient resolution to the succession problem. Furthermore, the agreement would secure England's northern border just when military intervention in the Low Countries looked unavoidable.

But there were serious caveats and imponderables. Could Mary be taken at her word? Could James? If he were associated with Mary as Elizabeth's heir, the pair would seem to bridge the religious divide and might introduce toleration for both faiths, a politique solution that would be unacceptable to those English who valued religious purity above all else. Yet even without the Association James still threatened Elizabeth and English Protestantism, since his religious preferences seemed uncertain. If Mary died, he appeared likely to inherit her following; and as a free monarch and an eligible bachelor, he was potentially a much more dangerous focus than Mary had been for conspiracies against the regime. As a result of such suspicions, many Elizabethan Councillors and diplomats preferred a covert alliance with the Anglophile, ultra-Protestant Scottish noblemen that would bring James to heel and once again secure a sympathetic government up north.

In the short run, that option won out and the so-called Ruthven Raid of August 1582, staged with English connivance, brought about the overthrow of Lennox and virtual captivity of James. What the English did not know for certain at that point, though they strongly suspected, was that the Association scheme provided a cover for an 'enterprise' or invasion of England via Scotland that was to have been coordinated by Mary's Guise cousins, Spain and the Pope, and assisted by Scottish Catholics, perhaps even the King.[73] The invasion never materialized. But it is easy to imagine the English regime's horror upon discovering a version of the plan in November 1583, when Walsingham sprung the so-called Throckmorton Plot. What role James would have played had any such undertaking been launched was unclear, though his escaping from Ruthven in June 1583 and rebuilding of an anti-Presbyterian regime boded ill.

So, with hopes that they could count on at least one decent Stuart as a fall-back successor seemingly in ruins, the English were reduced to casting about for expedients to contain the threat from both Mary and James even as the international situation deteriorated. Already that summer, probably in July, Leicester warned Elizabeth that Mary's 'yonge lusty sonne' was set to prove a foe more formidable than his devious mother and proposed legislation which would automatically exclude both from the succession, should anyone, whether Englishman or foreigner, venture to harm the Queen or her country, irrespective of whether either was aware of any such attempt.[74] This was collective responsibility with a vengeance, and though Elizabeth did not immediately countenance the proposal, it influenced both the Bond of Association and Act of Surety.

The years 1583–84 were turning into the English regime's worst nightmare, as it faced the seemingly united forces of Catholic Christendom and Stuart supporters within the British Isles hatching plots for invasion and assassination. The missionary priests and Jesuits were encouraging recusancy, and in a few cases conspiracy, while an unknown number of church papists were thought to be fellow-travellers just awaiting an opportunity to rise against the regime. Again Burghley resorted to propaganda. In his *The Execution of Justice* (1583) – a tract promptly reprinted and disseminated in Latin, Dutch and French, he denounced the papacy's temporal power and branded both Catholic priests and their harbourers as traitors. The 1584 Catholic counter-offensive, masterminded by the Jesuit Robert Persons, meanwhile, reiterated Catholic support for the Stuart claim, implicitly threatening civil unrest and foreign intervention should Mary come to any harm. The three hefty pamphlets issued under Persons's aegis at Rouen – the updated English version of Leslie's succession tract, the anonymous libel *Leicester's Commonwealth* and Cardinal William Allen's apology for the papal deposing power – also insinuated that James was about to convert to Catholicism.[75] Developments in Scotland contributed to the rising sense of alarm. The foiling of a fresh Presbyterian *coup* there in April was followed, in May, by the passage of the so-called 'Black Acts', which re-established bishops while proscribing presbyteries. Before long, the government learned of James's ill-concealed efforts to drum up military and/ or financial assistance from France, Spain and Rome.

Drastic measures were required to avert a Stuart succession in the event of a regicide. Confronted with the death of Anjou in June and assassination of the Prince of Orange in July 1584 amid reports of fresh conspiracies, the Privy Council moved on 19 October to mobilize the Protestant 'political nation' with the Instrument or Bond of Association. Cecil had conceived the idea of a loyalist association back in 1569.[76] Now he and Walsingham updated the device, most likely with reference to Leicester's letter of advice the previous year, to secure the cooperation of trustworthy men to put it in operation.[77] The ostensibly spontaneous Oath of Association bound subscribers to protect the Queen and pursue to the death the putative successor by or for whom any murderous design was attempted or actually carried out as well as his or her heir, no matter whether guilty or not. For Burghley, this was a constitutional solution that recognized the quasi-independent nature of local governors who had to be persuaded rather than ordered to defend the realm. As a further safeguard, the following summer the Privy Council sought to revive the institution of the lord lieutenancy in order to provide a more effective home-defence force; the assembling and drilling of the companies, moreover, was carried out by strong Protestants, who could be trusted to resist any Catholic attempts on Mary's behalf.[78]

The Bond has been routinely seen as targeting Mary, but at least one of its objectives was to prise mother and son apart. By the time of its launch, however, that was almost wholly superfluous. Having failed to garner support from Spain, France or the papacy, James realized that his best bet to secure the English crown would be to distance himself from Mary and mend fences with Elizabeth. Accordingly, he and his chief minister the Earl of Arran began making overtures to the English; in fact the Scottish envoy Patrick, Master of Gray, was due to arrive in London just as the Bond went public. While everyone agreed that to secure a friendly regime in Edinburgh was the priority, the question remained whether that might be more effectively achieved by another *coup* rather than by appeasement. Soon tensions were evident within the Privy Council, with Burghley, Walsingham and their godly allies keen to make the Bond law in the Parliament scheduled for November, in contrast to Hunsdon, Hatton and above all the Queen who preferred to negotiate with James and, if he proved amenable, avoid cutting him out of the succession.

Ultimately, the latter course prevailed (though the English did not neglect to coordinate potential opposition to James and Arran).[79] On 18 December

Elizabeth, reassured by Gray that the Scottish King was ready to abandon the Association, had Hatton instruct the Commons to frame the bill protecting her person so that the innocent heir of a treasonable pretender would not be penalized.[80] She also rejected interregnum proposals put forward during the parliamentary recess of winter 1584–85 that would license an acephalous parliament to elect her successor.[81] The discovery of the Parry Plot in February facilitated the smooth passage in March of the Act for the Surety of the Queen's Person, which kept James's title, such as it was, intact.

The English government could now turn its attention to concluding the Treaty of Nonsuch with the Dutch and opening negotiations for an Anglo-Scottish defensive league. Even so, many councillors remained highly suspicious of Arran, and, when a suitable pretext arose, Elizabeth agreed to connive in a *coup* to oust him. With Arran's removal in November 1585 and the Protestant lords in the ascendant, the Anglo-Scottish negotiations were resumed. The Treaty of Berwick, signed in July 1586, bound the two countries in a mutual defensive pact. Elizabeth granted James a pension, but refused to recognize him as heir presumptive.

Deprived of her son's cooperation and liable to prosecution under the terms of the 1585 Act of Surety should she step out of line, Mary had been largely defanged. True, she might endeavour to plot her way out of the predicament, but that was precisely what the government anticipated, hoping to entrap her. Meanwhile, the succession required further attention. Burghley and other members of the regime had been mulling over possible avenues for some time, their key priority being to endow the commonwealth with decision-making power without abandoning all semblance of legality. To that end (as also to refute the pro-Stuart pamphleteering), two substantial tracts were commissioned. One, written by the Somerset herald and Leicester's *protégé* Robert Glover, dismantled Leslie's case for Mary; the other, attributed to Burghley's client the City Recorder William Fleetwood, restated in painstaking detail the arguments against alien succession. For all their rehearsal of legal and historical precedents, the two tracts shared a strong commitment to the election of the next successor. The more conventional Glover attributed that capacity to the monarch in parliament; the more experimental Fleetwood asserted the right of the nobles and commons to choose a new ruler after the Queen's death even without a legislated interregnum.[82] Neither work mentioned James by name. Glover, though, suggested that Mary could have been made eligible by statute, despite her foreign birth, had she behaved with suitable probity. The implication was thus clear: Elizabeth and parliament could do the same for James. Furthermore, by early 1586, when the Anglo-Scottish treaty was practically a done deal, an anonymous position paper originating within the regime – we think its author was Sir Walter Mildmay, among whose papers it was found – bluntly spelled out the reasons for electing James.[83] Although as a foreigner he had no legal claim, James was simply the best man for the job, for where else would the English find a candidate who was a sovereign prince in his own right, a Protestant, a mature male and a fellow-Briton? Besides, being offered the crown as a gift rather than taking it by birthright, James would be honour-bound to respect the country's laws, a vital consideration.

It is impossible to say whether there was a realistic chance of James's election if Elizabeth had died naturally that spring. If so, he would almost certainly have had no scruples about trampling over his mother's right to gain the English throne. But Elizabeth lived, and by midsummer the window for some such eventuality had disappeared: the unmasking of the Babington Plot produced enough evidence (some of it manufactured) to bring Mary to the block.

MARY'S EXECUTION, ARMADA AND BEYOND

Mary's execution not only failed to resolve the succession problem but in some ways threw it wide open. While in its wake the Catholics came off worse, being deprived of their surefire candidate, there was no unanimity among Protestants either, especially given the Scottish King's erratic conduct in the run-up to his mother's beheading and its immediate aftermath.[84] Would he honour his pledge to assist England in the event of a Spanish invasion or even remain neutral? Or might he revert to something like the course he had pursued in 1583–84 and angle to benefit from any such assault? There was no way of knowing until crunch-time: hence, at the height of the Armada crisis in 1588, the English ambassador to Scotland, perhaps instructed by the Queen, gave greater promises in the matter of the succession than she would later vouchsafe. Thereafter the often fraught personal interaction between the two monarchs, no less than the ambivalent perceptions in England of James's religious policy, would continue to militate against unequivocal endorsement by Protestants of his claim.[85]

Whether the Stuart claim was vested in James meanwhile preoccupied the Spanish King and his English Catholic adherents. Back in 1586, Mary, despairing of her son's conversion to the Roman faith and frantic to win Philip over to the idea of military intervention on her behalf, had indicated her willingness to cede to the Spanish King her title to the English crown.[86] With preparations for the Armada underway, Spanish diplomats and agents went a-hunting after Mary's 'phantom will', while Allen, Persons and their allies spearheaded a print campaign in Latin designed to jog the Catholic powers into action.[87] Allen also prepared pamphlets in English that would have been distributed in the event of a successful Spanish conquest, which he portrayed as a papally sponsored crusade against the excommunicate usurping tyrant. His *Admonition to the Nobility and People of England and Ireland* (1588) did not dilate on the proprieties of the succession, but it made no bones that Philip was to be the man.

Following the Armada's failure, the Hispanophiles had to cast about for other ways to influence the outcome of the succession struggle. Might there be a chance of another Spanish onslaught? Could Spain, Rome and Catholic Englishmen be persuaded to agree on a single candidate? Could the Scottish King be 'turned'? Thirty years after Elizabeth's accession, Catholics were more divided than ever and had less to hope for on her death.[88] The prospects for Protestants looked brighter but were still uncertain.[89] All the way around, the problem of succession loomed increasingly 'doubtful and dangerous'. How it panned out eventually is the subject of the rest of this book.

By the 1570s religion became the fundamental factor shaping attitudes towards the succession and the main stimulus for novel constitutional ideas. Protestants had devised and advocated legal and constitutional processes that they hoped would ensure a succession safe for their purposes. These experiments went well beyond the Cecilian interregnum schemes and included a variety of elective solutions, all of which promoted the role of parliament. It was only when Persons appropriated election as a principle in the mid-1590s that Protestants drifted away from such expedients, and only after the Essex fiasco that virtually everyone affected to subscribe to hereditary succession and the Stuart title. But, given that the various confessional constituencies had diametrically opposed expectations of the Jacobean succession, this ostensible alignment masked the extreme conditionality of both constitutional principle and political allegiance. The victory of indefeasible hereditary right achieved by James's accession was consequently more apparent than real. The Catholic plots of 1603–5 were to threaten James's life and challenge his title, while the parliamentary debates on the British union in the sessions of 1604 and 1607 raised wide-ranging legal and constitutional questions about the nature of monarchy. Once out of the bottle, the genie of constitutional innovation was not easily put back.

NOTES

1 This view is implicit in Simon Adams's 'Eliza enthroned? The court and its politics', in Simon Adams, *Leicester and the Court* (Manchester, 2002), pp. 24–45. See also Stephen Alford, *The Early Elizabethan Polity: William Cecil and the British Succession Crisis* (Cambridge, 1998).

2 For the later relevance of this issue, see Chapter 11 of this volume.

3 John Fortescue, *A Learned Commendation of the Politique Lawes of Englande*, trans. Robert Mulcaster (London, 1567), p. 90.

4 Eric Ives, 'Tudor dynastic problems revisited', *Historical Research*, 81 (2008), 255–79.

5 Paulina Kewes, *This Great Matter of Succession: Politics, History, and Elizabethan Drama* (Oxford, forthcoming).

6 Glyn Parry, 'The monarchical republic and magic: William Cecil and the exclusion of Mary Queen of Scots', *Reformation*, 17 (2012), 29–47.

7 Victoria de la Torre, '"We few of an infinite multitude": John Hales, parliament, and the gendered politics of the early Elizabethan succession', *Albion*, 33 (2001), 557–82; Marie Axton, 'The influence of Edmund Plowden's succession treatise', *Huntington Library Quarterly*, 37 (1973–74), 209–26; Geoffrey De C. Parmiter, 'Edmund Plowden as advocate for Mary Queen of Scots: some remarks upon certain Elizabethan succession tracts', *The Innes Review*, 30 (1979), 35–53.

8 CUL, Gg.iii.34, fos 118–45. It is printed in the appendix to William Attwood, *The Fundamental Constitution of the English Government* (London, 1690).

9 *CSPSpan*, vol. 1, p. 262.

10 Gordon Donaldson (ed.), *Memoirs of Sir James Melville of Halhill* (London, 1969), p. 33, and Ian W. Archer *et al.* (eds), *Religion, Politics and Society in Sixteenth-Century England*, CS 5th series, vol. 22, pp. 108–9. For the 1563 Parliament, see T. E. Hartley, *Proceedings in the Parliaments of Elizabeth I*, 3 vols (Leicester, 1981), vol. 1, p. 87.

11 *CSPSpan*, vol. 1, p. 586.

12 *Ibid.*; Parmiter, 'Plowden', 45–6, 50–2.

13 *CSPSpan*, vol. 1, p. 297; J. G. Elzinga's *ODNB* article on Montague.

14 'An Answer to the Former Allegations against the Queen of Scots' Title', CUL, Gg.iii.34, fos 109–10.

15 Christopher Brooks, *Law, Politics and Society in Early Modern England* (Cambridge, 2009), pp. 73–4.

16 This question was raised in the 1563 Parliament when 'a pretended title' of Lady Margaret Douglas was 'motioned'. 21 March 1563, TNA, SP52/8, fo. 36.

17 Mortimer Levine, *The Early Elizabethan Succession Question* (Stanford, CA, 1966), pp. 89–162; Parmiter, 'Plowden'; and Kewes, *This Great Matter.*

18 *The Tragedie of Gorboduc* (London, 1565). For later Elizabethan drama's engagement with the succession, see Richard Dutton's Chapter 9.

19 On the Oxford disputation, see John Nichols (ed.), *The Progresses and Public Processions of Queen Elizabeth*, 3 vols (London, 1823), vol. 1, p. 213, n. 1. For Scottish protests about the Lincoln's Inn 'moot', see TNA, SP52/12, fos 117, 118; Samuel Haynes and William Murdin (eds), *A Collection of State Papers … Left by W. Cecill Lord Burghley*, 2 vols (London, 1740–59), vol. 1, p. 762.

20 Probably the work of the radical Protestant, Thomas Sampson, BL, Egerton MS 2636, fos 37–71.

21 Hartley, *Proceedings in the Parliaments of Elizabeth I*, vol. 1, pp. 92–3; *CJ*, vol. 1, p. 63.

22 Hartley, *Proceedings in the Parliaments of Elizabeth I*, vol. 1, pp. 58–62. The actual quotation is on page 59.

23 28 March 1563, *CSPSpan*, vol. 1, p. 315. A letter of 1563 also refers to a project to entail the Crown, see footnote 25.

24 'ffor restrayning of all persones from attemptes or hopes to the Quenes maiestie's perill', TNA, SP12/28, fo. 74.

25 Two different versions of the manuscript exist: one dated 10 February 1563 is printed in J. Payne Collier (ed.), *The Egerton Papers*, CS, vol. 12 (1840), pp. 38–9; the second, undated, in John Strype, *Annals of the Reformation*, 3rd edn, 4 vols (Oxford, 1824), vol. 2 ii, pp. 652–8.

26 Printed in *Historical Papers: Part I*, Roxburghe Club (London, 1846), pp. 5–40 (quotation at p. 36). For Edwardes, see Stephen Clucas, '"This paradoxall Restitution Iudaicall": the Apocalyptic correspondence of John Dee and Roger Edwardes', *Studies in History and Philosophy of Science*, 43 (2012), 509–18 (at pp. 510–12); Victoria Smith, 'The Elizabethan succession question in Roger Edwardes's "Castra Regia" (1569) and "Cista Pacis Anglie" (1576)', *Historical Research*, forthcoming.

27 Hartley, *Proceedings in the Parliaments of Elizabeth I*, vol. 1, p. 143; NLS, Advocates' MS 33.1.7, no. 24.

28 Stephen Alford, 'A politics of emergency in the reign of Elizabeth I', in Glenn Burgess and Matthew Festenstein (eds), *English Radicalism, 1550–1850* (Cambridge, 2007), pp. 17–36 (esp. pp. 26–8).

29 For a transcription of Cecil's clause, see Alford, *Early Elizabethan Polity*, pp. 225–8. The original is TNA, SP12/28, fos 68ʳ–69ᵛ.

30 Paulina Kewes, *This Great Matter*.

31 Sir Thomas Smith, *De Republica Anglorum*, ed. Mary Dewar (Cambridge, 1982), p. 47.

32 For the former, Michael Graves, 'The management of the Elizabethan House of Commons: the council's "men of business"', *Parliamentary History*, 2 (1983), 11–38; G. R. Elton, *The Parliament in England 1559–1581* (Cambridge, 1986), pp. 364–74; J. D. Alsop, 'Reinterpreting the Elizabethan Commons: the parliamentary session of 1566', *Journal of British Studies*, 29 (1990), 216–40; Stephen Alford, *Burghley* (New Haven and London, 2009), pp. 132–3; for the latter, J. E. Neale, *Elizabeth I and Her Parliaments*, 3 vols (London, 1953–58), vol. 1, pp. 137–40. We view the MPs not as Neale's 'puritan choir' but as 'forward' (and possibly 'froward') as in Patrick Collinson, 'Puritans, men of business and Elizabethan parliaments', *Parliamentary History*, 7 (1988), 187–211, pp. 192–3, 205.

33 www.historyofparliamentonline.org/volume/1558-1603 (accessed 24 August 2011).

34 TNA, SP12/40, fo. 195ʳ.

35 19 October, *CJ*, vol. 1, pp. 74–5; Hartley, *Proceedings in the Parliaments of Elizabeth I*, vol. 1, p. 143.

36 Hartley, *Proceedings in the Parliaments of Elizabeth I*, vol. 1, pp. 163, 151, 171–5.

37 Neale, *Elizabeth I and Her Parliaments*, vol. 1, p. 142.

38 Mortimer Levine, 'A "letter" on the Elizabethan succession question, 1566', *Huntington Library Quarterly*, 19 (1955), 13-38; Axton, 'The influence', pp. 221–22; Parmiter, 'Plowden'. Ives, 'Tudor dynastic problems revisited', 275 ignores the contradictory accounts, and thinks there was agreement that it was stamped.

39 Alford, *Early Elizabethan Polity*, pp. 199–206.

40 Parry, 'The monarchical republic and magic', pp. 43–5.

41 Neither these nor the later negotiations with Mary are mentioned in John Guy's *My Heart is my Own: The Life of Mary Queen of Scots* (London, 2004).

42 For the articles presented to Mary and her amendments dated 5 October 1570, see Haynes, *Collection*, pp. 608–14; for subsequent negotiations, pp. 615ff.

43 *Ibid.*, p. 623.

44 *A Discourse touching the pretended match betwene the Duke of Norfolke and the Queene of Scottes* (London, n.d. [1569?]), sig. Avii[v]. On this and later pamphlets, see Conyers Read, 'William Cecil and Elizabethan public relations', in S. T. Bindoff, Joel Hurstfield and C. H. Williams (eds), *Elizabethan Government and Society: Essays Presented to Sir John Neale* (London, 1961), pp. 21–55 (esp. pp. 31ff); Tricia A. McElroy, 'Executing Mary Queen of Scots: strategies of representation in early modern Scotland' (D.Phil. thesis, University of Oxford, 2005); Lake, 'The politics of "popularity"', pp. 59–94; Peter Lake, Ford Lectures, University of Oxford, 2011.

45 *A Discourse*, sig. Aiv[r].

46 *Ibid.*, sig. Bii[r].

47 The deletion was identified in M. A. R. Graves, *Thomas Norton: The Parliament Man* (Oxford, 1994), pp. 117–18.

48 James P. R. Lyell, 'A tract on James VI's succession to the English throne', *English Historical Review*, 51 (1936), 289–301 (esp. pp. 293–4); Paulina Kewes, '"Bastard succession established by parliaments"?: The idea of election in Elizabethan England', forthcoming.

49 13 Eliz. c. I.

50 *A Defence of the Honour of… Marie Quene of Scotlande* (London [*vere* Rheims], 1569). For discussion, see Margaret J. Beckett, 'The political works of John Lesley, Bishop of Ross (1527–96)' (Ph.D. thesis, University of St Andrews, 2002), chs 2–4; McElroy, 'Executing', ch. 3.

51 *A Treatise Concerning the Defence of the Honour of… Marie Queene of Scotland* (Louvain, 1571). See McElroy, 'Executing', ch. 3.

52 *De Maria Scotorum Regina* (London, 1571); *Ane Detectioun of the duinges of Marie Quene of Scottes* (n.p., n.d. [London, 1571]). The translator was most likely Cecil's colleague Thomas Wilson. See McElroy, 'Executing', ch. 2.

53 R. G., *Salutem in Christo* (London, 1571). Unlike Read, Alford attributes this pamphlet to Burghley. See Read, 'William Cecil', p. 34; Alford, *Burghley*, pp. 177–8.

54 Hartley, *Proceedings in the Parliaments of Elizabeth I*, vol. 1, pp. 259–418; Gerald Bowler, '"An axe or an acte": the Parliament of 1572 and resistance theory in early Elizabethan England', *Canadian Journal of History*, 19 (1984), 349–59; Patrick Collinson, 'The Elizabethan exclusion crisis and the Elizabethan polity', *Proceedings of the British Academy*, 84 (1994), 51–92, pp. 84–7.

55 Alford was suspected of Catholicism, but insisted he was Protestant. See Norman Jones, *The English Reformation: Religion and Cultural Adaptation* (Oxford, 2002), pp. 144–5.

56 Alexander Courtney's Chapter 7 explores the cross-confessional support for James after the Essex rebellion by focusing on the Scottish King's secret correspondence with the crypto-Catholic Lord Henry Howard and the Protestant Sir Robert Cecil.

57 *Treatise of Treasons* ([Louvain,] 1572). See Thomas H. Clancy, SJ, 'A political pamphlet: *The Treatise of Treasons*, 1572', in G. J. Eberle (ed.), *Loyola Studies in the Humanities*

(New Orleans, 1962), pp. 15–30; Beckett, 'Political Works', ch. 5; Peter Lake, '"The monarchical republic of Elizabeth I" revisited (by its victims) as a conspiracy', in Barry Coward and Julian Swann (eds), *Conspiracies and Conspiracy Theory in Early Modern Europe: From the Waldensians to the French Revolution* (Aldershot, 2004), pp. 87–111 (esp. pp. 92–101); and Peter Lake, Ford Lectures.

58 Lake, 'Conspiracy', pp. 102–4.

59 BL, Additional MS 48114, fos 73ᵛ–74. We wish to thank Victoria Smith for sending us her transcription and article discussing the tract.

60 *The Order and Usage of the Keeping of a Parlement in England* [London, 1575?], fo. 20ʳ⁻ᵛ.

61 *A Sermon made in the Chappel at the Gylde Halle in London* (London, 1575), sig. B4ʳ; Kewes, *This Great Matter*. For discussion of other sermons addressing the succession, see Chapter 8 of this volume.

62 TNA SP70/137, fo. 209ᵛ. Glyn Parry, 'Foreign policy and the Parliament of 1576', *Parliamentary History* (forthcoming). We are grateful to Glyn for sending us a copy of the article before its publication.

63 Hartley, *Proceedings in the Parliaments of Elizabeth I*, vol. 1, pp. 428, 438, 476. For Wentworth's later stance on the succession, see Kewes's Chapter 3.

64 Hartley, *Proceedings in the Parliaments of Elizabeth I*, vol. 1, pp. 463–4.

65 *The Discouerie of a Gaping Gulf* (London, 1579), sigs D1ʳ–D3ʳ.

66 Stubbes, *Discoverie*, sig. E5ᵛ.

67 Thomas M. McCoog, SJ, *"And Touching Our Society": Fashioning Jesuit Identity in Elizabethan England* (Toronto, 2013), ch. 2.

68 Collinson, 'The Elizabethan exclusion crisis', p. 53.

69 Susan Doran and Paulina Kewes, 'Associations and enterprises: the Scottish context of the Bond of Association' (forthcoming). See also D. M. Lockie, 'The political career of the Bishop of Ross, 1568–80: the background to a contemporary life of Mary Stuart', *University of Birmingham Historical Journal*, 4/2 (1954), 98–145; Patricia Basing, 'Robert Beale and the Queen of Scots', *British Library Journal*, 20 (1994), 65–82; Lake, Ford Lectures.

70 5 January 1581, Mary's commission to the Duke de Guise, Alexandre Labanoff (ed.), *Lettres, Instructions et Mémoires de Marie Stuart, Reine d'Écosse*, 7 vols (Londres, 1844), vol. 5, pp. 185–7; 28 August 1581, Mary's commission to James Beaton, Archbishop of Glasgow, SP53/11/59 translated in *CSPScot*, 6, pp. 45–6; 10 October 1581, Labanoff, *Lettres*, vol. 5, pp. 266–8, 271.

71 *De Titulo et Iure Serenissimae Principis Mariae Scotorum Reginae* (Rheims, 1580), sig. ē 1ʳ.

72 'The principall things to be considdered in the answer written to the Bussh. of Rosses booke' (Bodl, MS Eng. hist. b. 117). The upshot was a lengthy response by the Somerset herald Robert Glover. See Beckett, 'Political Works', p. 89, and below, pp. 36–7.

73 A. Lynn Martin, *Henry III and the Jesuit Politicians* (Geneva, 1973), pp. 68–74.

74 [July ?] 1583, Earl of Leicester to the Queen, TNA, SP12/161, fos 120–1, at 121ᵛ.

75 John Leslie, *A Treatise Touching the Right, Title, and Interest of ... Marie, Queene of Scotland, And of the most noble king Iames ... to the succession of the Croune of England* (Rouen, 1584); Anon., *The copie of a leter* ([Rouen,] 1584); William Allen, *A True ... Defence, of English Catholiques* (Rouen, 1584). See Lake, Ford Lectures; Kewes, *This Great Matter*;

Doran and Kewes, 'Associations and enterprises'. For later poetic treatments of the Stuart *mère et fils*, and Mary's gradual rehabilitation, see Richard A. McCabe's Chapter 10.

76 Read, 'William Cecil', p. 33.

77 Doran and Kewes, 'Associations and enterprises'; Neale, *Elizabeth I and Her Parliaments*, vol, 2, pp. 16–18. See also David Cressy, 'Binding the nation: the Bonds of Association, 1584 and 1696', in Delloyd J. Guth and John W. McKenna (eds), *Tudor Rule and Revolution: Essays for G. R. Elton from his American Friends* (Cambridge, 1982), pp. 217–34; Collinson, 'The Elizabethan exclusion crisis', pp. 63ff. For the text of the Oath, see 'Lincolnes Inne "Association for the defence of Queen Elizabeth"', in Collier, *Egerton Papers*, pp. 108–11.

78 Neil Younger, 'Securing the monarchical republic: the remaking of the lord lieutenancies in 1585', *Historical Research*, 84 (2010), 249–65.

79 By autumn 1584, the English had succeeded in reconciling two rival exile factions: the ultra-Protestant Lords led by Archibald Douglas, eighth Earl of Angus, and the Hamiltons, who had been banished by Angus's uncle Morton and were traditional rivals of his family. Significantly, John Hamilton was the next in line to the Scottish throne.

80 Hartley, *Proceedings in the Parliaments of Elizabeth I*, vol. 2, pp. 13, 77–8, 150.

81 Collinson, 'The Elizabethan exclusion crisis', pp. 66–7, 87–92; Doran and Kewes, 'Associations and enterprises'. The authors were Burghley and Thomas Digges, a client of Leicester. Whereas Burghley envisaged a conciliar interregnum and something akin to a parliamentary election to the crown only in the event of Elizabeth's assassination, Digges suggested it should be held also when she died of natural causes. The relevant documents associated with Burghley are: TNA, SP12/176/11; SP12/176/22 (in the same hand as no. 11; insertions in Burghley's hand); SP12/176/23 (attributed by *CSPDom, 1581–1590*, p. 224, to Walsingham; if so, Walsingham lightly amended by Burghley's underlines); SP12/176/28; SP12/176/29; SP12/176/30; SP12/176/25 [i.e. SP12/176, pt 1, fos 51ᵛ–52ʳ]; documents attributed to Digges are: SP12/176/26; SP12/176/32.

82 See Kewes, '"Bastard succession established by parliaments"'?, and Kewes, *This Great Matter*. Glover's tract survives in three manuscript versions: Northamptonshire Record Office, MS Fitzwilliam (Milton) Pol. 223 (with Mildmay's annotations); Bodl, MS Carte 105, fos 16–92ᵛ; and BL, Stowe MS 273 (the copy revised after the publication of the 1584 English edition of Leslie's tract). See Beckett, 'Political Works', p. 89, n. 12. Fleetwood's 'Certaine errors upon the Statute made the xxvth yeare of King Edward the third of children borne beiond ye sea...' in two versions: CUL, MS Additional 9212, appears to be a corrected autograph copy, and Bodl, MS Rawlinson C.85 a fair copy: we are grateful to Chris Brooks for advice on this matter; see also his *Law, Politics and Society*, pp. 74–8.

83 Northamptonshire Record Office, Document F(M)P214.

84 Susan Doran, 'Revenge her foul and most unnatural murder? The impact of Mary Stewart's execution on Anglo-Scottish relations', *History*, 85 (2000), 589–612.

85 See Doran, 'Revenge'; and Chapter 3 of this volume.

86 De Lamar Jensen, 'The phantom will of Mary Queen of Scots', *Scotia* 4 (1980), 1–15.

87 See Freddy Cristóbal Domínguez, '"We must fight with paper and pens": Spanish Elizabethan polemics, 1585–1598' (Ph.D. thesis, University of Princeton, 2011). We are grateful to Freddy for sending us a copy of his thesis.

88 For domestic and international aspects of the problem, see Chapters 4, 12 and 13 (of this volume) respectively. On allegations of involvement in a 'popish plot' levelled by and against Essex, see Chapter 6.

89 For intra-Protestant in-fighting and the government's exploitation of divisions among Catholics, see Chapter 5 of this volume.

Part II

Religion and politics

Chapter 3

The Puritan, the Jesuit and the Jacobean succession

Paulina Kewes

In recent years, a new consensus has begun to emerge among leading early modern historians about Puritan attitudes towards the succession after the execution of Mary Queen of Scots in February 1587. Fundamental to this consensus is the claim that as soon as the Catholic Mary died on the block, godly Englishmen who hankered after further reform of the Church embraced her Protestant son James VI of Scotland as their preferred candidate for the throne. Nicholas Tyacke, for example, assumes that from that point onward Puritans turned to James, who now represented 'the most plausible reversionary interest'.[1] In like vein, Patrick Collinson maintains that 'It must have been soon after the 1586 Parliament and the execution of Mary that the godly mafia had decided that James, the "young impe", had to be their man after all.'[2]

In this chapter I take issue with this influential interpretation. I argue, in particular, that it has too readily been concluded that the godly, dazzled by the apparent Presbyterian ascendancy north of the border, hastened to line up behind the Scottish King at that time. This is a misconception stemming partly from an unduly selective reading of the evidence; partly from concentration on developments in England to the virtual exclusion of those in Scotland; and partly from concentration on the conduct and writings of Protestants of various stripes, to the virtual exclusion of Catholics (with the sole exception of the Jesuit Robert Persons's *A Conference about the Next Succession to the Crowne of Ingland*).

For comments, conversation and advice, I owe a debt of gratitude to the late Pat Collinson, as also to Sue Doran, Tom Freeman, Paul Hammer, Tom McCoog, Roger Mason, Malcolm Smuts, Noel O'Sullivan, Glyn Parry, Alex Walsham and Arthur Williamson, and for expert research assistance to Tim Wales.

In reality, the situation was more complicated. Until the mid-1590s the Puritans – like so many other Protestants – were far from resolved on whom to pin their hopes, and James was almost certainly not at the top of their list. *Au contraire*, there is evidence that some of them wished to exclude the Scot in favour of a home-born candidate with more robust confessional credentials. Think of Peter Wentworth, the most prominent and well-connected Puritan commentator on the succession, whom Tyacke takes to have favoured James by 1593, and possibly as early as 1587, yet who in a tract of 1596 – in which he finally plumped for the Scottish King – confessed that he had 'fleeted and altered' in his view of the succession.[3] Persons, it seems, may not have been wide of the mark when he alleged in the *Conference* that 'The person most fauoured by the puritans hitherto in common voice and opinion of men, hath bin the earle of Huntington', and that Edward Seymour, Lord Beauchamp, elder son of Katherine Grey and the Earl of Hertford, was presently rising in their estimation at Huntingdon's expense.[4]

Wentworth's frank and somewhat mortified admission of his eleventh-hour conversion to the Stuart title, which he now urged fellow travellers – nay, all Englishmen – to accept, is never accorded the scrutiny it deserves. This is notwithstanding J. E. Neale's shrewd recognition, more than half a century ago, that Wentworth's 'conversion ... had probably been slow and only recent'.[5] What had precipitated the septuagenarian MP's change of heart? More generally, why did the godly turn to James in the mid-1590s, when the cause of reform lay in ruins?

PITHIE EXHORTATION

Wentworth addressed the issue of the succession in three distinct works written over roughly nine years, which circulated in clandestine scribal copies until their posthumous publication in 1598/9 The earliest, *A Pithie Exhortation to her Maiestie for Establishing her Successor to the Crowne* (c. 1587), had been conceived when the godly, though under siege, could still count on influential friends – Leicester, Mildmay, Walsingham. It sought to capitalize on the opportunities created by Mary's execution to secure the nomination of a successor sympathetic to the cause of further reform. But Wentworth did not raise thorny questions of doctrine or discipline. Rather, he focused on the ostensibly less divisive issue of the continued Catholic threat and how best to neutralize it. The papists, he warned, were feeding off the uncertainty surrounding the succession, and only a statutory settlement in Elizabeth's lifetime would avert a national catastrophe. As soon as the successor were appointed – or, rather, a whole raft of successors, for Wentworth urged the Queen and parliament to settle 'the succession of the crowne, successivelie to as manie, one after another, as the Lawe shal take notice of, to be inheritable thereunto'[6] – the papists, conscious that their lot was bound to worsen under the new monarch, would instantly cease any treasonable doings and instead join in prayers for the Queen's preservation.

Wentworth stressed 'the doubtfulnesse and ambiguitie of the title it self' (p. 48, 1st pag.) and studiously avoided naming names. He merely enunciated the principles according to which the determination should proceed. Those principles, however, were left fairly open. Wentworth indicated that birth would count for quite a lot, but he did not suggest that the claimant nearest in blood should necessarily succeed. The Queen and parliament, it seems, would have a good deal of discretion and latitude. Although Wentworth eschewed the word election, he was in effect proposing an elective succession akin to that tacitly advocated in much pre-1587 Protestant polemic.[7] He adopted that principle from expediency rather than conviction. All the candidates he had in mind had hereditary claims of some kind, and he expected the succession to return to its normal hereditary course in subsequent reigns. Wentworth did not elaborate why the elective principle – which he would openly repudiate in 1596 – should be followed on this occasion. He implied, however, that by authorizing parliament to choose the best Protestant for the job Elizabeth would 'break the neck of the Popishe hope of their golden day' and strengthen the 'Church throughout Christendome' (pp. 37, 96, 1st pag.).

Framed as a petition from the Lords and Commons, *Pithie Exhortation* seeks to convey an illusion of concord and unanimity. Protestants seem in a majority in the tract. Religious divisions, however, begin to encroach, as Wentworth's confessional taxonomy becomes uncomfortably contorted. The papists comprise those of state and of conscience, or, in modern parlance, conformists and recusants. Worse still, we learn that both papists (of either sort) and Protestants are vastly outnumbered by the army of neuters or 'worldlings' (pp. 66, 70, 1st pag.), ready to side with whoever has the upper hand.

The upshot of this exercise in mapping confessional difference is to subvert the rhetorical power of the fictive petition. For, once we subtract papists and neuters, what purports to be the voice of England emerges as a minority enterprise: by the end, only the few true believers are speaking. And even they might become alienated from the Queen if their just demands are not met (p. 36, 1st pag.). Ultimately, Wentworth's bid to harness confessional divisions falters both because of inconsistencies in the presentation of the Catholics – one moment they are a formidable enemy, the next a herd easy to overcome with one new statute – and because of the awkward identification of a legion of politic 'neuters', a by-product of Wentworth's half-hearted effort to paper over rifts within the Protestant camp. Under the circumstances, any suggestion that unity would be secured by appointing a successor rings distinctly hollow.

Is it possible, though, to discern whom Wentworth might have wished to see advanced to the throne around 1587? Or who was his *bête noire*? *Pithie Exhortation* does not trade in specifics. It neither mentions James nor overtly supports another candidate. In a 1593 deposition taken when the government swooped on Wentworth and his associates, Thomas Sparke, a godly Buckinghamshire minister who five years earlier had revised the tract at the author's request, pictures Wentworth as devoid of an ounce of partiality.[8] The depositions of Wentworth's other colleagues likewise deny that any of them endorsed a particular claimant. There is, however, internal evidence to suggest that Wentworth took a dim view of James in the *Pithie Exhortation*. He betrays his anti-Stuart bias in a brief retrospective on the perilous time when the Scottish Queen, 'a successor how weaklie soever supposed, yet mightily supported',[9] had been the focus of papist conspiracies. Surely, if Mary's title was weak, so is her son's. (Tellingly, in 1596 Wentworth would concede the strength of Mary's claim, which James inherited, while contrasting the evil mother and virtuous son.) The prominence of the biblical paradigm of King David's nomination of his younger son Solomon as heir – a conventional justification for excluding the next in line – likewise militates against Wentworth's espousal of James. So does his effusive praise of Henry VIII's forethought in providing for the country's future, for Henry's statutory regulations had over-ridden legitimacy by intruding his bastard daughters into the order of succession and his last will had arbitrarily bypassed the Stuarts.

Had Wentworth backed the Scottish King from the outset, it is reasonable to expect that he would have emphasized dynastic priority rather than promoting a quasi-elective expedient. Furthermore, *Pithie Exhortation* would probably have at least glanced at the British dimension of the problem, which is conspicuous by its absence. We cannot attribute Wentworth's reticence merely to caution, considering how reckless and egregiously rude the piece is in other respects. But what clinches the case against James is Wentworth's portrayal of the putative successor as a veritable hammer of the papists – 'hee shal…beat them with whippes, as slaves and dogs',[10] hardly a reputation the Scottish King commanded then or later. A more plausible contender for the starring role in Wentworth's morbid fantasy of persecution would have been Leicester's brother-in-law Henry Hastings, third Earl of Huntingdon, President of the Council in the North. Huntingdon's relentless hounding of Catholics and liberal patronage of radical ministers endeared him to the godly while attracting the severe opprobrium of papist pamphleteers.[11] Wentworth does not mention Huntingdon in *Pithie Exhortation*, but it is fair to speculate that he may have favoured the Earl when writing it.[12] In any case, there is no need for an alternative suspect to rule out the Scottish King as Wentworth's preferred candidate at this time.

JAMES VI OF SCOTLAND: A GODLY CHOICE?

What happened next? How did Wentworth's and his friends' thinking about the succession evolve in the later 1580s and beyond?

The accepted story is that James steadily rose in the estimation of the godly.[13] They were reassured by the fact that the King had refrained from any reprisals for his mother's execution and further heartened when Scotland loyally stood by England against the Spanish invaders in 1588. Meanwhile, James fostered a militant Protestant image in print, for instance in *Ane fruitfull meditatioun* (1588) on Revelation 20: 7–10. What further recommended him to Puritans was that after the fallout from the Marprelate controversy of 1588–89, he gave shelter to refugees from England, and in 1591 personally intervened on behalf of the Presbyterian Thomas Cartwright. By the autumn of 1593 Queen Anne was known to be pregnant, and the impending birth of an heir held out the promise of both dynastic and religious continuity. Were the Scottish King to take up reins in England and reform the Church after the Presbyterian model, the future of true religion in Britain would be assured.

This narrative, however, overlooks the less joyful news from Scotland during the five or so years since the Armada. Little if anything is made of the King's cosy relationship with the Catholic nobles, and how that soured his rapport with the Kirk, strained his relations with Elizabeth and compromised his standing among the godly, as also within the wider Protestant community.[14] At the same time, James's pronouncements on religion – such as the famous speech at the General Assembly in August 1590 stigmatizing the Church of England's alleged popish leanings that anyway may not have been widely known – are often quoted out of context. This obliterates their self-serving nature that would have been all too apparent to the original audience. In sum, whereas James's shifting and contested reputation in the mid-to-late 1590s has been well documented, our sense of his standing in the slightly earlier period is far less precise.

What did the godly make of James's stewardship of his country as it was being convulsed by revelations of successive Catholic conspiracies? English and Scottish reformers, we are often told, made, or hoped to make, common cause. But would there have been complete synergy in how the two groups approached the prospect of the Scottish King's enthronement in England? Scottish Presbyterians may have vehemently disapproved of James's reluctance to pursue alleged Catholic traitors and excoriated the inroads popery had made under his watch without necessarily linking any of this to the larger issue of the English succession. By contrast, their counterparts down south would have been acutely sensitive to the unsavoury implications for their homeland of James's well-attested intimacy with Scottish Catholic Lords, let alone his apparent tolerance of the Jesuit hydra. Presbyterian ministers routinely admonished their prince to govern his kingdom better, which, in the long run, would make him a better ruler of the whole island of Britain that was his by right.[15] But Puritans, for whom the succession had unique immediacy, may have been less inclined to wait for James to clean up his act. Wentworth, for one, comes across as willing to look for an heir closer to home.

1589

With *Pithie Exhortation* nicely copied out by a Banbury scrivener John Blundeville, Wentworth was ready to bring up the matter of succession in the 1589 Parliament, but ultimately desisted. Why? Neale thinks that Wentworth realized the time was unpropitious given the aftershocks of the Armada and was further disheartened by his failure to confer with Burghley who repulsed his many overtures during that session.[16] There may have been other reasons too. Coming at the climax of the Marprelate imbroglio, the Parliament had begun on 4 February with the Lord Chancellor Sir Christopher Hatton's speech condemning both papists and Puritans as equally pernicious enemies of Church and state.[17] The same message was relayed on 9 February from the pulpit at Paul's Cross by Hatton's chaplain (and Archbishop Whitgift's right-hand man) Richard Bancroft, who attempted to smear Puritan radicals as purveyors of seditious doctrine imbibed from Scottish Presbyterians.[18] This vendetta against reform had been facilitated by Leicester's death in September 1588.

Wentworth was not a timid man, but even he must have figured that Bancroft's sally dramatically altered the situation. Here was a well-connected cleric, evidently a cat's-paw of the regime's conservative wing, venturing an acerbic appraisal of Scottish ecclesiastical politics which boxed the godly into adopting one of two positions regarding James: either they could accept Bancroft's portrayal of him as still at odds with the Presbyterians, and, in defending the actions of the Kirk, end up trapped in the role of both religious and political subversives; or they could retort that he had been vilely traduced and that King and Kirk were as one – a taxing proposition. Since James's name would inevitably crop up in any debate about the succession, Wentworth may have concluded that it would be sensible to wait and see how the Scottish King and his clergy responded to Bancroft's charges. On the other hand, given Wentworth's serious doubts about James, why would the furore about Bancroft's sermon necessarily deter him from raising the succession issue? To play the devil's advocate, might this not actually have been an opportunity for Wentworth to separate the quest for a Protestant successor from the whole question of James? There are reasons why this would have been awkward, though, to do with the escalating charges of subversion against the reformers who now lacked a vocal patron on the Privy Council.[19]

What may also have swayed Wentworth against raising the touchy matter just then was some shocking news from Scotland. Towards the end of February the Catholic magnates closest to James – the Earls of Huntly, Erroll and Crawford – had been dramatically revealed to have conducted treasonable correspondence with Spain. In it, they lamented that the Armada had not landed on the Scottish coast and urged Philip to undertake a fresh assault on England via Scotland and Ireland. In addition, Huntly declared that his subscription to the King's Confession of 1581, essentially an anti-Catholic oath, had been a sham. The causes of the scandal were messy and complex,[20] but the facts that filtered through to the general public appeared simple and clear-cut: James consorted with Catholic nobles, who in turn harboured Jesuit missionaries, and now these magnates were exposed as agents of Spain. And yet the King forbore to punish the traitors. Even the momentary stand-off between forces loyal to the Crown and the now openly rebellious Catholic Earls, the so-called Brig o'Dee affair in April 1589, did not lead to a lasting banishment of the perpetrators from the court. Except for a fine, within months they were restored to former honours.

As a result, ministers of the Kirk who set out to rebut Bancroft's abrasive sermon found themselves in the unenviable position of having to defend their King's integrity and commitment to reform even as they themselves clamoured for him to discipline the Catholic Lords, expel the Jesuits and rid the court of suspected papists. In other words, they had to justify James as a particular kind of Protestant while not being entirely sure whether he was one at all. The Presbyterians were not altogether successful in that task,[21] as must have been glaringly obvious to their English acolytes.

What of Wentworth and his brethren? Equally disgruntled as their Scottish co-religionists by the aggressive conduct of Hatton and his clerical side-kick, they can hardly have felt reassured of James's religious steadfastness or political integrity.

1591

The protracted Bancroft saga coupled with the routing of reformers at home and repercussions of the Spanish Plot in Scotland alarmed Wentworth. Consequently, in May 1590, he was pleading with Burghley to help save the Church, now 'hanging upon more then half an untwisted thred, namelye, her Maties lyf'.[22] As Burghley again was failing to oblige, Wentworth then decided to approach the Earl of Essex, recently appointed commander of the Rouen expedition. In late summer 1591, he passed a copy of *Pithie Exhortation* to Dr Thomas Moffat, who would serve as physician to Essex's troops in Normandy.[23] When Moffat's carelessness in sending it out for copying brought the illicit tract to the attention of the Privy Council in mid-August, Wentworth was not at all dismayed. Rather, he saw this outcome as providential, for now his vital message would almost certainly reach the Queen. Once more appealing to Burghley, this time from the Gatehouse, Wentworth repeated that Church and commonwealth would go to wrack if the succession remained undeclared at Elizabeth's death.[24] Wentworth also reaffirmed his hope that the new prince would step up anti-Catholic policies,[25] scarcely a realistic prospect under James, of whom he sensed Burghley was no fan either. Wentworth's perseverance with this line shows that his reservations about the Stuart claim continued unabated.

This he made abundantly clear in the short essay, *Objection…Answered*, he drafted at the Gatehouse, probably in late October or November, in response to the following challenge from the Privy Councillors: 'Whereas the Scottish King is nowe our friend, if the successor were settled, and the title to the crown given from him to another, hee would, after, become our enemie. And for revenge hee would suffer the Spaniards with all their power to land in his countrie, & so to enter into ours'.[26] That was a timely concern given recent events in Scotland, especially since the discovery of the Catholic Earls' shady dealings with Spain and the restoration of Huntly to full royal favour. All the more surprising, therefore, that Wentworth's *Objection…Answered* has been completely neglected.

The piece suggests that James would be unwise to ally himself with Spain, for he would risk losing his own crown if Scottish papists sided with foreign ones. Whatever the odds that he might enter into such a compact, argues Wentworth, the English government would be nevertheless wrong to postpone grappling with the succession for fear of offending the Scot.[27] There is no reason, Wentworth asserts, why the King should demur at having his title examined by parliament. After all, he is seeking the English crown not by conquest but by right, so ought positively to welcome the chance to get that clarified. While not outwardly disrespectful towards James, the tract strongly betokens that parliament would be unlikely to recognize him as heir. Consider the following passage: 'If the successor were settled by Parliament, and the title of the crowne given from the Scottish king (lawfullie) to another…what cause hath he to become our enemie'?[28] What cause indeed! Or think of another, mocking the dubious benefits James would reap by consorting with Spain: 'Whither will his owne experience move him to expect better neighbourhoode at our soveraigne her hand during her life, & (after her decease) at the hand of an English Prince, or at the Spaniards hand, if he were king heere?'[29] How else to interpret this but as a broad hint in support of a home-born candidate?

Wentworth's *Objection…Answered*, unlike its Anglo-centric predecessor, situates the succession firmly within the British context. But it makes no reference to the possibility of an Anglo-Scottish union and instead dwells on relations between the two kingdoms, already linked by amity and common religion, now and in the post-Elizabethan future. In defiance of papist pamphleteers and Bancroft alike, Wentworth suppresses differences between English and Scottish Churches. The highest priority, he contends, should be the securing of a Protestant succession in England, or else both realms will fall prey to the satanic forces of the League of Trent.

Whereas in *Pithie Exhortation* Wentworth addressed his Queen directly, if under the guise of a parliamentary petition, here he was angling for the attention of Privy Councillors. The shift of emphasis comes across vividly in his plea to leaders of both England and Scotland, seen here as two 'monarchical republics', to solve this 'British' question for the common good: 'Let such…as rule the stearns of both the commonwealths of England & Scotland, lovinglie & kindlie conferre, consult and prevent the overthrows of both Church and commonwealths in both their countries, & that spedily'.[30] Wentworth's phrasing echoes the remonstrance with which Kirk ministers had nearly presented Elizabeth in January 1590. They too talked of the burning need for 'the wise and godlie of both the realmes' to ensure the two kingdoms showed a united front in the face of dangers from within and from without.[31] There is a distinct sense in both epistles that the prince, whether Elizabeth or James, must be compelled to do the right thing.[32] Wentworth's parting shot is to threaten James with divine vengeance lest he refuse to submit to 'this godlie and quiet triall'[33] and abide by its verdict. And yet the process would be humiliating in the extreme, James having to plead in person or else hire lawyers to speak on his behalf, the whole thing ominously redolent of his mother's treason trial. Besides, the constant harping on parliament's capacity to give the title away from the Scottish King presages that he could well end up excluded.

Wentworth may have been foolhardy but he was no fool. While directing his memorandum to the Privy Council, he plainly understood that the councillors represented a range of often divergent positions. He took Burghley to be sympathetic to his mission, quite unlike Hatton. During interrogations Hatton apparently accused Wentworth of waging a concerted propaganda offensive by dispersing copies of 'a booke of the heyre apparante', which, the Chancellor alleged, 'came owte of coblers & taylors shoppes'.[34] In other words, Wentworth was being located by Hatton within a subversive underground network of the kind the mad reformer Edmund Coppinger had masterminded as recently as July, in the run-up to his harebrained venture to proclaim as messiah the no less deranged William Hacket, and so oust the rotten political and ecclesiastical establishment.[35] Before long Wentworth would be overtly vilified for allegedly 'encouraging' Coppinger 'as the Lord did *Iosuah*' in Bancroft's fresh diatribe against radical dissent, *Daungerous Positions* (1593).[36]

By writing and circulating *Pithie Exhortation* Wentworth had flagrantly violated the provisions of the 1571 Treasons Act. So we might well wonder why anyone on the council should have invited him to pen answers to hypothetical objections, and why he was then let off the hook. Wentworth's exceedingly gentle treatment only becomes intelligible when related to ongoing intra-conciliar disputes. To counter Whitgift and Hatton's drive against reform, Burghley was about to avail himself of the well-tried formula of anti-popery and Hispanophobia, and to that end drafted *A Declaration of Great Troubles Pretended against the Realme by a Number of Seminarie Priests and Jesuists [sic]*.[37] The proclamation was ready and printed by 18 October, though temporarily withheld from publication.

With the conservatives in temporary disarray, owing to Hatton's illness and later death on 20 November, Burghley wasted no time in unleashing his anti-popish tirade, which implemented the harshest and most sweeping set of anti-Catholic measures yet. Nor did he forget about the old Puritan trouble-maker. Wentworth was released from the Gatehouse and placed under house arrest on 21 November, the day after Hatton's demise; by mid-February 1592 he was a free man.[38]

1593

In some respects, 1593 looks like a re-run of 1589. The year opened with lurid reports from Scotland of another popish plot starring Huntly and his *confrères*, the so-called Spanish Blanks affair, and James was at the receiving end of the same tired complaints from Elizabeth and the Kirk about his dereliction in punishing the chief culprits. Meanwhile, Lord Keeper Sir John Puckering instructed the Parliament which met on 19 February to leave contentious matters alone. Whitgift, with the blessing of the Queen, renewed moves to extend anti-Catholic legislation to encompass Protestant dissidents, and even before the draconian penal measures were put in place, had three separatists executed under the terms of the 1581 statute originally targeting Catholics. Wentworth likewise doggedly stuck to his guns. After a spell of electioneering to 'procure such Burgesses, as might further the same cause',[39] he arrived in London with his pockets full of writings on the succession, among them a brand new copy of *Pithie Exhortation*.

Wentworth's abortive attempt to coordinate a petitioning campaign in the 1593 Parliament has been scrupulously chronicled by Neale. The contours of the godly network-in-the-making have been further elucidated by Tyacke and Collinson, and a fresh trawl through the archives reveals it to have been yet more extensive than even they realized.[40] None, however, has paid heed to the Scottish context of the undertaking or its wider international reverberations. If the Privy Council had been worried beforehand about James's potential collusion with Spain, their misgivings only grew with the disclosure of the Spanish Blanks scandal, which both they and the Kirk viewed as another bout in the ongoing Counter-reformation crusade against true religion.[41] Huntly, chief royal favourite, appeared up to his neck in the conspiracy, but how far was the

King embroiled? Would he not get into still deeper waters if alarmed that the English Parliament was poised to disallow his claim? With the French war of succession at a critical juncture, and mounting anxiety about a fresh Spanish onslaught, the last thing the regime needed was a bunch of overzealous MPs holding forth on titles and contenders. The Scottish King must be weaned away from the Hispanophiles, not aggravated and practically driven into their arms. Quite apart from Elizabeth's perennial distaste for having the succession thrust into the open, this would have been the worst possible time to try to broach it.

And so the clampdown was swift and severe. Wentworth and his godly brigade had held their first (and, as it turned out, last) conference about the succession on 21 February, two days after the formal opening of the Parliament. Wentworth was apprehended and interrogated on the 23rd, and further arrests and interviews followed. The various depositions reveal that his associates had been taken aback by the intemperate tone of Wentworth's missives.[42] No less tellingly, the conferees had prevailed upon Wentworth to seek counsel from more experienced parliament men, and he duly approached James Morice, a renowned Puritan lawyer whose career had chiefly been facilitated by Burghley. But Morice poured cold water on the whole project, for 'if we shold enter into dealing wth titles of the Crowne we had nede (I thinke) holde a parleament a whole yeare long'.[43]

This is a significant remark, not least from someone occupying the same end of the confessional spectrum as Wentworth. While the absence from the depositions of any hint of preference for a specific candidate could be construed as a sign of wariness, Morice's recognition that to reach consensus quickly would be impossible implies that the godly did not have a firm – and plausible – favourite at this stage. At a minimum it suggests that James was not necessarily seen as an uncontested front-runner. This impression is reinforced by the deponents' concern that for parliament to delve into his title would be a 'cause of griefe' to the Scot, not something they would have worried about if the object of the exercise had been to make James king.[44] It is further confirmed by a memorandum which Sir Walter Ralegh obligingly sent to the Queen on hearing of the Wentworth imbroglio. Ralegh mocked 'thes great patriots' for their indecision about whether to advance James, whose recent conduct had been deeply disconcerting, or the childless Huntingdon, or someone else altogether. And he dismissed their plan for 'an election' as divisive, seditious and ineffectual.[45] All in all, had it come to a formal discussion in 1593, many godly MPs – not just mainstream Protestants apprehensive that the Scottish King would bring in presbyteries – might have opposed his candidacy. And with good reason, for James's credentials, as Ralegh bluntly pointed out, were becoming murkier and murkier.

True, in June 1592 James had finally approved legislation entrenching presbyteries – the so-called 'Golden Act' – and a concomitant repeal of selected 'Black Acts', as well as an act against Catholicism. But this had been done under duress.[46] Besides, as everyone could see, popery prospered in Scotland and official counter-measures were not being strictly enforced; in consequence, the militants' homilies were getting increasingly abusive towards their King and questioning of his creed.[47] What about the Spanish Blanks? How might that brouhaha have affected his image? The royal proclamation of 5 January 1593 painted James as the intended victim of this newest popish conspiracy. His oversight of the subsequent investigation and later expedition up north to discipline the Catholic earls strengthened this perception. (One wonders how far James was timing these to coincide with the opening of the English Parliament.) But thenceforth, this hopeful scenario began to unravel. The King returned from the north on 10 March, having achieved next to nothing, and on the 18th when the newly arrived English ambassador urged him to declare war against Spain, he politely but firmly declined, citing his disappointment that the English had not made good their promises regarding the succession proffered at the height of the Armada crisis.[48] Any credit the Scottish King might have garnered by his resolute proceedings earlier in the year rapidly dissipated.

Nor did the official account of the Spanish Blanks affair necessarily boost his prestige among the godly or anyone else in England. *A Discouerie of the Unnaturall and Traiterous Conspiracie of Scottisch Papists, against God, his Kirk, their Natiue Cuntrie, the Kingis Majesties Persone and Estate*, probably compiled by John Davidson, was printed in Edinburgh 'at the special commaund of the Kingis Maiestie' and instantly reprinted in London.[49] The pamphlet positions itself in the long line of agitprop purporting to dissect popish treason for the edification of an expectant public. But familiar trappings aside, there is more going on. Even a cursory reading of the documentary evidence reproduced by Davidson reveals that the treason had been festering for years – several of the letters date to 1589 and the Brig o'Dee fiasco; that the real culprits, above all royal bosom-friend Huntly, were still at large; and that the King was either complicit or gullible, and in any case woefully indolent. Admittedly, the title page *pro forma* lists James among the targets – after God, Kirk and country – as does the preamble, though why the papists should have conspired against him is baffling given his goodwill towards them; and nothing in the correspondence actually proved that they had. Quite the reverse – there is a distinct sense that they had not anticipated opposition from that quarter, and may in fact have counted on tacit consent.

Furthermore, Davidson implies that justice is yet to be done and stints to say anything positive about James. The best he can do is note, in a margin, that the papists 'count our King amongst the heretickes'.[50] And when the prefatory epistle trenchantly admonishes 'euery one according to his calling and place…to withstand these desperat attempts before they passe remedie, and timely to preuent the farther danger, by assisting the execution of Iustice vpon the rest of the detected traitors without respect of persons',[51] James manifestly is the main addressee. Unless he bestirs himself, it seems, his godly subjects may well take matters into their own hands. And they would scarcely lack ammunition even against their royal master, for they had seized – though for the time being suppressed – the private rumination, in his own hand, on the pros and cons of invading England in cahoots with Spain![52]

Would the Puritans have warmed to James on reading the pamphlet? I doubt it. For the prospect of a monarch who cannot maintain order in his own house would have looked distinctly unappetizing. The latent anti-Scottish bias would likely have flared up and got superimposed on hatred of popery amid reports of the Hispaniolized Scots' wicked designs against England, outweighing any confessional solidarity with the Scottish Presbyterians, who seemed themselves less than pleased with their King. Under the circumstances, the indefatigable Bancroft's latest bid to drive a wedge between the godly and the Scottish King in the mammoth *Daungerous Positions* would have rung disconcertingly true. The most charitable interpretation of James's conduct by the end of 1593 was to see him, like Elizabeth, as a 'seduced king'.[53]

PERSONS THE KINGMAKER?

The 1593 Parliament precipitated a decisive shift in the focus and direction of pamphleteering by English Catholic exiles whom Albert J. Loomie, SJ, has dubbed 'the Spanish Elizabethans'.[54] Since the execution of Mary Queen of Scots and defeat of the Armada, these writers were struggling to find a voice on the succession. Cardinal William Allen's *Admonition to the Nobility and People of England and Ireland* (1588) had none too subtly implied that the crown should go to Philip II.[55] But with the Spanish invasion an unmitigated failure and no immediate prospect for another, Hispanophiles had to retreat from pushing the Habsburg claim. So the raft of publications issuing from Richard Verstegan's press in Antwerp, while laudatory towards Philip, concentrated on lambasting the Elizabethan regime, above all the Cecils, and only vaguely reflected on the dangers for the country of an uncertain succession, blamed here on the self-serving designs of such atheistic monsters. That was part and parcel of the papists' bid to picture England in terminal crisis: riven with religious divisions, isolated on the international scene and fearful for the future. Burghley's 1591 proclamation added fuel to the fire, and the pro-Spanish polemicists accordingly ratcheted up the tone of their abuse. But however adept the libels may have been at riling the government, vitriol was no substitute for policy. In the absence of a plausible Catholic contender around whom to rally openly, they had to develop a different tack, at least until such time as Spanish conquest again became viable. And that in turn required taking a stand on the candidacy of James VI, son and heir of their *quondam* hope.

The contrast between the initial post-Armada efforts and Persons's work composed in 1593 is striking.[56] The former mostly stayed away from specifics, though on occasion came close to conceding the strength of the Stuart claim. Verstegan's *The Copy of a Letter* (1589) evinced longing for a successful invasion, meanwhile stressing the ambiguity of the title and concomitant likelihood of internecine strife.[57] The riff on 'the incertitude of the succession' also reappears in Verstegan's *An Advertisement written to a Secretarie of my L. Treasurers* (1592), itself a summary of and puff for Persons's Latin *Philopater* (1592).[58] In the same year, Verstegan's *Declaration of the True Causes of the Great Troubles* (1592) portrayed James as a consummate dissembler who, though quiescent for now so as not to 'cut him-self from the possibilitie of that crowne', once firmly in the saddle would avenge 'the cutting of of his owne mothers head'. Expert punning aside, this attempt to blacken James in the eyes of the English and in particular to spook Burghley, architect of Mary's beheading, would be rather counterproductive if Verstegan did not at the same time insinuate that even in terms of strict dynastic precedence the Jacobean succession was far from clear-cut.[59]

So that is where Hispanophile propaganda stood on the succession as the furore broke out over Wentworth's bid to raise the taboo topic in parliament. If in Mary's lifetime all papist polemicists had repeatedly avowed that she was the only competitor with an unassailable claim, the Spanish Elizabethans were now beginning to peddle the uncertainty principle. Far from transferring allegiance from mother to son (whom, some thought, she may in fact have disinherited in favour of Philip in her last will),[60] they now undertook to discredit James to make him odious and threatening in the eyes of the English. Yet so far they had not produced a proper succession tract, merely broaching the issue in passing.

The news of Wentworth's arrest provided the ultimate stimulus – really a reminder of how much the regime wanted to keep the thorny problem under wraps – and by the end of the year Persons completed two pamphlets dealing with the succession. *Newes from Spayne and Holland* was ready by 1 September 1593, and *A Conference* by 31 December. The former was printed and disseminated forthwith; the latter, though printed early in 1594,[61] would not be released for publication until the summer of 1595, which may explain why its rootedness in the events of 1593 is often ignored. While *A Conference* has always enjoyed the scholarly limelight, *Newes* is only ever cited as an advertisement of sorts for the later, more substantial treatise. This, though, is to underestimate its importance and miss a signal shift in the Jesuit's tactics. A *faux* newsletter, *Newes* is a transitional text which fuses insistence on the robustness of the Catholic cause plus evil councillor rhetoric with the more novel, reason-of-state approach to religion and the succession. The first part dissects England's international isolation stemming from her supposedly idiosyncratic religious settlement and bad foreign policy, the second zooms in on bitter confessional divisions which are tearing her apart. Unlike *A Conference*, which will analyse how these could influence the outcome of the succession struggle, *Newes* speculates on how they might pan out in the remainder of the reign and then under the new monarch. The concluding section pretends to give an overview of a conference about the succession held in April in Amsterdam by 'divers gentlemen, captaynes, schollers, and others, as wel Inglish, Scottish, Irish, & French, as also some Italians & Dutchmen'.[62]

Whereas Wentworth's *Pithie Exhortation* sought to create a sense of unity, Persons exploits the free-flowing format of the dialogue to illustrate, and further foment, conflict and unease. The old fault-line between Protestants and Romanists, he argues, has been compounded by the increasingly acrimonious split between Protestants and Puritans manifest in the recent outpouring of mutual invective in print courtesy of Martin Marprelate and his detractors, the execution of the three separatists, and now the passage of punitive legislation targeting Puritans and papists alike (to which Persons's translation into Latin, and pungent appraisal, of the relevant documents simultaneously alerted Continental audiences).[63] The Jesuit's quasi-forensic take on dynastic titles demonstrates that, far from there being a clear front-runner, the race is still wide open. And in a masterstroke, Persons spices up the noxious brew with a dash of conspiracy theory. He insinuates that to retain power at all cost Burghley will engineer the accession of a docile candidate, say Arbella Stuart, whom he can manipulate the way he has Elizabeth.

Because the *Newes* supposedly relays what the motley crew said on the occasion of the conference, the various allegations hardly need to hold together, and indeed they do not. The object is simply to sow confusion and vilify the Scottish King. Not only does Persons falsely indicate that the Stuart title was 'cut of' by Mary's attainder.[64] He also mocks her son as the pawn of seditious Scottish clergy: 'the king is tossed and tumbled by troblesome people as it pleaseth the ministers without heades, to blow into their eares' (fo. 32[v]). This diminishes James's regal stature but does not posit that he is on a collision course with the Presbyterians. Rather, Persons leaves open the possibility that on arriving in England James might side with the Puritans out of sheer political calculation – a clever way to alarm anyone committed to the established church.

Finally, the Jesuit turns to the role of Queen and parliament in sorting out England's future. '[W]hy is ther not order taken by parliament for so great an inconuenience', asks another of his mouthpieces, 'and how commeth it to passe that we heare out of Ingland that some were committed to prison this last parliament for offering to treate in this affayre?' (fo. 38[r-v]). What follows reads like a point-by-point rebuttal of Wentworth's *Pithie Exhortation*. Whereas Wentworth criticized the Queen's inaction and called for a prompt parliamentary settlement, Persons appears to defend the royal policy of permanent deferral. To deal with the succession in Elizabeth's lifetime, he contends, would be to imperil the Queen's personal safety, the peace of the realm, even the interests of leading competitors. If an heir apparent were declared now, he or she would be Elizabeth's mortal enemy, for 'ther is none to succed that may be presumed by the neernes of bloode to desire more the Queenes safty then ther own commodity' (fo. 38ᵛ) – another nasty dig at James; the disappointed pretenders would take to arms; and the loyalties of the English would predictably shift from Elizabeth to her successor, from the setting to the rising sun. For the Queen to keep the succession unresolved, therefore, is both prudent and advantageous – note the echoes of Ralegh's argument, but the lack of a settlement will unquestionably lead to a bloody civil war once she is gone.

Newes from Spayne and Holland was a new departure. Adopting the feignedly aloof perspective of reason of state, it explicitly situated the succession quandary against a backdrop of acute religious tensions and, with the introduction of the civilian and the common lawyer, adumbrated a legal case proving that there are a multitude of bidders for the crown, none with a foolproof claim. But aside from the one reference to Mary's attainder, the pamphlet did not challenge James's claim with any specifics, and certainly did not plump for another. This changed in the far more exhaustive *Conference* which, maintaining the pretence of detachment, systematically demolished the Scottish King's pretensions and implicitly promoted the Spanish Infanta, Isabella Clara Eugenia.

Persons finished *A Conference* in December 1593 and, as the swift Antwerp printing suggests, fully intended to have it published in the New Year. Had the edition appeared as scheduled, 1594 would have marked the first time James was so openly and sweepingly rejected by a Catholic in print. There are several reasons why Persons penned the hostile tract. Unlike his fellow-Jesuit, the Scot William Crichton,[65] he never had high hopes of James's conversion and anyway recognized that such sway as Huntly and the Catholic Lords had enjoyed was irrevocably on the wane. Now that the French crown had eluded Spain, Persons judged that the time was ripe to persuade Philip to turn his attention once again to England. Another significant factor was that James's Queen was known to be pregnant, and Persons, keenly aware of the kudos that the birth of the Stuart heir, especially if male, would confer on James, planned for his attack to anticipate or coincide with that event. Besides, Persons also angled to capitalize on Essex's February appointment to the Privy Council to stir up factional tensions in England. That is why, having harped on Burghley's near-omnipotence in *Newes*, he now performed a stunning volte face and designated the Earl as the unquestioned kingmaker.'[66]

The 1593 Parliament and its aftermath provided Persons with an ideal pretext for the assault. The preface highlights the continuing relevance of the Wentworth fiasco, naming both him and Sir Henry Bromley as victims of government crackdown, and the main text dwells on deadly religious dissension that fuelled the recent penal laws.[67] How better to hit out at both English and Scottish crowns, and provoke heretics across Britain, than by twinning succession and religion and bringing the explosive mixture into the open, all under cover of impartiality and concern for the public good?

There is no need to rehearse the Jesuit's case for elective monarchy and resistance which effectively crystallizes the assumptions latent in Wentworth's *Pithie Exhortation*, or his tortuous genealogical divagations. The key point is that *A Conference* comprehensively undercut James's claim not only by marshalling a host of supposed legal impediments but also on the grounds that the Jacobean succession would be plain bad for the country. Ergo, reason of state dictates that James, whose power base anyway is negligible, must be excluded. The Spanish Infanta, the book insinuates, would be a far more auspicious choice.

Reflecting on the 'wonderfull diversity in matters of religion',[68] Persons describes the rival factions of Protestants, Puritans and papists, and affects to decipher the likely inclinations of each. Although he is adamant that to advance a prince of a contrary religion is both a sin and a grave error in policy, irrespective of one's religion, the Jesuit nevertheless dangles the trump card of potential Catholic support before the Scottish King. The papists, he explains, are buoyant despite, or perhaps because of, ongoing persecution, and their vote may well prove decisive. Besides, unlike the other two groups, they are neither committed to a specific title nor divided among themselves. To gain them, however, James would either have to convert, like Henry IV of France, or else guarantee freedom of worship.[69] Naturally, the argument against advancing or even accepting a candidate of a different faith applied in reverse, for what Protestant would promote a Spanish papist princess, whatever the putative advantages of her accession? But that is altogether irrelevant, for, as Persons knew better than anyone, only a successful conquest could make Spanish succession viable.

When the book hit the underground market in the late summer of 1595, the situation was in many ways less propitious; and some aspects of the argument, *au courant* back in early 1594, would have seemed positively dated. Nonetheless, *A Conference* caused an international furore, and determined the course of the succession debate for the remainder of the reign. Much ink has been spilled in attempts to chart the impact of Persons's treatise. Here I concentrate on how it persuaded Peter Wentworth and his Puritan brethren to abandon their reservations about the Stuart claim.

THE PURITAN'S CONVERSION

Wentworth's was the first of many rejoinders to the 'Spanish harted papist'.[70] Penned in 1596, his fourth year in the Tower, *A Treatise ... Concerning the Person of the True and Lawfull Successor* made crystal clear his preference for James. Wentworth begins with a confession: 'I have somewhat fleeted and altered concerning some pointes of this question: yet at this present I am of that minde, and so, as I thinke, shal be stil, that the right shall be found in this king of Scots'.[71] In order to justify James's title, Wentworth had to renounce principles which he once held dear and defended in writing.

Erstwhile advocate of parliamentary sovereignty and petitioner to Elizabeth for naming a successor, Wentworth now vehemently opposes election and royal nomination alike. Instead, he argues that 'bastard succession established by Parliaments' would be ineffectual and the elected monarch weak. As for claims that Elizabeth has the power to name an heir, first, there is no parliamentary act to that effect; secondly, such arbitrary 'pretended willes' only bring 'horrible miseries'; and, thirdly, the Queen herself has already declared for the Scottish title in her conversation with Maitland of Lethington back in 1561 and should remain true to both her word and her motto '*Semper Eadem*'. To drive the point home, Wentworth quotes Elizabeth's *ipsissima verba* straight from Buchanan's Latin history, providing a translation for the unlearned reader.[72]

Wentworth pronounces James's right virtually unassailable. That right, moreover, comes from God, which is why, he argues, to challenge it would be the height of injustice 'if the religious and wise king of Scots ... be willing to governe us according to our owne lawes (as no question he will)'.[73] *A Treatise* leaves unclear whether (and if so how) a guarantee of abiding by the laws should be extracted from the Scottish King or whether the coronation oath would be sufficient unto the purpose. Ultimately, Wentworth contends that James's right cannot be taken from him, whereas in both *Pithie Exhortation* and *Objection ... Answered* he implied that it could. *A Treatise* concludes with a prayer that we 'may give the crowne and Realme with cheerefulnesse and peace to that man, to whome [God] hath beene pleased to give the right'.[74] The 'giving' of the crown will be a *pro forma* act, a mere ratification of divine appointment.

Wentworth may have ditched whole swathes of his prior constitutional assumptions but does not seem to have revised his view of the sort of ecclesiastical policy James would likely pursue on his accession. In *Pithie*, we recall, Wentworth was hopeful that the new incumbent would hammer the papists, a sign that the Scottish King was not uppermost in his mind. Now that he is rooting for James, Wentworth changes course. In an implicit concession to the Jesuit's insistence that the Catholic vote will most certainly count, Wentworth affirms that the Scottish King will practise far-reaching toleration, 'for none of them could ever expect greater favour at anie successors handes, then at his, who hath already shewed himself too too remisse in punishing so manie of his owne subjectes of their profession'. Even so, Wentworth is sanguine about James's own faith, and commends 'his rare wisdome and love of Religion'.[75]

With the cause of reform virtually broken, and no home-born candidate remaining who could revive it, James's *cachet* among the godly had obviously gone up. In a transparent allusion to Huntingdon's death the previous December (and his champion Leicester's a few years earlier), Wentworth remarks, somewhat ruefully, that 'The removal of the moste wise, heroicall and popular competitors and their favourers which might have opposed, doeth smooth and plaine a way for him to come in'.[76] In addition to Huntingdon's passing, the Seymour claim had been damaged by the involvement of Sir Michael Blount, the lieutenant of the Tower, in a plot that came to light in late 1595 to hold the Tower for Edward Seymour, Earl of Hertford in the event of Elizabeth's death (resulting in Blount's dismissal, the arrest of the Earl of Hertford and his sons, and a renewed scrutiny of Wentworth). It was harmed again in mid-1596 by Sir John Smythe's bizarre outburst in praise of the younger Seymour at the Colchester musters. The Stanley claim had also been badly bruised by the mysterious death in 1594 of Ferdinando, fifth Earl of Derby; the marriage of William, the sixth Earl, to Burghley's granddaughter; and the struggle over the inheritance between Earl William and Earl Ferdinando's dowager countess.[77] All of these events weakened rival options to James.

It is not a little ironic that while Scottish Presbyterians, distinctly disillusioned with their King, were hatching another *coup* whose dismal failure precipitated a powerful backlash against James's Presbyterian critics,[78] Wentworth and his godly associates at long last threw their weight behind his succession. Ultimately, their grudging and drawn out switch to the Scottish King – as gauged by Wentworth's writings – was less an ideological drift away from the elective option than a function of circumstance. In their conversion to the Stuart title, moreover, the Puritans were not alone: just as Wentworth was writing up his case for James in the Tower, the Archbishop of York, Matthew Hutton, defended the Jacobean succession in a sermon at court.[79]

CODA: THE REHABILITATION OF THE SCOTTISH KING

Like Elizabeth who, as Alexandra Walsham has shown, owed her elevation as a Protestant icon largely to recurrent Catholic attempts to assassinate and depose her,[80] James could be taken – with only a pinch of salt – to have in some respects owed his position as the most compelling Protestant candidate for the English throne to the Jesuit's nasty attack in *A Conference*. Hitherto, post-Armada Catholic pamphlets had either ignored the Scottish King altogether or fired isolated volleys, while the intercepted correspondence of the likes of Huntly made public by Davidson evinced papist hopes that James might convert to Catholicism – and that of course fanned suspicions of the Kirk and all manner of Protestants in England. Once *A Conference* was in circulation, in later 1595, James's title was for the first time comprehensively impugned in print – and his 'heretical' *bona fides* acknowledged – by a papist author. Thereafter opposition to the Stuart claim would be explicitly associated with Spain and Catholicism or, more precisely, militant Catholicism epitomized by the Society of Jesus.

To be sure, a host of important external factors variously contributed to the process of rendering Jacobean succession both viable and desirable. James now had a son who was being brought up by the Protestant Earl of Mar; Essex had become a close ally and brought a lot of the godly into James's camp; the episcopate's mistrust of him abated; Huntingdon was no more; the Huntly problem had been essentially resolved; and with Henry IV back in the Roman fold, James could pose as the international champion of militant Protestantism. Last not least, whereas in the past the Elizabethan regime had feared a Hispano-Scottish Catholic invasion from the north, James was now considered a declared enemy of Spain – Wentworth cites approvingly his recent belligerent proclamation to that effect – and none of his shifty diplomacy in dealing with the papacy, Catholic powers or Tyrone would dispel that impression in the public mind. Should the Scottish King end up fighting for the English crown because Elizabeth chose to exclude him, as he feared she might, he would be leading an army of Protestant Scots and Protestant nations. Nonetheless, Persons's *Conference* provided a signal boost to James's credentials, even though he himself did not necessarily see it that way.

NOTES

1 Nicholas Tyacke, 'Puritan politicians and King James VI and I, 1587–1604', in Thomas Cogswell, Richard Cust and Peter Lake (eds), *Politics, Religion and Popularity in Early Stuart Britain: Essays in Honour of Conrad Russell* (Cambridge, 2002), pp. 21–44 (esp. pp. 22–3).

2 Patrick Collinson, 'The religious factor', in Jean-Christophe Mayer (ed.), *The Succession Struggle in Late Elizabethan England: Politics, Polemics and Cultural Representations* (Montpellier, 2004), pp. 259–60.

3 Tyacke, 'Puritan politicians', p. 23; Peter Wentworth, *A Pithie Exhortation to her Maiestie for Establishing her Successor to the Crowne Whereunto is added a Discourse Containing the Authors Opinion of the True and Lawfull Successor to Her Maiestie* ([Edinburgh,] 1598), p. 6 (2nd pag.). See also J. E. Neale, 'Peter Wentworth: II', *English Historical Review*, 39 (1924), 175–205, to which the accounts of Tyacke and Collinson are both indebted.

4 R. Doleman [Robert Persons], *A Conference about the Next Succession to the Crowne of Ingland* ([Antwerp], 1594 [1595]), pp. 242–3 (2nd pag.).

5 J. E. Neale, *Elizabeth I and Her Parliaments*, 3 vols (London, 1953–58), vol. 2, p. 262.

6 Wentworth, *Pithie Exhortation*, p. 91 (1st pag.)

7   Paulina Kewes, *This Great Matter of Succession: Politics, History, and Elizabethan Drama* (Oxford: forthcoming).

8   BL, Harley MS 6846, fo. 101ʳ.

9   Wentworth, *Pithie Exhortation*, p. 82 (1st pag.).

10 *Ibid.*, p. 71 (1st pag.).

11 Claire Cross, *The Puritan Earl: The Life of Henry Hastings, Third Earl of Huntingdon, 1536–1595* (London, 1966); Peter Lake and Michael Questier, *The Trials of Margaret Clitherow: Persecution, Martyrdom and the Politics of Sanctity in Elizabethan England* (New York, 2011), p. 117 *passim*.

12 Neale thinks that in Mary's lifetime, Wentworth may have looked to Huntingdon or the sons of the Earl of Hertford ('Wentworth', p. 198).

13 For example, Tyacke, 'Puritan politicians', p. 23.

14 See, for example, Helen Georgia Stafford, *James VI of Scotland and the Throne of England* (New York and London, 1940), pp. 41ff.

15 For example, Robert Bruce, *Sermons upon the Sacrament of the Lords Supper* (Edinburgh, 1591), sig. A2ᵛ; cf. Robert Bruce, *Sermons Preached in the Kirk of Edinburgh* (Edinburgh, 1591).

16 TNA, SP12/232, fo. 25ʳ.

17 T. E. Hartley, *Proceedings in the Parliaments of Elizabeth I*, 3 vols (Leicester, 1981), vol. 2, pp. 414–24 (esp. 419–20).

18 Richard Bancroft, *A Sermon Preached at Paules Crosse* (London, 1589). See Gordon Donaldson, 'The attitude of Whitgift and Bancroft to the Scottish Church', *Transactions of the Royal Historical Society*, 4th ser., 24 (1942), 95–115 (esp. 104–60); Owen Chadwick, 'Richard Bancroft's submission', *Journal of Ecclesiastical History*, 3 (1952), 8–73; Chapter 5 in this volume.

19 Private communication from Paul E. J. Hammer.

20 See Ruth Grant, 'The Brig o' Dee Affair, the Sixth Earl of Huntly and the politics of the Counter-Reformation', in Julian Goodare and Michael Lynch (eds), *The Reign of James VI* (East Lothian, 2000), pp. 93–109; Thomas M. McCoog, SJ, '"Pray to the Lord of the Harvest": Jesuit missions to Scotland in the sixteenth century', *Innes Review*, 53 (2002), 127–88, at pp. 146ff.

21 For example, the piece probably drafted on behalf of the Kirk by the fiery preacher John Davidson though never sent, 'To the most Mightie Princes … Elizabeth Qwene of England, & c.', in David Laing (ed.), *The Miscellany of the Wodrow Society*, [9] (1844), pp. 489–96; and Davidson's *D. Bancrofts rashnes in rayling against the Church of Scotland* (Edinburgh, 1590).

22 Wentworth to Burghley, 9 May 1590, TNA, SP12/232/16; cf. the letter of 12 May, SP12/232/19.

23 Neale, 'Wentworth'. For Essex's infelicitous attempt in mid-1589 to establish rapport with James, see Paul E. J. Hammer, *The Polarisation of Elizabethan Politics: The Political Career of Robert Devereux, 2nd Earl of Essex, 1585–1597* (Cambridge, 1999), pp. 91–2.

24 Wentworth to Burghley, 27 September 1591, TNA, SP12/240/21 and enclosure SP12/240/21.i.

25 *Ibid.*

26 *Objection…Answered*, in Wentworth, *Pithie Exhortation*, p. 109 (1st pag.).

27 *Ibid.*, p. 117 (1st pag.).

28 *Ibid.*, p. 115 (1st pag.).

29 *Ibid.*, p. 112 (1st pag.).

30 *Ibid.*, p. 118 (1st pag.).

31 Laing, *Miscellany*, p. 492.

32 *Objection … Answered*, in Wentworth, *Pithie Exhortation*, p. 119 (1st pag.).

33 *Ibid.*, p. 121 (1st pag.)

34 Wentworth to Burghley, TNA, SP12/240/21.i.

35 Alexandra Walsham, '"Frantic Hacket": prophecy, sorcery, insanity, and the Elizabethan Puritan movement', *Historical Journal*, 41 (1998), 27–66.

36 [Richard Bancroft], *Daungerous positions and proceedings published and practised within the iland of Brytaine, vnder pretence of reformation, and for the presbiteriall discipline* (London, 1593), p. 174.

37 Paul L. Hughes and James F. Larkin (eds), *Tudor Royal Proclamations*, 3 vols (New Haven, CT, and London, 1964–69), vol. 3, no. 738, pp. 86–93; Glyn Parry, *The Arch-conjuror of England: John Dee* (New Haven, CT, and London, 2011), ch. 19; Victor Houliston, 'The Lord Treasurer and the Jesuit: Robert Persons's satirical *Responsio* to the 1591 proclamation', *The Sixteenth Century Journal*, 32 (2001), 383–401; Freddy Cristóbal Domínguez, '"We must fight with paper and pens": Spanish Elizabethan Polemics, 1585–1598', Ph.D. thesis, University of Princeton (2011), pp. 200ff.

38 BL, Additional MS 24664, fo. 51[r].

39 Robert Lynford's deposition, 11(?) March 1593, BL, Harley MS 6846, fo. 96[r].

40 For instance, in 1593 Sparke admitted to having read *Pithie Exhortation* aloud to two fellow ministers, 'm[r] Harrys of Hardwick & to m[r] Egerton of Adstock' ('M[r] doctor [Thomas] Sparkes his Confession', BL, Harley MS 6846, fo. 101[r]).

41 Ruth Grant, 'George Gordon, Sixth Earl of Huntly and the Politics of the Counter-Reformation in Scotland, 1581–1595', unpublished Ph.D. thesis (University of Edinburgh, 2010), pp. 305ff. Cf. Thomas M. McCoog, SJ, *The Society of Jesus in Ireland, Scotland, and England: 1589–1597: Building the Faith of Saint Peter upon the King of Spain's Monarchy* (Farnham and Rome, 2012), pp. 80–5; T. G. Law, 'The Spanish blanks and Catholic earls, 1592–94', in P. Hume Brown (ed.), *Collected Essays and Reviews of Thomas Graves Law* (Edinburgh, 1904), pp. 244–76.

42 BL, Harley MS 6846, fos 86[r], 97[v].

43 BL, Harley MS 6846, fo. 108[r–v].

44 Oliver St John's deposition, BL, Harley MS 6846, fo. 88[r].

45 Walter Ralegh, letter to the Queen, Hatfield, Cecil Papers, vol. 83, fos 35a–36b and 'Reasons why her M should not name a successor', vol. 139, fos 139a–140b, printed in Pierre Lefranc, 'Un Inédit de Raleigh sur la Succession', *Etudes anglaises*, 13 (1960), 38–48, at pp. 44–5.

46 Alan R. MacDonald, 'The Parliament of 1592: a crisis averted?', in Keith M. Brown and

Alastair J. Mann (eds), *The History of the Scottish Parliament*, vol. 2 (Edinburgh, 2005), pp. 57–81.

47 David Calderwood, *History of the Kirk of Scotland*, ed. T. Thomson, 8 vols (Edinburgh, 1842–49), vol. 5, p. 191.

48 *Ibid., passim.*

49 *A Discouerie of the Unnaturall and Traiterous Conspiracie of Scottisch Papists, against God, his Kirk, their Natiue Cuntrie, the Kingis Majesties Persone and Estate* (Edinburgh[, 1593]). On Elizabeth's covert attempts to create, via the Cecils, an Anglophile Protestant faction in Scotland centred on the Earl of Bothwell, and Essex's dealings with Huntly undertaken at her command in the summer and autumn 1593, see Hammer, *The Polarisation of Elizabethan Politics*, pp. 165–6.

50 *A Discouerie*, sig. D2^r.

51 *Ibid.*, sig. A3^v.

52 Law, 'Spanish blanks', pp. 270–1; Stafford, *James VI of Scotland*, pp. 87–9.

53 John Bruce (ed.), *Letters of Queen Elizabeth and King James VI of Scotland*, CS 46 (1st series, 1849), p. 98.

54 Albert J. Loomie, SJ, *The Spanish Elizabethans: The English Exiles at the Court of Philip II* (New York, 1963).

55 William Allen, *Admonition to the Nobility and People of England and Ireland* (n.p. [Antwerp], 1588), esp. p. LIV.

56 Domínguez, 'Spanish Elizabethan Polemics', recognizes that this year marks a turning point (p. 220), but does not link the change to the 1593 Parliament.

57 Richard Verstegan, *The Copy of a Letter lately written by a Spanish Gentleman* (n.p. [Antwerp], 1589), p. 32.

58 Richard Verstegan, *An Advertisement written to a Secretarie of my L. Treasurers of England, by an Inglishe Intelligencer as he passed throughe Germanie towardes Italie* (n.p. [Antwerp], 1592), pp. 10, 30; Andreas Philopater [*vere* Robert Persons], *Elizabethae Angliae Reginae Haeresim Calvinianum Propugnantis* (n.p. [Antwerp], 1592).

59 Richard Verstegan, *Declaration of the True Causes of the Great Troubles* (n.p. [Antwerp], 1592), pp. 47, 51.

60 De Lamar Jensen, 'The phantom will of Mary Queen of Scots', *Scotia*, 4 (1980), 1–15.

61 Peter Holmes, 'The authorship and early reception of *A Conference About the Next Succession to the Crown of England*', *Historical Journal*, 23 (1980), 415–29, p. 421; Thomas M. McCoog, SJ, 'Harmony disrupted: Robert Parsons, S. J., William Crichton, S. J. and the question of Queen Elizabeth's successor, 1581–1603', *Archivum Historicum Societatis Iesu*, 73 (2004), 149–220, at 165–7.

62 Robert Persons, *Newes from Spayne and Holland* ([Antwerp,] 1593), fo. 21^v.

63 *Acta in comitiis parlamentaribus Londini die X. Aprilis huius anni praesentis 1593. tam contra Catholicos quam Puritanos seu Caluinistas rigidos* (Antwerp, 1593). See Peter J. Holmes, 'Robert Persons and an unknown political pamphlet of 1593', *Recusant History*, 17 (1985), 341–7.

64 Persons, *Newes*, fo. 36^v.

65 Crichton abandoned James's cause after his refusal to support the Armada only to

regain faith by the end of 1593 that the Scottish King would convert to Catholicism. See McCoog, 'Harmony disrupted', p. 154 *et passim*.

66 Doleman [Persons], *A Conference*, sig. *3ʳ.

67 *Ibid.*, sig. B1ᵛ, pp. 233ff (2nd pag.).

68 *Ibid.*, sig. B3ᵛ.

69 See also Chapter 4 in this volume.

70 *Treatise*, in Wentworth, *Pithie Exhortation*, p. 4 (2nd pag.).

71 *Ibid.* pp. 6–7 (2nd pag.).

72 *Ibid.*, pp. 57, 56, 37, 39–42 (2nd pag.).

73 *Ibid.*, pp. 46–7 (2nd pag.).

74 *Ibid.*, p. 95 (2nd pag.).

75 *Ibid.*, pp. 66, 71 (2nd pag.).

76 *Ibid.*, pp. 66, 71 (2nd pag.).

77 Hammer, *The Polarisation of Elizabethan Politics*, pp. 355, 385 and private communication; Neale, 'Wentworth', 198–9, 201–2; Roger Manning, 'The prosecution of Sir Michael Blount, Lieutenant of the Tower of London, 1595', *Bulletin of the Institute of Historical Research*, 67 (1984), 216–24.

78 Julian Goodare, 'The Scottish Presbyterian movement in 1596', *Canadian Journal of History*, 45 (2010), pp. 21–48.

79 Sir John Harington, *A briefe view of the state of the Church of England as it stood in Q. Elizabeths and King James his reigne* (London, 1653), pp. 187–91.

80 Alexandra Walsham, '"A Very Deborah?" The myth of Elizabeth as a providential monarch', in Susan Doran and Thomas S. Freeman (eds), *The Myth of Elizabeth* (Basingstoke, 2003), pp. 143–68.

Chapter 4

Taking it to the street? The Archpriest controversy and the issue of the succession

Peter Lake and Michael Questier

The Archpriest controversy was an intra-Catholic dispute between a group of secular priests and their Jesuit foes. It is conventionally taken to have started in the prison at Wisbech where the Catholic priests incarcerated there by the government had created, by the mid-1590s, something of a model clerical community and mission centre. However, from 1595 on, that idyll was disrupted by a series of rancorous altercations. The initial flashpoint had been attempts by the Jesuits and their supporters to impose their idea of order, but the disputes quickly came to encompass wider political issues. Similar animosities at the English College at Rome, also centred on resentment of the Jesuits and emergent suspicion of their commitment to the Spanish monarchy and latterly to the Infanta as their preferred candidate for the English throne, compounded these tensions and prompted the appointment of Robert Persons as the head of the English College and of an archpriest, George Blackwell, to reduce the English Catholic community to something like order. These moves appeared to the opponents of the English Jesuits to be nothing short of a Jesuitical take-over and prompted a series of appeals to Rome against the authority of the archpriest; hence the name of the controversy and the moniker of the anti-Jesuit camp as Appellants.

Much of the resulting dispute was phrased in the often dizzying technicalities of canon law, and a good deal of it was conducted in public and in print, often in the most vitriolic of terms. The affair has tended to attract the attention mostly of Catholic historians, many of whom have viewed it with a mixture of distaste and embarrassment.[1] In what follows we want to argue that the controversy was a genuinely significant aspect of the Elizabethan *fin de siècle*, with much to tell us about the political dynamics of the post-Reformation and the politics of incipient regime change (aka the succession).

To make that case we have to start with Robert Persons's two great books of the mid-1590s, *A Conference about the Next Succession* and the so-called *Jesuit's Memorial for the Intended Reformation of England*.[2] In the first of these he did three things. Firstly, he produced an account of England as an elective monarchy; a polity in which power flowed from the commonwealth to the ruler in such ways that an errant monarch could be constrained and even removed if his or her actions clashed overtly with the demands of the common good and in which the course of hereditary succession, which (under normal circumstances) represented the best way to regulate the transfer of power, could be diverted, again if the common good so dictated.

Secondly, he examined the case to be made for various claimants to the English throne after the death of Queen Elizabeth, whose demise without an heir of her body was now both certain and relatively imminent. His main point was that the situation was complex since there was no one candidate whose case was incontrovertible but rather a number of almost equally strong hereditary claims, a point he sought to make through a dizzying, positively obfuscatory, array of historical and genealogical detail. While Persons denied that he was a partisan for any particular candidate, the upshot of all this elaborate argumentation was the undermining of the seemingly clinched case for James Stuart and the advance of an alternative one for a Habsburg, the Infanta Isabella Clara Eugenia of Spain.

Thirdly, Persons produced an account of the current political scene, and indeed of the terrifying series of events likely to be unleashed by the death of the Queen, cast in terms of a number of religiously defined interest groups or parties. Given the confused nature of the succession, the Queen's demise was likely to be followed, he claimed, by a power struggle – indeed by an outbreak of dynastic conflict, even civil war – as each of the claimants and perhaps their foreign (as well as domestic) allies pushed their claim to the throne through any and every means available. The outcome would likely be determined by the relative strength of the various religious groups that now made up the inherently divided political and cultural terrain of post-Reformation England. Persons discerned three main groups – Protestants, Puritans and Catholics – and he provided an account in which the internal divisions between the Protestants and Puritans were set centre stage and the claims of different candidates – Lord Beauchamp, Arbella Stuart, the Earl of Huntingdon, or James Stuart – on various Puritan and Protestant constituencies were emphasized.[3] Over and against this actually or potentially fragmented Protestant camp, Persons set the English Catholics, who were presented as relatively united and as yet undecided as to whom they would support as Elizabeth's successor.

A conference, at least in its English recension, was an utterly public document.[4] Dedicated, in the most provocative of terms, to the Earl of Essex, the book represented a supreme act of political provocation, intended not merely to identify but also to exacerbate and exploit precisely the range of anxieties, tensions and lines of force and division that it purported merely to be analysing for the benefit of an English people and commonwealth, long kept in the dark on these crucial matters by the narrow clique that had governed in the Queen's name since Elizabeth's accession; a clique which, having, for its own sinister purposes, succeeded in keeping the Queen unmarried and the succession unsettled, was now about to reap the whirlwind; an eventuality which Persons, along with a succession of other Catholic commentators, had been prophesying, awaiting and eagerly trying to bring to pass since at least the early 1570s and from which he now claimed to be trying to rescue his countrymen.

The other book in question, Persons's *Memorial*, was anything but such a public text. Written in English and it seems in Spanish, it remained, and circulated, in manuscript. The text envisaged a radically reformed Church and state, with the interests and property of the traditional religious orders subjugated to the imperatives of a root and branch reformation. At the centre of the scheme was a reformed episcopate with the bishops acting as epitomes of religious zeal, local political bosses and key counsellors to the king. Only conviction Catholics, those who had either kept their consciences clean even at the height of heretical rule or been thoroughly spiritually examined, purged and publicly reconciled to the Church, would be admitted to office. The polity thus created was a form of mixed monarchy with the constituent parts consisting of prince, pope (or rather bishops) and parliament.[5]

Viewed as a one-two punch, the two texts represent an extraordinary mixture not only of Counter-Reformation zeal with Leaguer political thought, but of both with a prudential, artfully destabilizing account of politics as the art both of the possible and of dissimulation. Here was Parsons playing for all the marbles; seeming to dangle the political support of a unified English Catholicism, comprising both recusants and church papists, zealots, fellow travellers and malcontents, before all comers. Seeking to fish in troubled waters, Persons was making it known to James VI that he would need to concede something really significant – his own conversion or some form of toleration? – if he were to win over English Catholics, even as he tried to persuade the Spaniards that there remained all to play for in England; that in the Infanta they had a more than viable candidate; that in English Catholics they had assets worth supporting and in England the opportunity to construct, if not *ex nihilo*, then at least on a *tabula rasa* created by years of heretical rule now crushed by Spanish conquest, a church more reformed, more spiritually pure, more truly Catholic, than even the Council of Trent had dared to envisage.

Here was a spiritual, social and political transformation so thoroughgoing as to rival the similar schemes for national religious and political regeneration being put forward by the English Presbyterian movement and, just like those schemes for godly reformation, Persons's blueprint for reform, and the ongoing political projects and manoeuvres with which he pursued it, provoked a reaction amongst the more conservative sections of English Catholic opinion; a reaction from which the Archpriest controversy took much of its ideological origins and subsequent emotional force. In short, we might argue that the origins of the Archpriest controversy lay in debates and anxieties about, and in manoeuvres around, the succession.

To their opponents, the Jesuits' attempts to effect a reformation of manners at Wisbech represented a power play, part of a conspiracy to impose what Robert Fisher called a 'spiritual monarchy over all England' or what William Watson termed a 'Japonian monarchy', to be established over England, Scotland and Ireland.[6] And central here was the succession. Thus Thomas Bluet alleged that eighteen students had been ejected by Persons from the English College in Rome because 'they would not consent that the book of titles', i.e. the *Conference*, 'should be publicly and daily read in the college'.[7] Others claimed that similar readings had actually taken place in the seminaries in Spain. According to Christopher Bagshaw, Charles Paget reported that Persons had instructed the English Catholic seminarians in Spain to 'subscribe that', when they 'came into England', they should, in 'all conferences', 'advance the Infanta's title, not intending thereby to expect her Majesty's death, but by all means to remove her from the present possession of her royal estate'.[8] In Wisbech, in late 1598, Bluet claimed that the anticipated conferral on William Weston, the leading Jesuit there, of superiority over the other clergy would mean that orders would come from Rome to Weston to 'swear all the priests to the obedience of the infanta of Spain', just as Persons had 'caused the priests that were in Spain to be sworn', though Bluet assured the keeper of the gaol that he and his friends would never do such a thing.[9]

When Persons denied that any of this was true,[10] William Clarke started naming names: claiming that 'there be divers yet that will depose the same against him', most notably the priest Jasper Lothbury (who had signed the appeal drawn up at Wisbech on 17 November 1601) who 'was the man [that] should have read the same, but he rejected it, utterly refusing to meddle with such stuff'.[11] On this basis, the financial subsidies made available by the Spaniards for the English seminary colleges were little better than blood money 'by reason of Father Parsons's treacherous practises, thereby to promote the Spaniards' title for our country'.[12]

THE JESUIT CONSPIRACY EXPLAINS ALL

What is emerging here is a picture of a Jesuit and Hispanophile conspiracy to take over the English Catholic community, commit the exile community and all the new priests being trained in the seminaries to the cause of the Infanta and thus to entrust the future of English Catholicism to the triumph of Spanish arms and of the Jesuits and to the succession of a foreigner to the English throne. This dastardly plot fitted well with what was emerging as a coherent narrative of Jesuit political insurgency and Hispanophile conspiracy that stretched back to at least the 1580s. As early as 1591 a seminary priest named John Cecil had spilled the beans about his role as an agent of Robert Persons and Cardinal Allen, sent to assure English Catholics that the King of Spain had no designs on the throne but intended only the 'reformation of religion'; to ascertain how many English Catholics would support a Spanish invasion; and then to exaggerate the numbers of such people in order to encourage Philip to intervene militarily again. Cecil fingered Allen and Persons as 'the capital enemies not only of the present state but of the Catholics themselves in England' and offered Burghley a deal whereby the Catholics might attain some indulgence 'in matter[s] of conscience' in return for assuring the regime of their 'fidelity'. Burghley, Cecil suggested, should emulate Henry IV by employing Catholic moderates and loyalists to counteract the activities of the extremists; proposals which represent a remarkable anticipation of the Archpriest controversy.[13] Perhaps unsurprisingly, Cecil was one of the Appellant Proctors who went to Rome in 1602.

Charles Paget, ironically himself once up to his neck in the very plots and conspiracies which he now denounced, gave coherent voice to the resulting vision in 1597. Looking back, the whole thing now made sense: 'Father Parsons and the rest of the Jesuits first sent into England had orders not to deal in matters of State, but only to gain souls; nevertheless Parsons so broiled in matters of State that some Catholics, now dead, desired him to retire out of the country, or they would discover him, whereupon he went to France, without the privity of his general'. While in France, 'he did not cease to deal in State matters', and he wrote the work known popularly as 'Leicester's Commonwealth'. This book he 'sent…to England by a lay brother'. Persons 'was one of those that advanced' the MP William Parry's and the Babington plotter John Savage's 'practices to kill the Queen'. His associates in France, notably the Jesuit Claude Matthieu, 'were the chief dealers with the Duke of Guise, to his ruin, to enter with 5,000 men into England, where Father Parsons promised he should have been seconded with some English, for the sudden surprising of the queen's person, and of London. An Italian Jesuit in Paris gave Parry his absolution for killing the queen, and another in England animated Savage'. Persons 'assisted Cardinal Allen to make the book that should have been divulged against the queen, at such time as the Spanish army was to invade England, and has ever since, until lately, remained in Spain, to advise practices for the ruin of her Majesty and her estate'. He also 'made the book of the pretenders to the Crown of England', i.e. the *Conference*. He 'caused it to be printed', and by the agency of William Holt and Hugh Owen dispatched it to England. He even had the gall, after he was relocated to Rome and was confronted about it by the pope and his own superiors, to deny that he had written the book; 'yet the original copy with his own hand is extant'. The book was a blueprint for rebellion: 'immediately after the making of this book, he caused all priests sent out of Spain to take their oath that at their arrival in England, by all means they would advance the title of the infanta of Spain'. His meddling knew no end, for he had made 'another book, not yet printed, for the reformation of England, to the prejudice of the nobility, ancient customs and laws of England', i.e. Persons's manuscript *Memorial*. Paget was clear where the fault lay – with the Society of Jesus in general, and with Robert Parsons, in particular; 'I mean not to include herein religious or secular priests who only deal in matters of religion', he added.[14]

Versions of this same Jesuit conspiracy went on to provide the bedrock of the printed works of the Appellants. The 'epistle to the reader' to Bagshaw's *Sparing Discovery*, a book which, in effect, expanded Paget's manuscript narrative about the Jesuits' and Persons's enormities into a printed screed of some seventy pages, outlined the Jesuits' 'Machiavellian' 'maxims, axiomaes or rules' which justified as 'lawful, profitable, commendable and necessary' 'lying, perjury, swearing, foreswearing, murder, incest, sacrilege, simony, idolatry'. The Jesuit political play-book contained all that was necessary to 'canton a kingdom' and 'to refine a monarchy into the form of a province' as well as to 'alien[ate] the minds of most loyal subjects and draw them to consent to what unnatural invasion, conspiracy, riot or what else … and when and how to colour treacheries, treasons and popular tumults under glorious styles of commonwealths and zealous actions'.[15]

Not that such views were anything like original. Throughout the 1580s and 1590s the French opponents of the Catholic League had produced just such a vision of an Hispanophile, monarchomach, Jesuited conspiracy against all true authority in Church and state. Many works pushing that line had been translated into English and sold in London, and the Appellants themselves drew expressly upon them. This kind of anti-Jesuit rhetoric was a vehicle for contemporary absolutist political theory which underwrote the new monarchy in France. For Appellant writers that new monarchy was clearly a model for the way in which the Stuart family might rule in England after Elizabeth was gone. As Lisa Ferraro Parmelee stresses, several factors, not least the mixed reception which the Appellants were getting at Rome, were in any case driving them towards a form of Gallicanism which stressed the power of the national Church over and against the papacy and which emphasized the authority of the episcopate at the expense of the privileges of the religious orders.[16]

Viewed from this perspective, the appointment, at the Jesuits' behest, of the archpriest to exercise authority over the English Catholic clergy looked like the continuation of a very sinister and consistently pursued Jesuit and Spanish plot. Watson averred that Blackwell's 'authority extend[ed] to all England, Scotland and … Ireland, with many agents in them all'; the groundwork for it was in fact to be found in Persons's *Memorial*.[17] On Watson's account 'the spider's web' of authority created by the (arguably) canonically irregular archpresbyterate made 'vent for invasion both of England and Scotland, the archpriest's twelve assistants being dispersed in every corner with the laity, to work by North and South, persuading it to be for the Scots' good to join with Spain'.[18]

In short, what was claimed to be merely a way of governing the secular clergy would serve as a means to advance the interests of the Spaniards and the Jesuits. In the interim, Blackwell's power would be deployed to silence any of their secular-clergy critics who raised their voices against the archpresbyterate, the Jesuits or their Hispanophile purposes and plots.

SPAIN AND THE JESUITS, THE JESUITS AND PURITANS

Thus, for the Appellants, the imposition of the archpriest was a continuation of the political agenda laid out in Robert Persons's *Conference* which had contested James's assertion of his hereditary right to succeed Elizabeth. As Watson phrased it, the new archbpresbyterate was 'at least…and…in many respects…more prejudicial to the Scottish king and commonwealth' than to Elizabeth, 'because the institutor Parsons had before written his book of titles or succession in most apparent prejudice and ignominious slander of the said king very saucily and rudely abasing both his royal Majesty and his whole realm'.[19]

In any case, asked William Clarke, on what grounds could Catholics agitate for a Catholic successor? They had no credible candidate, since the Infanta had no better claim than

> every gentleman in England that can any way derive himself from any noble house that hath any way matched in the blood royal (as the most ancient gentlemen's houses in England have done). Neither is there any probability of her obtaining the sceptre unless we be willing to become slaves to Spaniards and aliens.

Nor was it incumbent upon Catholics 'without all humane respect to dispose themselves for such a competitor as must be a Catholike'.[20] Watson explained what (good) Catholics should and would do:

> if the heir apparent of any Catholic king or other prince were either addicted to heresy, or should become an apostata, I, being borne to be his subject, would use my uttermost endeavour to reclaim him; but if that purpose would not prevail with him…I hold it were a very impious part, either in me or in any other private person, being his subject, if we should seek to prevent him of his right or, if it lay in our powers, should take upon us to give it unto another, were he never so good a Catholic that had no right thereto.

Persons, on the other hand, 'cares not who it is, from whence he comes, or what right he has to the crown of this kingdom, that, when the time comes, shall be able to catch it, so he be a Catholic'.[21]

But while Persons claimed to be all about religion, he was in fact acting for

Spain. The Appellants maintained that the claims made (in the *Conference* and elsewhere) that the Spaniards had no plans for permanent temporal dominion over England were mere dissimulation. Clarke wondered, sarcastically, whether the Spaniards' military preparations 'were to catch butterflies upon the seas'. 'Was the book of titles (wherein the king's daughter, the lady infanta was entitled to all her Majesty's dominions) written to no purpose but to exercise Father Parsons's wit?'[22] Clarke also insisted that Persons's *Memorial* for England's reformation was predicated upon a Spanish invasion and derided the second part of the *Conference*, which he insisted disabled every other claim except that of the Infanta.[23] John Mush, like several others, argued that *Conference* was a renewal of the 'mortal dissentions between the families of York and Lancaster, laying perilous grounds for most cruel works and bloodshed in time to come; and drawing all to some particular person whom he affects above the rest'.[24]

None of this was surprising, the Appellants argued, when you looked at the political doctrines underpinning the *Conference*. Addressing Persons in print, Clark claimed: 'when I perused it [*A Conference*], me thought I was reading all the while your master in that art Buchanan, the Scot, his book *De iure regni apud Scotos*: unto whom you are very much beholden', since the 'full scope' of both books 'is how they may set up the people against their sovereigns'.[25] William Watson, who produced the longest and most detailed account of the Puritans and Jesuits proclivity for popular agitation, thought that 'Parsons and the…Jesuits that writ of the deposition of Henry III' were 'exceedingly beholden' to 'Buchanan that archtraitor of Scotland'. Thus, while Watson's attack on 'statizing' in his eighth *quodlibet* is, initially, designed almost entirely to denounce 'the consistorian discourses, letters, libels and practices of Knox, of Buchanan, of Beza, of Cartwright, of Barrow, of Browne, of Field, of Gibson, of Davison, and many others', he also claims that 'the Puritans and Jesuits jump together in statizing'. If Buchanan was an 'enemy to all regal soveraignty' so were Persons and his Jesuit friends.[26] Watson pointed to what he termed the Jesuits' 'gross anstatisticall principle…that they, of their exorbitant word and authority, might call a parliament, and enact what they pleased, without consent of king, queen or other state', just as the Protestant Scots had done in 1560.[27]

This was crucial for the Appellant argument about loyalty and toleration. If all opponents of sovereign authority were basically the same (and equally intolerable) whatever their confessional label, equally tolerable were all those who understood monarchical power correctly. Furthermore, in this context, what was true for the state applied to the Church as well. Clarke trotted out the Appellant mantra that 'popularity in the civil state doth not well digest a monarchy in the ecclesiastical'. Both Jesuits (and, for that matter, all supporters of the archpresbyterate) and Puritans aimed at the eradication of episcopal authority.[28] On Watson's account, both Puritans and Jesuits were equally keen to 'overthrow both states ecclesiastical and temporal' and to bring 'both head and members of the body political to be a plebeian hotch-potch of popularity void of all name, nurture or nature of any state'. When Watson was picking out the characteristics that Puritans and Jesuits shared, he zeroed in on the Puritans' 'scoffing, scolding and ignominious disgracing speeches that may be, with most infamous libels against the bishops and English clergy' and on the Jesuits' 'use [of] the like against all the bishops and prelates of the Roman clergy'.[29] According to Watson, the Jesuits preferred the authority of an archpriest to that of a bishop, not because (as they claimed) the appointment of a bishop would provoke the regime into intensifying the persecution against English Catholics, but because 'the Jappon island could not then have been governed absolutely by them as is intended by excluding all bishops and other authority'.[30] Thus, if the Puritans were bad, the Jesuits (Watson concluded) were worse.[31]

But what was true of the Jesuits (and the Puritans) was definitely not true of the secular clergy: 'never shall our adversaries be able to upbraid us or stain our priestly function and Catholic profession with a Calvinian or a Buchananian or Cartwrightian, or a huf muf Puritanian popularity, which is the only mark the Jesuits aim at'. And 'never shall her Majesty nor the State suspect us for any bill exhibited by us or our means in her high court of parliament, for any alteration and change of the ancient laws and customs which both Puritans and Jesuits do greedily gape after and labour for'.[32] The same, of course, could hardly be said of the Jesuits, who, again just like the Presbyterians, held that 'the inferior magistrate or people, by direction (forsooth) of the ministry, might lawfully and ought (if need required), even by force and arms, to reform it [the Church] themselves'.[33]

It was in many ways in Watson's *Decacordon* that all the other Appellant critiques of the Society and its patrons were brought together. The result of the Jesuits' meddling, on Watson's account, was a veritable world turned upside down.[34] It was on that basis that the Appellants were able to portray their own seemingly dissident and insubordinate behaviour as the epitome of order. When, in 1601, Anthony Copley heard that Bishop Tobie Matthew had 'made a sermon at Paul's Cross…against a toleration to us by the state', he contended that in response the Catholics should simply 'dis-Jesuit themselves' and 'seek to be beholding rather to' 'the state' 'than to Spain'.[35] Capitalizing on the recent conversion of Henry IV, Copley asked, 'why should not we the Catholics of England suit our fidelities and love (I say not our religion) to our Protestant princess as well as the Protestants of France do theirs to their Catholic king?'[36]

PRAEMUNIRE ANYONE? GETTING THE RELATION BETWEEN POLITICS AND RELIGION STRAIGHT

We can gain an insight into the nature and origins of the consequent contacts between the anti-Jesuit elements amongst the Catholic clergy and the Elizabethan regime from a remarkable letter sent by William Watson to the attorney-general in April 1599. Watson started out by rejecting all the rumours that, he said, had been spread about him by his Jesuited enemies; rumours calculated to equate opposition to Spain and the Infanta and animosity towards the Jesuits with religious apostasy, political betrayal and an actively seditious support for the Scottish claim.[37] Thus, when Watson returned to London from Scotland and the North he found that it was rumoured everywhere that he had been working for various elements in the regime, that he had 'slandered Dolemans book' and 'with other seminarists sought to bring in the Scot'. Also, it was said that he 'was become an apostata, an excommunicate person and suspended from the altar, and neither might hear Mass, hear confessions, nor use any other priestly functions'; that, in fact, he 'cared for no religion, was an atheist, sought to set up heresy, and preferred rather the Scot, an heretic than the Spaniard, so sound a Catholic'; and that he was 'a deadly enemy to all the Jesuits, and sought by all means possible to get them banished out of the land'.[38] Watson's response was simple: 'be the Scots king as he is, yet I will ever prefer him before the Spaniard, both in word and writing'.[39]

Watson had indeed been working on a reply to Doleman, but 'ere ever [he] set pen to paper, or in good faith intended it', he had got word that the Council was more than well affected to Catholic attempts to refute Persons's work.[40] Having consulted his colleagues, including Dr Bagshaw, Watson let it be known: 'indeed I was about a piece of work which I meant only should go amongst Catholics to show what men the Jesuits were and whereunto their ambitious Spanish pretence did incline'. However, his unwavering honesty and loyalty to the Queen meant that he had no intention of 'setting out any book or other work that might touch the title in particular'.[41] Thereupon, he started writing a dialogue designed to 'make one of Doleman's works confute another'. However, when he had finished just fifteen sheets or so he was arrested and his papers seized. What he had written was then 'perused with great good liking (as I was told) of her Majesty, my lord of Essex, my Lord Chamberlain, Mr Secretary, Mr Comptroller and others'. The Queen kept 'one copy and my lord of Essex another of the sum or contents of the whole work'. Cecil saw the dedicatory epistle (in Essex's possession) and disliked Watson's use of the word 'toleration', maintaining that 'her Majesty would not grant it'. So Watson altered it. But Essex was impressed and said 'that he could wish with all his heart that we might have liberty of conscience'.[42] Watson then rounded off this remarkable performance by insisting that the Protestant critics of the Appellants were all Puritans. Their attacks were revenge, Watson opined, for his characterization of the Puritans as soul-mates of the Jesuits.

As early as 1599, therefore, Watson had outlined to the regime, how the (religious) profession of Catholicism was entirely compatible with (political) loyalty to the crown, adherence to the cause of hereditary legitimacy, and therefore opposition to the Infanta, hostility towards the Jesuits and hatred of Spain and what he called 'the Spanish faction' amongst English Catholics. But such a position did not amount to a factional attachment to the Scottish claim. Far from it. Rather, it represented a defence of the English nation and of traditional (English) forms of both monarchical and episcopal legitimacy against the Jesuit (and Puritan) threat/s.

In making that case the Appellants made great play with the 'old law' of *prae-munire* 'enacted as well by our Catholic bishops and prelates, as by the prince, above 300 years ago'. Fear of infringing this statute had made the Appellants wary of wielding any 'external jurisdiction' over one another. But, claimed William Bishop, the introduction of archpresbyteral authority was a praemunire offence.[43] For William Clarke, so 'exorbitant' was 'this authority of the archpriest' that no 'Catholic prince' worth his salt 'would admit thereof, or consent thereto (were the times Catholic)'. How any man could 'be excused from the penalty of that law in admitting an external jurisdiction without the knowledge of their prince and against her consent' Clarke could not imagine. Not to obey the Queen in this respect was 'wilfully, without all reason or necessity, to contemn her princely prerogative', and therefore, he continues, 'no excuse of religion, conscience or the like can (in my conceit) free any man'.[44]

We have here a vision of the right relation between politics and religion, between the temporal and the spiritual, between, in fact, Church and state, based on the law of *praemunire* and thus stretching back far before the Reformation. Thus could the current policies of the Elizabethan regime towards its Catholic subjects, the behaviour of the Appellants themselves and even their request for toleration all be justified in ways which, however seemingly novel, disruptive, disorderly and even un-Catholic they might appear to their enemies, were in fact entirely 'traditional', quintessentially 'English' and both utterly 'loyal' and completely 'orthodox'. Such arguments underpinned the Appellants' wider claim that, Catholic though they were, they were also loyal to the state and were not challenging the authority of the Queen, even while, of course, they refused to make other (religious) concessions which the regime demanded of its Catholic subjects. The Appellants were responding here to what they took to be the Queen's own line, and that of her more moderate councillors, on the relationship between temporal and spiritual authority.[45]

It was on that basis that the Appellants petitioned the state for toleration. For, Watson asked, had not toleration brought relative peace to the Empire and even to France?

> Did it not as well animate the Huguenots to join with King Henry of the house of Valois, then a Catholic in show, howsoever the Jesuits censure of his heart, as it did of like sort the Catholics to join with the now most Christian and Catholic king Henry the 4, then a Protestant? Yea, and did they not stick as sure and fast to his Christian Majesty as if he had been of their own Catholic religion and profession, and that with great alacrity of mind, in regard of his present right to that crown, and their future hopes of his conversion to their church and faith, as afterward it hap-pened, God sweetly so disposing.[46]

For French Catholic loyalist opponents of the League, read the Appellants, and for Henry IV read James VI and I.

THE RESPONSE OF THE REGIME

The regime responded to these overtures favourably; not, of course, by offering anything like toleration but rather by aiding the secular priests' efforts in appealing to Rome against the archpriest. The 'banishment' of Christopher Bagshaw, Anthony Champney, Thomas Bluet and Francis Barnaby (though John Mush replaced Bagshaw and John Cecil replaced Barnaby) was a mere sleight of hand which allowed the 1602 appeal to the papacy, this time with French support, to proceed. On 6 October 1601 Bancroft wrote to Cecil heartily praying him 'to dispatch as [he] may the commission for banishment', for it was 'time they were gone and of some importance'.[47]

Bancroft and others provided the Appellants with a certain amount of patronage and protection, often against the hostile activities of the regime's own agents.[48] Thus in September 1601 Thomas Bluet wrote to Bancroft informing him: 'a friend of mine, a priest, that from the beginning assisted me both with counsel and other means, and being, at this present, about my affairs in procuring hands for me', i.e. subscription to the Appellant cause, was 'fallen into prison at Westchester' and was liable to be proceeded against with the full rigour of the law. He reassured Bancroft both that the man was 'one who always behaved himself as one clear from practice of matters of state, as appeared plainly when Parsons would have thrust him into the armada which perished between Lisbon and Ferrol', and that his life would 'more pleasure the state than his death'. For, he continued, 'unto me and my fellows his death will be a great blot and hindrance both within and without England'. Bluet begged Bancroft to intervene: 'your word with the council would easily effect a greater matter, but haste is requisite, the assizes being at hand and the judges perhaps not truly informed of his condition'.[49]

But perhaps most remarkably of all, the Appellants' pamphlets were helped into print by the authorities, with Bancroft ceding them access to royal presses for the purpose. In a remarkable burst of print publicity, Bagshaw published his *True Relation of the Faction Begun at Wisbech*, William Watson arranged the publication of Thomas Bluet's *Important Considerations*, Bagshaw's *Sparing Discovery* and Anthony Copley's *A Dialogue betwixt a Secular Priest and a Lay Gentleman*. Watson then produced a massive diatribe against the Jesuits, his *Decacordon of Ten Quodlibeticall Questions* and Copley the thoroughly Hispanophobe *Answer to a Letter of a Jesuited Gentleman*. At one point during all this William Watson was actually living with Bancroft.[50] What was going on here? Most obviously, perhaps, a policy of divide and rule. That certainly was how Bancroft explained himself to Sir Robert Cecil, on 3 August 1601: 'I do find by the priests themselves that the recusants amongst us are grown to be of another spirit than they were wont; and that they were never so like to join with the enemy as they are now, if opportunity serve'. He identified 'Blackwell, the archpriest (whom the Catholics do wholly follow, some few excepted), and Garnet, the provincial of the Jesuits' as the 'wicked and treacherous instruments' of Persons, who 'you know is as vile a traitor to her Majesty as any man living; and (as the case yet stands) he directs all the Catholics almost that are in England', by their means.

> So as the Jesuitical humour does now reign amongst all that generation, which is a disposition to entertain all manner of traitorous designments against her Majesty and their country, for the promoting of the Spaniard, and consequently, as they are taught, of the Pope's religion. Of this matter sundry priests have given their judgments, and do think themselves, that as the lay Catholics are now instructed, the State is more carefully to prevent the worst, and in times of danger to look unto them.[51]

By 18 August, Bancroft was writing to Cecil to inform him:

> at the receipt of your letter Mr Watson was with me. I find him very tractable to whet his pen against the Jesuits, and to omit that other great matter [i.e. the succession]. I hope you will read the treatise which I left with you, and send it back to me with your opinion of it: I have another of the same party's which I think will please you.[52]

On 22 December 1601, William Sterrell recorded that Bancroft had 'caused 50 of the Apologies', i.e. by Persons, 'to be new printed here by the queen's printer' in order to keep the fracas bubbling away.[53] This could, in other words, be represented as completely compatible with the best interests of the Queen and the state. In February 1602, when the Council authorized Bancroft to continue his dealings with the Appellants, they did so that he 'might be privy to their courses in laying open the malicious practices of the Jesuits, and to receive overtures from them of dangerous purposes contrived against the State, in which respect [he has] been driven sometimes to restrain and sometimes to relieve them'.[54]

Whether it was prepared to admit it or not, the regime was clearly indulging in exactly the same kind of analysis of the political scene as Persons: pointing out and playing up the incompatibility of various religious interest groups and parties. In *A Conference*, Persons had sought to exacerbate the internecine disputes between Puritans and conformists while emphasizing the unity of the Catholics. The outbreak of the Archpriest controversy not only gave the lie to that, it also provided the regime, or at least elements within it – Bancroft and Cecil, if not Cecil's brother Lord Burghley, Archbishop Hutton and the Council in the North – with a perfect opportunity to play on and widen those divisions.

There was, moreover, an international, even a geopolitical, aspect to these manoeuvres. By allowing or helping the Appellants to secure French backing for their appeal at Rome, the regime could use the continuing rivalry between the two great Catholic powers, France and Spain, to undermine Persons's claim to speak for a monolithic English Catholic interest; claims crucial to his attempts to get the papacy and Spain to intervene in the succession question by backing the Infanta. Hence Bancroft's jubilation when the curia found that the Appellants' refusal to obey Blackwell had not amounted to schism.[55]

While many contemporaries saw Bancroft's conduct as merely an attempt to divide and rule,[56] not everyone was so complaisant. Amongst the godly, the regime's machinations looked distinctly threatening. But, as Tobie Matthew's sermon at Paul's Cross during the 1601 Parliament showed, it was not only Puritans who took offence and alarm.[57] One notable pamphlet, *Humble Motives for Association to Maintain Religion Established, published as an antidote against the pestilent treatises of the secular priests*, adopted a distinctly Personian mode of analysis. Viewing the contemporary political scene in terms of the relative strength and unity of various religious interest groups, it claimed that divisions between the Jesuits and the seculars were a mere pretence, one that 'tendeth to the increasing, and not diminishing, of the popish party'. Lamenting current attempts to cosy up to Catholic priests while the state's greatest supporters, the Puritans, were kept down, the tract muttered darkly about the presence near the centre of power of a crypto-Catholic fifth column, while harking back to the anti-papal solidarities of the high Elizabethan era, when big beasts like Leicester and Burghley had roamed the land.[58] The tract both got the attention of the regime and provoked further responses from various Catholic authors.[59]

Here, therefore, was another crucial facet and effect of the Archpriest controversy – its publicness, the creation and encouragement of public discourse, of argument and counter-argument, conducted in both the pulpit and in print, as well as through the rumour mills and newsletter networks of both the godly and of various Catholic factions, about a range of issues in contemporary politics, issues which were more usually confined to council, court and parliament; and, furthermore, these arguments were very frequently centred implicitly, and also sometimes explicitly, on the forbidden subject of the succession.

JUST WHO WAS USING WHOM AND FOR WHAT? BREAKING THE SILENCE ON THE SUCCESSION

We can, of course, draw obvious connections between Bancroft's conduct in relation to the Archpriest controversy with his earlier, both official and unofficial, use of the press and performance, anonymous knock-about and more formal polemic, in his campaigns against first Marprelate and then the classis movement.[60] Moreover, as Peter Lake has argued elsewhere, in the course of its propaganda campaigns against the Catholics the regime had (with increasing frequency) either ventriloquized or co-opted the voice of English Catholic loyalism to unmask the evil conspiracies of the Spanish, of the papacy and of their clerical, and often Jesuit or Jesuited, agents and allies.[61] Viewed from that perspective, Bancroft's conduct during the Archpriest controversy was entirely in line with his own (not to mention Burghley's) past practice. All that was involved here was a final sophistication whereby a fully fledged dissident Catholic faction was enlisted and enabled to do the job instead.

But there was something else going on here as well. For in allowing the Appellants to go public through print, the regime (or elements within it) was permitting, albeit at one remove, the public discussion of the succession. We say at one remove because the Archpriest controversy never quite became an overt discussion of the succession. Or at least none of the major participants would admit that that was what it was or that they were acting as cheerleaders for particular interests or claimants. Thus, just as the Appellants typed Persons as the creature of the Spaniards, so he was eager to characterize them as a 'Scotist' faction, who, careless of the demands of religious principle, were desperate to push the claims of the heretic James VI for their own private and political advantage.[62] This, of course, the Appellants furiously denied.[63] But whatever they *said*, their denunciations of Persons's Spanish sympathies, their rubbishing of the claims of the Infanta and their espousal of legitimist hereditary principles all constituted a very public discussion of the rights and wrongs of the succession issue and all pointed towards the accession of James VI.

Thus one effect of the regime's patronage of the Appellants was to end, in rather a spectacular and sustained way, decades of public silence on the subject of the succession. Indeed it may not just be a coincidence that the printed propaganda campaign only picked up after the death of Essex had removed James's former point man from the scene and rendered the opening of the secret correspondence possible. Thus did the regime in effect break its own laws and taboos, sending very public (as well as, in the secret correspondence, entirely private) reassurances northwards that James was indeed now the man. Such public reassurances were particularly in order after the Essex debacle, since James's and the Earl's belief that Cecil and others might be prepared to sell the Stuart claim down the river in negotiations with the Spaniards had been integral to the tensions that had produced the Essex rebellion and James's near disastrous implication therein. Indeed, at his trial, Essex had even gone public with his suspicions on this score, citing Sir Robert Cecil's conversance with the *Conference* as his clinching evidence.[64] What better way now to reassure James than (semi-publicly) to back the most vociferously rabid Catholic opponents of Spain, the Infanta and indeed of Robert Persons? These dots were rendered all the easier to connect by the fact that, before his fall, Essex had been the focus of loyalist Catholic hopes for toleration, of the sort now being articulated, with the regime's connivance, in print by the Appellants.[65]

Here we might suppose were the English equivalents of the printed replies to Persons's *Conference* produced under James's aegis in Scotland in 1598/9. Where

James had relied on the works of a disgraced English Puritan, Peter Wentworth, and indeed on his own anonymous *True Law of Free Monarchies*, to do the job, the Elizabethan regime was able to let the Appellants discharge essentially the same functions for them. In both cases the proprieties, or at least a fig leaf of plausible deniability, were preserved, but in both cases, if not everyone, then many people, and certainly everyone who mattered – not only in London and Edinburgh, but also in Paris, Rome and Madrid – knew perfectly well what was happening.[66]

But, of course, the regime was not the only one sending messages James-ward in and through the Archpriest controversy. So too were the Appellants themselves. Indeed we might conclude that central features of the pitch they were making were specifically designed to echo central features of James's own position. Their espousal of legitimist principle, their impassioned expressions of political loyalty, their pleas for religious toleration, their denunciations of the popular methods and the 'allobrogical' style of rule preferred by both the Puritans and the Jesuits, and their consequent equation of the Jesuit and Puritan threats, all spoke directly to James's publicly stated concerns. The pitch being made here was clear: since they were amongst the most outspoken supporters of his claim to the English throne and were also the most rabid opponents of James's chosen *bêtes noires*, for all their Catholicism, here were the sort of men with whom James could do business; men who, having read and inwardly digested the stated principles of Jacobean king-craft, could be accommodated within the new Stuart regime, which was shortly to be installed in England and Ireland, with relative ease.[67]

The Appellants and the likes of Bancroft and Sir Robert Cecil had always only been allies of convenience. While the Appellants might have fantasized about the conversion of the Queen or a grant of toleration by her government to the right sort of Catholic, it seems fair to say that, throughout, their eyes were fixed firmly on James rather than on Elizabeth. Thus while Bancroft *et al.* enabled their books and activities in order to divide and disrupt the English Catholic interest, fracturing English Catholics, as they hoped, into warring factions and separating at least some of them from their most threatening sponsors in Rome and Madrid, while sending reassuring messages of public (as well, of course, as private) support to James in Edinburgh, the Appellants themselves took what they could get and used the resulting opportunity for very public utterance to make their own pitch to the man they fervently hoped and expected would be the next king of England. In that sense, the Archpriest controversy really was all about the succession.

But if we can use the succession to reflect back upon the Archpriest controversy, what happens when we reverse the process? What emerges is a far more contested and open-ended process than conventional accounts allow. Here are a variety of groups, not merely factionalized and dissident Catholics, struggling with their opponents not just in England but in Rome, or different sorts of (moderate or radical) Puritans, alternately alarmed and exhilarated by the prospect of the accession of James VI, but central elements in the regime – Bancroft certainly, but behind him surely Sir Robert Cecil and others, not to mention James himself – all playing a high stakes game, at least some of the time in public, as they attempted to manipulate a politico-religious scene composed, as they thought, of highly factionalized religious groupings, each with its different backers and support bases both at home and abroad.

For none of these people can the 'Elizabethan settlement' be said to have settled much; a great deal seemed to be up for grabs, and all sorts of expedients and manoeuvres called for, if events were to be shaped according to one's own rather than one's rivals' interests. Thus, far from the fall of Essex ushering in the control of the sensible tendency, thus rendering the accession of the first Stuart all but inevitable, what we have is another round of fevered manoeuvre and counter-manoeuvre, of anxiety and expectation, of calculation and risk-management; the next stage, in fact, in a rolling accession crisis that arguably would not end before the Gunpowder Plot and the failure of the union between England and Scotland. But that, thankfully, is another subject.[68]

NOTES

1 The best recent discussion is Arnold Pritchard, *Catholic Loyalism in Elizabethan England* (London, 1979), esp. chs 7–11. Also see John Bossy, *The English Catholic Community 1570–1850* (London, 1975), pp. 42–8, and Peter Holmes, *Resistance and Compromise: The Political Thought of the Elizabethan Catholics* (Cambridge, 1982), ch. 17. For the distaste and embarrassment of modern Catholic historians, see, for instance, J. H. Pollen, *The Institution of the Archpriest Blackwell* (London, 1916), pp. 13–14; J. J. Scarisbrick, *The Reformation and the English People* (Oxford, 1984), pp. 160–1.

2 R. Doleman [Robert Persons], *A Conference about the Next Succession to the Crowne of Ingland ([Antwerp], 1594 [1595])*; A. F. Allison and D. M. Rogers, *The Contemporary Printed Literature of the English Counter-Reformation between 1558 and 1640*, 2 vols (Aldershot, 1989–1994) [ARCR], vol. 2, no. 167; E. Gee, *The Jesuit's Memorial for the Intended Reformation of England, Under Their First Popish prince* (London, 1690).

3 The 'political theory' was contained in book one of *A Conference* and the genealogical material in book two. The discussion of the relative strength of the religious parties in England is at pp. 235–48.

4 For the distribution in manuscript of other, rather different, versions of *A Conference* in Spanish and Latin, see Cristóbal Domínguez, '"We must fight with paper and pens": Spanish Elizabethan Polemics, 1585–1598', Ph.D. thesis, University of Princeton (2011).

5 J. J. Scarisbrick, 'Robert Persons' plans for the "true" reformation of England', in N. McKendrick (ed.), *Historical Perspectives: Studies in English Thought and Society in Honour of J. H. Plumb* (London, 1974), pp. 19–42; T. H. Clancy, 'Notes on Persons's "memorial for the reformation of England" (1596)', *Recusant History*, 5 (1959), 17–34.

6   Peter Lake with Michael Questier, *The Antichrist's Lewd Hat: Protestants, Papists and Players in Post-Reformation England* (London, 2002), pp. 285–99, quotation at page 293; Thomas Graves Law (ed.), *The Archpriest Controversy*, CS, 2 vols (1896, 1898), vol. 1, pp. 92–3, 95.

7   Robert Persons, A *Brief Apologie, or Defence of the Catholike Ecclesiastical Hierarchie* (n.p. n.d. [Antwerp,1601]), fo. 153ʳ; see also Archives of the Archdiocese of Westminster (AAW), A:vi, no. 89, pp. 332–3; Thomas Bluet, *Important Considerations, which Ought to Move All True and Sound-Catholikes* (n.p. [London], 1601), sig. ✱✱✱ʳ⁻ᵛ; Christopher Bagshaw, *A Sparing Discoverie of our English Iesuits* (n.p. [London], 1601), pp. 62–3.

8   Bagshaw, *A Sparing Discoverie*, p. 57; John Mush, *A Dialogue betwixt a Secular Priest, and a Lay Gentleman* (Rheims [imprint false; printed at London], 1601), p. 92; ITL, Petyt MS 538, vol. 38, no. 82, fo. 184ᵛ.

9   ITL, Petyt MS 538, vol. 38, no. 150, fo. 399ʳ.

10 Robert Persons, *A Manifestation of the Great Folly and Bad Spirit of Certayne in England Calling Themselves Secular Priestes* (n.p. [Antwerp], 1602), fos 49ᵛ, 50ʳ.

11 William Clarke, *A Replie unto a Certaine Libell* (n.p. [London], 1603), fo. 69ʳ. See also Mush, *A Dialogue*, p. 93; ITL, Petyt MS 538, vol. 38, no. 82, fo. 185ʳ; G. Anstruther, *The Seminary Priests*, 4 vols (Ware and Great Wakering, 1968–1977), vol. 1, p. 213.

12 Clarke, *A Replie*, fo. 52ʳ.

13 Thomas M. McCoog, SJ, *The Society of Jesus in Ireland, Scotland, and England: 1589–1597: Building the Faith of Saint Peter upon the King of Spain's Monarchy* (Farnham and Rome, 2012), pp. 22–4; Anstruther, *Seminary Priests*, 1, pp. 64–5.

14 *CSPDom, 1598–1601*, pp. 68–9; *ARCR*, vol. 2, no. 31.

15 Bagshaw, *A Sparing Discovery*, from the 'the epistle to the reader' by W[illiam] W[atson], sig. a2ʳ. Also see Pritchard, *Catholic Loyalism*, ch. 10.

16 Lisa Ferraro Parmelee, *'Good Newes From Fraunce': French Anti-League Propaganda in Late Elizabethan England* (Woodbridge, 1996), *passim*, and pp. 147–51.

17 Law, *Archpriest*, vol. 1, p. 95; William Watson, *A Decacordon of Ten Quodlibeticall Questions* (n.p. [London], 1602), p. 144.

18 Watson, *A Decacordon*, p. 166; see also Law, *Archpriest*, vol. 1, pp. 97–8.

19 Watson, *A Decacordon*, pp. 162–3.

20 Clarke, *A Replie*, fo. 76ʳ⁻ᵛ; see also Watson, *A Decacordon*, pp. 297–8.

21 Watson, *A Decacordon*, pp. 292–3.

22 Clarke, *A Replie*, fos 65ᵛ–6ʳ.

23 *Ibid.*, fos 74ʳ, 77ʳ.

24 Mush, *A Dialogue*, pp. 91–3.

25 Clarke, *A Replie*, fo. 76ʳ.

26 Watson, *A Decacordon*, pp. 298, 224–5.

27 *Ibid.*, p. 227.

28 Clarke, *A Replie*, fo. 76ʳ⁻ᵛ.

29 Watson, *A Decacordon*, pp. 224, 27–8.

30 Law, *Archpriest*, vol. 1, p. 97.

31 Watson, *A Decacordon*, p. 26. Although, he quickly added, 'their doctrine', purely respecting matters of faith, was not yet 'so absurd' as that of the Puritan: 'even the worst and baddest Jesuit' was, in that respect, better than 'the best and saintliest seeming Puritan'.

32 Bluet, *Important Considerations*, sig. ***2[r–v] [sic] [sig. A2[r–v]].

33 Watson, *A Decacordon*, p. 225.

34 *Ibid.*, pp. 321–2.

35 He was also probably exploiting the fact that Matthew was known to be less than enthusiastic about James VI as Elizabeth's successor.

36 Anthony Copley, *An Answer to a Letter of a Iesuited Gentleman, by his Cosin, Maister A.C.* (n.p. [London], 1601), p. 71; W. Richardson, 'The Religious Policy of the Cecils 1588–1598' (D.Phil. thesis, University of Oxford, 1993), p. 203; Helen Georgia Stafford, *James VI of Scotland and the Throne of England* (New York and London, 1940), pp. 58, 91–2; David Marcombe, 'The Dean and Chapter of Durham, 1558–1603' (Ph.D. thesis, University of Durham, 1973), p. 70; R. P. Sorlien (ed.), *The Diary of John Manningham of the Middle Temple 1602–1603* (Hanover, NH, 1976), p. 245.

37 Law, *Archpriest*, vol. 1, pp. 215–16.

38 *Ibid.*, pp. 217–18.

39 *Ibid.*, p. 219.

40 *Ibid.*

41 *Ibid.*, p. 220.

42 *Ibid.*, pp. 222–3.

43 William Bishop *The Copies of Certaine Discourses* (Rouen [imprint false; printed at London], 1601), p. 6; see also Clarke, *A Replie*, fo. 35[v]; Watson, *A Decacordon*, p. 12; Robert Charnock, *A Reply to a Notorious Libell* (n.p. [London], 1603), pp. 120–2.

44 Clarke, *A Replie*, fo. 36[r].

45 Persons was having none of it. For him it was no accident that 'the statute of praemunire… was begun to be treated about the time that Wickliffe rose up, when emulation was in heat against the clergy'. Its 'chief purpose' was 'to prohibit appellation to Rome in the first instance'. Only 'the worst kings of England ever since have most urged it, and it was not made… "by our Catholic bishops and prelates"' but rather 'against their wills'. It 'passed in parliament by the stream of temporal power and emulation against them', Persons, *Brief Apology*, fos 15[r–v]; also see Persons, *A Manifestation*, fos 14[v]–15[r].

46 Watson, *A Decacordon*, p. 275.

47 *HMC Sal*, XI, p. 410. They first visited the Flanders nuncio (at Nieuport) and Thomas Worthington at Douai (where they arrived on 5/15 December). They apparently secured his support and went via Paris (which they reached on 7/17 December 1601) in order to secure the backing of the French court, John Bossy, 'Henri IV, the Appellants and the Jesuits', *Recusant History*, 8 (1965), 80–122; Pollen, *Institution*, p. 66; *APC, 1601–4*, p. 298.

48 See Bossy, *English Catholic Community*, pp. 44–5.

49 *HMC Sal*, XI, pp. 389–40; AAW, A:vii, no. 39 (transcript at Farm Street library and archive, Rivers Correspondence, pp. 60–1).

50 Gladys Jenkins, 'The archpriest controversy and the printers, 1601–3', *The Library*,

5th series, 2: 2–3 (1948 for 1947), 180–6. William Watson was living at Fulham Palace, Bancroft's residence in London, by September 1601, Nicholas Cranfield, Richard Bancroft, *ODNB*, citing TD, III, p. cxlvii.

51 *HMC Sal*, XI, p. 318.

52 *Ibid.*, p. 350.

53 Rivers Correspondence, p. 35.

54 *CSPDom 1601–3*, p. 155. Also see the royal proclamation of 5 November 1602, denouncing all Catholic clergy, Jesuits and seculars alike, P. L. Hughes and J. F. Larkin (eds), *Tudor Royal Proclamations*, 3 vols (London, 1964–9), vol. 3, no. 817. For the Appellants' response, see *HMC Sal*, XII, pp. 631–2.

55 As reported by Persons's correspondent William Sterrell, AAW, A:vii, transcript at Farm Street library and archive, Rivers Correspondence, p. 96. As both John Bossy and Peter Holmes have emphasized, the French connection was crucial throughout. See Bossy, 'Elizabethan Catholicism; the link with France' (Ph.D. thesis, University of Cambridge, 1961) and 'Henri IV'; Holmes, *Resistance and Compromise*.

56 N. E. McClure (ed.), *The Letters of John Chamberlain*, 2 vols (Philadelphia, 1939), vol. 1, p. 171; Rivers Correspondence, p. 35.

57 Copley, *Answere to a Letter*, p. 71.

58 *Humble Motives for Association to Maintaine Religion Established. Published as an Antidote Against the Pestilent Treatises of Secular Priests* (n.p., 1601). We hope to address this remarkable text and its contexts in Peter Lake and Michael Questier, '"Protestants", "Puritans" and "papists": Robert Parsons, Sir Francs Hastings and the contested religio-political arithmetic of the Elizabethan *fin de siècle*" (forthcoming).

59 Edward Coke to Sir Robert Cecil [n.d.], *HMC Sal*, XI, pp. 572–4; Bancroft to Cecil, 20 February 1602, *ibid.*, XII, p. 56; Thomas Fitzherbert, *A Defence of the Catholyke Cause* (n.p. [Antwerp], 1602) and *A Brief Censure upon the Puritane Pamphlet: Entitled, (Humble Motives…)* (n.p. [printed secretly in England], 1603). Two other Puritan tracts of 1602, *An Antiquodlibet, or an Advertisement to Beware of Secular Priests* and *Let Quilibet Beware of Quodlibet*, declared that the quarrels between Jesuits and secular clergymen were a charade.

60 Patrick Collinson, 'Ecclesiastical vitriol: religious satire in the 1590s and the invention of Puritanism', in John Guy (ed.), *The Reign of Elizabeth I: Court and Culture in the Last Decade* (Cambridge, 1995), pp. 150–70; Lake and Questier, *Antichrist's Lewd Hat*, pp. 509–63; J. Black, *The Marprelate Tracts* (Cambridge, 2008), pp. lx–lxxiv.

61 Lake, Ford Lectures, Univ. of Oxford 2011. See Burghley's own *The Copie of a Letter Sent out of England to Don Bernardin Mendoza Ambassadour in France for the King of Spaine Declaring the State of England* (London, 1588) or, later, Lewis Lewkenor's *The Estate of the English Fugitives under the King of Spain and his Ministers* (London, 1594). The *State of Christendom*, the tract identified by Alexandra Gajda as having been written by Anthony Bacon on behalf of the Essex faction in 1594–5, also took this form, as did the translation into English of Antonio Perez' memoirs, also prepared for Essex in 1595; see her 'The State of Christendom: history, political thought and the Essex circle', *Historical Research*, 81 (2008), 423–46 and *The Earl of Essex and Late Elizabethan Political Culture* (Oxford, 2012), pp. 87–8.

62 Persons consistently claimed that he had never sought anything other than order, decorum and, primarily, true religion. For example, on 24 January 1600 Persons

had written a semi-public letter to the Earl of Angus, which was seen by various people in England on its way to Scotland. Persons mentioned that six months before, he had written to the Earl to allay his suspicions about the *Conference*. Apparently Persons' second missive never arrived, so now he wrote again (on 4/14 November 1600). In both letters, Persons explained how his (former) opposition to James VI was only for the sake of religion. See *CSPScot*, 13, pp. 613–17; AAW, A:vi, no. 101, pp. 371–5; Thomas M. McCoog, SJ, 'Harmony disrupted: Robert Parsons, S.J., William Crichton, S.J. and the question of Queen Elizabeth's successor, 1581–1603', *Archivum Historicum Societatis Iesu*, 73 (2004), pp. 202–8; Holmes, *Resistance and Compromise*, pp. 221–2; *CSPDom 1598–1601*, pp. 423–5, 430, 434–5; Charnock, *A Reply*, p. 82; ABSI, 46/12/3–6 (transcripts of letters written by Robert Persons, archived at Farm Street library and archive), pp. 1113–14.

63 Mush, *Dialogue*, pp. 129–30.

64 See Stafford, *James VI of Scotland*.

65 See Gajda, *Earl of Essex*, esp. ch. 3.

66 Peter Lake, 'The king (the queen) and the Jesuit: James Stuart's *true law of free monarchies* in context/s', *Transactions of the Royal Historical Society*, 6th series, 14 (2004), 243–60. Appellant Catholic approaches to the Scottish court and James's own negotiations with a range of Catholics caused the Elizabethan regime some alarm, while in Ireland, it could be argued, a more alarming and certainly more violent version of aspects of the Appellant controversy was being played out in the confrontation between Tyrone and some of the leaders of the Anglo-Irish community. We hope to pursue the 'British' aspects of this elsewhere.

67 See Henry Constable's *Discovery of a Counterfeit Conference … For the Advancement of a Counterfeit Title* (Paris [imprint false; printed in Cologne], 1600), which echoes very closely James's *True Law*. Constable was an ex-associate of Essex and a close friend of Bagshaw and other appellants. See G. Wickes, 'Henry Constable, poet and courtier, 1562–1613', *Biographical Studies*, 2 (1953–54), 272–300.

68 One we hope to address in a monograph speculatively entitled, 'The queen is dead, long live the king; the accession crisis of James VI and I'.

Chapter 5

◆

Bishop Richard Bancroft and the succession

Patrick Collinson

This is not quite a non-subject, but it comes pretty close. We have no means of knowing what Richard Bancroft, Bishop of London from 1597, may have thought, hoped or feared about the succession to the throne of England. If Bancroft ever chose to put pen to paper on this delicate subject, his views are no longer on record.

There was, and in the nature of things could be, no episcopal 'line' on the succession. There was no legitimate forum in which the bishops could have formed a collective opinion or policy on such a matter, and there was no way that they could have advanced their position in public debate. If the clergy of England had been ordered by the government of the day to declare from their pulpits that, say, Lady Arbella Stuart or the Spanish Infanta should succeed, and they had refused to act in accordance with the order, then there might have been a situation like that of 1688, when seven bishops, including the Archbishop of Canterbury, were sent to the Tower for their refusal to comply with a command to publish James II's Declaration of Indulgence. But of course no such scenario was conceivable in the 1590s, and the episcopate had little of the backbone, the freestanding resilience, which it would acquire in the age of Anglican triumphalism, the last years of Charles II.

Insofar as they constituted one of the estates of the realm, or part of it, which was as lords of parliament, the bishops appear to have been silent on the issue in 1593, 1597 and 1601, and for that matter in convocation, which met at the same time as parliament; this contrasted with the role their predecessors had played in 1572, when, it seems through the pen of Archbishop Edwin Sandys, they had demanded the head of Mary Queen of Scots on a platter and had come perilously close to threatening Elizabeth with deposition

---

I acknowledge the helpful advice of John Craig, Pauline Croft, Kenneth Fincham, Arnold Hunt, and Alexandra Walsham.

if she failed to deliver.[1] That might suggest that by the 1590s the bishops had become poodles under the throne, in the more coercive climate of what has been called the second Elizabethan reign.[2] However, we have every reason to believe that the 1572 memorandum was drawn up at the political bidding of William Cecil, Lord Burghley, so perhaps they had always been poodles.[3]

Which raises a very relevant question about Bancroft's conduct in the last Elizabethan years, and particularly his role in supping with a group of Catholic priests, with a not so long spoon, the story we shall reach later in this chapter. In a political minefield, was Bancroft capable of navigating solo, or only at the behest of Burghley's son Sir Robert Cecil, or that of 'the state', a word which enters the political lexicon at about this time? But so far as pronouncements on the succession were concerned, there would not and could not have been any such bidding. For there was no formal ministerial position on this matter of such great delicacy, only secret correspondence with Scotland involving first Essex and then Cecil.[4] A certain understanding between Cecil and Bishop Bancroft, which we shall come to, may perhaps be construed as arising from Cecil's Scottish correspondence, and from the direction in which it was pointed. The exclusion crisis, which culminated in the execution of Mary Queen of Scots, was very different from the later Elizabethan succession crisis which followed her elimination.[5] Everyone, not least the bishops, was now stumbling around in a fog, like that parody of a Shakespeare history play in 'Beyond the Fringe'.

However, bishops individually did have a voice, which they could have exercised in correspondence or discreet conversation; and even more publicly when it fell to them to preach in the Chapel Royal, in the very face of the sovereign. One bishop who ventured a transgressive sermon on the edge of this dangerous subject was Anthony Rudd, the relatively young and financially challenged bishop of the Welsh see of St David's, hoping for better things. The year was 1596, the season Lent, when excoriating sermons were in order. Elizabeth was in her sixty-third year of age. Rudd chose to preach on Psalm 9: 12 ('teach us to number our days') and he entered into some mystical arithmetic, while reminding the Queen of her age and approaching mortality. According to the gossipy Sir John Harington, the Queen, sitting *vis-à-vis* the pulpit in her closet, made her displeasure plain, and with the sermon ended said that Rudd should have kept his arithmetic to himself: 'but I see said shee the greatest clerks are not the wisest men'. But, Harington reported, her displeasure was short-lived, and the episode was made an excuse to assure anyone listening that she still had all her faculties, good eyesight and hearing, and a voice for singing and fingers still capable of playing the virginals.[6]

This little drama may or may not have had something to do with Richard Bancroft and his prospects for advancement from London to Canterbury. According to Thomas Fuller, writing a generation later, the Queen had been so 'highly affected' by an earlier sermon of Rudd's that she had instructed Archbishop Whitgift to tell him that he would be his successor if the archbishopric were to fall vacant in her time. Whitgift duly passed this good news on to Rudd, adding that the Queen, growing weary of wittily contrived sermons, liked nothing better than something 'plain', which, of course, is what she got on that Sunday in Lent 1596. Fuller professed to be reluctant to believe that Whitgift would have intentionally laid 'a train to blow up this archbishop-designed', although that is what happened. Rudd 'lost his reversion of the archbishopric of Canterbury', and remained at St David's on £400 a year until his death nineteen years later. Fuller suggested a motive: no more did Whitgift welcome talk of who should succeed him than did the Queen herself.[7] But perhaps Whitgift was already grooming Bancroft for the Canterbury succession. Bancroft's reputation had been made as the hammer of the Puritans, whereas Rudd was almost a fellow traveller, aligning himself with the Puritan spokesmen at the Hampton Court Conference in 1604 and later an opponent of Bancroft's drive for conformity in the years that followed.[8] Harington was indulging in gossip, his own motivation, as with everything that he wrote, shrouded and convoluted.[9] Fuller too was a gossipy writer, and his nineteenth-century editor poured cold water on both versions of the story.[10] But when it comes to accounting for the emergence and promotion of bishops, historians have little choice but to make what use they can of such dodgy materials. There may have been politics in all of this. Were the pulpits of episcopal preachers tuned? Someone who may have had more realistic hopes of Canterbury than poor Rudd was Tobie Matthew, Bishop of Durham. According to Harington again, the hot money was on Matthew, not so much as a matter of patronage as on account of his reputation as a learned man and an indefatigable and eloquent preacher. But James preferred Bancroft 'as a man more exercised in affairs of the State', thus making a distinction – to be found at the heart of Kenneth Fincham's study of the Jacobean episcopate, *Prelate as Pastor* – between pastoral, preaching bishops like Rudd and Matthew and capable administrators. Here we are not wholly dependent upon Harington. Dr John Johnston, writing to that veteran Cecilian Sir Michael Hicks in May 1604, reported: 'The Bishop of Durham hath certaine word now, for his remove to Canterbury'.[11] It looks as if there was everything to play for in the summer of 1604. According to Fincham, it was the strenuous parliamentary campaign mounted at that time by the Puritans which persuaded the King that Bancroft would be a safer pair of hands than Matthew.[12] So Bancroft's long end-game as the nemesis of militant Puritanism finally, after twenty years, paid off.

However, that tells us a good deal less than we would like to know about early Jacobean episcopal politics, the motives which advanced Bancroft to Canterbury and Matthew to York, for Matthew had been *persona non grata* with James, or at least James with him. The Bishop of Durham ruled a palatinate (so he was not just a preacher), and Matthew's long years of service on the Scottish frontier as the government's principal agent in the far north had served to make him hostile to the Scottish interest. The only surviving copy of Harington's pro-Scottish *Tract on the Succession to the Crown* is to be found among Matthew's papers, a copy presented by the author, and Matthew has filled the margins with critical annotations.[13]

In March 1602 Matthew sent Robert Cecil a damaging report, purporting that for all the 'intercourse' between Cecil and James VI, of which Matthew clearly had some knowledge, he wanted Cecil to know that in private James had shown him scant respect, and that a 'libel' denouncing Cecilian government had been found in James's bed. It is not clear what game Matthew was playing. Did he favour one of the other aspirants to the throne? It seems unlikely. But soon after Elizabeth's death, preaching before the King as he entered his new dominion at Berwick, Matthew had to eat humble pie, craving pardon for his 'opposition heretofore, with promise of faythful service'.[14] But in another sermon preached at Newcastle, Matthew still sailed close to the wind. The sermon is no longer extant. But we know that his text was 2 Chronicles 15: 1–2: 'The Lord is with you, while ye be with him; and if ye seke him, he wil be founde of you, but if ye foresake him, he wil forsake you'.[15] Elizabeth had become accustomed to being addressed in these almost threatening terms; James too, sitting on his humble stool under those Scottish pulpits. There was a homiletical and rhetorical convention operating here, the principle that the preacher should not be a flatterer. But James would not be so happy to accept such frank admonition when seated in the privileged immunity of the English royal closet.

The cool relations between James and Matthew contrast with the fulsome letter which James sent from Newcastle (at the very time of Matthew's sermon) to Archbishop Matthew Hutton of York, in response to a letter 'whearby wee cleerely perceave your most loving affection towardes us, as…wee have oftentymes heretofore understood'.[16] James will have known that in a sermon preached before the Queen in 1596, Hutton had dared to name the King of Scots from the pulpit as her preferred successor, and that he had been rewarded with a 'sharpe message'.[17] If Hutton had not been on his last legs, James might well have translated him from York to Canterbury.

BANCROFT AND THE KIRK

As for Bancroft's primatial prospects, to bring us a little closer to our subject, Harington had to concede that 'some imagined he had…given the King some distaste' by his writings against 'the Genevising and Scottizing Ministers'.[18] Well you could say so! That was not something that Harington had made up. In 1589 Bancroft had provoked not only royal offence but a diplomatic incident by wading gratuitously into Scottish ecclesiastical politics in his bitterly anti-Puritan sermon preached at Paul's Cross at the time of the literary outrage of the Marprelate Tracts.[19] It was a turbulent time in the affairs of the Scottish Kirk, when hardline Presbyterians, disciples of Andrew Melville, were locking horns with the King, whose chosen instrument to assert control over the Kirk was a somewhat effete episcopate. Bancroft's understanding of these intricate matters was crude – that of a tabloid newspaper – and he depended upon dubious sources, including an account of the Scottish situation by the lapsed English Separatist, Robert Browne. Bancroft was never too fussy about his sources. A glaring error was to attribute to James himself a declaration against the Presbyterians which had in fact been drafted by that poor relation of Whitgift north of the border, Archbishop Adamson of St Andrews. 'A moment's thought might have reminded [Bancroft] that James's struggle with the Melvillians could only be aggravated by a public intervention from a noted English opponent of English presbyterians.'[20] Whatever James's solution to the challenge to his regality, it was not an English solution. He knew that he was neither Henry VIII nor even Elizabeth. Bancroft's gaffe was made worse by his proud identification of himself, on the title page of his published sermon, as 'Chaplain to the Right Honorable Sir Christopher Hatton Knight, Lord Chancellor of England'.[21] Did that mean that the sermon had some official sanction from the English government? One of the Scottish hardliners, in a pamphlet entitled *D. Bancrofts Rashnes in Rayling Against the Church of Scotland,* made much play of this: the chaplain 'as he will needs be styled', 'whose chaplaine so ever he be'.[22]

The English government was better informed about Scottish affairs by its own representatives in Edinburgh, who warned that James was disturbed by the likely damage done by Bancroft's sermon to Anglo-Scottish relations (which of course embraced his own hopes for the English succession). The consequence was that Burghley summoned Bancroft before him, swept aside the defence which Bancroft had already prepared, and presented him with a submission to be sent to the King of Scotland. This Bancroft elaborated, at length. Burghley was assured that Bancroft knew very well that the pulpit was not the place to deal with the affairs of princes – 'and god knoweth my harte, how farre it was from my entent, to have offended therin, especially against so renowned and vertuous a kinge'. But Bancroft went on to offer a robust defence of his understanding of matters north of the border, justifying his attribution of the Declaration of 1584, if drafted by Adamson, to the King. Yet,

> your Lordship I trust did never esteem me as a madde man: and surely I have been little better (consideringe the inviolable league of perfect love and amitye betwixt the Quenes majestie our dread soveraigne Lady and his highnes) if I should wittingly have spoken any thinge that might have turned to his dishonor.

'I hope his Majestie will accept my offer of satisfaction', he added. This so-called 'submission', more than 4,000 words in length, was an extraordinary mixture of humility and defiance. It ended with an almost threatening plea and a whiff of blackmail. Burghley should prevent the matter reaching the ears of the Queen, otherwise Bancroft would be forced to seek 'for helpe els where [Hatton?], which [he] wold be loth to doe'. James didn't think much of Bancroft's submission, and initially demanded that he should retract what he had said in another Paul's Cross sermon. Further diplomatic exchanges ensured that Bancroft would not have to grovel in public.[23] The King declared himself satisfied.

Bancroft was only politically, not genuinely, repentant. Three years later, in two books called *A Survay of the Pretended Holy Discipline* and *Daungerous Positions and Proceedings*, he launched a much more extensive attack on 'Genevating' in Scotland and what he chose to call 'Scottizing' in England. 'Once again, Bancroft's expressed sympathy with the King only served to highlight his weakness.'[24] These two books were published anonymously, for obvious reasons, but they were ascribed to Bancroft by Whitgift, and others.[25] Bancroft was profoundly mistaken in supposing that James, as King of Scotland, favoured a Church constitution in any way resembling that of England. In 1598, James told the General Assembly: 'I minde not…to bring in Papisticall or Anglican bishopping.' He had renounced the model of 'our neighbour kirk in England', pronouncing it 'an eville said masse in English, wanting nothing but the liftings'.[26] These were the politically motivated utterances of a much subtler politician than Bancroft. They help to explain why Bancroft must have been alarmed at the prospect of a Scottish succession. To sharpen the question and turn it around: how was it that James chose Bancroft, with such a crime sheet, to be his Archbishop of Canterbury?

The most straightforward answer to our question must be that James, having arrived in England and having confronted the English counterparts of his old Presbyterian opponents in Scotland (perhaps fatally misunderstanding and misrepresenting those moderate men who appeared before him at Hampton Court), impressed with Bancroft's performance in the conference, and troubled by the consequential reverberations in parliament, decided that Bancroft was after all the man to enforce discipline, and conformity, in a no bishop no king situation.[27] Perhaps that was what the dying Whitgift had advised. And it is practically certain that the man of the hour, Robert Cecil, now Viscount Cranborne and soon to be Earl of Salisbury, was of the same disposition.

BANCROFT AND THE PURITANS

But if that is all that has to be said, this chapter could have remained unwritten. That Bancroft leant in such an exaggerated anti-Genevan, even anti-Calvinist, direction, to the verge of paranoia, is at least partly explicable by his religious background and formation. Bancroft grew up in the large and very conservative, not to say Catholic, parish of Prescot, in south Lancashire. It is probably relevant that Richard Barnes, in turn Bishop of Carlisle and Durham, seven years his senior, was born and raised in the same little neck of the woods. For Barnes would be Archbishop Grindal's only enemy in the episcopate at that watershed moment, Grindal's sequestration after resisting the Queen on the matter of the prophesyings. Barnes took the same view of the affair as Bancroft's patron Sir Christopher Hatton, who may have engineered the archbishop's downfall. But what Bancroft may have thought about that affair, which determined the future course of the Elizabethan Church, is not on record.

Bancroft's first patron, a great uncle, was Hugh Curwen, the temporizing Archbishop of Dublin whom other more Protestant Irish bishops loathed and denounced. Curwen made Bancroft a prebendary of St Patrick's Cathedral when Bancroft was still an undergraduate, which gave him a lifelong interest in Irish affairs.[28] Bancroft's Prescot background made it easy, to say the least, to have more or less comfortable relations with the quieter Catholics of Elizabethan England, a cordiality he was incapable of cultivating with moderate Puritans.

The fact that Bancroft made his entry to the Cambridge scene via Christ's College, already an evangelical hothouse, had nothing to do with hot Protestantism and, probably, everything to do with the fact that he had been educated at a grammar school founded by Bishop William Smith of Lincoln, another local worthy, whose patron was the mother of Henry VII, Lady Margaret Beaufort, later Countess of Derby, living near Bancroft's home turf.[29] Lady Margaret was the foundress of Christ's, which Bancroft soon left for the more congenial and conservative environment of Jesus College, one of whose members, perhaps Bancroft's pupil, would soon be denounced in Suffolk, with reference to his college, as a 'Jesuit'.[30]

It may have been Bancroft's wounding experience at the hands of the godly mafia of Christ's which turned him into a lifelong enemy of the hot Protestantism we know as Puritanism. By the early 1580s, he was composing a string of polemical treatises denouncing the Puritans and all their ways, which he had observed with all the dedication of Dostoevsky's policeman in pursuit of Raskolnikov.[31] Much of Bancroft's field work had been conducted in and around Bury St Edmunds, where in 1582 he and other Jesus men had been drafted in to combat the ascendancy of the Puritan preachers and their gentry patrons, at war with Bishop Edmund Freke of Norwich.[32]

That was the start of a career which turned Bancroft, through the machinery of the High Commission for Ecclesiastical Causes, into a virtually full-time policeman for the established Church, thanks to the support of his patron, Archbishop Whitgift's only staunch supporter in the government, Sir Christopher Hatton, whom he served as speech-writer on ecclesiastical matters. When a frustrated Puritan faction went ballistic in the scandalous and satirical Marprelate Tracts, Bancroft went into top gear. Raids on ministers' studies yielded a mass of incriminating evidence which was deployed in the Star Chamber in a trial of a select bunch of Puritan ministers, headed by Thomas Cartwright. The trial was inconclusive. But Bancroft soon found another use for the fat dossier of evidence which he had compiled of the machinations of the Presbyterians. That was in those two books published in 1593, with the dossier largely digested in *Daungerous Positions*.[33]

Bancroft was not wilfully ignorant of Scottish Church and state politics.

Far from it. A whole volume of nearly 150 folios in one of the manuscript collections in his library at Lambeth consists entirely of letters and papers relating to Scottish affairs. They date from 1572 until 1612. Very many of the documents are endorsed and occasionally annotated in Bancroft's hand. They include a copy of the letter which he sent to the Scottish clergy, defending his offensive Paul's Cross sermon, and endorsed with the words 'The copie of my letter to the ministers of Scotlande'.[34] It nevertheless seems that Bancroft's observation of Scottish matters was really all about England. Events in Scotland were meant as a warning to England not to go down the same road. And insofar as Bancroft contemplated the possible, even probable, accession to the English throne of the King of Scotland, he was perhaps entitled to be alarmed. It is inconceivable that his thoughts about the English succession should not have been haunted by Scottish nightmares. Sir John Harington had quoted a satirical definition of Puritans as 'Protestants scar'd out of their wits'.[35] But it was Bancroft, as the anti-Puritan foremost among English episcopalians, who may have been scared out of his wits as the 1590s progressed towards the inevitable denouement.[36]

BANCROFT AND THE CATHOLICS

But now Bancroft professed to being scared out of his wits by the Society of Jesus. This indefatigable collector of intelligence had a new agenda. He was compiling a new dossier, employing some of the same methods he had deployed to document and expose the activities of John Field and the Presbyterians involved in the Puritan conferences, or classes. Once again he was looking from the outside at the inner affairs of a cabal of religious dissidents, but now they were Catholics rather than Puritans. To what end is what we have now to consider, and, in particular, what this may have had to do with the succession. That is almost the same question as asking how far Bancroft's new interest was intended to restore his credibility with the most likely successor to the throne of England.

The dossier, once filed away in the library which Bancroft, as archbishop, created at Lambeth Palace, and to which much of the contents was restored by certain transactions in the sale room in the twentieth century, consisted of the correspondence and other papers of a motley collection of seminary priests opposed to the imposition from Rome of a newly invented entity, an 'archpriest', one George Blackwell, whose appointment was attributed by his enemies to the alleged power-hungry machinations of the English Jesuits. The Lambeth archive is evidence of Bancroft's extensive contacts and dealings with these anti-Jesuits, known from their appeals to Rome against the appointment of Blackwell as the 'Appellants'.[37]

This split in the Catholic ranks had its origins partly in bitter disputes in the English College in Rome, where students prepared for the English mission but were frequently distracted by the frictions that are often found in isolated, expatriated communities, and partly in what were called 'stirs' among the Catholics in claustrophobic custody in that mild Elizabethan version of Guantanamo, Wisbech Castle in Cambridgeshire, in which Bancroft had taken a close interest. Penelope Renold, the editor of materials relating to the Wisbech stirs and running on into what became the Archpriest controversy has remarked on the sheer bulk of what she calls 'Bishop Bancroft's "Dossier"'. 'The reconstruction of the dossier involves in all about 460 items of varying lengths, from those of one or two pages to one long Memorial of over eighty pages.' She notes 'a constant and unifying thread', a large number of comments and endorsements in Bancroft's own hand or in the hands of those assumed to have been on his staff.[38] Moreover, the manuscripts now at Lambeth include two indices to these papers which are typical of Bancroft's own methodology, as exemplified in the early 1580s in the manuscripts now in St John's College Cambridge and edited in modern times as *Tracts Ascribed to Richard Bancroft*. These papers are headed: 'Treatises and resolutions in Q. Eliz. tyme etc.', and include an entry 'Of the iarres amongst the seculer Priests themselves and with the Jesuits ab. Anno 1592 ad Anno 1600 exclusive'.[39]

When did Bancroft begin to interest himself in these internecine squabbles? Probably a couple of years before he became Bishop of London. One of the most revealing of the Wisbech documents, Christopher Bagshaw's letter 'to a certain gentleman in Norfollk', is endorsed in the hands of Bancroft and his collaborator: 'Dr Bagshaw of the separation to certayne gentilmen in Norfolk'. There are other letters with similar Bancroftian endorsements dating from 1595 to 1597, but when they came into Bancroft's hands we cannot tell. The sources in most cases were (proto) Appellant rather than Jesuit or Roman, suggesting that for the most part Bancroft was being fed a one-sided story. The endorsements are brief and laconic summaries of what the letters contain, in no way polemical, resembling, one hopes, the summaries which a modern police force might make of evidence from Islamist sources.[40]

One document from this stable of particular importance was entitled 'Forty-five Articles of Enquiry', which T. G. Law thought furnished 'the key to the whole collection', and which he attributed to Bancroft. This amounted to a nearly exhaustive investigation into everything concerning the English Jesuits since their first appearance in England: forty-five propositions all beginning 'it appeareth' or 'it seemeth'. The Articles were presented to the leading Appellant, Bagshaw, and are accompanied in the surviving manuscript by his answers.[41]

This is evidence of the extent to which Bancroft chose to work hand in glove with this small and very far from representative party of English Catholics. He entertained one of them, Thomas Bluet, an elderly priest with a drink problem, as his house guest at Fulham and assisted them with the publication of a whole string of anti-Jesuit books and pamphlets. He released four of the Appellants into 'exile', but in truth left them free to make their journey to Rome to advance their cause, whence Bluet kept in close touch with Fulham.[42] The difference between this intelligence operation and that which Bancroft had mounted against the Puritans was that while some of the material was 'seized'(?) from Bagshaw on more than one occasion, so that a great authority, J. H. Pollen, could refer to the whole collection as 'Dr Bagshaw's dossier', much of it appears to have been voluntarily shared with the Bishop of London, who in a (compromising) sense was himself a party to these dodgy dealings.[43] Bancroft's conduct of these negotiations, and especially the practical tolerance – and even the hospitality he extended to several of the Appellants – sailed close to the legal and political wind.

On one occasion Bancroft demanded, more or less, that a leading Appellant, Cuthbert Trollope, a vocal opponent of Persons, should not face trial in York but be sent down to London 'and disposed of here as afterwards it shall be held meet'. The Council in the North was obliged to do what the Privy Council (Cecil?) accordingly required, to send Trollope and another seminary priest, Edmund Calverley, down to London. But the Lord President of the Council, Cecil's half brother, was not best pleased: 'The like precedent was never seen in this place. I pray God the good that is intended thereby may take good effect, but in the meantime it has a little distasted this government, that has heretofore proceeded severely in these cases.'[44]

At about the same time Bancroft took into his service a man, evidently a staunch Protestant, who very soon smelled a rat. He knew that the Appellant William Watson, Bancroft's house guest in an arrangement authorized by the Privy Council,[45] was a priest and, he thought, author of the Appellants' anti-Jesuit polemical tracts often referred to collectively as the *Quodlibets*, 'wherein were many very great treasons'; and he strongly suspected that Watson's servant, ostensibly a tailor, was also a priest. The matter reached the Lord Chief Justice, John Popham, and Bancroft had to write an extraordinary letter to Popham asking him, in effect, to lay off.[46] These incidents occurred in June and July 1602. Later, with James on the throne, Bancroft had good reason to detach himself from the same 'Mr Watson', whose involvement in the absurd Bye conspiracy took him to a scaffold. Bancroft now called his old friend 'the chief contriver, deviser and setter on of this mysterious plot'.[47] There is a tradition that the execution of Watson at Winchester was carried out on the orders of Sir John Popham.[48]

Above all, Bancroft was all but incriminated by the role he played in assisting the Appellants in the publication, from presses in England, of the *Quodlibets*: the eccentric title of the most notorious of these libels, by William Watson, is *A Decacordon of Ten Quodlibeticall Questions concerning Religion and State: Wherein the Author framing himselfe a Quilibet to every Quodlibet, decides an hundred crosse interrogatorie doubts, about the generall contentions betwixt the seminarie preiets and Iesuits at this present* (1602). This was no pamphlet but a tome of 362 pages. It was later plausibly alleged that Bancroft had arranged for the printing of no fewer than thirteen Appellant tracts, some of them in Staffordshire.[49]

This caught up with Bancroft in 1604 when the Puritan printer, William Jones, intercepted the Speaker of the House of Commons on his passage through Westminster Hall to present him with a bill indicting Bancroft of treasonable practices for his involvement in the printing of 'popish books', 'An Acte for declaration of certayne practises of the Bishop of London to be Treason'. The bill was duly read in the Commons on 15 May, but the King intervened to prevent its further passage.[50] The King could forestall an impeachment, but he could not put a stop to malicious gossip. After Bancroft's death an epigrammatic obituarist accused him of having kept open the back door 'to let in the strumpet of Rome'.

> Here lyes my Lords Grace at six and seaven.
> And if I do not lye his soule is in heaven.
> I wish with my hart it may be to his leeking
> Since all the world knows it was never his seeking.[51]

Bancroft may have lived with such suspicions for much of his career, much like his patron, Sir Christopher Hatton. Why else did Archbishop Whitgift feel it necessary to affirm in the reference he wrote in 1597: he 'is certainly no papist'.[52] When Sir George Paule published his life of his old master, Archbishop Whitgift, Daniel Featley wrote, commenting on Paule's intention to follow this up with a life of Bancroft. But Featley knew that Bancroft had been under fire for entertaining Romish priests in his house and making use of them. Although the King had publicly supported Bancroft's conduct at the Hampton Court Conference, Featley thought that if Bancroft had favoured popery, he would not encourage Paule to proceed. So there was a tinge of lingering suspicion in even the most respectable religious circles.[53]

The key to a certain affinity, however opportunistic, between Bancroft and some of the Appellant priests may lie in the fact that the Appellants, with their professed concern for an ecclesiastical order of a traditional kind, not so unlike episcopacy as practised in the Elizabethan Church, compared the Jesuits to the Puritans in their radical contempt for hierarchy and the proper order of things. Much of this was tittle tattle, insults about 'Genevists' hurled across the dinner table in Wisbech. But Bancroft too may have found it easy to bracket in his mind the character and methodology of the Jesuits with his old Puritan-antagonists. In *A Survay of the Pretended Holy Discipline* he had written of 'puritane-popish assertions', comparing Presbyterians to 'the rankest Jesuits in Europe'.[54] In a sense he was dealing with the same phenomenon. And we find the same strange symbiosis which had cemented Bancroft to Elizabethan Presbyterianism. Bancroft was a natural conspirator who warmed to conspiracy, and for whom intelligence-gathering was second nature.

By some historians of English Catholicism, the Archpriest controversy has been seen as essentially a matter of politics, closely related to the question of allegiance, whether to the pope or to Queen Elizabeth; and to the burning issue of the day, the succession.[55] The English Jesuits, and especially their most radical, polemical as well as capable leader Robert Persons, now as rector making peace in the disturbed English College in Rome, leant towards the Spanish interest. In 1594 Persons ghosted, under the pseudonym of R. Doleman, *A Conference about the Next Sucession to the Crowne of Ingland* which wrapped its preference for the succession of the daughter of Philip II of Spain, the Infanta, in a sophisticated dialogic investigation of the constitutional rights and wrongs of the matter. The Appellants, as with those at Wisbech and Rome who had resisted Jesuit control of their affairs, were unhappy about the Jesuit-Spanish connection. Hence the stratagem of Bancroft, and behind Bancroft Cecil, to make use of these awkward customers who were rocking the Catholic boat.

But the stratagem could only have a limited utility, if the intention was to create a kind of *laissez faire* settlement between the English state and the English Catholics, which is what Roland Green Usher thought was going on.[56] John Bossy has rightly insisted that the split between the Jesuits and the Appellants was more religious than political, even more clerical, having most to do with the internal affairs of the English Catholics, and especially the organization and control of the clergy, matters of little concern to the aristocratic Catholic laity, who tended to assume that it was they who employed the priests as their household chaplains; and of no interest to the English government, except as something to be conveniently exploited. The Appellants, although denounced by Archpriest George Blackwell as troublesome schismatics, were ecclesiastical conservatives, interested in the restoration of traditional structures of discipline and government. Bossy, always interested in the difference between lay and clerical Catholicism, has suggested that insofar as there was a politics beyond the internal affairs of the Catholic community, if some of the Catholic gentry wanted to be shot of the Jesuits in order to affirm their allegiance to the Elizabethan regime, the priests offered declarations of allegiance to the regime in the hope of getting shot of the Jesuits.[57]

As a means of incorporating the English Catholics into an ecumenical toleration, this was not going anywhere, since even the Appellants could never have disowned their spiritual loyalty to the Roman curia, which no amount of distinction between politics and religion could make tolerable to the Elizabethan state. After all, their repeated appeals to Rome, for all that they were facilitated by Bancroft, were in direct and obvious contravention of the statute of 24 Henry VIII which had prohibited appeals to Rome.

But for Bancroft, and for Robert Cecil, these were promising waters to fish in, either to secure the allegiance of a substantial body of English Catholics or, more plausibly, to divide their ranks, to the detriment of the Jesuits, whose politics were the immediate threat, not least in respect of the succession. The archpriest made it easy for them. George Blackwell was an awkward autocrat, skilled at rubbing people up the wrong way. When, in 1598, the first two Appellant delegates – a couple of political innocents, William Bishop and Robert Charnock – were totally outclassed in the politics of the Roman curia, the anti-Jesuits duly submitted. But Blackwell, instead of celebrating the return of peace and fraternity, demanded that his opponents acknowledge that they had incurred the guilt of schism. This they refused to do, acquiring from the University of Paris a ruling that there had been no schism: a judgement which Blackwell promptly dismissed. The Appellants now resorted to the printing press, aided and abetted by Bancroft; and in September 1601 four Appellants, nominally 'banished', were in effect licensed to go to Rome, armed with a second appeal. The outcome, a papal compromise, condemned the polemical writings of both sides, cleared the Appellants of the charge of schism and forbade Blackwell to consult the English Jesuits on the affairs of the mission. But also, critically, it upheld the authority of Blackwell as arch-priest, although he was required to choose at least six of his assistants from among the Appellants.[58]

At about this time, in October 1602, Bancroft began to detach himself from the affairs of the English Catholics, although he continued to offer hospitality to Thomas Bluet, perhaps in genuine friendship. The Appellants had served their purpose. Jesuit sources, which are inherently suspect, regularly reported that Bancroft rejoiced when the Appellants went public in their condemnation of the Jesuits, since 'this was that he looked for all the while, viz. that one should write against another'. Bancroft had 'termed both sides knaves, but the Appellants good instruments to serve the state'.[59] Was Bancroft really that cynical? As for 'the state', a proclamation of 5 November 1602, which was the first governmental utterance to admit the existence of the Appellants, banished all priests from the realm. There is evidence that Bancroft assisted with the drafting of the proclamation and may even have been the author of it.[60]

BANCROFT, CONSPIRACY THEORY, AND
THE JACOBEAN SUCCESSION?

We have now to try to resolve the question of what Bancroft was really up to in these questionable dealings; how far they were, primarily, his dealings; and, in particular, what they may have had to do with the succession. According to one reading of the situation, by the late 1590s everyone, most Catholics included, knew that James VI would become James I of England. Most Catholics, clerically the Appellants but surely including much of the politically aware Catholic laity, were distancing themselves from the Jesuit-led Hispanophile party.[61] Did Bancroft, and Cecil, know that that was the case; even would they have wanted to believe that that was the case? Thanks to Doleman/Persons, they, and not only they, were in the grip of a conspiracy theory. There is good evidence of that in the instructions which Bancroft initially gave to the preachers of London in the wake of the Essex revolt: that in their sermons they should charge Essex with having corresponded with the Pope and other Catholic powers.[62] Often quoted is a letter from Bancroft to Cecil of August 1601, his inform-ants among the Appellants assuring him that the hardline recusants 'were never so like to join with the enemy as they are now, if opportunity serve. Parsons you know is as vile a traitor to her Majesty as any man living.' 'The Jesuitical humour' was now in the ascendant, entertaining traitorous designs and favouring the Spaniard.[63] Whether Bancroft fully believed this, or merely wanted to believe it, is not easy to say. At the very least he appears highly susceptible to what the Appellants told him, just as years earlier he had been quick to smell a kind of conspiracy in the operations of the 'Genevisors'. The suggestion that the issues between the Jesuits and the Appellants were of little interest beyond small clerical cliques is belied by the huge number of books published on both sides of the dispute. Someone must have been reading them. Can we be so sure that the Catholic laity were hostile to the Hispanophile party? If so, why all those books? Alex Walsham has told me: 'It wouldn't surprise me at all if there were more pro-Jesuit lay Catholics about than we have been led to believe.'[64]

In the perception of Joel Hurstfield, the explanation of what the Appellants were up to in their covert negotiations with 'the heretics' was simple. It lay in 'their resolution to prevent a Spanish succession to the English throne, and in their hope of obtaining a religious toleration under some other candidate'.[65] The question for us is whether Bancroft–Cecil participated in the first of these resolutions while holding out hopes of the second. Were their dealings with the Appellants mainly or even entirely motivated by the need to prevent the Spanish succession, the promise of religious toleration for 'good' Catholics no more than the bait in a trap?

In resolving this question we are mercifully free from what was Hurstfield's main concern in his essay 'The succession struggle in late Elizabethan England', which was to exonerate Cecil, in his factional contest with Essex, from having favoured the claims of the Infanta, as alleged by the Jesuit historian Father Leo Hicks.[66] But we are not absolved from considering what Bancroft's motives may have been, if this was what the Appellant conspiracy was all about. We must also consider the question, without necessarily resolving it, whether the idea of doing business with the Appellants origi-nated with Cecil (as Hurstfield, at work on a biography of Cecil, seemed to assume) or with Bancroft, the answer given by Roland Green Usher, Bancroft's panegyrist.

We shall not get much closer to resolving that issue than a series of letters from Bancroft to Cecil, preserved at Hatfield House.[67] There are no fewer than twenty-three letters concerned mainly with the Catholic question, written and received between July 1601 and July 1603. Almost all are in Bancroft's own hand, which must be significant. At the very least they are evidence of a high level of mutual confidence between the two men. If we need evidence of friendship, it is provided by the fact that Bancroft, on his return from a diplomatic trip to Emden in 1600, brought Cecil six score gallons of good Rhenish wine, a gift reciprocated on Cecil's part by haunches of venison.[68] Bancroft and Cecil had been singing from the same song sheet since the hectic February days of the Essex revolt, when the bishop had been active in securing the streets of the city and tuning the London pulpits, always following Cecil's instructions.[69] It is also worth noting that no other bishop, no other part of the ecclesiastical machine, such as the High Commission, seems to have been involved in these dealings; least of all Archbishop Whitgift himself, who appears to have been silent on the issue, and for that matter on much else. Was Bancroft already the archbishop-in-waiting? There was a later tradition that that was the case – Bancroft 'in effect Archbishop while Bishop' – a view shared by a modern authority.[70] There is a revealing letter from Whitgift to Cecil, with a valetudinarian feel to it, in which the archbishop expresses gratitude that Cecil should have spoken kindly about him to Bancroft, as if Bancroft were now the up-and-coming man, and rather oddly goes on about what Whitgift's career had owed to both of Cecil's parents. Well that was true, but why should he have needed to say so?[71]

Throughout the Bancroft–Cecil correspondence, Bancroft is supplying information, Cecil receiving it, Bancroft proactive, Cecil reactive. I know of only one letter travelling in the other direction, but it is illuminating: 'I see you haue your Part in slander and Malediction. It sufficeth that we haue conscience strong against all these Calumniations.'[72] It is in any case inconceivable that Bancroft could have conducted himself as he did, particularly in licensing, in effect, illegal books, without the support of the Privy Council, which may be as much as to say, Cecil. Bancroft received an official letter endorsing his activities:

> You have divers times had cause to confer privately with Romish priests…in which respect you have been sometimes driven to retain, and sometimes to relieve them. As these proceedings have tended to her Majesty's honour, we let you know that she approves thereof and is pleased you continue them at discretion.

But a communication with Cecil, dated 8 February 1602, makes it clear that it was Bancroft himself who drafted that helpful letter, just as he seems to have had a hand in the proclamation of 5 November 1602.[73]

We are left with the question of the extent to which Bancroft's sustained intervention in Catholic affairs was motivated by his own, or his and Cecil's, hopes and intentions with respect to the succession. There could be a simple answer. Bancroft was frustrating the schemes of the Jesuits, and of Persons in particular, which he equated with the Spanish interest, which meant, in addition to the threat of invasion, the Spanish pretender, the Infanta.

But we do not have to believe that Bancroft's mind was that tightly focused. It is possible that he had a genuine interest in trading political allegiance for some measure of toleration, which is what the Appellants wanted to believe. Several more than respectable historians have wanted to believe it too. But it's still hard to believe, and there is no evidence that such a toleration was ever seriously considered. Another more plausible explanation for the operation was that it was intended to spike the guns of the Jesuits, not so much with Pope Clement VIII, who was unlikely to be persuaded by a heretic to take sides against the Society, as with an English Catholic audience, parts of which perhaps needed to be persuaded that the Jesuits were bad news.

In support of the view that the succession was at the heart of all this, there is copious evidence that the Appellants, and those who thought and planned as they did, were unhappy about the pro-Spanish machinations of the Jesuits and their supporters. Little doubt about that. Bancroft wanted the priest Trollope to be transferred from York to London, specifically because he had opposed the reading of Doleman's *Conference* at mealtimes in Rome.[74] Archbishop Hutton, writing to Bishop Matthew in May 1604, suggested that Bancroft's dealing with the secular priests 'was done only to advance his Maiesties title against the Spanish faction'.[75] The only trouble with this post-1603 testimony is that it benefited from hindsight; interested hindsight at that.

On the whole, it seems that the crudest explanation of what Bancroft was up to is the best, which also may be most in character. The bishop was in the serious business of dividing the Catholic ranks, particularly to the detriment of the Jesuits, and for whatever advantage might come from that. We have to employ with some caution the Jesuit sources which make such allegations, but Bancroft's own letters to Cecil generally support that diagnosis. That the entire operation was planned simply to secure the succession of James VI and to defeat the aspirations of the Infanta, or of any other Catholic candidate, is at best not proven.

We can, I think, get no deeper in these murky waters than some things that were said at the Hampton Court Conference. The moderate Puritan spokesman from Oxford, Dr John Rainolds, was understood (misunderstood, according to Rainolds) to have complained about Bancroft's activities in facilitating those Appellant books. James I told Rainolds:

> If his meaning were, to tax the bishop of London for suffering those books between secular priests, lately published, so freely to passe abroad, his majesty would have him and his associates to know, and willed them also to acquaint their adherents and friends abroad therewith, that the said bishop was much injured and slandered in that behalf, who did nothing therein but by warrant from the lords of the councel, whereby, both a schism between them was nourished, and also his majesties cause and title handled: the lord Cicil affirming thereunto, that therefore they were tolerated, because, in them, was the title of Spain confuted.[76]

And that might seem almost to settle the question surrounding the secondary succession issue touched on in this essay: how it was that Richard Bancroft, we might almost say, of all people, became the seventy-third Archbishop of Canterbury.

NOTES

1   T. E. Hartley, *Proceedings in the Parliaments of Elizabeth I*, 3 vols (Leicester, 1981), vol. 1, pp. 274–82. On Sandys's probable responsibility, see Collinson's article in *ODNB*; and Kathryn Murphy, 'The date of Edwin Sandys's Paul's Cross sermon: "At what time a maine treason was discouered"', *Notes and Queries*, 53 (2006), 430–2. I owe the latter reference to John Craig.

2 John Guy, 'The 1590s: the second reign of Elizabeth I?', in John Guy (ed.), *The Reign of Elizabeth I: Court and Culture in the Last Decade* (Cambridge, 1995), pp. 1–19.

3 For William Cecil, Lord Burghley, and the bishops, see Brett Usher, *William Cecil and Episcopacy, 1559–1577* (Aldershot, 2003).

4 *CJRC*. See Michele Vignaux, 'The succession and related issues through the correspondence of Elizabeth, James and Robert Cecil', in Jean-Christophe Mayer (ed.), *The Succession Struggle in Late Elizabethan England: Politics, Polemics and Cultural Representations* (Montpellier, 2004), pp. 65–88.

5 Patrick Collinson, 'The Elizabethan exclusion crisis and the Elizabethan polity', *Proceedings of the British Academy*, 84 (1994), 51–92.

6 Sir John Harington, *A Briefe View of the State of the Church of England* (London, 1653), pp. 160–3; there is a modern edition of Harington's book, *A Supplie or Addicion to the Catalogue of Bishops to the Yeare 1608*, ed. R. H. Miller (Pontomac, 1979). Jason Scott-Warren, *Sir John Harington and the Book as Gift* (Oxford, 2001), pp. 219–30; *ODNB*, John Rudd. Manningham's version of the Queen's reaction to the sermon was: 'M[aster]-D[octor], you have made me a good funerall sermon; I maye dye when I will.' R. P. Sorlien (ed.), *The Diary of John Manningham* (Hanover, NH, 1976), p. 194.

7 Thomas Fuller, *The Church History of Britain*, ed. J. S. Brewer, 6 vols (Oxford, 1845), 5, pp. 435–7.

8 Patrick Collinson, 'The Jacobean religious settlement: the Hampton Court conference', in Howard Tomlinson (ed.), *Before the Civil War: Essays on Early Stuart Politics and Government* (London, 1983), pp. 39, 49; BL, Sloane MS 271, fo. 23ᵛ; Kenneth Fincham, *Prelate as Pastor: The Episcopate of James I* (Oxford, 1990), pp. 65–6, 215, 229–30. See also Patrick Collinson, *Richard Bancroft and Elizabethan Anti-Puritanism* (Cambridge, 2013).

9 Scott-Warren, *Sir John Harington*.

10 Fuller, *Church History*, 5, pp. 436–7.

11 Harington, *A Briefe View*, pp. 10–14; BL, Lansdowne MS 89, fo. 19. I owe this reference to Arnold Hunt.

12 Fincham, *Prelate as Pastor*, p. 27.

13 Patrick Collinson, 'The religious factor' and Gerard Kilroy, 'Sir John Harington's protesting Catholic gifts', in Mayer, *Succession Struggle*, pp. 264, 229–30.

14 *HMC Sal*, XIV, pp. 211–12; Sorlien (ed.), *Diary of John Manningham*, p. 245.

15 Peter E. McCullough, *Sermons at Court: Politics and Religion in Elizabethan and Jacobean Preaching* (Cambridge, 1998), p. 103.

16 James Raine (ed.), *The Correspondence of Dr Matthew Hutton, Archbishop of York*, Surtees Society, 17 (1843), pp. 168–9.

17 Harington, *A Briefe View*, pp. 186–90.

18 *Ibid.*, pp. 10–11.

19 *A Sermon preached at Paules Crosse the 9. of Februarie, being the first Sunday in the Parleament, Anno 1588, by Richard Bancroft Dr of Divinitie and Chaplaine to the Right Honorable Sir Christopher Hatton Knight L[ord] Chancellor of England* (London, 1589); Patrick Collinson, *The Elizabethan Puritan Movement* (London and Berkeley CA, 1967), p. 397.

20 Jenny Wormald, 'Ecclesiastical vitriol: the kirk, the puritans and the future king of England', in Guy (ed.), *The Reign of Elizabeth I*, pp. 173–91.

21 *Ibid.*, p. 178.

22 John Davidson, *D. Bancrofts Rashnes in Rayling against the Church of Scotland* (Edinburgh, 1590), sigs 3ᵛ, 6ʳ. Davidson reported that Bancroft 'is presently as far out of his maiesties favour (let the Bishopists of England trust the intelligence given of him to those of the contrary so much as they list) as ever before he seemed to be in it' (sig. 6ʳ).

23 Owen Chadwick, 'Richard Bancroft's submission', *Journal of Ecclesiastical History*, 3 (1952), 58–73.

24 Wormald, 'Ecclesiastical vitriol', p. 179.

25 CUL, Mm.i.47, fo. 333. The Appellant priest William Watson's books included what Watson called 'the bishop of London's Genevian platfourme'. See Mark Nicholls's *ODNB* article on Watson.

26 Wormald, 'Ecclesiastical vitriol', pp. 187, 190, 177.

27 Fincham, *Prelate as Pastor*, p. 27.

28 I owe my knowledge of Bancroft's origins to Stella Fletcher, who if the young Bancroft were still alive would be her close neighbour in what is now a suburb of Warrington. This runs contrary to earlier accounts of his religious background as Protestant, even hot Protestant. See, for example, R. G. Usher, *The Reconstruction of the English Church*, 2 vols (London and New York, 1910), vol. 1, pp. 22–4. I am equally indebted to Dr Fletcher for knowledge of the origins of Bishop Barnes. For Barnes and the Grindal affair, see Patrick Collinson, *Archbishop Grindal 1519–1583: The Struggle for a Reformed Church* (London, 1979), pp. 193–4, 264–5. See also *ODNB* articles on Bancroft, Curwen. Barnes, Curwen, Hatton: these are names with which to track an alternative, less evangelical, trajectory for the Elizabethan Church.

29 My indebtedness is, again, to Stella Fletcher.

30 John Craig, *Reformation, Politics and Polemics: The Growth of Protestantism in East Anglian Market Towns, 1500–1610* (Aldershot, 2001), p. 100; BL, Egerton MS 1693, fos 89ᵛ–90ʳ, Lansdowne MS 37, no. 28, fo. 61. The Bury gentleman Thomas Badby was brought before the High Commission in London for this aspersion, where he explained that he did not mean that Oliver Phillips, was 'a papisticall Jesuyte', alluding only to Phillips's college.

31 Albert Peel (ed.), *Tracts Ascribed to Richard Bancroft* (Cambridge, 1953).

32 Craig, *Reformation, Politics and Polemics*, pp. 88–111.

33 Collinson, *Elizabethan Puritan Movement, passim*.

34 LPL, MS 3471.

35 Harington, *Briefe View*, p. 7. At the Hampton Court Conference this aphorism was attributed to 'master Butler of Cambridge': 'A puritan is a protestant frayed out of his wits'. Edward Cardwell, *A History of Conferences* (Oxford, 1849), p. 184.

36 Wormald, *Ecclesiastical vitriol*, pp. 178–91.

37 Papers, now known in part as the Laud–Selden–Fairhurst Papers, were removed from Lambeth by John Selden and passed into the hands of his friend and executor Sir Matthew Hale. Some found their way into the Petyt manuscripts in the Inner Temple Library. Many other documents remained with the Hale family until they

were acquired in 1946 by the businessman James Fairhurst. They were restored to Lambeth in 1963 and 1988. The Lambeth volumes which mainly concern the affairs of the Appellants, including their dealings with Bancroft, are MSS 2006, 2007, 2014. Other related documents are preserved in the archives of Westminster Cathedral. The Petyt material was published by T. G. Law in *The Archpriest Controversy: Documents Relating to the Dissensions of the Roman Catholic Clergy, 1597–1602*, CS, n.s. 56, 58, 2 vols (1896 and 1898). Law was unaware of the original provenance of these materials, although he did know that Bancroft had had a role in their interception and preservation; P. Renold (ed.), *The Wisbech Stirs (1595–1598)*, Catholic Record Society, 51 (1958), pp. xviii–xxii. For a general account of the Archpriest controversy, and of the role of the Appellants, see Arnold Pritchard, *Catholic Loyalism in Elizabethan England* (Chapel Hill, NC, 1979), *passim*; Peter Holmes, *Resistance and Compromise: The Political Thought of the Elizabethan Catholics* (Cambridge, 1980); Stefania Tutino, *Law and Conscience in Early Modern England, 1570–1625* (Aldershot, 2007). For the resonance of the Appellant position with the matter of the succession, see Sandra Jusdado, 'The Appellant priests and the succession issue', in Mayer, *Succession Struggle*, pp. 199–216; and Chapter 4 in this volume.

38 Renold (ed.), *The Wisbech Stirs*, pp. xviii–xx.

39 *Ibid.*, pp. xx.

40 *Ibid.*, pp. 14–18, 22–9, 36–8, 41–3, 70–9, 83–4, 86–7, 90–5, 99–101, 105–6, 112–14, 119–23, 132–4, 138–9, 141–4, 179–82, 185–7, 189–94, 207–9, 219–21, 225.

41 Law, *The Archpriest Controversy*, 1, pp. 226–41. (ITL, MS Petyt 538.47, fo. 107–13.)

42 Pritchard, *Catholic Loyalism*, pp. 125–9.

43 Renold (ed.), *The Wisbech Stirs*, p. xix.

44 *HMC Sal*, XII, pp. 194, 232, 238.

45 Law, *The Archpriest Controversy*, 2, p. 127

46 Bancroft to Popham, 5 June 1602, BL, Harley MS 360, fo. 36.

47 *HMC Sal*, XV, pp. 183–4.

48 *ODNB*, Watson.

49 H. R. Plomer, 'Bishop Bancroft and a Catholic press', *The Library*, 2nd series, 8 (1907), 164–76. See also N. P. Brown, 'Paperchase: the dissemination of Catholic texts in Elizabethan England', in Peter Beal and Jeremy Griffiths (eds), *English Manuscript Studies 1100–1700*, 2 vols (Oxford, 1989), vol. 1, pp. 120–43; and Peter Milward, *Religious Controversies of the Elizabethan Age: A Survey of Printed Sources* (Ilkley, 1977), pp. 116–24.

50 *CSPDom. James I*, 8, pp. 21–5; *CJ*, vol. 1, pp. 210–12.

51 Bodl, Ashmolean MS 1463, fos 17, 18.

52 CUL, Mm.i.47, fo. 333.

53 Bodl, Rawlinson MS D47, fo. 19. I owe this reference to Kenneth Fincham.

54 [Richard Bancroft,] *A Survay of the Pretended Holy Discipline* (London, 1593), pp. 259–60, 266–7.

55 A. O. Meyer, *England and the Catholic Church under Queen Elizabeth* (with an introduction by John Bossy) (London, 1967), pp. 411–64.

56 Usher, *Reconstruction of the English Church*, vol. 1, chs 7 and 8, 'The Catholic Problem

in 1600', 'Fostering Catholic Disunion'.

57 John Bossy, *The English Catholic Community 1570–1850* (London, 1975), pp. 35–48. And see Bossy's Introduction to the 1967 edition of Meyer, *England and the Catholic Church*. But for a rather more nuanced analysis which helps to explain how this storm in a clerical teacup generated so much documentation, see Michael Questier, *Catholicism and Community in Early Modern England: Politics, Aristocratic Patronage and Religion, c.1550–1640* (Cambridge, 2006), pp. 250–9.

58 Pritchard, *Catholic Loyalism*, pp. 127–8.

59 Henry Foley (ed.), *Records of the English Province of the Society of Jesus*, 3 vols (London, 1875–8), vol. I, pp. 23–5, 38–40, 41–3.

60 Paul L. Hughes and James F. Larkin (eds), *Tudor Royal Proclamations, 3: The Later Tudors (1588–1603)* (New Haven, CT, and London, 1969), pp. 250–5; *HMC Sal*, XII, p. 457.

61 Peter Lake with Michael Questier, *The Antichrist's Lewd Hat: Protestants, Papists and Players in Post-Reformation England* (New Haven, CT, and London, 2002), pp. 285–92.

62 Arnold Hunt, 'Tuning the pulpits: the religious context of the Essex revolt', in Lori-Anne Ferrell and Peter McCullough (eds), *The English Sermon Revisited: Religion, Literature and History, 1600–1750* (Manchester, 2001), pp. 86–114. At his trial, Essex reversed the charge, claiming that Cecil favoured the claims of the Infanta: all the more reason for Cecil to back Bancroft in his dealings with the Appellants. For unfounded allegations about Cecil and the Spanish interest, see Joel Hurstfield, 'The succession struggle in late Elizabethan England', in S. T. Bindoff, Joel Hurstfield and C. H. Williams (eds), *Elizabethan Government and Society: Essays Presented to Sir John Neale* (London, 1961), pp. 369–96; and Chapter 6 in this volume.

63 *HMC Sal*, XI, pp. 318–19.

64 A view expressed in correspondence.

65 Hurstfield, 'The succession struggle', p. 387.

66 *Ibid.*, pp. 374–9.

67 *HMC Sal*, XI, XII. I have compared the versions of these letters in the *Calendar* with the originals in the microfilms held, by courtesy of the Marquess of Salisbury, in the British Library; and find that the *Calendar*, so far as these materials are concerned, provides what are virtually modern-spelling transcriptions of the originals.

68 *Ibid.*, IX, p. 235; XI, p. 176.

69 *Ibid.*, XI, pp. 52, 55–6, 76, 88–9.

70 D. Lloyd, *State Worthies or the Statesmen and Favourites of England since the Reformation* (London, 1670), p. 764; A. G. Dickens, *The English Reformation* (London, 1989), p. 368.

71 *HMC Sal*, XI, p. 232.

72 Cecil to Bancroft, undated, Westminster Diocesan Archives, vol. 7 (1601–5), no. 82. I owe this reference to Arnold Hunt.

73 TNA, SP12/283/40; *HMC Sal*, XII, p. 47.

74 *Ibid.*, XII, p. 194.

75 Raine (ed.), *Correspondence of Dr Matthew Hutton*, pp. 304–5.

76 Cardwell, *Conferences*, pp. 189–90. Daniel Featley later referred to James's endorsement at the Hampton Court Conference of Bancroft's dealings with the Catholics. (Bodl, MS Rawlinson D47, fo. 19.)

Part III

The court

Chapter 6

Essex and the 'popish plot'

Alexandra Gajda

In the late morning of 8 February 1601, Robert Devereux, second Earl of Essex, sallied out of Essex House, leading over a hundred nobles, gentlemen and assorted followers. As the company processed east, seeking armed support from Sheriff Smythe, they appealed in the Queen's name for protection from murderous enemies. Essex also implored the London citizens to take arms for an even graver cause: 'the crowne of England was offred to be sould to the infanta' by his own would-be assassins, Sir Walter Ralegh, Henry Brooke, Lord Cobham and Sir Robert Cecil, the Principal Secretary.[1] Beseeched to disband his company, Essex refused with stirring rhetoric: 'Now or never is the tyme for you to pursue your liberties…for you are sold for slaves to the Infant of Spain'.[2] The Earl's strident oratory fell on ears stupefied with surprise. The horrified Sheriff refuted promises of military assistance; the citizens failed to rally. After a scuffle at Ludgate, the Earl's depleted following beat a forlorn retreat to Essex House where they surrendered soon after nine.

The regime's condemnation of Essex's so-called rebellion expended little energy denouncing these allegations of a 'popish plot' to sell the crown to Spain. If this dreadful act of rebellion was about a succession conspiracy at all, the enthroning of Essex – as King Robert I – had been the rebels' aim.[3] At their trial on 19 February, when Essex and his accomplice the Earl of Southampton defended their belief in a Hispanophile conspiracy, their voices sounded ill-assured. When Southampton cited a second-hand report of Sir Robert Cecil's positive remarks about the Jesuit Robert Persons's *A Conference about the Next Succession to the Crowne of Ingland*, the Secretary, piously aghast, proclaimed his innocence of all underhand dealings with Spain.[4] How could Essex truly believe that the son of Burghley, scourge of Mary Queen of Scots, had plotted for the accession of a Catholic queen? In a letter to Patrick, Lord Gray, Cecil insisted that Essex had later confessed that all accusations *'fully urged against [him] concerning the Infanta'* were a fabrication employed that he might '*pretend reason for private revenge to gather company*' (Cecil's additions to the clerk's draft in italics).[5]

Accounts of Essex's rising have tended to follow the shape of the official post-rising narrative of events, dismissing his description of a plot to sell the crown to Spain. Essex had been in political disgrace since his return from his military campaign in Ireland in September 1599, when he had shockingly forced his way into Elizabeth's bedchamber to justify the causes of an unauthorized truce that he had concluded with Hugh O'Neill, the rebel Earl of Tyrone. When Elizabeth failed to renew his patent of sweet wines at Michaelmas the following year, Essex faced financial ruin as well as ongoing exclusion from the court. Essex's 'exposure' of a succession plot has been seen as a rhetorical fig-leaf cynically employed to legitimize a second unlawful attempt to force access to the Queen, and to impose his ascendancy over political rivals. Otherwise, the animus that Essex expressed against Cecilian conspiracy has been defined as the product of a deep paranoia that warped his political vision.[6]

Essex possessed, though, a far more developed conception of a succession plot than the accusation levelled at trial. On 25 December 1600, he had written to James VI of Scotland, with an urgent warning that James's title to the throne was imperilled. The Queen, Essex explained, no longer ruled in England. Instead, a 'raigninge faction' tyrannized, who would 'overawe the people, bury freedome, usurpe soverainety for the present'. These odious caterpillars were Essex's bitterest personal foes – but they were also the enemies of James and of the English state, and worked covertly for a popish succession: they 'practise for the Infanta of Spain...[with] divelish plots...against your [Majesties] person and life'. Now, Essex explained, he was obliged to act: 'Now am I summoned of all sides to stop the malice, the wickednes and madnes of these men, and to releeve my poore cuntry'. If James would send a trustworthy ambassador to England by 1 February, the Earl would embark on 'this great worke' – the protection of James's succession.[7]

Here, enshrined, was Essex's conception of a Spanish succession plot, a plot that drew direct parallels between the Earl's misfortunes and a threat to James's title. A detailed account was revealed after the rising in the confession of Henry Cuffe, the Earl's secretary. Describing instructions that would have been delivered to John Erskine, Earl of Mar, Essex's preferred choice of Scottish representative, Cuffe defined a clique of pro-Habsburg agents who monopolized the court, the finances and the military resources of the English kingdom. Ralegh and Cobham, Essex's loathed rivals at court, were Governor of Jersey and Warden of the Cinque Ports respectively; the Lord Treasurer, Buckhurst, commanded 'the treasure, the sinnews of actionn'; and 'the navye, the walles of this realme' were in the charge of Charles Howard, the Lord Admiral and Earl of Nottingham. All of these enemies of Essex and James were willing puppets controlled by 'the principall Secretary, Sir Roberte

Cecill'.[8] Essex's actions, however disastrously enacted on 8 February, had a threefold goal, intimated in his Christmas letter to James: the removal of his enemies, the restoration of his own political fortunes, and the formal declaration, ideally by Queen-in-Parliament, of James's title.[9]

Rather than dismissing the Earl's theory of a Cecilian-led plot to subvert the succession as a manipulated fiction or a raving hallucination, I argue that Essex's claim to act in defence of the endangered Scottish succession rested on an interpretation of contemporary politics that strongly resembled the popish conspiracy plots of the seventeenth century. Essex's equation of his personal misfortunes with opposition to a supposed party for the Infanta was certainly warped by personal ambition. Since at least the mid-1590s he had desired to play the kingmaker in the succession, and to dominate politics after the death of Elizabeth.[10] But Essex also viewed the world of the court through ideological lenses that gave apparent coherence to a Spanish succession plot and imposed a plausible narrative on the complex interplay of domestic and foreign politics in late-Elizabethan England.

As Thomas M. McCoog, SJ, demonstrates in Chapter 13, a group of English Catholic exiles, led by Persons was, indeed, restlessly intriguing for a Spanish-endorsed Catholic succession. In 1955, Father Leo Hicks argued that Essex was far from wrong to believe that an embryonic party for the Infanta also existed at the English court.[11] With evidence from secret intelligence filtered back to Madrid from a well-connected contact of Persons, Hicks showed that a cluster of leading councillors – headed by Cecil – were thought to have initiated approaches to the Spanish King to endorse a particular candidate. Joel Hurstfield's account of the late-Elizabethan 'succession struggle', however, which has had greatest currency in modern accounts, dismissed Hicks's argument, which was based, he argued, on Persons's and his agent's wildly creative interpretations of Cecil's intentions.[12] Albert J. Loomie provides a balanced reappraisal: while it seems most unlikely that the Infanta had a group of convinced supporters on the Privy Council, it was natural that the regime would attempt to ascertain the opaque attitudes of Philip III towards the succession by indulging in clandestine communication with Spain and Brussels; meanwhile the Infanta's supporters hoped to convince Philip to make a firm declaration about the English succession by cultivating prominent English statesmen.[13] So, while there was no 'popish plot', it is understandable why Essex thought otherwise. Just as in Madrid, Persons's reports of sympathy for the Infanta at Elizabeth's court were taken seriously, shaping Philip III's attitudes towards the succession, so too in England, Essex interpreted what he knew of English communications with Brussels and Spain as evidence of a devilish alliance of all of his enemies to enthrone the Infanta and perpetuate their power.

I further demonstrate here that the main source of Essex's political strength in 1601 was his certainty that James VI would believe his revelations. The Earl's ambition to be the steer of the succession rested on the relations that he and his closest friends had forged with the Scottish King over the previous decade. There were also secure foundations to Essex's assumption that James would be hostile to a Cecilian clique and would easily be convinced by his adumbration of a 'popish plot', centred on the courts of London, Brussels and Madrid. Cuffe's compilation of evidence of the succession plot rested on seven points of proof, the very first to be revealed by Mar himself, 'because the Earl of Essex was informed that the King was able to produce cleare evidence thereof'.[14] Before the Earl paraded onto the London streets on 8 February 1601 a succession crisis seemed to loom in the minds of both Essex and his rivals that entwined their fates with the Scottish King's title to the English throne.

THE 'POPISH PLOT' IMAGINED

The notion of 'popish plot' that fruited in Essex's mind had taken root within conceptual frameworks deriving from the broader literary culture of the 1590s. Essex and his associates adopted a self-consciously intellectual approach to the interpretation of politics, which sensitized them to theories of conspiracy that hinged on the succession. In a letter written to the Earl's close friend Sir Fulke Greville, perhaps by Essex himself, perhaps by Francis Bacon, a scholar was advised to compile maxims on 'the uncertainty of succession' – one of the 'sufficient causes to ruin the greatest monarchy'.[15] Similar guidance was provided by the ancient historians prized by Essex. The first vernacular edition of Tacitus, produced by the Earl's scholarly mentor Sir Henry Savile in 1591, would also have focused the attention of the reader attuned to draw connections between political malaise and succession crisis. The first four books of Tacitus's *Histories*, translated by Henry Savile, narrated the dense wave of civil wars fought over the contested imperial throne, following the deposition of the tyrant Nero.[16]

As Essex's fortunes declined, this Tacitean matrix sharpened his recourse to an age-old rhetoric of political corruption which he invoked to explain the frustrations of his own career. The Christmas letter to James enshrines a conventional if viscerally expressed conceptualization of Essex's enemies as archetypal evil counsellors, who tyrannize over the Queen and repress her virtuous subjects. It is these men's lust for power that inclines them to support the illegitimate title of the Infanta. Essex's familiarity with these tropes was not new in 1600. Since at least the mid-1590s his close associates had slurred those whom they perceived to be his rivals as grasping Machiavellians: Essex's close associates, Lord Henry Howard and Anthony Bacon, developed a private vocabulary of casual slander of the Lord Treasurer as 'the old fox', and his son 'Robert the Devil' (*Roberto il Diabolo*) as Cecil's 'cub', whose avarice and greedy ambition, they argued, contrasted stunningly with Essex's heroic virtues.[17] Essex's disgrace after Ireland gave a much wider public currency to this discourse. A rash of libels spread about City and court, blaming the Earl's fall from power on his vicious enemies. Controlling all was the hunchbacked Cecil, denounced as the 'Crookback spider', the usurping Richard III reincarnate. In a libel that drew on the tradition of the allegorical beast fable, the Secretary was lampooned as a deceitful camel, who controlled the 'kingdomes sterne', enchanting the Queen with sugared potions.[18]

But the conceptual model of the Machiavellian favourite and minister who possessed designs on the succession also derived most immediately from the spate of libellous histories recently authored by Catholic polemicists to slander and embarrass the Protestant government. Scholars have noted that Essex's repudiation of a Cecilian cabal in 1601 mirrored concepts of a *regnum Cecilianum*, or 'Burghley's Commonwealth', found in tracts authored by Robert Persons and Richard Verstegan in the early 1590s.[19] In these works Burghley was denounced as an atheistic, over-mighty subject who smothered the Queen and plotted the perpetual stranglehold of his dynasty over the English realm.[20] In 1593 Essex began deliberately to appeal to moderate Catholics to broaden the base of his political support; in doing so, he was conscious that Burghley's unfavourable depiction in Jesuit-authored libels might be turned to his advantage.[21] Anthony Bacon, who controlled Essex's intelligence network, was deeply involved in coordinating an 'Essexian' response to recent Catholic polemic.[22] Taking assiduous notes from Spanish news in December 1592, Bacon had marked up slander of Burghley, noting rumours of the 'pretended wedlock betwene his honors little sonne & dame Arbella' – Arbella Stuart, whose claim to the English throne was deeply vexing to James VI.[23] To Essex's ardent admirers it seemed natural that Burghley would pass this thirst for dominion to his son.

Of course, a succession crisis was the fate imagined for England in that most famous Catholic treatise entwined with Essex's fortunes. The brilliant dedication of *A Conference* to Essex was an ingenious attack by friendly fire: in one short commendatory epistle, dripping with praise for the ambitious Essex, Persons pointed a glaring finger at the Earl's desire to play the pre-eminent role in the succession.[24] The purpose of the dedication was almost certainly to undermine Essex's relationship with the Queen and James VI and to unsettle his growing body of Puritan and Catholic supporters. All of these relationships survived this assault-by-dedication intact. In less ostensible ways, though, the *Conference* exerted a powerful influence on the Earl's mentality. First, the tract invoked the dreadful spectre of civil war that would likely follow Elizabeth's death if the succession were not settled. And the *Conference* seemed to be proof that the Infanta's claim had serious support – and from ingenious enemies of Essex. For the Earl, the notion that his Machiavellian rivals at court covertly approved of Persons's treatise required no great imaginative leap.

PEACE, THE *APOLOGIE* AND THE SPANISH SUCCESSION

At Essex's trial, Cecil complained that the Earl's suspicion of his attitudes towards the Infanta had emerged in 1598, in the specific context of negotiations about peace with Spain.[25] During the negotiations surrounding the Franco-Spanish Treaty at Vervins on 2 May (NS), the Privy Council had discussed the proposition that England and the United Provinces also negotiate for settlement. As the foremost proponent of aggressive militarism, Essex stridently opposed peace on ideological grounds, expressing his views in his polemical *Apologie… against those which fa[l]sly and maliciously taxe him to be the onely hinderer of the peace, and quiet of his countrey* (1600).[26] Mainly written and revised over the spring and summer of 1598, the treatise was circulated in manuscript, probably deliberately by Essex and his associates, before it received its first unauthorized print publication in May 1600.[27] Anticipating that Philip II's son would replicate his father's aggression towards England more fiercely, the Earl argued that the Spanish monarchy so obviously possessed an insatiable ambition to tyrannize over Christendom that peace at present would be extraordinarily dangerous. Essex's arguments countered the more favourable attitudes towards peace expressed by Burghley and other councillors, who feared the long-term impact of war on the English economy, especially while Ireland was engulfed in rebellion. In Camden's account, arguments on the Council were extremely bitter; Burghley accused Essex of an irreligious thirst for war.[28]

The *Apologie* thus documents an important turning-point in Essex's relation to the rest of the government. As Paul E. J. Hammer has shown, it was only in the course of differences over foreign policy that tensions between Essex and the Cecils tipped into factionalism.[29] Essex's treatise framed his arguments against the peace as a *personalized* defence of his reputation from 'malicious' detractors who queried his war record and his civic virtue. As he would in 1601, the Earl defined his critics as dire threats to the state, whose sympathy for peace endangered the Queen, the state and religion: 'Iniurious…to the countrey which bredde them…Iniurious…to her Maietie who hath ruled them', and 'Iniurious and most vnthankfull to God himselfe'.[30]

The *Apologie* was also important, though, because it linked this personal attack on 'peacemongers' explicitly to fears about the Infanta's title to the English throne. In a letter to the Queen, written probably in the summer of 1597, Essex had warned that no peace could be achieved with Spain until Philip II's 'ambitious humor of entitleinge his daughter the Infanta' had been quenched.[31] These suspicions were only deepened by the betrothal of Isabella to Archduke Albert of Austria, and Philip II's donation to the couple of the sovereignty of the Netherlands on 6 May 1598 (NS). Installed directly across the channel, warned Essex, would be 'the Infant, the person whose title to the crown of *England, Parsons* so laboured to prooue'; an invasion of England could be launched with terrifying ease.[32]

If peace negotiations were reckless, Essex also gave voice to more insinuating fears that a party at court would be targeted and bought with Habsburg gold. The Earl described a thwarted plot by the English Jesuit Joseph Creswell and Spanish ministers to suborn Elizabethan dignitaries with pensions, under the 'pretence of making an overture of peace'.[33] In the *Apologie*, Essex did not accuse advocates of peace on the Privy Council of taking Habsburg bribes, but the possibility was clearly present in his mind. After the rising, Cuffe revealed he had received information that Cecil had been 'consigned' a payment of 10,000 crowns from Archduke Albert.[34]

In fact, Essex's understanding of a succession conspiracy mirrored almost exactly the intelligence used by English Catholics to try to persuade the kings of Spain to endorse the Infanta's title. Thomas Fitzherbert, Philip III's English secretary, wrote to William Sterrell on 1 March 1599 of strategies to 'wynne a party in England' for the Infanta, secured with 'negotiations here and pensions'.[35] An informant of Robert Persons at the English court claimed to be in direct contact with a clique of privy councillors including Cecil, Lord Buckhurst, and the Lord Admiral: these men who 'fear the Scot' favoured a Derby succession, but were positively disposed to the succession of the Infanta, having little care for the confessional identity of the future monarch.[36] Cecil and his party seem to have opened communications to glean information about Spanish intentions.[37] Persons's intelligence, though, about a Cecilian cabal sympathetic to the Infanta was influential in the ways that he intended it to be. In early February 1601, Philip III finally agreed to heed the Council of State's recommendation that he work to secure his sister's title to the English throne. As Thomas M. McCoog, SJ, shows in Chapter 13, Philip's decision was far from a resounding endorsement; no public declaration was made. He did, however, agree to purchase English support and, on 28 February 1601 (NS), Philip assured Balthasar de Zúñiga, the Spanish envoy in Flanders, that Cecil, Howard, Buckhurst and Thomas Egerton the Lord Chancellor would all back a Catholic candidate after Elizabeth's death.[38]

During the intrigues of English Catholics for a Spanish succession, negotiations for peace resumed between England, Brussels and Madrid, hardening Essex's inclination to define his personal enemies as dangerous pacifist friends of the Infanta. The embassy of Audencier Verreycken in February 1600 resulted in further talks between the English and the Spanish at Boulogne in May. The negotiations failed, but confident rumours had circulated for months that peace was much desired by the Queen and the majority of the court.[39] Those other enemies whom Essex had named as part of the succession conspiracy were also strongly associated with friendly attitudes towards Brussels and Spain. Cobham was known to cultivate Flemish and Spanish intelligence.[40] On the Privy Council itself, Buckhurst was the most ostensibly zealous of the peacemongers; but even Ralegh, famously as Hispanophobic as Essex, made 'great Sute' to be named a commissioner at the Boulogne negotiations.[41] The lynchpin of negotiations, though, was Cecil. While Ireland remained in rebellion, the Secretary was not optimistic about the feasibility of an end to the Spanish war. Nevertheless, he was known to be friendly to the Archdukes, commissioning portraits of Albert and Isabella in the autumn of 1599.[42] Another of Cuffe's proofs against Cecil was his willingness 'for the better compassing of somme purposes … to entertayne the Treatie againe'.[43]

THE FALL OF ESSEX AND THE *REGNUM CECILIANUM*

Essex's conception of a 'popish plot', though, only emerged congruently with the implosion of his career and his growing alienation from Queen and regime. In early July 1598 Essex quarrelled violently with Elizabeth and was exiled from the court. When he returned in September, drawn by the crisis in Ireland, Essex had become convinced that his courses were thwarted by implacable enemies. Before he departed as Lord Lieutenant of Ireland on 27 March 1599, the Earl foretold that these adversaries would hinder his campaign against the rebel Tyrone, and would ruin his credit with Elizabeth.[44]

Even as Essex's energies were consumed by the immense preparations for the campaign, the question of succession still haunted his thoughts. As discussed in Chapter 14, John Hayward published *The First Part of the Life and Raigne of King Henrie IIII* in February with a most unwelcome dedicatory epistle to Essex. With strong echoes of 'Doleman's' dedication of the *Conference*, the Earl was praised as 'great indeed, both in present judgment and in expectation of future time', his virtues likened to those of Henry Bullingbrook.[45] Essex was far from flattered by another treatise that implicitly yoked his ambition to control the succession to a 'politic' analysis of the deposition of Richard II, and commanded John Whitgift, archbishop of Canterbury to investigate the printing of the history. In other contexts, Essex may have been less guarded about his expectations of political change. The French ambassador reported an extraordinarily frank conversation in which the Earl, about to leave for Ireland, predicted the desperation of many councillors who were certain to fall from power in the next reign. From this insinuation, the ambassador deduced the worst-kept secret at the Elizabethan court: Essex was rooting for the accession of the King of Scots; Cecil, it was implied, would be the casualty.[46]

This reported conversation accurately captured Essex's hopes that James's accession would destroy his personal rivals once and for all and would win him the unrivalled ascendancy that he craved. While he was fighting his doomed Irish campaign, though, that ascendancy slipped further out of his grasp. All his fears and predictions fulfilled, Essex saw his 'enemies' increase their power in his absence. The appointment of Buckhurst as Lord Treasurer on 15

May 1599 was an elevation that Essex had tried previously to hinder;[47] while in August, Thomas Cecil Lord Burghley, the Secretary's older brother, was installed as President of the Council of the North, a post that Essex and Anthony Bacon had once hoped would fall to their friend Lord Willoughby.[48] Again, it was precisely this vision of the *regnum Cecilianum* – outlined by Cuffe in 1601 – that was enthusiastically noted by Persons in his correspondence, who argued that the dominance of Essex's enemies was good news for the Infanta's chances. In his investiture as Master of the Court of Wards – a post obtained in May 1599 – the Secretary had won a rich office, coveted by Essex himself.[49]

While his rivals flourished, Essex blamed his military difficulties in Ireland on their machinations. In particular, he became convinced that his enemies deliberately deprived him of supplies needed to attack the rebels in Ulster.[50] When the Earl pursued a course of military consolidation in Leinster and Munster, thus abandoning the offensive strategy he had agreed to follow, Elizabeth responded with infuriated letters, haranguing him for his failings and commanding him to assault Tyrone. Convinced that the Queen had been poisoned against him, Essex contemplated in August bringing soldiers back to England to launch an attack on the court. Only the forceful counsel of Sir Christopher Blount and the Earl of Southampton persuaded the Earl to reject this desperate, treasonable action.[51]

As Rory Rapple argues in Chapter 12, the shadow of succession had hung over the course of Essex's inglorious Irish campaign. When Essex made the fateful decision to talk alone with Tyrone at Bellaclinthe Ford on 7 September, it seems highly likely that the two noblemen discussed James VI's title and courses for action that would bring mutual benefit when Elizabeth died.

Disgraced and arrested after his extraordinary return on 28 September, Essex was stripped of public office at a trial on 5 June 1600. Although released from house arrest on 26 August, he remained exiled from the court and was denied access to Elizabeth's presence. Throughout these months of humiliating disgrace, though, Essex continued to rally because of one particularly sustaining tonic: his certainty of the sympathy of James VI, whose succession to the English throne would turn all his fortunes around.

ESSEX AND JAMES VI

Forging the relationship between Essex and James was Anthony Bacon, who facilitated the intelligence links that Essex had established with Edinburgh by the autumn of 1593.[52] Bacon and Essex had also long realized that the Earl could be in an extremely strong position *vis-à-vis* a Scottish succession, because James blamed Burghley for the death of his mother, Mary Queen of Scots.[53] Furthermore, Elizabeth invariably used William and Robert Cecil as the front for those policies that the Scottish King found most offensive, including delays in the payment of his pension. In particular, the Cecils coordinated the tacit support made by Elizabeth to the Protestant rebel Francis Hepburn, Earl of Bothwell, intended to pressurize James into punishing the rebel Catholic earls who conspired with Spain, most recently in the Spanish Blanks farrago of 1592. English meddling in Scottish politics was utterly infuriating to James, and a spur to his initiation of direct contact with Essex. The King expressed hopes that the Queen would choose to take counsel first and foremost from 'a nobleman of the ranke ye are of', cannily flattering Essex's pride in his lineage.[54] On 6 October 1595, James wrote more furtively to Essex: 'I am glad that he who rules all there is begun to be loathed at by the best and greatest sort there, since he is my enemy'.[55] Of Essex's affection he could be certain: with typically unadvisable candour, the Earl assured the King, 'whatsoever I am ... I consecrate unto your regal throne'.[56]

Here, then, was a relationship founded on both men's attempts to exploit latent hostility to a *regnum Cecilianum* in the other. Bacon and his Scottish agents fuelled the fire, sniping at Cecil for spying on Essex's Scottish communications.[57] More informal associations also suggest the outline of mutual interest groups focused on the Scottish succession. Nicholas Tyacke has shown that the English Puritan Sir Henry Bromley and the Scottish envoy David Foulis, one of Bacon's agents, were probably responsible for smuggling Peter Wentworth's succession tracts to Scotland for publication in Edinburgh in 1598 or 1599.[58] Bromley was acquainted with some of Essex's most secret counsels. In the summer of 1600 he plotted with Henry Cuffe, his 'dear brother', to release Essex from house arrest. Summoned by Lady Penelope Rich, Bromley failed to turn out on the day of the rising itself, but his brother, Edward, played an active role.[59]

Similarly connected to Essex's associates was Walter Quin, an Irish poet employed as the tutor to the Earl of Mar's son, who also vilified the Cecilian ascendancy as threatening to James's title. In late 1595 Quin impressed the King with a manuscript of poems which (through some rather tortuous allusions to Arthur's Seat) hailed James as a glorious King of Britain reborn.[60] Quin also corresponded with Anthony Bacon, to whom he sent a flattering poem in the late spring of 1596.[61] In language very similar to that used by Bacon himself, Quin warned James about the machinations of William Cecil, the Spenserian fox, whose avaricious desire to advance his offspring – 'ses petits Renardeaux' – was, he warned, a dangerous stumbling block to James's inheritance.[62]

Contacts at the Anglo-Scottish border were also essential to Essex's plans to safeguard a Scottish succession – especially if military intervention would be needed. Essex was successful in aiding the suit of his friend, Peregrine Bertie, Lord Willoughby of Eresby, who was appointed Governor of Berwick-upon-Tweed and Warden of the East March in March 1598. A tough, travelled soldier, Willoughby, though friendly in correspondence with Burghley and his son, also participated in the anti-Cecilian slander that characterized Essex's private communications.[63] Essex's letter of December 1600 was transmitted through Willoughby at Berwick, via the book-seller John Norton.[64]

More positively, Essex established a warm relationship with Mar, the ambassador James would dispatch to England in February 1601 with Edward Bruce, Commendator of Kinloss.[65] As the custodian of the young Prince Henry, Mar was a powerful figure. In June 1600, when James appealed for support at the Scottish Convention to secure his title, it is notable that Mar and Bruce were amongst the most vocal advocates of raising money.[66]

Thus a group existed that ostensibly recognized that James's interests were best served by a network of Essex's followers. But Essex could also hope that James's anti-Cecilian sentiments might be focused on a more alarming threat to his title. Most recently James's hostility to Robert Cecil had been vocally aired within broader criticisms of English diplomacy, criticisms that articulated precisely the insinuations that Essex had made about the existence of an English party for the Infanta.

The Earl's warnings about dangerous English peacemakers had been noted in Scotland; James had read a manuscript of Essex's *Apologie*, mentioning it in conversation with Henry Leigh, Deputy Warden of the West March, in the autumn of 1599.[67] On 12 January 1600, George Nicolson reported to Cecil the King's displeasure at ongoing negotiations with Brussels; James's councillors interpreted them as a threat to their master's title.[68] When Cecil sent word that he had no desire to see England subject to Spain, James's response was grim. This protracted, murky diplomacy, James insisted, was deeply suspicious: clearly it was intended to facilitate the 'plotting and traffickinge' of ambassadors for darker purposes, 'which wold be to his hurte'. He was aware that many of Elizabeth's courtiers would be bought by bribes.[69]

The absence of further evidence of direct communication between Essex and James about the succession may have been caused by the burning of secret papers at Essex House on the day of the rising.[70] The whereabouts of Anthony Bacon during the revolt are mysterious; there are hints that his ongoing involvement in Scottish correspondence was deliberately concealed.[71] The subsequent confessions of Essex's closest advisors, however, startlingly revealed that direct appeals to James to take action had been made in 1599 and 1600. Most worryingly, these had been spearheaded by Charles Blount, Lord Mountjoy, the lover of Essex's sister Penelope Rich, who had replaced Essex in Ireland as Lord Deputy. In the early months of 1600, as Essex fretted in custody, Mountjoy formed a plan to engage James. Following up overtures made the previous summer, when he had written with assurance of his own and Essex's good will, Mountjoy proposed to take 4,000–5,000 soldiers from the Irish army, to join with English forces to free Essex and declare James as Elizabeth's heir. James was to show force on the borders.[72] Southampton wrote with similar intent, affirming friendship and loyalty. The Scottish King must have viewed the destruction of the power of his most prominent supporter at the English court as alarming as peace negotiations with Brussels; he made no firm declarations, but promised to 'putt himself in a rediness'. James was certainly entertaining thoughts of military intervention. In November 1599, he had sworn his nobility to a General Band to support his succession; in December and June of the following year he sought money from Convention for the same purpose.[73] James, though, was all too aware of a pressing problem should he choose to associate directly with the suggestions of Essex's party. Under the terms of the 1585 Act for the Queen's Surety, if he engaged in actions that endangered Elizabeth's life, his own claim to the throne was voided. Mountjoy and Southampton, similarly sensitive to slurs of treason, insisted that they had sworn oaths to protect the Queen.

No concrete actions emerged from these overtures. After Essex's release from house arrest, Mountjoy's concerns for his friend's safety receded. When Essex tried to rekindle his support for a *coup* later in the summer, the Lord Deputy refused to participate. But political disgrace had not defanged Essex's threat to his self-defined enemies. Even Gloriana, despite the protestations of court poets, was not immortal: the spectre of civil war over the succession had not yet been banished by Essex's fall from grace.

A SUCCESSION CRISIS AVERTED?

From the point of view of the regime, the Earl's stake in succession politics now necessitated his removal. Essex's absolute antagonism towards his 'enemies' placed him beyond the bounds of any feasible reconciliation. With the arrest of Henry Leigh, Mountjoy's envoy to James, in April 1600 the Council may also have gained specific awareness of the intrigues of Essex and his supporters.[74] With Essex alive, implacable, and allied to the King of Scotland and Lord Deputy of Ireland, many councillors must have viewed the natural death of Elizabeth with growing alarm.

When Ralegh brutally insisted that Essex – 'this tirant' – had to be killed, Cecil was certainly listening.[75] Although Essex was reprieved in June 1600 of charges of disloyalty to Elizabeth, the Council steadily collated charges of treason to use against him. The interrogation of Essex's former chaplain, William Alabaster, a Catholic convert, ironically provided material for a spurious allegation that Essex had flirted with Jesuit schemes to enthrone the Infanta! The Earl was accused of plotting with Tyrone to divide power in England and Ireland between them, and seditious approval of Hayward's *Life and Raigne of King Henrie IIII*.[76] Had Elizabeth enjoyed her father's paranoid suspicions of treason, privy councillors could have prepared the gallows. Instead, as they contemplated bringing a vague amalgamation of insinuations to the Queen about her fallen favourite, they would have remembered Elizabeth's furious response to those she deemed responsible for conniving at the execution of Mary Stuart.

These tentative strategies to destroy Essex collided with his own burgeoning plans to make some form of intervention. In early February 1601, Essex's closest advisors compared strategies for striking at the Tower and the court, or appealing to London for support. Meanwhile Essex waited for the arrival of the Scottish embassy. The Council moved first, summoning Essex to appear in person on 7 February. Fearing – probably correctly – that he was going to be charged with treason, Essex refused and panicked: the outcome was his shambolic rising the following day. Although difficult to prove, it seems likely that Essex was tricked into taking precipitate action before he had orchestrated a more coherent plan.[77]

For if Essex had not blinked first, his plotting might have had a much more significant outcome – where James's own clandestine dealings would have been revealed. Unaware of the immediate turn of events in London on 8 February, James drew up instructions to his ambassadors which indicated that he took the warnings of Essex's December letter seriously. On their arrival in London, Mar and Bruce were to listen to the counsel of James's 'friends'; if convinced by Essex and associates, they were to 'give them full assurance of [James] assisting them accordingly'.[78]

While playing this dangerous game, James must have been fully aware of a brilliant irony: his communication with Essex's party resembled nothing so much as the interventions that had long been practised in Scottish politics by Elizabeth and Burghley when giving covert support to the Scottish Protestant nobility, supporting rebels such as Bothwell to exert pressure on the King. Ralegh's letter had (unwittingly?) drawn the parallel exactly, when he described Essex as Elizabeth's 'Bothwell...the canker of her estate'.[79] James's relations with Essex threatened to give Elizabeth a dose of the patronising medicine usually administered to the King of Scotland by the Queen of England.

On the momentous occasion, though, when Elizabeth had intervened in the politics of the Scottish succession, the eventual result had been the enforced abdication of Mary Queen of Scots in 1567. That these traumatic events might be mirrored in England over thirty years later was a feasible outcome, and one with which James was desperate to disclaim association. Mar was instructed to assure Essex that he was 'willing and ready to supply that place as they canbe to desire me, *only with that old reservation of the safety of the Queen's person, which ye maun take them sworn to* (my italics)'.[80] James need not have worried in this respect: the emphatic vows of loyalty sworn to the Queen's person by Essex and his companions on 8 February were maintained by the 'rebels' at their trials and on the scaffold. Only Blount's confession and execution speech admitted that the outcome might have been bloody, and Elizabeth harmed, if Essex had seized control of the court.[81]

Paul E. J. Hammer has recently argued that the action planned by Essex – as well as the strange parade on the streets of London – was thus no rebellion or even attempted *coup*, but a form of loyalist action. Essex and his associates insisted relentlessly on their allegiance to Elizabeth: their desire was to gain access to the Queen's presence where the scheming of her counsellors would be revealed; thus enlightened, she would willingly consent to be rescued from their tyranny.[82]

Essex was forced to define his actions within this loyalist framework. A professed fidelity to the monarch was, of course, the classic rhetoric employed by all those denounced as 'rebels' by the crown who were intent on effecting political change through autonomous forms of protest. In Essex's case, though, the need to defend his revolt as a lawful action that would preserve Elizabeth's life had little to do with chivalric codes of loyalty or reverence for divine right monarchy. As the language of James's instructions to Mar indicates, any intervention by Essex on behalf of the Scottish title had to be compatible with the Act for the Queen's Surety. If James were found complicit in a deposition plot, his claim would be outlawed.

In their public performances after the rising, both Essex and the authorities played roles that saved the King from his worst fears: at trial and on the scaffold, the Earl colluded with the resounding silence about his contacts with James, for the greater good of the *patria*, perhaps. Scared post-rebellion that the depths of his involvement with Essex would be revealed, James was more than ready to discard his dislike of Cecil's parentage; popish conspiracy plots were forgotten with hearty mutual intent. As Alexander Courtney demonstrates in Chapter 7, the passage to James's peaceful accession was facilitated by relationships established by the Secretary and Lord Henry Howard, Essex's erstwhile friend. In 1604, and an altered world, Cecil and James would work together as architects of Anglo-Spanish peace. To this extent, the lasting legacy of Essex's revolt – the most bathetic of 'Tudor rebellions' – was positive: Essex's self-destruction meant that the regime could finally plan for the smooth accession of 1603. But this happy outcome for all parties other than Essex was not anticipated at the turn of the seventeenth century, as political rivalries and the pressures of war with Spain and rebellion in Ireland created a culture of paranoia and tension. The drama of Essex's death provided the clearest assurance that succession crisis – the stuff of so many nightmares for so many decades – would be avoided.

NOTES

1   TNA, SP12/278/51, fo. 73v, examination of Roger Manners, Earl of Rutland, 12 February 1601; Cecil MS 76/91, examinations of eyewitnesses, 18 February 1601. The classic study of Essex's rising is Mervyn James, 'At a crossroads of the political culture: the

Essex revolt, 1601', in his *Society, Politics and Culture: Studies in Early Modern England* (Cambridge, 1986), pp. 416–65; for the most important recent account, see Paul E. J. Hammer, 'Shakespeare's *Richard II*, the play of 7 February 1601, and the Essex rising', *Shakespeare Quarterly*, 59 (2008), 1–35.

2 Cecil MS 83/57, Timothy Willis to Sir Robert Cecil, 10 February 1600.

3 TNA, SP12/278/63, fos 108ʳ–109ᵛ, 'Directions for the preachers', 14? February 1601; these instructions formed the text of the sermon preached at Paul's Cross on 15 February: *HMC Sal*, XI, pp. 55–6. For the post-rising propaganda, see Arnold Hunt, 'Tuning the pulpits: the religious context of the Essex revolt', in Lori Anne Ferrell and P. E. McCullough (eds), *The English Sermon Revised: Religion, Literature and History, 1600–1750* (Manchester, 2000), pp. 86–114. See also Francis Bacon, *A Declaration of the Practices & Treasons Attempted and Committed by Robert Late Earle of Essex and his Complices* (1601): Essex's allegations about the Infanta are covered in Bacon's synopsis of the arraignment (sigs H2ʳ–H3ᵛ), but not emphasized in the main account.

4 TNA, SP12/278/101, fo. 177ʳ, account of the trial of Essex and Southampton. Slightly variant accounts of the trial circulated in the early seventeenth century, although they do not differ substantially in content. See also the printed version in T. B. Howell (ed.), *Cobbett's Complete Collection of State Trials and Proceedings for High Treason and Other Crimes and Misdemeanours*, 33 vols (London, 1809–26), vol. I, pp. 1333–60.

5 TNA, SP52/67, fo. 90ʳ, April 1601.

6 See in particular, Lacey Baldwin Smith, *Treason in Tudor England: Politics and Paranoia* (London, 1986), pp. 192–276; Joel Hurstfield, 'The succession struggle in late Elizabethan England', in S. T. Bindoff, Joel Hurstfield and C. H. Williams (eds), *Elizabethan Government and Society: Essays Presented to Sir John Neale* (London, 1961), pp. 369–96.

7 BL, Additional Manuscript, 31022, fos 107ʳ–108ʳ.

8 *CJRC*, pp. 82–3.

9 An anonymous correspondent of Anthony Bacon described Essex's main aim to be the settling of James's title by act of parliament: Bodl, Rawlinson MS D1175, fo. 107ʳ⁻ᵛ.

10 See Paul E. J. Hammer, *The Polarisation of Elizabethan Politics: The Political Career of Robert Devereux, 2nd Earl of Essex, 1585–1597* (Cambridge, 1999), pp. 91–2, 167–70, 392–3.

11 Leo Hicks, SJ, 'Sir Robert Cecil, Father Persons and the succession, 1600–1601', *Archivum Historicum Societatis Iesu*, 24 (1955), 95–139.

12 Hurstfield, 'The succession struggle', pp. 374–9.

13 Albert J. Loomie, 'Philip III and the Stuart succession in England, 1600–1603', *Revue Belge de Philologie et d'Histoire*, 43 (1965), 492–514 at pp. 498–9.

14 *CJRC*, p. 83.

15 Authorship is disputed between Paul E. J. Hammer and Brian Vickers; Vickers has printed the letter in his edition of selected works, *Francis Bacon* (Oxford, 1996), pp. 102–6, quotation at p. 104; authorship is discussed in *ibid.*, pp. 557–8 and Hammer, 'The Earl of Essex, Fulke Greville, and the employment of scholars', *Studies in Philology*, 91 (1994), 167–80.

16 Paulina Kewes, 'Henry Savile's Tacitus and the politics of Roman history in late Elizabethan England', *Huntington Library Quarterly*, 74 (2011), 515–51; R. Malcolm

Smuts, 'Court-centred politics and the uses of Roman historians, *c*.1590–*c*.1630', in Kevin Sharpe and Peter Lake (eds), *Culture and Politics in Early Stuart England* (Basingstoke, 1994), pp. 21–43; David Womersley, 'Sir Henry Savile's translation of Tacitus and the political interpretation of Elizabethan texts', *Review of English Studies*, 42 (1991), 313–42; Hammer, *The Polarisation of Elizabethan Politics*, pp. 335–6.

17 See correspondence in Bacon's papers: LPL, MS 660, fos 107ʳ, 145ʳ, 220ʳ, 235ʳ–236ᵛ; for context see Hammer, *The Polarisation of Elizabethan Politics*, pp. 357–8.

18 Bodl, MS Don C54, fos 19ʳ–20ʳ.

19 Natalie Mears, '*Regnum Cecilianum?* A Cecilian perspective of the court', in John Guy (ed.), *The Reign of Elizabeth I: Court and Culture in the Last Decade* (Cambridge, 1995), pp. 46–7.

20 See Victor Houliston, *Catholic Resistance in Elizabethan England: Robert Persons's Jesuit Polemic* (Aldershot, 2007), pp. 41–70.

21 For Essex's decision to appeal to loyalist Catholics, see Hammer, *The Polarisation of Elizabethan Politics*, pp. 173–81.

22 See Alexandra Gajda, '*The State of Christendom*: history, political thought and the Essex circle', *Historical Research*, 81 (2008), 423–46.

23 LPL, MS 648, fo. 140ʳ.

24 R. Doleman [Robert Persons], *A Conference about the Next Succession to the Crowne of Ingland* ([Antwerp], 1594 [1595]), sigs *2–[*3ʳ].

25 TNA, SP12/278/101, fo. 177ʳ; compare SP12/278/102, fo. 195ʳ, a second account of the arraignment.

26 For the diplomatic context, see R. B. Wernham, *The Return of the Armadas: The Last Years of Elizabeth's War against Spain* (Oxford, 1994), pp. 191–249 and *passim*.

27 Addressed to 'Maister Anthony Bacon', the treatise was reprinted in 1603; I am thankful to Hugh Gazzard for sending me his forthcoming study of extant texts of the *Apologie*, which will highlight the minor discrepancies between the redrafted manuscript versions of the treatise and the printed versions. Quotations used here differ only slightly in spelling from the 1603 edition.

28 William Camden, *Annales Rerum Anglicarum et Hibernicarum Regnante Elizabetha* (London, 1717), pp. 765–71.

29 Paul E. J. Hammer, 'Patronage at court, faction and the earl of Essex', in Guy (ed.), *The Reign of Elizabeth I*, pp. 65–86.

30 *Apologie*, sigs D2ᵛ–D3ʳ.

31 TNA, SP12/45, fo. 64ʳ.

32 *Apologie*, sig. C3ᵛ.

33 *Ibid.*, [B4ᵛ].

34 *CJRC*, p. 88.

35 TNA, SP12/270/47, fo. 76ʳ.

36 See reports of 25 April and 3 May 1600, cited in Hicks, SJ, 'Cecil, Persons and the succession', 112–17; see also the discussion in Chapter 13 of this volume.

37 See Loomie, 'Philip III and the Stuart succession', pp. 498–9.

38 Henri Lonchay and Joseph Cuvelier (eds), *Correspondance de la Cour d'Espagne sur les Affaires des Pays-Bas au XVIIe Siècle*, 6 vols (Brussels, 1923), vol. 1, pp. 63–4.

39 Arthur Collins (ed.), *Letters and Memorials of State … [of the Sidney family] … From the Originals at Penshurst Place in Kent*, 2 vols (London, 1746), vol. 2, pp. 169–79.

40 André Hurault, Sieur de Maisse, *A Journal of All That Was Accomplished by Monsieur De Maisse Ambassador in England from King Henri IV to Queen Elizabeth, Anno Domini 1597*, ed. and trans. G. B. Harrison and R. A. Jones (London, 1931), pp. 44–45; Cecil MS 72/52, Cobham to Cecil, 11 August, 1599; Cecil MS 68/62, Cobham to Cecil, 1 March 1600.

41 De Maisse, *Journal*, pp. 44–45, 107; H. S. Scott (ed.), *Journal of Sir Roger Wilbraham, Master of Requests*, Camden Miscellany, 10 (3rd series, 1902), pp. 49–50; Collins, *Letters and Memorials*, 2, p.178.

42 *HMC Sal*, IX, pp. 345, 391, 440.

43 *CJRC*, p. 83.

44 Cecil MS 58/86, Essex to Lord Willoughby, 4 January 1599.

45 John J. Manning (ed.), *The First and Second Parts of John Hayward's The Life and Raigne of King Henrie IIII*, CS 42 (4th series, 1991), p. 61 (editor's translation of the Latin epistle). See Manning's introduction, pp. 1–34, for the publication and censorship of the text, and Chapter 14 of this volume.

46 Pierre Paul Laffleur de Kermaingant, *L'Ambassade de France en Angleterre sous Henri IV. Mission de Jean de Thumery, Sieur de Boissise 1598–1602* (Paris, 1886), p. 483.

47 See Rivkah Zim's *ODNB* article on Thomas Sackville, first Baron Buckhurst and first earl of Dorset.

48 LPL, MS 658, fo. 11^r, Anthony Bacon to Dr Henry Hawkins, Essex's agent in Venice, 10 July 1596.

49 See advice of Persons to his English intelligence contact written on 3 June 1600, cited in Hicks, 'Cecil, Persons and the succession', p. 114. On 7 August 1598 Dudley Carleton remarked to John Chamberlain that Essex was likely to get the post: TNA, SP12/268/18, fo. 33^r.

50 See L. W. Henry, 'The Earl of Essex in Ireland', *Bulletin of the Institute of Historical Research*, 32 (1959), 1–23.

51 *CJRC*, pp. 107–8, from the examination of Sir Christopher Blount.

52 An earlier attempt to establish contact made by Essex and his sister, Penelope Rich, in 1589, had been snubbed by James. For Essex and Bacon's contacts with James VI, see Helen Georgia Stafford, *James VI of Scotland and the Throne of England* (New York and London, 1940), pp. 203–20; Hammer, *The Polarisation of Elizabethan Politics*, pp. 91, 163–73.

53 Laffleur de Kermaingant, *Mission de Jean de Thumery*, p. 483.

54 James was asking Essex to facilitate his protest to Elizabeth about her support of Bothwell: James VI to Essex, 13 April 1594; G. P. V. Akrigg (ed.), *Letters of King James VI and I* (Berkeley, CA, 1984), p. 131.

55 *Ibid.*, pp. 142–3. For secrecy, this letter was addressed directly to 'my goode friend SHB'.

56 Thomas Birch (ed.), *Memoirs of the Reign of Queen Elizabeth, From the Year 1581 till her Death*, 2 vols (London, 1754), vol. 1, p. 176: the letter, dated 17 May, was probably written in 1595.

57 See Bacon's complaints to Essex on 20 December 1596: Birch, *Memoirs*, vol. 2, p. 233.

58 Nicholas Tyacke,'Puritan Politicians and King James VI and I, 1587–1604' in Thomas Cogswell, Richard Cust and Peter Lake (eds), *Politics, Religion and Popularity in Early Stuart Britain: Essays in Honour of Conrad Russell* (Cambridge, 2002), pp. 35–7.

59 Cecil MS 179/131, Bromley to Cuffe, 29 July 1600; TNA, SP12/279/10, fos 13^r–14^r, examination of Edward Bromley, 2 March 1601.

60 The verses are published in full in *CSPScot*, 12, pp. 79–86. For Quin, see Chapters 10 and 11 in this volume.

61 LPL, MS 657, fos 173^r, 174^r.

62 *CSPScot*, 12, p. 85.

63 See Cecil MS 59/10, Willoughby to Essex, 21 January 1599; *HMC Report on the Manuscripts of the Earl of Ancaster, Preserved at Grimsthorpe* (Dublin, 1907), pp. 331–2, 337.

64 *CJRC*, p. 90.

65 See LPL, MS 655, fo. 218^r, Essex to Mar, 9 February 1596; LPL, MS 656, fo. 177^r, Mar to Essex, 10 March 1596; Hammer, *The Polarisation of Elizabethan Politics*, p. 171.

66 TNA, SP52/66, fos 37^r–38^r, George Nicolson to Sir Robert Cecil, 29 June 1600.

67 TNA, SP59/38/1169, fo. 300^r, declaration of Henry Leigh, 12 April 1600.

68 *CSPScot*, 13(ii), pp. 612–13.

69 TNA, SP52/66, fo. 21^r, Nicolson to Cecil, 20 April 1600.

70 *CJRC*, pp. 80–1, 90.

71 *Ibid.*, p. 90. After Essex's rising, Archibald Douglas wrote that James needed to be wary of Bacon's professions of loyalty: TNA, SP12/52/67, fo. 330^r, copy by George Nicolson of a letter by Archibald Douglas to Richard Douglas, August? 1601.

72 *CJRC*, pp. 95–107.

73 Susan Doran, 'Loving and affectionate cousins? The relationship between Elizabeth I and James VI of Scotland 1586–1603', in Susan Doran and Glenn Richardson (eds), *Tudor England and its Neighbours* (Basingstoke, 2005), pp. 203–34 (pp. 225–6).

74 TNA, SP59/38/1169, fos 298^r–304^r, declaration of Henry Leigh, 12 April 1600; *CJRC*, pp. 86, 103–4. Leigh's extant interrogation reveals nothing usefully damning, but he may have revealed more verbally. In November 1600, when Sir William Eure was arrested for his contacts with James, Lord Willoughby was alarmed that his own involvement in intrigues would be revealed: see his defensive letters from 7 and 12 December 1600, TNA, SP59/39/1294, 1297, fos 278^{r-v}, 286^{r-v}.

75 Ralegh to Cecil, February/March 1600, printed in Agnes Latham and Joyce Youings (eds), *The Letters of Sir Walter Ralegh* (Exeter, 1999), pp. 185–7.

76 TNA, SP12/275/33, endorsed by Cecil, 'An Abstract of the Erl of Essex his Treasons'. Though dated 22 July 1600 in the calendar, the charge appears to have been compiled over a number of months after the earl's trial at York House on 5 June: Hammer, 'Shakespeare's *Richard II*', pp. 20–1.

77 Dr Giles Fletcher was told on the evening of 7 February that Essex had been summoned on the fabricated pretext that Spanish ships were off the coast: TNA, SP12/279/12, fo. 19ʳ, confession of Dr Fletcher, 3 March 1601. See also Hammer's observations about Ralegh's possible involvement: 'Shakespeare's *Richard II*', 15.

78 James apparently revised his instructions after news of Essex's insurrection reached Edinburgh, around 12 and 13 February; still he believed that he and 'friends' might make a stand about the succession: Akrigg (ed.), *Letters of King James*, pp. 169–71.

79 Latham and Youings, *Letters of Sir Walter Ralegh*, p. 186.

80 Akrigg (ed.), *Letters of King James*, p. 170.

81 *CJRC*, p. 109, examination of Sir Christopher Blount; Bodl, Rawlinson MS C774, fo. 34ᵛ, account of Blount's execution.

82 Hammer, 'Shakespeare's *Richard II*'.

Chapter 7

The Scottish King and the English court: the secret correspondence of James VI, 1601–3

Alexander Courtney

Freshly proclaimed as King of England, James VI and I addressed his thanks to Sir Robert Cecil: 'How happy I think myself in the conquest of so faithful and so wise a counsellor'.[1] The peaceful manner of James's accession to the English throne was, to many contemporaries, astonishing; but no less remarkable was the survival into the new reign of Cecil as the monarch's leading counsellor. Since the middle of the previous decade, James's greatest supporters in England had been anti-Cecilian, while for a time the King himself was apparently convinced that his claim was opposed by William Cecil, Lord Burghley, and his son Robert. How surprising it must have seemed, therefore, that the shift from the last Tudor to the first Stuart should prove a 'change changeless', that the King of Scotland should accede to the throne without trouble and that Robert Cecil should remain in favour.

The secret correspondence between James and Cecil, carried on during the last two years of Elizabeth's life, helped to make that smooth transition of 1603 possible for both men. James was in contact with others in England, independently of his connection with Cecil, though such dealings have left very few traces. No substantial evidence survives of such regular and extensive communication between James VI and other English courtiers and councillors at that time; the letters that passed between Cecil, James and their co-correspondents thus present historians with unique insights into how James saw the English court and how some there sought to ingratiate themselves with their future King. These clandestine contacts played an important role in preserving friendly relations between the two kingdoms after the defeat of the Essex rebellion and helped to determine the shape of the early Jacobean regime in England.

Yet despite its significance, the secret correspondence of 1601–3 between James, Cecil and others has rarely been analysed in any depth and is often treated merely as evidence of Cecil's immense political skill and foresight. Thus Joel Hurstfield contended that Cecil 'saw clearly what was necessary to achieve a peaceful transfer of power'.[2] Similarly for John Guy, Cecil's 'purpose' in February 1601 'was to create the atmosphere in which he could engineer the smooth succession of James VI'. Cecil 'paved the way' for James's peaceful accession.[3] In Richard Rex's words, by 'Cecil's secret diplomacy with James VI' the succession to the throne was 'wrapped up' before Elizabeth's death.[4] The extent of Cecil's initiative in opening contact with James is, however, exaggerated by such accounts and they leave largely unexplored the question of exactly *how* these letters contributed to the 'wrapping up' of the succession problem, just as James's own intentions in corresponding with a man he had previously regarded as his enemy are overlooked. This chapter reconsiders James's relations with Cecil in 1601–3. It examines how and why their correspondence was established, as well as its content and nature, before assessing the part it played in the spring of 1603 in helping to bring James peacefully to the English throne.

THE OPENING OF THE CORRESPONDENCE

James VI's understanding of English court politics was not subtle. He thought that Elizabeth was prey to the influence of those around her and that the malice of certain of her courtiers and counsellors served in no small part to explain friction between the two monarchs. At points of crisis in their relations he was thus prepared to stand up to Elizabeth and to trade insults with her as to which of them was the more 'abused' or 'seduced' by their counsellors. In April 1594, for example, as tensions increased over the affair of the Spanish Blanks and English support for the rebel Earl of Bothwell, James declared to Elizabeth that she presented 'the spectacle of a seduced queen': 'that so wise…a prince, having so long and happily governed, should be so sylid [i.e. deceived]…it is hardly to be believed', he wrote, 'if I knew it not to be a maxim in the state of princes that we see and hear all with the eyes and ears of others'.[5] Again, in September 1600, James expressed to the Queen his 'uonder, that…your earis shoulde yett be so oppen to such as goes about, by all the meanis they can, to burie and abolishe, by the force of lyes and calumnies, that happie amitie standing betuixt us'.[6] A few months later, in the aftermath of the Essex rebellion, James instructed his ambassadors to London to 'plainlie declaire unto [Elizabeth]…that the greattest reuenge that euer I shall take of her shall be to praye to god to oppen her eyes & to lett her see hou farre she is urongid by such base instrumentis about her as abusis her eare'.[7] James's use of such rhetoric of evil counsel was formulaic and his assessment that Elizabeth was unable to take her own line in policy, independent of the preferences (or prejudices) of those around her, was not well informed. Nevertheless, such views were significant in shaping his relations with English courtiers: if Elizabeth was 'seduced' and 'abused' by enemies of the Anglo-Scottish amity and James's claim to the throne of England, then it followed that the influence of such 'base instruments' in her counsels needed to be countered. This clear, if un-sophisticated, understanding of English court politics led James in the 1590s to draw the Earl of Essex into his service and then, following Essex's demise in early 1601, to seek to recruit Sir Robert Cecil as his chief ally at Elizabeth's court and in her counsels.

During the years before 1601, James identified the Cecils as the most influ-ential of Elizabeth's evil counsellors and turned to Essex to defend his interests at her court. As James wrote to Essex on 13 April 1594, he expected the Earl to 'move and assist the Queen with [his] good advice not to suffer herself to be so…abused any longer with such as prefer their particular and unhonest affections to the Queen's princely honour and peace of both the realms'.[8] There can be no doubt, as Alexandra Gajda demonstrates in Chapter 6, that James had the Cecils in mind here. Slackness in the payment of his English pension, aid given to Bothwell on the Borders, and the disparaging letters that James so often received from Elizabeth – all these the King blamed upon Burghley and his son Robert. Moreover, James felt that Burghley, who had so vehemently opposed his mother, also opposed his claim to the English throne and 'favour[ed] the house of Hartforde'.[9] James hoped that Essex would act for him as a counterbalance to the Cecils' supposedly nefarious influence and a correspondence between the pair was duly established during the summer of 1594, with the Scottish courtier David Foulis and Essex's agent Anthony Bacon acting as intermediaries.[10] Thereafter Essex certainly maintained 'intel-ligence' with James, in some form or another, until early 1601.[11]

Essex's usefulness as James's ally in Elizabeth's counsels would not last, however. The failure of the Earl's career in Ireland and at court in 1598–1600 coincided with developments that weakened the Anglo-Scottish amity and made James more restive over his claim to the English crown. Edmund Ashfield and William Eure were arrested after visiting James, and Elizabeth refused to declare (in a manner which James found satisfactory) that the Scottish King was not involved in the alleged plotting of Valentine Thomas against her life, thus raising the fear that the Act for the Queen's Surety might one day be invoked against James and his title by his 'undeserved haters'.[12] More impor-tantly, James, like Essex, opposed peace negotiations between England and Spain, believing that any settlement would favour a Spanish title to the throne. Both men suspected Robert Cecil of seeking to promote such a peace and a diversion of the succession to a Spanish claimant. As Susan Doran has argued, James took very seriously the arguments in favour of the Infanta Isabella advanced in Robert Persons's *A Conference about the Next Succession to the Crowne of Ingland*.[13] Philip II's *donacíon* of sovereignty over the Low Countries to the Infanta in 1598 only made such arguments more disturbing for James: was she not now ideally placed to launch an invasion of England in defence of her claim? In such circumstances James believed that peace between England and Spain would be unsafe; yet Essex, banished from court and then under house arrest in 1599–1600, could only push the case against peace from the sidelines: a printed edition of his *Apologie*, arguing against negotiations with Spain in part explicitly on the grounds of the Infanta's claim, appeared in May 1600, neatly coinciding with talks underway at Boulogne between Flemish and English commissioners.[14] James needed more than such printed intimations of Essex's continuing goodwill. Without a useful man of business at the English court, James could not feel assured that his right to succession would not be bypassed or stymied for lack of a party to speak and act effectively on his behalf. It was clear that Essex was no longer in a position to 'move and assist the Queen with [his] good advice', as James required.

There is some evidence that James considered offsetting Essex's decline in favour and influence by making tentative efforts to develop new channels of communication with the English court in late 1600. His agent James Fullerton was despatched to London in August and December 1600, possibly with the aim of sounding out Robert Cecil.[15] These initiatives failed, however, to forge links between the English Secretary and the King. Encouraged by the alarmist reports of an increasingly desperate Essex, James remained mistrustful of Cecil and his allies, and in February 1601 was prepared, from a safe distance, to countenance whatever action Essex intended to resolve finally the perceived problems with their mutual 'enemies' around Elizabeth.[16]

The opportunity for James to acquire another supporter at Elizabeth's court thus only came with the failure of the Essex rebellion and the Earl's execution on 25 February 1601. James remained wary of Cecil but, in keeping with his understanding of English politics, he believed that Essex's demise left Cecil as simply *the* dominant figure in the Privy Council and at court. In early April James accordingly advised his two special ambassadors to London, John Erskine, Earl of Mar and Edward Bruce, Commendator of Kinloss, that Cecil was 'king thaire in effect'. If the Queen now granted James's requests – including renewal of her promise not to do anything 'in præiudice of [his] future richt', an increase in his pension and a legally recorded declaration that James was innocent of involvement in any plotting against her – then it would reflect her 'principall gydairis…affections' towards him. Although he expected that Cecil and his 'follouairis' on the Privy Council would ensure that Elizabeth gave the ambassadors no satisfaction in their talks with her, James also indicated that he was willing to extend his favour to Cecil if he 'preast to deserue the same'.[17] James's instrumental view of English court politics, in which Cecil simply led Elizabeth, had caused the King to distrust the Secretary. But now that James's chosen counter-weight to Cecil's influence over the Queen was dead, that same view of the English court meant that it made sense to mend fences with Cecil, for the latter's influence might equally well be used to James's advantage.

If Elizabeth responded favourably to the Scottish ambassadors, therefore, James felt that it would be down to Cecil. However, from their arrival at London on 6 March 1601 through to the end of April, Mar and Kinloss got nowhere in their talks with the Queen. She received them fairly but denied all their master's requests. On 23 April Elizabeth chose the Earl of Derby to succeed to Essex's stall as a Garter knight, while the next day the Earl of Hertford was promoted to the lord lieutenancies of Somerset and Wiltshire. No slight to the Scots may have been intended by these appointments, yet, as the French ambassador Thuméry de Boissise speculated at the time, James might well have taken umbrage at them, since 'ledict Darby et les enfans dudict Hertford sont les plus proches en Angleterre pour succéder à la Couronne'.[18]

Elizabeth's intransigence left Mar and Kinloss in an awkward position. They were Anglophiles, and James relied mainly on them and a few associates at his court to advise him on English affairs. If they returned to Edinburgh empty handed, their position at court would be weakened. As a last resort, therefore, they complained directly to Cecil on 29 April 1601 about the Queen's 'cauldnes' and urged him to consider the likely impact of their embassy's failure. James's 'confidence' in them would diminish and others less well affected to the Anglo-Scottish amity would be promoted in his counsels:

> in stead of [such] Servants and Ministers as might have suppressit enemies, in all their indirect attempts, by our evil success, the same enemies will make their awin fortune, and establish their opportunities, quhilk throughly considered can be na good change for her Majesty.[19]

James had indeed left hanging over their embassy a prospective mission to France, to be led by the Duke of Lennox, to resurrect the 'auld alliance'. The precise nature of Lennox's mission was dependent upon Mar and Kinloss's success in England.[20] 'Throughly considerid', their failure would be 'na good change' for Cecil either: 'to yourself we conclude', they wrote, 'that there is ane greit difference between vigilancy and credulity'. Eager to advance their business and preserve their favour with the King in Scotland, Mar and Kinloss equated that favour with the maintenance of friendly relations between James and Elizabeth. The implication was clear enough: Cecil could choose to be over-cautious and so undermine those Scots who were the best advocates of the amity, wrecking the chances he might have had of gaining James's favour at their hands in the process, or alternatively he could help to promote their master's interests.

Though several historians have suggested otherwise, it appears that Cecil was not, in fact, quick to seize the opportunity offered by the arrival of James's ambassadors to establish a confidential correspondence with the Scottish King.[21] The initiative seems to have been more the Scots' than the Secretary's. We should note that, in his first letters to James, Cecil clearly stated that he had responded to the 'embassadors sommons' and their 'ouvertures'.[22] In any case, it was only after the Scots had made their representations to him about the dangers posed to all parties by his too great caution, that Cecil persuaded Elizabeth to increase James's pension to £5,000 per annum. For the first time, Elizabeth committed to regular, twice-yearly payment of a fixed sum. The King's straitened finances made such an addition especially welcome.[23] So, contrary to James's expectations, his ambassadors had not received 'nothing but a flatte & obstinate denyall' from Elizabeth and her 'principall gydairis'. In accordance with their instructions, therefore, Mar and Kinloss approached Cecil to extend their master's favour to him at some point in early May. He then agreed to correspond with James. Though disappointed in most parts of their business with Elizabeth, the embassy had achieved a great success. Their main aim was to obtain from the Queen and her counsellors 'a suretie for holding of[f] euill', as James had put it in his instructions, and this they had done. Assured of the support of Elizabeth's leading counsellor, James would have no cause to fear the 'craft of the counsall'.[24]

THE NATURE OF THE CORRESPONDENCE

James's rapprochement with Cecil was arranged at a meeting between the Secretary and the Scottish ambassadors at the Duchy House on the Strand.[25] The secret correspondence which resulted was carried between the parties (unbeknownst to him) via the English diplomatic agent in Scotland George Nicolson. The letters travelled by the ordinary diplomatic post to London from Edinburgh, dressed as packets from the Scottish court to French Huguenot noblemen, Rohan, Bouillon and La Tremoille; replies from London passed back along the same route. (Duped in this way into performing the role of James and Cecil's messenger, Nicolson was referred to in the correspondence as 'the pigeon'.)[26] Geoffrey Elton's claim that Elizabeth knew about Cecil's activities cannot be substantiated.[27] Although James and Cecil did occasionally write themselves, most of the correspondence was conducted through intermediaries. On the Scottish side, Kinloss was the main correspondent, while David Foulis and Mar's cousin Sir Thomas Erskine were privy to at least some of the letters' content. None of Mar's letters survive. The main English correspondent was Lord Henry Howard, brother to Thomas Howard, the executed fourth Duke of Norfolk, and an associate of Essex. Howard, James's 'long aproued and trustie 3', as he was known in these letters, had already been in correspondence with the King for some time, possibly since 1588 or 1589. His role was to be 'a sure interpretoure betwixt 30 [James] and 10 [Cecil] in the opening up of euerie one of thaire myndis to another'.[28]

The letters which passed between James and his English correspondents were written in terms appropriate to the new relationship that each party hoped to nurture: that between a monarch and his faithful and learned counsellors. The letters' tone has in the past been misconstrued. Thus James's hostile modern biographer David Harris Willson asserted that the King's sudden expressions of 'thankefulnes and…constant loue' to his erstwhile enemy Cecil were merely evidence of his shallowness – his 'unbounded and dancing delight was that of the self-centred opportunist'. Henry Howard's lengthy and obscure letters, meanwhile, dripped with the kind of 'unctuous adulation' bound to appeal to such an egotist.[29] The tone and style of the correspondence are better understood, however, in the light of contemporary conventions of political discourse. James expressed his 'love' to Cecil and signed himself as the Secretary's 'most louing freinde' as part of an exposition of the proper relationship between king and counsellor: James extended to Cecil his friendship, the *amicitia* which would encourage freedom of speech and good counsel in return. Writing to Cecil, James himself spelled out this commonplace equation of friendship and counsel: 'friendshippe without freedome is nothing but a fontaine of affectate complementis'.[30] Meanwhile the floridity of Howard's letters was meant not only to flatter but also to persuade the reader. Though admittedly Howard, a Reader in Rhetoric at Cambridge during the 1560s, laid it on rather thickly, the purpose was to impress upon James a sense of his correspondent's learning and aptitude as a counsellor, and in this Howard succeeded. In one passage he might pile clause upon clause, quote Pliny, cite a moral sentence, and deploy extended similes about astronomers, labourers and physicians.[31] Even as he tired of reading long pages of Howard's cramped handwriting, James recognized the techniques and indulged in a clever and good-humoured put-down in response: to these 'ample, asiatike & endless uolumes', James answered in his own contrastingly 'lakonike style'.[32] Early in their correspondence, James averred to Cecil: '[I shall] reule all my actions for aduauncing of my future hoapes by youre aduyce, euen as ye waire one of my owin counsaillouris'. For their part, Cecil and Howard gratefully acknowledged the role James expected them to play: 'Our office is to present the matter', Howard wrote to the King, 'your wisdom to dispose'.[33]

What counsel was thus offered? Cecil used his very first letter to offer James advice on how to 'secure the heart of the Highest [Elizabeth]'. He urged the King not 'to be busy, to prepare the vulgar beforehand', but rather to trust in 'a choyce election of a feaw at present', and not to importune Elizabeth with 'needles expostulations, or over much curiosity in her…actions'.[34] This counsel can indeed be credited with improving relations between James and

Elizabeth during her last years, as Helen Stafford and others have argued. There were no further embassies to England to seek a grant of the Lennox lands, an acknowledgement that James was untouched by plots against the Queen, or public recognition of his claim. The tone of letters between the monarchs improved and James offered the use of Scottish men against Elizabeth's Irish rebels. Over the next two years the amity was secure. James accepted Cecil's counsel: 'goode gouuernement at home, firme amitie uith the queen, and a louing caire in all things that maye concerne the uell of that state, are the onlie three steppes quhairby I thinke to mounte upon the hairtis of the people'.[35]

The loss of so many of the Scottish letters of the correspondence makes it impossible to establish how demanding James was of Cecil, but we should not assume his passivity. Some obscure references to James's instructions to his English supporters survive in the letters, such as his 'opinion hou ye shall behaue youre self in that maitter' or the King's 'owne iudiciall commandments, set downe in [Kinloss's] lettre'.[36] His stance on one issue, however, is clear. Writing in late 1602 or early 1603, James urged Cecil against supporting peace with Spain, since it would be 'most perrelouse for [his] iust claime'. Peace would allow more open discussion in England of a 'spanishe title', encouraged by Habsburg diplomats and agents who would 'corrupte the myndes of all corruptible men' in favour of a Spanish-backed claimant.[37] Pauline Croft has argued persuasively that continuing rebellion in Ireland was the major obstacle to an English peace with Spain before 1603. If so, James had little cause for concern and Cecil needed to do nothing to prevent negotiation of an agreement that would not occur until Ireland had been secured and Spanish interference there had become less feasible.[38] Nonetheless, James's hostility to settlement with Spain before he was securely upon the English throne could not simply be ignored by Cecil. So Howard claimed in one letter to James that the once 'pacificus' Cecil had shifted to 'earnest opposition' to peace because of James's views. Cecil himself alleged to the King that the Earl of Nottingham, a new addition to the correspondence in 1602, now professed 'coldnes' towards peace 'for your only respect'. A record of discussion in the Privy Council on 24 May 1602 notes that Cecil and Nottingham were among those who advised against negotiating a settlement of the conflict, since Ireland remained in arms *and* as there was 'no safetie to have peace with Spaine, for that the Enfanta makes title of succession'.[39] Whatever actual influence over English policy-making James was able to exert through Cecil, it was certainly in his correspondents' interest to make it *appear* to him that they were daily active on his behalf and in accordance with his wishes.

Most of that work of keeping up appearances to James was carried out by Henry Howard. A crypto-Catholic supporter of Mary Queen of Scots and the brother of an alleged traitor, Howard had been long out of favour with

Elizabeth.[40] As something of a political outsider then, Howard had much to gain from his new association with Cecil and, perhaps, from occasionally depicting Cecil as more active in promoting James's interests in Elizabeth's counsels than he really was or needed to be in 1601–3. From the very start Howard described Cecil as 'able to bringe anie matter of effect to passe' through his influence over Elizabeth. Thus when Archduke Albert made Elizabeth 'honorable and constant offers of sownd amitye' following the Essex rebellion, Howard claimed that 'poor 10 [Cecil] had much adoo to bear vp a good caus agaynst so manie violent & artificiall assaultes'. Nevertheless, Cecil had 'cast it in a sleep again by drawing the quenes eie from admiratione of that forward offer' and 'by puzzelinge the peace with such other difficultis and perplexities as could not by any meanes be cleered'.[41] Howard's depiction of Cecil was not so far from James's earlier notion that he was 'king thaire in effect'. Both Cecil and Howard had an interest in encouraging James in his long-established view of Elizabeth as malleable and in persuading him that, when a problem with the Queen did arise, 'No ma[n] could awnser more iudiciously and honestly then 10. to eury pointe, temperinge hir feares…and abating passion'.[42]

The connection between Mar, Kinloss, Cecil and Howard was above all a political (rather than a diplomatic) alliance, the survival of which depended upon maintenance of their privileged position in James's counsels, to the exclusion of rival groupings of Scottish and English courtiers. James already believed that Cecil held sway over Elizabeth and her Council. The correspondence needed to keep up that impression and to persuade him that Cecil was using his powerful influence to advance and protect the King's interests. Moreover, if Cecil's 'intelligence' with James were uncovered and Elizabeth made aware of it, then his perceived usefulness to the King would be at an end and Howard and his Scottish allies deprived of their best means to James's favour. Similarly, all their interests would be damaged if other Scottish courtiers were to muscle their way into the management of James's English affairs, by disgracing Mar and his Scottish associates, or by opening up alternative channels of communication between the King and the English court.

Much of the correspondence, therefore, was concerned not so much with policy matters as with discussion of the threats, real and imagined, that others posed to James and his correspondents' ambitions. Nicolson and other agents in Scotland reported to Cecil throughout 1601 and much of 1602 that Queen Anne was plotting the disgrace of Mar and his cousin Sir Thomas Erskine. Anne wanted the guardianship of her son Henry to be removed from Mar and, with the Duke of Lennox, was jealous of Mar and Erskine's closeness to the King and their involvement in James's dealings with England. In April 1602 Anne allegedly declared that she would 'gladly…intercept' the letters which the King wrote for England, so as to 'break' Erskine and Mar. Cecil even received vague reports that Anne was plotting 'against the king's person (if not against his life) and against the lives of some of his most trusty councillors and servants'.[43] Such factional rivalry within James's court, by threatening Mar and his circle, also threatened Cecil and Howard's position. Cecil divulged these reports to Howard, who then used the information to warn Mar, Kinloss and James of the dangers they faced. Though his efforts to persuade James to beware of his wife met with a cold response, Mar and Kinloss did take heed and, in June 1602, took steps to protect the passage to Berwick of their despatches.[44]

Henry Howard was not only troubled by the supposed machinations of Mar's Scottish rivals. Ambitious for preferment in the next reign, he sought to depict as worthless other English courtiers who might also lay claim to positions of influence under James. Moreover, one way of assuring his Scottish correspondents of his and Cecil's usefulness was to make out that they were daily vigilant against the King's supposed enemies around Elizabeth. Large tracts of Howard's rhetorically elaborate letters to James and his servants were thus given over to denigrating the 'accursed duality' of Sir Walter Ralegh and his friend Henry Brooke, Lord Cobham – men who, as Essex's opponents, may well have been regarded with suspicion by James already.[45] Ralegh indeed attempted to make contact with James through Lennox, during the latter's visit to London on his return from France in November 1601. Meanwhile both Cobham's proximity to Elizabeth and his marriage in the summer of 1601 to one of her Privy Chamber ladies, Frances, dowager Countess of Kildare, suggested to Howard that he posed a threat. Cobham made no attempt himself to curry favour north of the border, but before their marriage Kildare, the daughter of the Earl of Nottingham, had been in correspondence with James.[46]

Neither Ralegh nor Cobham had secured advancement to the Privy Council upon Essex's death. However, Howard feared that their ambition to promote themselves with Elizabeth and/or James would come at his (and Cecil's) expense. Sensing that James might perhaps be keenly interested in the allegiance of Cobham and Ralegh if either could gain influence over English policy, Howard privately urged Cecil to consider means to 'dissolue them befor they ascende into thos highe regions' and himself set about describing them to the King, Mar and Kinloss as dangerous though foolish conspirators.[47] If one crucial element of the depiction of Cecil as James's strong supporter in Elizabeth's counsels was that he opposed peace with Spain, then it made sense to portray Cobham and Ralegh as promoters of such a settlement and as evil counsellors who were trying to foster in the Queen's mind 'idele apprehensiones' of Cecil's allegiance to the King of Scots. Howard alleged that the pair not only dealt 'in the matter of this peace' but also 'nourishe[d] a certain muddy springe of intelligence' at 'the Archdukes courte'.[48] Given James's well-known anxiety about the Archduchess Isabella's claim to the English throne, the implications of such remarks cannot have been lost on him. Whether or not any of this was fair or true, by painting the late Elizabethan court as divided, as 'a world … of fractiones' – with Cecil and his friend Howard aligned (secretly) on James's side and against Cobham and Ralegh, the supporters of peace and opponents of James for their own ambitious ends – Howard was able to emphasize Cecil's and his own continuing usefulness.[49]

THE CORRESPONDENCE AND JAMES'S ACCESSION

In June 1603, after his peaceful accession, James boasted to the French ambassador that 'in Scotland, long before the death of [Elizabeth], he had directed her whole council, and governed her ministers, by whom he was better served and obeyed than herself'.[50] His claim was exaggerated, but he was certainly led to believe that, thanks to Cecil (and Mar, Kinloss and Howard), this was the case. By the summer of 1602 pledges of support from two more English privy councillors, Nottingham as '40' and possibly Lord Treasurer Buckhurst as '50', were conveyed through the correspondence.[51] With the inner ring of the Privy Council thus apparently engaged in a 'happie and honest concurrence for my uell', as James put it, keeping the 'quenis mynde from the poison of iealouse præiudice' and 'ualiantlie resist[ing] the crooked courses of … seditiouse spirits', he was firmly convinced that he was 'settelid … in the only richt course for my goode'.[52] He had no cause to appeal directly and provocatively to Elizabeth for various public tokens of her support for his claim, since he no longer feared that her 'guiders' were abusing her ear: in Cecil's own later words, 'what could more quiet the expectation of a successor so many ways invited to jealousy, than when he saw [the Queen's] ministry, that were most inward with her, wholly bent to accommodate the present actions of state for his future safety … ?'[53]

The true value of this clandestine alliance with powerful figures on the English Privy Council was proven in March 1603, as Elizabeth neared death. During the three weeks of the Queen's last illness the Council made efforts to preserve public order, banning unlawful assemblies, suspending plays, rounding up vagabonds, and setting extra guards around prisons and important London buildings. Close watch was placed upon James's English cousin, Arbella Stuart.[54] More significantly, measures were taken to lend the Council's decisions greater legitimacy. While Elizabeth lived the Privy Council's writ still ran, but their authority would be terminated by her death. So, from 17 March the Privy Council began to draw in members of the nobility on hand at court to aid in their deliberations.[55] The French ambassador, Beaumont, who was well informed about the Council's doings at this time, reported on 18 March that the councillors had resolved 'soudain apres le decez de la Reine d'assembler avec eux les plus grands du Royaume qui se trouveront à la Cour et par leur consentement comun faire proclamer le Roy d'Ecosse Roy d'Angleterre'. By 22 March he was able to write that 'Messieurs du Conseil ont déja commencé d'appeller avec eux les Comtes et Barons du Royaume'.[56] On Sunday 20 March a larger 'conference' of councillors and noblemen abiding in and near London had indeed been held and letters were then sent out inviting 'sondrie Earles and Barons' to join them upon the Queen's death in a 'Grand Counsell' of former privy councillors and lords temporal and spiritual.[57] Cecil's draft of the proclamation of James's accession was forwarded to Scotland by Henry Howard following this meeting of 20 March, perhaps after discussion there. By the time of Elizabeth's death on 24 March James had read the proclamation and could thus be certain that 'the counsel and state standeth for ws in a constant and resolut wnion to aduance owr ryghtfull hopes'.[58]

Despite the tense atmosphere of Elizabeth's final weeks, the correspondence with Cecil undoubtedly calmed James's nerves. In March 1603 he received 'many letters from gentillmen of good accompt' in England, including from the Tower of London, signed in ciphers and penned by the Tower's Lieutenant, Sir John Peyton. Peyton had in all likelihood been in touch with James through the King's agents David Foulis and James Hudson for some time, perhaps providing a means for the King's imprisoned supporters in his charge, like the Earl of Southampton and the Catholic gentleman Edmund Ashfield, to communicate with the Stuart court. Peyton now was in receipt of daily reports about the Queen's health from 'an Immynent parsonne' at the court at Richmond and had called to his side unnamed individuals of 'e[x]traordinary qualytye and powre to doe [James's] seruyse'. These so-called 'cyphers of the toure' requested that James send Foulis to London 'in all possyble haste' to act as a special ambassador. Such a 'minister' was needed, the writers claimed, to provide 'corresspondence & derectyon' to affairs. They hinted darkly at 'stronge opposition' to James planned by the 'popishe factyon' and backed by 'the forraynge imbassadors'. It is significant that James did not take alarm but instead calmly referred these reports from the Tower to Mar and Kinloss for them to seek Cecil and Howard's advice as to whether the sending of Foulis as ambassador to London would be 'agreable'. Similarly, when Southampton wrote to James to request his liberation from the Tower upon Elizabeth's death, James deferred to Cecil's better judgement of what was 'expedient'. Despite the 'multitud of advertisments' coming out of England, the King, as Kinloss assured Howard and Cecil, meant 'to sall by no wther compass then your consell and aduise in all thinges'.[59]

The secret correspondence had thus succeeded in creating a bond of trust between its participants. James benefitted from this immediately as the inwardness established by the correspondence was translated rapidly into effective collaboration between his trusted Scottish and English servants. As James started on his journey south to claim his throne in early April, Howard posted northwards to advise him in person, while Kinloss and Foulis joined Cecil in London to open the King's mind to his new councillors and furnish them with further authority to act in his name. Kinloss and the leading members of Elizabeth's Privy Council – Cecil, Nottingham, Buckhurst and Lord Chancellor Egerton – worked closely together in London, writing to the court as it journeyed south and drafting 'royal' commands on pre-signed blank sheets that Kinloss had brought with him. Some of these were used to reword James's own letters slightly, so as to keep the nobles gathered in the capital contented by holding out the prospect of promotion to James's Privy Council, for example. Others were used to prevent some courtiers from rushing northwards to present themselves and their petitions to the new King: one such was used to deny Ralegh access.[60] Howard, shortly to be made a privy councillor, was already by the King's side, as the newsletter writer John Chamberlain recorded, 'to possesse the Kinges eare and countermine the Lord Cobham'.[61] The King was not the only beneficiary of the correspondence with Cecil; in seeing his enemies frozen out and securing his own place on James's Privy Council, Howard now gained massively from it too.

CONCLUSION

Of all James VI's strategies to help secure his inheritance, as Susan Doran has recently argued, his gaining of support from English courtiers, councillors and noblemen ultimately proved the most successful.[62] Some, such as Henry Clinton, Earl of Lincoln, and Sir John Harington, sent him gifts with messages of goodwill in the last year of Elizabeth's life.[63] He continued to communicate with and enjoy the backing of his former Essexian friends Mountjoy and Southampton.[64] From early 1602 onwards, he received assurances of loyalty from the Earl of Northumberland. Reluctant to turn away the messenger of a major landowner with Catholic connections, James ignored Henry Howard's warnings about the Earl – who, with Cobham and Ralegh, allegedly formed part of a 'Diabolicall triplicitie' and was James's 'sworne enemye'– and engaged in a guarded correspondence with him.[65] Finally, when the Queen died, a contact among her ladies, Lady Philadelphia Scrope, used her brother Sir Robert Carey to return James his earlier present of a sapphire ring, so as to prove that his time had come.[66]

Sir Robert Cecil's support was, however, the most significant. Essex's death provided the context in which James, at first deeply distrustful of the Secretary, was prepared to consider reconciliation with Cecil; the embassy of Mar and Kinloss to London in March–May 1601 secured this. There can be no doubt that this connection with Cecil paid off handsomely in the end. It was the relationship of trust and service established and maintained through the secret correspondence that made the 'translation of [the] monarchy' in March–May 1603 easier to manage.[67] The letters from Cecil and Howard did not 'instruct James in the duties that would one day await him in London', nor did they contain detailed discussions of what would be done for James when Elizabeth died; still less did they lay before the King any of the 'routine business' of governance in England.[68] Thanks to the 'intelligence' kept up between them previously, during the days and weeks surrounding Elizabeth's death James was happy to trust to the judgement of Cecil and his allies, and they collaborated closely to promote his (and their) interests. It was in this sense that the secret correspondence 'paved the way' for James's peaceful accession.

Nevertheless, although ultimately successful, James's approach to English courtiers and court politics during these latter years of Elizabeth's reign should not be judged too positively. His conduct was certainly clear, consistent and, within its own terms, logical. He believed that Elizabeth was strongly influenced by her counsellors and he accordingly sought backing at her court to defend his interests. He had thus drawn Essex into his service during the 1590s and then (eventually) extended his favour to Cecil in May 1601. From James's point of view, his policy – of seeking to balance Elizabeth's counsels in his favour, when he recruited Essex, and winning important friends at her court and in her Council when he could be sure of their disposition – was vindicated by his peaceful accession to the English throne. Yet while clear in its rationale, James's secretive engagement with certain English courtiers during these years was predicated upon a limited understanding of English court politics. For years he had seen – and been encouraged by his English court correspondents to see – the Elizabethan political scene in terms of his own succession claim. Thus he perceived that the unsettled succession had divided Elizabeth's court and Council over whose claim to support and, connectedly, over the matter of peace or continued war with Spain. Furthermore, he was all too ready to believe in the power of faction over the Queen: that Elizabeth's coldness towards him was the result of 'seduction' and 'abuse' by her 'guiders', that she could easily be led to think the worst of him, that his interests were threatened by his 'enemies' around her. Confident of the justice of his claim to the English throne, James certainly was; but he was not, contrary to the arguments of Jenny Wormald, 'confident…of the succession'.[69] Up to 1601 Essex was able to play upon his fears of Cecil's influence over Elizabeth, and Howard was subsequently able to persuade him of the existence of a similar 'threat' from Cobham and Ralegh. In March 1603 James had good reason to be happy with his 'conquest' of Cecil, a 'faithful and…wise…counsellor'; but his approach to English court politics ironically left *him* prone to manipulation by his supporters.

NOTES

1   G. P. V. Akrigg (ed.), *Letters of King James VI & I* (Berkeley, CA, 1984), p. 209.

2   Joel Hurstfield, 'The succession struggle in late Elizabethan England', in S. T. Bindoff, Joel Hurstfield and C. H. Williams (eds), *Elizabethan Government and Society: Essays Presented to Sir John Neale* (London, 1961), reprinted in his *Freedom, Corruption and Government in Elizabethan England* (London, 1973), pp. 104–34 (pp. 130–2).

3   John Guy, *Tudor England* (Oxford, 1988), pp. 452–4.

4   Richard Rex, *Elizabeth I: Fortune's Bastard* (London, 2003), p. 144.

5   Akrigg (ed.), *Letters of King James*, pp. 128–30.

6   John Bruce (ed.), *Letters of Queen Elizabeth and King James VI of Scotland*, CS 46 (1st series, 1849), pp. 132–3.

7   James to Mar and Kinloss, 8 April 1601, NLS, Advocates' MS 33.1.7, Denmilne State Papers, XXI, item 42, fo. 3ᵛ.

8   Akrigg (ed.), *Letters of King James*, pp. 130–1.

9   Paul E. J. Hammer, *The Polarisation of Elizabethan Politics: The Political Career of Robert Devereux, 2nd Earl of Essex, 1585–1597* (Cambridge, 1999), pp. 167–70.

10 Foulis to Bacon and Essex, 18 May to 4 November 1594, BL, Additional MS 4125, fos 157, 160, 162, 164, 167, 169, 170, 172–3, 174.

11 Hammer, *The Polarisation of Elizabethan Politics*, pp. 169–70; *CJRC*, p. 86.

12 Akrigg (ed.), *Letters of King James*, pp. 157–63 (James's letters to Elizabeth on Valentine Thomas), quotation on p. 160.

13 Susan Doran, 'Loving and affectionate cousins? The relationship between Elizabeth I and James VI of Scotland 1586–1603', in Susan Doran and Glenn Richardson (eds), *Tudor England and its Neighbours* (Basingstoke, 2005), pp. 203–34; Susan Doran, 'James VI and the English succession', in Ralph Houlbrooke (ed.), *James VI and I: Ideas, Authority, and Government* (Aldershot, 2006), pp. 25–42.

14 Richard B. Wernham, *The Return of the Armadas: The Last Years of the Elizabethan War against Spain, 1595–1603* (Oxford, 1994), pp. 239–40, 349; *To Maister Anthonie Bacon. An Apologie of the Earle of Essex* (London?, 1600), sig. C3. See also, Alexandra Gajda, 'Debating war and peace in late Elizabethan England', *Historical Journal*, 52 (2009), 851–78.

15 David Edwards, 'Securing the Jacobean succession: the secret career of James Fullerton of Trinity College, Dublin', in Seán Duffy (ed.), *The World of the Galloglass: Kings, Warlords and Warriors in Ireland and Scotland, 1200–1600* (Dublin, 2007), pp. 209–12; see also Helen Georgia Stafford, *James VI of Scotland and the Throne of England* (New York and London, 1940), p. 214.

16 *CSPScot*, 13(ii), pp. 755–7; *CJRC*, pp. 80–1, 82–4, 85, 86, 89–90, 99–100 (examinations and confessions of Essex, Southampton and Henry Cuffe, 1601).

17 NLS, Advocates' MS 33.1.7, Denmilne, XXI, item 42, fos 2, 3ᵛ.

18 '[T]he said Derby and the children of the said Hertford are nearest in England to succeed to the crown'. Boissise to Henry IV, 14 and 30 April [OS] 1601, TNA, PRO 31/3/32, fos 46ᵛ–47ʳ, 55. I am grateful to Neil Younger for information on Hertford's lieutenancies.

19 *CSPScot*, 13(ii), pp. 812–13. See also James Hudson's letters to Cecil in March–April 1601, making similar points: *ibid.*, pp. 791–2, 800–1, 804–5.

20 *CSPScot*, 13(ii), pp. 769–70, 773, 810, 823–4, 829.

21 Cf., among others, David Harris Willson, *King James VI & I* (London, 1956), p. 153; Maurice Lee, Jr, *Great Britain's Solomon: James VI and I in His Three Kingdoms* (Urbana and Chicago, IL, 1990), p. 102; Wallace T. MacCaffrey, *Elizabeth I* (London, 1993), p. 444; Mark Nicholls, *A History of the Modern British Isles, 1529–1603: The Two Kingdoms* (Oxford, 1999), p. 310.

22 *CJRC*, pp. 4, 12.

23 Julian Goodare, 'James VI's English subsidy', in Julian Goodare and Michael Lynch (eds), *The Reign of James VI* (East Linton, 2000), pp. 113, 116.

24 NLS, Advocates' MS 33.1.7, Denmilne, XXI, item 42, fos 1ᵛ–2ᵛ.

25 *CJRC*, p. 8.

26 Stafford, *James VI of Scotland*, pp. 255–7; '3' [Howard] to '30' [James], 24 August [1602], and '3' to '8' [Kinloss], 27 April [1602], NLS, Advocates' MS 33.1.7, Denmilne, XXI, items 6, 15; *CSPScot*, 13(ii), p. 1114 (note of packets sent by George Nicolson, March 1603).

27 G. R. Elton, *England under the Tudors* (2nd edn, London, 1974), p. 474.

28 Foulis to Mar, 3 December 1601, National Archives of Scotland, GD124/15/21; Henry Howard, Earl of Northampton, to Robert Carr, Viscount Rochester [1613], CUL, Dd.iii.63, fo. 21; *CJRC*, pp. 1–2.

29 *CJRC*, p. 2; Willson, *James*, pp. 154–6.

30 *CJRC*, pp. 11, 32; John Guy, 'The rhetoric of counsel in early modern England', in Dale Hoak (ed.), *Tudor Political Culture* (Cambridge, 1995), pp. 292–310.

31 '3' [Howard] to '30' [James], 24 August [1602], NLS, Advocates' MS 33.1.7, Denmilne, XXI, item 6; Linda Levy Peck, *Northampton: Patronage and Policy at the Court of James I* (London, 1982), p. 8.

32 '30' [James] to '3' [Howard], undated [September 1602?], NLS, Advocates' MS 33.1.7, Denmilne, XXI, item 39. For the terms 'ample', 'Asiatic' and 'laconic', see Morris W. Croll, '"Attic" prose in the seventeenth century', in J. Max Patrick and Robert O. Evans (eds), *Style, Rhetoric, and Rhythm: Essays by Morris W. Croll* (Princeton, NJ, 1966), pp. 68–71; Peter Mack, *Elizabethan Rhetoric: Theory and Practice* (Cambridge, 2002), pp. 42–3.

33 *CJRC*, p. 10; NLS, Advocates' MS 33.1.7, Denmilne, XXI, item 6.

34 *CJRC*, pp. 7–8.

35 *Ibid.*, p. 11.

36 *Ibid.*, pp. 26, 28.

37 *Ibid.*, pp. 30–1.

38 Pauline Croft, '*Rex Pacificus*, Robert Cecil, and the 1604 peace with Spain', in Glenn Burgess, Rowland Wymer and Jason Lawrence (eds), *The Accession of James I: Historical and Cultural Consequences* (Basingstoke, 2006), pp. 145–6. See also Paul E. J. Hammer, 'The crucible of war: English foreign policy, 1589–1603', in Doran and Richardson (eds), *Tudor England*, pp. 261–2.

39 '3' [Howard] to '30' [James], no date [early 1602?], NLS, Advocates' MS 33.1.7, Denmilne, XXI, item 13; *CJRC*, p. 35; H. S. Scott (ed.), *The Journal of Sir Roger Wilbraham, Solicitor-General in Ireland and Master of Requests, for the Years 1593–1616'*, Camden Miscellany, 10 (3rd series, 1902), pp. 49–50.

40 Pauline Croft's *ODNB* article on Howard.

41 '3' [Howard] to '8' [Kinloss], no date [summer 1601?], BL, Cotton MS Titus C VI, fo. 65^v.

42 '3' [Howard] to '8' [Kinloss], no date [April 1602?], NLS, Advocates' MS 33.1.7, Denmilne, XXI, item 5.

43 *CSPScot*, 13(ii), pp. 773, 829, 899, 902–3, 932, 941, 945, 970–1, 976, 1029, 1049–50, 1091–2.

44 '3' [Howard] to '30' [James], 24 August [1602], and '3' [Howard] to '8' [Kinloss], no date [summer 1602?], NLS, Advocates' MS 33.1.7, Denmilne, XXI, items 6, 25; *CSPScot*, 13(ii), p. 1001.

45 NLS, Advocates' MS 33.1.7, Denmilne, XXI, item 5. See Chapter 6 in this volume.

46 Mark Nicholls and Penry Williams, *Sir Walter Raleigh in Life and Legend* (London, 2011), p. 181; Mark Nicholls's *ODNB* article on Cobham; *CJRC*, p. 43; '3' [Howard] to '8' [Kinloss], no date [May? 1602], and '3' to '8' and '20' [Mar], 27 August [1602], NLS, Advocates' MS 33.1.7, Denmilne, XXI, items 16, 35; '3' to '20' [Mar], 22 November [1601], NAS, GD124/15/26/1. Diana Newton's claim that Cobham offered James his services in 1601 is mistaken: see her *The Making of the Jacobean Regime: James VI and I and the Government of England, 1603–1605* (Woodbridge, 2005), p. 14; HMC Sal, XV, pp. 64–5.

47 Undated draft memorandum, [Howard] to [Cecil], BL, Cotton MS Titus C VI, fo. 387^r.

48 '3' [Howard] to '8' [Kinloss], 4 December [1601], and '3' to '30' [James], no date [early 1602?], NLS, Advocates' MS 33.1.7, Denmilne, XXI, items 9, 13.

49 *Ibid.*, item 9. On Cobham's support for peace, see Chapter 6 in this volume. For Cobham and Ralegh's implication in treasonous contact with Flemish diplomats after James's accession, see Mark Nicholls, 'Two Winchester trials: the prosecution of Henry, Lord Cobham and Thomas, Lord Grey of Wilton, 1603', *Historical Research*, 58 (1995), 26–48; Mark Nicholls, 'Sir Walter Ralegh's treason: a prosecution document', *English Historical Review*, 110 (1995), 902–24.

50 Judith M. Richards, 'The English accession of James VI: "national" identity, gender and the personal monarchy of England', *English Historical Review*, 117 (2002), 513–35 (quotation at p. 527).

51 Letters of '3' [Howard] to '30' [James] and '8' [Kinloss], 1 May to 24 August [1602], NLS, Advocates' MS 33.1.7, Denmilne, XXI, items 6, 14, 16, 25; *CJRC*, pp. 77–8.

52 *CJRC* p. 15 (3 June 1602).

53 Hurstfield, 'The succession struggle', p. 129.

54 R. C. Munden, 'The politics of accession: James I and the Parliament of 1604' (M.Phil. dissertation, University of East Anglia, 1975), pp. 80–2; Mark Nicholls, *Investigating Gunpowder Plot* (Manchester, 1991), p. 113; Stafford, *James VI of Scotland*, pp. 288–90.

55 *CJRC*, p. 73.

56 '[A]t once after the Queen's death to assemble the greatest in the kingdom who are then at court and, by their common consent, to proclaim the King of Scotland as King

of England'; 'Members of the Council have already begun to call together the earls and barons of the kingdom'. Beaumont to Henry IV and Villeroy, 18 and 22 March [OS] 1603, BL, King's MS 123, fos 11ʳ, 13ᵛ, 16ᵛ. By the end of April 1603 Beaumont had been 'so curious' in the Council's affairs that James had to dismiss him as ambassador: James VI & I to Sir Thomas Parry, 25 April 1603, BL, Cotton MS Caligula E X, fo. 195ʳ.

57 *HMC Sal*, XV, pp. 11–12; *APC*, 32, p. 493; Cecil and Kinloss to Howard, 9 April 1603, TNA, SP14/1/16, fo. 30ᵛ.

58 *CJRC*, p. 47.

59 [Sir John Peyton and others] to James VI, undated and 10 March [1603], NLS, Advocates' MS 33.1.7, XXI, items 4, 44; Peyton to Cecil and the Privy Council, 10 October 1603, TNA, SP14/4/14, fos 27–9; *CJRC*, pp. 48, 51.

60 Egerton, Buckhurst, Nottingham and Cecil to Thomas Lake, 10 April 1603, TNA, SP14/1/18, fos 36ᵛ–37ʳ; SP 14/1/16, fo. 30ʳ.

61 Norman Egbert McClure (ed.), *The Letters of John Chamberlain*, 2 vols (Philadelphia, 1939), I, p. 192.

62 Doran, 'James VI and the English succession', p. 41.

63 Declaration of William Wright, 21 July 1602, TNA, SP12/284/82; Jason Scott-Warren, *Sir John Harington and the Book as Gift* (Oxford, 2001), pp. 193–7. See also Lincoln to the Privy Council, 21 September 1603, TNA, SP14/3/77, fo. 134ᵛ.

64 '3' [Howard] to '30' [James], 24 August [1602], NLS, Advocates' MS 33.1.7, Denmilne, XXI, item 6.

65 Letters of '3' [Howard] to '8' [Kinloss], 4 December [1601], undated [April 1602?], and 1 May [1602], NLS, Advocates' MS 33.1.7, Denmilne, XXI, items 5, 9, 14; *CJRC*, pp. 53–76; Nicholls, *Gunpowder Plot*, pp. 99–101; Mark Nicholls's *ODNB* article on Thomas Percy.

66 F. H. Mares (ed.), *The Memoirs of Robert Carey* (Oxford, 1972), pp. 63–4.

67 Akrigg (ed.), *Letters of King James*, p. 208.

68 Cf. Hurstfield, 'The succession struggle', p. 130; John Cramsie, *Kingship and Crown Finance under James VI & I, 1603–1625* (Woodbridge, 2002), p. 73.

69 Jennifer M. Brown [Wormald], 'Scottish politics 1567–1625', in Alan G. R. Smith (ed.), *The Reign of James VI and I* (London, 1973), p. 37; Jenny Wormald's *ODNB* article on James VI.

Part IV

Imaginative writings
and
the wider public world

Chapter 8

The succession in sermons, news and rumour

Arnold Hunt

S ermons on the succession, in late Elizabethan England, might be thought to be conspicuous by their absence. It would have been a bold preacher who dealt openly with the succession question from the pulpit. The Treasons Act of 1571, which prohibited 'contentious and seditious spreading abroad of titles to the succession to the crown', did not necessarily prevent preachers from handling the subject in general terms, without naming names – and, as we shall see, some did precisely that – but most preachers understandably preferred not to confront an issue of such acute political sensitivity. When the Lincolnshire minister Henry Hooke presented James I with a copy of his treatise 'Of succession to the Crowne of England' in 1603, he prefaced it with a set of Latin verses declaring: 'what is now laid open was formerly a high crime [*grande nefas*] to spread abroad either in speech or writing'.[1] His words reveal the pent-up frustration that many preachers must have felt in the late Elizabethan period, and the palpable sense of relief after 1603 when the succession was at last resolved.

But silence on the succession had not always been the rule. Indeed, early in Elizabeth's reign, it seemed as if preaching might play a critical role in opening the succession question to wider discussion. In a sermon preached at the opening of Parliament in 1563, Alexander Nowell subjected the Queen to a very public scolding, warning her that her failure to marry and provide an heir was likely to prove a 'plague' to the kingdom, and confronting her with some decidedly awkward questions: 'If your parentes had beene of your minde, where had you beene then, or what had become of us nowe?' Nowell went on to describe the 'continuall voyces and lamentations' of the people during the Queen's recent sickness, 'saying Alas what trouble shall we be in, even as great or greater than France, for the succession is so uncerten and such division for religion, Alack what shall become of us?' In his peroration, Nowell gestured to the royal tombs around him in Westminster Abbey, including the 'ruinous monument' of Henry III, 'the longest reign that ever was, and yet his crown in the dust', and the funeral places of Edward VI, Mary I and Lady Jane Grey, all serving as a reminder that death is 'the most certain thing that can be' and yet 'uncertain when the hour shall be, or how soon'.[2] Nowell was evidently aware of the intention to raise the succession question in parliament, and his sermon was the prelude to a petition drawn up by a Commons committee later that month calling on the Queen to marry and designate a successor.

Nowell's sermon, once thought to have been sponsored by Robert Dudley in support of his courtship of the Queen, is now seen as part of a concerted action by the Privy Council to force a debate on the succession. It thus reflects the conciliarism rather than the factionalism of early Elizabethan politics, and illustrates the public/private strategy which Peter Lake has labelled the 'politics of popularity', whereby the Queen's councillors urged a course of action on the Queen in private while simultaneously using the press, the pulpit and other public media to exert additional leverage.[3] But Nowell did not simply regard himself as the mouthpiece of the Privy Council. His sermon also asserted the role of the wider political nation, including parliament and, by implication, godly preachers such as himself, in offering counsel to the Queen on the government and good order of the realm. Having made his hearers' flesh creep with dire predictions of the imminent ruin of the kingdom, Nowell ended his sermon on a more optimistic note. He had, he declared, been on the point of despair, 'but then again when I heard of the calling of this Parliament I was thereby encouraged, hoping and not doubting but there should be such order taken and good lawes established which should agayne erect up the decay of the same'.[4]

Yet in the frankness of its language, its assertion that the succession was a matter of legitimate public concern and its warning of future catastrophe if the issue were not addressed, Nowell's sermon has few parallels in the Elizabethan period. Other preachers were far more cautious in their pulpit utterances, and with good reason. In 1577 Tobie Matthew, Dean of Christ Church and future Archbishop of York, was censured for a sermon at Paul's Cross in which he touched on the succession. According to his own account, he had prayed that the gospel might 'in perpetuall succession of all ages remayne amongst us', and told his hearers that 'if we have a dutiful regarde of succession in [God's] service, he cannot but cast a fatherly respect to our quiet government', adding, 'this is the succession that we shoulde seke and sue for'. In his defence, Matthew claimed, a little disingenuously, that he had merely been referring to the succession of the Protestant religion, not the succession to the throne. He had also taken care to safeguard himself by stating that 'succession of other maters and persons' was 'a cause that concerneth the prince and the peers to consider of how and when it shall please god and them', while admonishing his audience not to 'busy their tongues or witts therein as a mater far unmete for them to intermedle withall'.[5] Matthew was protected by his patron, Robert Dudley, Earl of Leicester, and does not seem to have suffered any lasting ill-effects as a result of his sermon, but the incident nonetheless demonstrates that any mention of the succession, however carefully qualified, was liable to land a preacher in trouble.

By the 1590s Elizabeth's refusal to name an heir or to countenance any discussion of the succession meant that it was impossible to raise the issue in public. One of the reasons for the destabilizing effect of Robert Persons's *A Conference about the Next Succession* (1594/5) was that the government was unable to mount any counter-propaganda in pamphlets or sermons, apart from the semi-clandestine Appellant tracts.[6] The result was a deafening public silence, as preachers retreated from political engagement and took refuge in platitudes. Sir John Harington was so disgusted by a sermon he heard on the Queen's accession day in 1598 that he responded with an epigram 'against an extreame flatterer that preached at Bathe on the Queens day the fortith yeare of her Raigne', in which he launched into a ferocious prophetic denunciation of a nation that had lost its way:

> You that extoll the bliss of this our nation,
> And lade our eares with stale and loathsome prayse
> Of forty yeares sweet peace and restfull dayes,
> Which you advaunce with fayned admiration,
> Much better would yt sute your high vocation,
> To beat down that your flattring tongues do rayse,
> And rather seeke some words of Commination,
> For times abounding with abhomination,
> Say that gods wrath against us is provoked,
> And tell us 'tis to us the scripture sayes
> I forty yeares have dur'd this generation,
> And sayd theise people have not known my wayes.
> For law with lust and rule with rape is yoaked,
> And zeale with schisme and Symony is choaked.[7]

The sermon that aroused Harington's ire does not survive, but Thomas Holland's accession-day sermon at Paul's Cross the following year provides a sample of the stale preaching that infuriated him so much. Holland's sermon consists of a long-winded panegyric of Elizabeth, comparing her to the Queen of Sheba who 'came from the ends of the earth to hear the wisdom of Solomon' (Matthew 12: 42): 'by sexe…a woman; by vocation, a Queene; in wealth, abundant; in knowledge, a rare Phoenix; in travail, laborious; in disputations, learned; in observation, discreet; in behaviour, honorable and wise; in traine, magnificall; in rewardinge Salomon, heroicall; in religion, studious, zealous and fervent'.[8] There is no mention of the succession apart from a casual remark that the Queen of Sheba had left her kingdom to her 'lawful successors', which in the light of the uncertainty over the English succession must have seemed blatantly evasive.

David Colclough has contrasted 'the general timidity of Elizabethan preachers and the relatively restricted conditions under which they operated' with the 'culture of outspoken preaching' under the early Tudors.[9] The dismal trajectory I have sketched here, from political activism in the 1560s to political quietism in the 1590s, would seem to bear this out. But while discussion of the succession may have gone underground, it had not gone away. Harington's treatise on the succession, probably written around 1602, shows that even before Elizabeth's death the likelihood that James would succeed her was already being widely though cautiously discussed: 'the people as I heare, specially Northwarde, talke broadly of it already, but for us in the West wee have tutors, look better to our tounges, but our heartes ar thinking and our pennes are scribling as warilie as we can'.[10] Preaching, so closely concerned with issues of authority and obedience, inevitably fed into this debate and offered unusual opportunities for public discussion of the succession, albeit in coded and indirect forms. In a speech in Star Chamber in November 1599 the Lord Keeper, Thomas Egerton, complained of 'stirrers of sedition' who criticized the Queen 'as though … her highnes did fayle in care and providence to provide for her dominions and people', and singled out preaching as an example: 'some of late have played Preachers, and under generall speeches, have used such particular designations, as their malicious meaning hath appeared to their simplest Auditors'.[11] This suggests that there is more political content in late Elizabethan sermons than has generally been recognised.

PREACHING THE SUCCESSION, 1590–1603

By the 1590s there was an ever-expanding flow of political news and rumour circulating both in manuscript and by word of mouth. It is not surprising, therefore, to find Egerton trying to stem the tide of seditious words, including 'politique discourses of Princes, Kingdomes and Estates' in inns and alehouses, and 'false and seditious Libells' scattered abroad in the court and city. The role of sermons in this news culture has been rather neglected, perhaps because they have generally been categorized as religious rather than political discourse. But sermons could respond to news; they could help to circulate news; and they could also, on occasion, become news themselves. This was particularly true of the sermons preached at Paul's Cross, whose proximity to the bookshops in Paul's Churchyard and the newsmongers in Paul's Walk placed them right at the heart of the London information network. When Richard Bancroft preached a controversial sermon at the Cross in 1595, the news immediately travelled to the Suffolk gentleman Sir Thomas Cornwallis, who immediately passed it on again in a letter to his London agent John Hobart: 'it ys reportyd here that doctor bancrofte made a strange sermon at pawles Crosse on Sonday laste'.[12] When Stephen Gosson let drop some tactless remarks in a Paul's Cross sermon in 1596, the news again spread very rapidly: as Gosson later recalled, 'it was told me to my head fortie miles hence in the presence of an honourable man, that I had stricken at some great person, and should be called in question for it'.[13] Preachers did not always welcome this appetite for news – Henry Hooke warned that matters of state ought not 'to be made common, to be handled and dandled trivially, to be chatting and chaffing matter for tavernes and alehouses' – but they could not easily control the way their sermons were used, or prevent them from being recycled into the gossip mill.

Henry Smith's sermon *The Magistrates Scripture*, preached before the Lord Mayor, possibly at Paul's Cross, is not as politically tendentious as the sermons Egerton may have had in mind, but shows how a preacher could use 'general speeches' to point to 'particular designations'. Smith's text, provocatively, was Psalm 82: 6–7, 'I have said ye are gods ... but you shall die like men, and fall like one of the princes', and the sermon is an extended *memento mori*, reflecting on the inevitability of death and reminding princes and magistrates that 'though they be above other, yet they shall die like other: and though they judge here, yet they shall be judged hereafter'.[14] There was nothing particularly original about the sermon, which drew on familiar commonplaces and similes much as Nowell had done in his remarks on the royal tombs in Westminster Abbey. 'One hundred Princes of England are dead and but one alive, the rest are gone to give accounte how they ruled heere when they sustained the person of god ... How soone the flower of this world is faded! There lie the men which were called gods, and thus ends the pilgrimage of kings, princes and rulers.' The simple moral message of the sermon helped to establish its popularity well into the seventeenth century, when it was still being reprinted in collected editions of Smith's sermons. But even within this fairly hackneyed formula it was still possible to deliver a pointed warning about the mortality of princes. 'Thus I have proclaymed to all, kings, Princes, Judges, counsellers and magistrates that which Isaiah foretold to one, Set thy thinges in order for thou shalt die.' In the context of the 1590s there could be little doubt as to what Smith meant by setting things in order. This was an allusion to Elizabeth's advancing age and a message to her to settle the succession.

Smith's sermon remained safely within the limits of acceptable criticism. It thus provides an instructive contrast with a sermon by Anthony Rudd, Bishop of St David's, preached before the Queen in Lent 1596, which disastrously overstepped the mark. Rudd's sermon is well known from the accounts in Harington's *Supplie or Addition to the Catalogue of Bishops* (1608; first published

1653) and Thomas Fuller's *Church-History of Britain* (1655) as an example of the hazards of preaching at the Elizabethan court. According to Fuller, Rudd had been inadvertently or deliberately misled by Archbishop Whitgift, who told him: 'the Queen now is grown weary of the vanities of wit and eloquence, wherewith her youth was formerly affected; and plain Sermons, which come home to her heart, please her the best'. Acting on this advice, Rudd unwisely chose to preach on old age and mortality, 'personally applying it to the Queen, how age had furrowed her face, and besprinkled her hair with its meal. Whereat Her Majesty (to whom *ingratissimum acroama* to hear of death) was highly displeased', and Rudd lost his chances of preferment, as Whitgift had perhaps intended.[15] Harington adds a further detail, that the Queen 'said she thankt god that neither her stomacke nor strength nor her voyce for singing, nor fingring for instruments, nor lastly her sight was any whit decayed', then took out 'a little jewell that had an inscription of very small letters' and read it aloud to prove that her eyesight was as keen as ever.[16]

A closer reading of Rudd's sermon, which survives in several contemporary manuscripts and a printed edition published shortly after the Queen's death in 1603, supplements the accounts in Fuller and Harington and helps to explain why the sermon went so spectacularly wrong.[17] Preaching on Psalm 90: 12, 'O teach us to number our days that we may incline our hearts unto wisdom', Rudd urged his hearers to practise 'a divine Arithmeticke, or arithmeticall Divinitie' in the reckoning of their days, 'not the bare numbring of the years of our life…but in deeply considering the shortnesse, frailtie and uncertaintie of this life which is lent unto us for the setting foorth of Gods glorie in it'. He cited various examples from scripture, including Jacob, who 'rightly numbred the dayes of his pilgrimage to be few and evil', and Samuel, 'who when he was become olde, made his sonnes Judges of Israell, because he was not able to beare the charge'.[18] Harington describes what happened next: the Queen 'perceaving wherto yt tended, began to be troubled with yt', and Rudd, 'discovering all was not well, for the pulpet stands there vis a vis to the Closet', hastily brought the sermon to a conclusion with 'an excellent prayer by waie of *Prosopopeia* in her Maiesties person'. 'The Queene (as the manner was) opened the window, but she was so far from giving him thanks, or good countenance, that she said plainly, he should have kept his Arithmetick for himselfe, but I see (said she) the greatest Clerks are not the wisest men; and so went away for the time discontented.' According to Harington, Rudd was briefly banished from the court and ordered 'to keepe his house for a time', but pardoned after a few days. In fact the consequences seem to have been more severe, as Rudd wrote to Cecil on 9 April 1596, twelve days after the sermon, 'from the place of my commitment', asking him to intercede with the Queen for his release.[19]

It was the prayer that caused most of the offence. Prosopopoeia, an imaginary speech in the voice of another person, was a common figure in early modern rhetoric, and it is not particularly unexpected to find it employed in a court sermon before a rhetorically cultivated audience.[20] However, Rudd not only assumed the voice of Elizabeth herself but, with breathtaking audacity, took his audience into the Queen's private closet to eavesdrop on her prayers and meditations. 'I know mine iniquitie, and my sinnes are ever before me', he made her declare, in the words of scripture (Psalm 51: 3), as she pleaded with God not to punish England for her 'former sinnes'. He then imagined her reflecting that she was 'now entred a good way into the Climactericall yeare of mine age, which mine enemies wish and hope to be fatall unto me', but that she trusted in God to deliver her, as he had done by the defeat of the Spanish Armada in 1588. This led him on to even more sensitive territory as he imagined her thoughts turning to old age and the approach of death:

> Lord, I have now put foote within the doores of that age, in the which the Almond tree flourisheth: wherein men begin to cary a Calender in their bones, the senses begin to faile, the strength to diminish, yea all the powers of the body daily to decay…So direct me with thine holy spirit, that I may daily waxe elder in godlinesse; wisedome being my gray haires, and an undefiled life mine old age…[for] what availeth this my long temporall life in surviving others, unless I myselfe lead always a spirituall life while I continue upon earth, in hope to enjoy an eternall life when I am dead?

The reference to the 'climactericall yeare' was particularly pointed, as Elizabeth was then in her sixty-third year, the 'grand climacteric' thought to be a particularly critical or dangerous year of a person's life. In his defence, Rudd claimed that he had not intended to encourage belief in the grand climacteric but rather to discourage it by citing Jeremiah 10: 2, 'be not dismayed at the signs of heaven', and that the remainder of the sermon had simply been misinterpreted.

> Assuredly I refuted the fansye of the Climactericall yeare both by the doctryn of the prophet Jeremye, and also by th'example of 88 in the which was a strange Constellatyon and yet all things fell out prosperously to hir Highnesse. And that which I spake of old age in generall, is made personall. Somewhat also which in sense ought to receave a future constructyon hath found a present understanding. Finally, divers things were mistaken.

Rudd's version of events, therefore, was that the Queen's objection to the sermon had taken him by surprise; he had, he protested, merely intended 'to encourage hir in welldoinge, even by those speeches which proved so offensive'. Harington, too, assumed that Rudd had simply miscalculated: 'I dare undertake he thought, and so should I if I had not bene somwhat better acquainted with her humor, that it would have well pleasd her or at least no waie offended her'. However, it is significant that Rudd began his sermon with a robust assertion of the preacher's right to counsel the monarch. 'David had need to have Nathan and Gad to admonish and advise him', Rudd pointed out. 'And to be short, where prophesying faileth, there both the Prince and the people must needs perish in the end.' His use of prosopopoeia also makes more sense as a protective strategy designed to shield him against future reprisal. Putting words into the Queen's mouth may seem astonishingly risky, but it was also a way of avoiding any direct address to the Queen by way of admonition or reproof. The reason for this defensiveness emerges at the very end of the sermon, where Rudd imagines Elizabeth praying that God would spare her life until 'I have met with dangers present, or imminent, and established the state for the time to come'. Like Smith's exhortation to 'set things in order', this was quite clearly a warning to settle the succession, only lightly veiled by the polite rhetorical fiction that the preacher was merely expressing what the Queen was already thinking. This makes it implausible to see Rudd as a naïve or inexperienced preacher who accidentally misjudged the royal mood. The careful rhetorical positioning of the sermon suggests that he was perfectly well aware of treading close to the limits of what could safely be said from the pulpit.

As this episode shows, court preachers occupied a highly exposed yet powerful position, with opportunities to counsel the Queen and command her attention, that few other courtiers could equal. But apart from Rudd, almost the only preacher who dared to touch on the delicate matter of the succession was Archbishop Matthew Hutton, in a sermon at Whitehall in which he not only urged the Queen to name her successor but went so far as to state plainly 'that the expectations and presages of all wryters went northward, naming without anie circumlocution Scotland'.[21] These were exceptional cases. It should be emphasized that court sermons were not intended for the monarch's ears alone; preachers were also conscious of addressing a wider audience, and in this respect it may be misleading to bracket off court sermons from other forms of preaching, as they were plugged into the same public discourse, the same news culture, regardless of whether they were delivered inside or outside the court.[22] The presence of that wider audience is acknowledged in the preface to the printed edition of Rudd's sermon, which notes that the sermon 'bred much speech long ago, and the sight of it was greatly desired by many'.[23] The diary of John Manningham allows us to watch the process of oral transmission at work, as the sermon was gradually smoothed and polished into an anecdote through repeated retellings. In February 1603, a few months before the printed edition came out, Manningham recorded a garbled account of it, confusing the text with that of Henry Smith's sermon, 'you shall die like men and fall like one of the princes', and reporting that Rudd had preached a 'discourse of death' which had prompted the Queen to reply: 'you have made me a good funerall sermon; I may dye when I will'.[24]

Nor was it only in London and at court that preachers took the opportunity to broadcast political messages. Henry Robinson, provost of Queen's College, Oxford, dealt with the succession issue in an accession-day sermon probably preached at Oxford in the mid-1590s.[25] His text (Psalm 132: 11–18) was another provocative choice in the reign of a childless queen: 'The Lord hath sworn in truth unto David, saying, Of the fruit of thy body will I set upon thy throne'. Robinson began by stressing how easily the line of succession could be broken: 'When Moses the servant of God was dead, the government of the people was geven awaie from his house to Josua who was of another tribe. Likewise after Josua it went one time to one tribe, another time to another. Saul was the first and last kind of his familie.' David therefore had good reason to be thankful for God's promise to continue the kingdom to his descendants. But God would only guarantee the succession, Robinson argued (fo. 89ᵛ), as long as the prince and the people were obedient to him:

> God did long forbeare the disobedient children for their fathers sakes, but when both Prince and people had sold themselves to work wickednes, when there was no remedie, then did hee ridd the good land of evill inhabitants…And though a remnaunt came againe after their captivitie, yet the crowne never returned to the house of David.

God's promise was also a threat. As with the Hoseads and Jeremiads that formed the staple fare of so much early modern preaching, the covenant was presented in highly conditional terms: God's blessings would be taken away if God's people broke their side of the bargain.

Robinson then proceeded to apply this to England, praising Elizabeth for remaining faithful to the Protestant religion throughout her reign. 'The great Princes her neighbours did labour to discourage her from attempting anie reformation of Religion, as the borderers of Benjamin and Juda sought to discourage Nehemiah from building the walls of Jerusalem', but she was not dissuaded: 'shee cleansed the houses of God throughout her dominions; tooke upon her the defence of the truth', and unlike Solomon and many other kings of Judah, who began in the right path only to forsake their religion in their old age, 'shee hath not onlie mainteined this word of salvation without chainge within her owne territories, but hath bene the greatest protection under God to those of other countries' (fo. 94ʳ). Beneath this fairly standard panegyric of Elizabeth as the Protestant Deborah lay a more subtle message: that Elizabeth could be trusted to favour a Protestant successor (by implication, James), and that the long continuation of the Protestant religious settlement was the best guarantee of future political stability.[26] This echoes the message of Tobie Matthew's Paul's Cross sermon of 1577, in which the succession of the gospel was implicitly equated with the succession to the throne.

Finally, Robinson defended the Queen against 'the mouthes of repining

Mal-contentes' by answering various grievances about the economic problems of the realm. To the common complaint 'that since the reformation of Religion all things have bene sold at a farr higher rate, than theie were in former times', he replied (fo. 94ᵛ) that this price inflation was common to the whole of Europe:

> If theie would looke into the dominions of Italie and Spaine, where Poperie, which theie count devotion, is mainteyned, I think theie should finde the same alteration of prises. Neither doth this come of penurie of victualls, but partlie of the different rates of money in severall Princes times, partlie of the encrease of Gold and Silver which hath bene brought into the Land.

As for the high price of grain, this was not just the result of poor harvests, but of a lack of social responsibility and a failure to give work or wages to the poor. In the 1580s grain had been far cheaper, yet 'the crie was litle lesse because of cheapnes, than it was in the deare times; the artificer cold not utter his wares, the poore could not be sett on work, the farmer was not able to paie his rent and his servauntes wages'. If only the richer sort had been contented with 'sobrietie in meates and apparell', instead of wasting their money on 'superfluities', then 'the manie yeares of plenty under her majesties blessed raigne could not have been eaten up with so fewe deare yeares … and the Realme for wealth … should by this time have bene the flowre of all Christendom'. Thus it was clear, Robinson concluded, that 'the complaint of dearth proceedeth of our murmuring, not of anie want of Gods blessinges' (fo. 95ᵛ). This is a sermon deeply engaged with public opinion and with the perception of a country in crisis.

Public insecurity reached a peak in the summer of 1599, as rumours swept the country of the Queen's death and an imminent Spanish invasion. Again, sermons were closely scrutinized for hints of what was going on at court. On 23 August, by which time the panic was beginning to die down, John Chamberlain reported to Dudley Carleton that the army had been mustered in London and that 'the Lord Generall [the Earl of Nottingham] with all the great officers of the field came in great bravery' to the sermon at Paul's Cross on 12 August and dined with the Lord Mayor. According to Chamberlain, 'the vulgar sort cannot be perswaded but that there was some great misterie in the assembling of these forces, and because they cannot finde out the reason of yt, make many wilde conjectures, and cast beyond the moone', leading to speculation 'that the Quene was daungerously sicke' or that the mustering of the army was intended as a snub to the Earl of Essex, 'with many other as vaine and frivolous ymaginations as these'.[27] These rumours spread with astonishing speed. On 13 August, the day after the sermon at Paul's Cross, two Cornish husbandmen were out on the downs near Falmouth when one told the other 'that he harde that her maiestie was dead, and that there was an armye in the feilde about London wherein was brought forth only her maiesties picture but her selfe in person was not there'.[28] On 15 August this was reported to the governor of Pendennis Castle, and the following day a record of the whole incident was despatched by special messenger to Robert Cecil, suggesting that it took only a week for the rumour to make its way from London to Cornwall and back again.

The same febrile atmosphere of rumour and speculation is captured in the testimony of a young Cambridge don, Thomas Myriell, fellow of Pembroke College, who happened to be spending the week at his father's house in Harleston, on the Norfolk–Suffolk border.[29] On 14 August Myriell was in Norwich, where he met Richard Carlton, master of the cathedral choristers, at the White Horse Inn, and asked him: 'What news?' 'Nothing but troubles and miseries', Carlton replied, and when Myriell asked what he meant, answered: 'you know, it is in every man's mouth'. 'What news from court?' Myriell enquired, to which Carlton responded: 'What court? Where is the court?' adding darkly: 'the queen hath not been seen these seventeen days'. Later that day Myriell met one of his Cambridge acquaintances, Dr William Branthwaite, fellow of Emmanuel College, on horseback in the street, and put the same question to him: 'Do you hear any news?' 'No', replied Branthwaite, 'do you hear any?' Eager to pass on the gossip he had just heard, Myriell informed him that there was 'a muttering in the town about *vita Principis*', but hastily added: 'if you hear not this of others, tell it not from me'. The following Saturday, 18 August, Myriell's father returned home from Great Yarmouth and was greeted by his neighbours with the inevitable question: 'What news at Yarmouth?' to which he replied 'that a shipp of Yermouth coming crosse the seas, mett with a scottishe shipp cominge from London, and the Scott asked the Yermouth men whether he heard anie newes, who answered no; then said the Scott I can tell you some, your bonny Queene is deade'. After evening prayer the following day, Myriell fell into conversation with Mr More, curate of Harleston, and told him of a letter that 'one Baxter (a soldier of Harlston) had written to his wife' announcing the same news, 'that hir Maiestie was deade'.

This episode is of interest for several reasons. It shows the importance of the clergy in disseminating news, and also shows that even a small village like Harleston was closely connected with news networks in Norwich, Yarmouth and further afield. But the rumours of the Queen's death, which in that anxious week in August were being repeated all over the country, would probably not have warranted much investigation but for the fact that Myriell had also participated in some very indiscreet conversations about the succession. Hauled up before the authorities, he at first denied having spoken to anyone about the succession but admitted that 'since his last coming into Norfolk he hath seene a pece of a booke called Leicesters comonwealth wherein such matter is handled'. However, Peter Raye, rector of Starston in Norfolk, reported that Myriell had told him 'he thought ther would be some controversie about the succession, betweene the Kinge of Scotts and the Ladie Arbella', and 'he wished and desired that the Lords of the privie counsayle, and nobility might soe agree in one, as might be most for the peace and quietnesse of the common welth'. Confronted with this evidence, Myriell claimed not to remember the words about Arbella Stuart, but admitted that he and Raye had 'talked about the booke called Leicesters common wealth entreating upon succession &c'. He also volunteered the information 'that he heard some of the common people say, that this kingdome should be governed according to the government now used in the Lowe Countries'. This was said in self-defence, to give the impression that he was merely repeating what was being said by everyone – 'the muttering hath been so generall' – but nonetheless suggests that the values of the monarchical republic might, on occasion, shade into speculation about a republican alternative.

We know relatively little about how these rumours might have been reflected in preaching at a local or parochial level. However, a manuscript of sermons preached, probably in Coventry, between 1600 and 1603 gives us a rare glimpse of preaching outside London and the court.[30] On 17 November 1602 a Mr Hutton preached an accession-day sermon on Hosea 13: 10–11, an ominous text: 'Where is the king that should help thee in all thy cities? ... I gave thee a king in mine anger, and I took him away in my wrath'. The Israelites, Hutton declared (fo. 142^v), were restless and easily dissatisfied:

> they were a fickle headed people for the lord gave them Samuell who was gret and famous in his sight, but yet he would not serve the turne, but they would have a kinge ... In this people we se our people and declineinge age, for we are as they were after fulnes and plenty, mutable and discontent.

Samuel was despised for being old (1 Sam. 8: 5), yet 'old age is a signe of much peace and quietnes', and 'vertuous old age is a crowne of glory': therefore, Hutton pleaded, 'learne beloved to reverence ould and aged princes, and magistrates that be in authoritie'. The sermon was remarkably candid in admitting the popular desire for a new monarch (fo. 148^r):

> Some fickle headed amongst us are wery of the state, and finde fault with old age as Israell did and therfore would have a change, and cry give us a kinge, but let such malecontentes knowe that they have cause to rejoice, and to give god thankes for his longe preservation of our dred soveraigne, and us under her protection, and not to murmur against soe good and loveing a god, for god hath given us such a prince as noe nation upon the earth hath the like.

Only four months later, on 27 March 1603, Dr William Hinton, archdeacon of Coventry, stood in the pulpit to preach on the Queen's death. His choice of text was suitable for the occasion: 'Thou hast turned my mourning into joy' (Psalm 30: 11–12). The mourning was of course for Elizabeth; the joy, as

Hinton explained, was for the smooth transition to a new monarch. After some fairly perfunctory praise of Elizabeth as a defender of true religion, a father to the fatherless and a mother to the distressed, he went on to give thanks that the hopes of those 'discontented and lustfull after alteration and change' had been disappointed. 'Who would have thought this?' Hinton exclaimed. 'One would have thought we should rather have stoode on our guarde'. But God has given us a king 'whom we voluntarily with one consent have received and proclaimed knowing and seeing in conscience that the imperiall crowne of this kingdome is his by right of inheritance':

> It is good for us to knowe this, that he is borne of English blood, and descended truly and lineally (to the crowne of England) of the bodye of margrete eldest daughter to that wise prince Henry the seventh Kinge of England of famous memory, soe that *lege naturae* by the law of nature, and the right line of succession it commeth to him and this is it that god will blesse when it cometh lawfully and by right without any usurpation. (fo. 187ᵛ)

Hinton extolled James for his relative youth, noting that he was 'not yonge, but of the ripest yeares even 36 yeares of age, neither old, but in his best time, and therfore best able to governe, and to performe soe grete a charge'. And 'although his mother was soe addicted to papistrie and that false superstitious worship even untill her death', he had been brought up in the true religion, 'ever hateinge and detesteing all popery and superstition', and 'his bookes declare the same wherin he doth teach and instructe his sonne in the exercise of pietie and religion' (fo. 188ʳ). The fact that Hinton was able to present such a well-turned case for James's succession, only four days after the Queen's death, tells its own story. These sentiments were already familiar from private circulation but could now be presented publicly for the first time.

CONCLUSION: SERMONS AND NEWS CULTURE

These examples only give us a few snapshots of preaching in the final years of Elizabeth's reign. Even so, they make it clear that preaching took place against a constant background chatter of political discussion and speculation. As one Jacobean poet remarked a few years later, 'The Court's full of news, London's full of rumours'.[31] Most of this ephemeral talk is lost to us, except in a few cases where it happened to attract the attention of the authorities. In April 1600, for example, three Roman Catholic gentlemen held a meeting at the house of the printer Thomas East, where they handed round a copy of Persons's *A Conference*; we only know about this because, unfortunately for them, two of East's apprentices were listening at the door and heard them discussing the claims of a Spanish successor and agreeing that 'the world would never be at a better stay until all people were under one government or religion'. This gathering has been described as 'an event of great magnitude in the public affairs of the time', but I would argue that it is significant precisely because of its commonplace nature. Discussions like this must have been going on behind closed doors all over England.[32] If the rumour mill went into overdrive in the later 1590s, it was partly because the Queen was appearing less often in public and there was consequently less news coming out of the court. Rumour spread so easily because, like Kremlinologists in the last days of Brezhnev, court observers were looking in from outside on a closed system, with very little access to inside information. This is reflected in Harington's anecdotes of Elizabeth's last years which, as Jason Scott-Warren has pointed out, are part of his self-fashioning as a court insider but actually reveal his lack of access to the inner workings of the privy chamber.[33]

But this fascination with news went along with an awareness of its risks and dangers. These were 'ticklish times', as Peter Wentworth remarked, and newsletters from the 1590s are full of nervous requests for privacy and secrecy. 'I know you will burn my letters', wrote the newswriter Rowland Whyte to Sir Robert Sidney in 1599, and again in another letter, 'I beseach you lett my poore scribling be burnt, for I wold be sory this should fall to any other hands'.[34] In such a climate, sermons took on particular importance as one of the few ways in which anxiety about the succession could be publicly articulated. As we have seen, preachers took advantage of their privileged position, not just by the time-honoured method of 'criticism and compliment', wrapping an implied reproof inside a panegyric, but also by selecting suitable examples from the wide repertoire of Old Testament texts dealing with the death of princes and the fall of commonwealths. It is significant how often, in the examples discussed above, the choice of text is used to signal the political purpose of the sermon. Harington's account of Matthew Hutton's controversial sermon at court includes a vivid description of the audience's response, which began with 'so generall a murmur of one frend whispering to another, then such an erected countenance in those that had none to speake to, lastlie so quiet a scilence and attention … as I have never observed either before or since'. Not the least interesting aspect of this story is that it was the mere announcement of the text that sparked off the excitement. Even before Hutton had uttered a word of the sermon, his choice of text, 'the kingdoms of the earth are mine, and I do give them to whom I will' (Jeremiah 27: 5–7), was enough to lead the audience to anticipate 'some straunge doctrine where the text it selfe gave away kingdomes and scepters'.[35]

It was not only sermons that deployed scripture in this way. Wentworth's *Pithie Exhortation* uses many of the same texts, the same comparisons between Israel and England and the same applications, arguing, for example, that as David had named Solomon as his successor, so Elizabeth should name an heir during her lifetime to avoid a power struggle between rival claimants after her death:

Wherefore as the state of Israell then mooved David to make his successor knowne:
so nowe the state of England ought to move you … Think therefore (moste gratious
soveraigne) that these facts of Moses and David are thus recorded in the holie sto-
rie, not onlie that you should knowe that God his Magistrates thus governed: but
especiallie, that hereby you may learne to governe to the safetie of your subiectes,
as they did.'[36]

Wentworth's decision to cast his tract as a lay sermon can be seen as an
attempt to assert a preacherly authority and lay claim to a privileged space,
a kind of textual pulpit from which to admonish the Queen without fear of
reprisal. His attempt was unsuccessful, but the biblical examples used in *A
Pithie Exhortation* – with which, it is clear, many preachers were familiar –
then found their way back into sermons. Even if *A Pithie Exhortation* failed
to influence the Queen as Wentworth had hoped, it succeeded in making its
arguments part of public discourse. Sermons played a crucial role here in
giving wider oral circulation to the succession tracts and fuelling the culture of
news and rumour that we have encountered so often in this chapter running
parallel to the culture of preaching.

Much of this public discussion of the succession had perforce to take place
indirectly. But preaching on the succession was not just a matter of nods and
winks and subtle hints. Patrick Collinson has written perceptively of the 'prophetic mode' of preaching typified by the sermons at Paul's Cross, in which
England was envisioned as a nation chosen by God yet perpetually balanced
on a knife-edge, with the ever-present threat that God's blessings might sud-
denly be withdrawn. One reason why this style of preaching was so effective
was that it bore more than a passing resemblance to the actual state of the
nation – and here I have to take issue with Collinson's characterization of
it as 'intellectually impoverished and almost unbearably repetitive'; on the
contrary, it seems to me a highly flexible and adaptable mode of preaching,
which worked well because there was a basic fit between pulpit rhetoric and
political reality.[37] Thus William Hinton, in a sermon preached shortly before
Elizabeth's death, could switch almost automatically into the prophetic mode
to warn that the Queen's peace might come to an end at any moment: Christ
'came not to send peace but a swialorde, soe therfore let us beware how we have
used this peace lest we have deserved a sword, I meane the abuse of this peace
and our unthankfulnes for the same have deserved a sword which god shall
send as a just punishment and recompence for our sins'.[38] In this sense, the
succession issue is almost omnipresent in the sermons of the 1590s. If references to it appear to us to be few and far between, perhaps that is only because
we have not learned how to recognize them.

NOTES

1 Henry Hooke, 'Of Succession to the Crowne of England', BL, Royal MS 17.B.XI, printed in Jean-Christophe Mayer (ed.), *Breaking the Silence on the Succession: A Sourcebook of Manuscripts and Rare Elizabethan Texts* (Montpellier, 2003), pp. 261–309 (ref. p. 270).

2 'Mr Noels Sermon at the Parliament before the Queens Maiestie', printed in G. E. Corrie (ed.), *A Catechism Written in Latin by Alexander Nowell*, Parker Society (Cambridge, 1853), pp. 223–9.

3 Peter Lake, 'The politics of "popularity" and the public sphere: the 'monarchical republic' of Elizabeth I defends itself', in Peter Lake and Steven Pincus (eds), *The Politics of the Public Sphere in Early Modern England* (Manchester, 2007), pp. 59–94. On Nowell's sermon, see also G. R. Elton, *The Parliament of England 1559–1581* (Cambridge, 1986), p. 358; Susan Doran, *Monarchy and Matrimony: The Courtships of Elizabeth I* (1996), pp. 61–2; and Simon Adams, *Leicester and the Court: Essays on Elizabethan Politics* (Manchester, 2002), pp. 103–4.

4 'Mr Noels Sermon at the Parliament', p. 229. See also Stephen Alford, *The Early Elizabethan Polity: William Cecil and the British Succession Crisis* (Cambridge, 1998), pp. 104–5, for the argument that Nowell saw parliament as a royal council with a duty to advise on the succession.

5 'Doctor Mathewes writing to my Lord of Lecester having geven occasion of offence in a sermon at Paules crosse concerning succession': Folger Library, Washington, V.b.317, fos 11–12. My thanks to Dr Mary Morrissey for generously sharing a photocopy of this manuscript. On Matthew, see also Rosamund Oates, 'Puritans and the "monarchical republic": Conformity and conflict in the Elizabethan Church', *English Historical Review*, 127 (2012), 819–43, which draws attention to another copy of Matthew's letter to Leicester in Bodl. MS Top. Oxon c.5.

6 I owe this point to Susan Doran: see her 'Three late Elizabethan succession tracts', in Jean-Christophe Mayer (ed.), *The Succession Struggle in Late Elizabethan England: Politics, Polemics and Cultural Representations* (Montpellier, 2004), pp. 91–117 (ref. p. 95).

7 Gerard Kilroy (ed.), *The Epigrams of Sir John Harington* (Aldershot, 2009), p. 196. Contemporary manuscripts of this poem survive in the hands of Sir Thomas Tresham (BL, Additional MS 39829, fo. 93) and John Stow (BL, Harley MS 367, fo. 144), suggesting a significant Catholic or crypto-Catholic readership.

8 Thomas Holland, *Panegyris D. Elizabethae…A Sermon Preached at Pauls in London the 17. of November Ann. Dom. 1599* (Oxford, 1601), sig. G1^v.

9 David Colclough, *Freedom of Speech in Early Stuart England* (Cambridge, 2005), p. 86.

10 Sir John Harington, *A Treatise on the Succession to the Crown (AD 1602)*, ed. C. R. Markham (London, 1880), p. 51.

11 Speech by Lord Keeper Egerton, 1599, TNA, SP12/273, fo. 60.

12 Cornwallis to Hobart, 21 Nov 1595, quoted in Jason Scott-Warren, 'News, sociability, and bookbuying in early modern England: the letters of Sir Thomas Cornwallis', *The Library*, 7th series, 1 (2000), 381–402 (ref. p. 393).

13 Stephen Gosson, *The Trumpet of Warre* (London, 1598), sig. G5^r.

14 Henry Smith, *The Magistrates Scripture* (London, 1590), sig. A2^v (p. 2). A contemporary

manuscript of the sermon, entitled 'A sermon preached before the L. Maior, taken by charactery' and with some textual variations from the printed edition, is in BL, Lansdowne MS 377, fos 67–85.

15 Thomas Fuller, *The Church-History of Britain* (London, 1655), X, 69 (sig. 413ʳ).

16 John Harington, *A Supplie or Addicion to the Catalogue of Bishops to the yeare 1608*, ed. R. H. Miller (Potomac, Maryland, 1979), pp. 151–3. On Harington's anecdotes and their interpretation, see Jason Scott-Warren, 'Harington's gossip', in Susan Doran and Thomas S. Freeman (eds), *The Myth of Elizabeth* (Basingstoke, 2003), pp. 221–41.

17 Extracts from the sermon survive in the papers of Anthony Bacon (LPL, MS 656, fo. 369) and Robert Cecil (Hatfield House, CP 39/106–8).

18 Anthony Rudd, *A Sermon Preached at Richmond before Queene Elizabeth of Famous Memorie, upon the 28 of March 1598* (London, 1603), pp. 10, 30 (sigs B5ᵛ, C7ᵛ). See also Chapter 5 in this volume.

19 Rudd to Cecil, 9 April 1596, Hatfield House, CP 39/108 (*HMC Sal*, VI, p. 139).

20 On early modern prosopopeia, see Gavin Alexander, 'Prosopopoeia: the speaking figure', in Sylvia Adamson, Gavin Alexander and Katrin Ettenhuber (eds), *Renaissance Figures of Speech* (Cambridge, 2007), pp. 97–112.

21 Harington, *Supplie or Addicion*, p. 172.

22 Natalie Mears, *Queenship and Political Discourse in the Elizabethan Realms* (Cambridge, 2005), pp. 133–4.

23 Rudd, *Sermon Preached at Richmond*, preface, A2ʳ.

24 R. P. Sorlien (ed.), *The Diary of John Manningham* (Hanover, NH, 1976), p. 194. I am not convinced by James Shapiro's suggestion that this refers to a sermon on a different occasion: see his *1599: A Year in the Life of William Shakespeare* (London, 2005), p. 88.

25 Robinson's sermon is in LPL, MS 113, fos 87–98. It cannot be precisely dated, but probably predates 1598, when Robinson was appointed Bishop of Carlisle. A reference to the universities (fo. 95ᵛ) suggests that this is an Oxford sermon, though the possibility of its being a Paul's Cross sermon cannot be ruled out.

26 On the Elizabeth-as-Deborah trope, including the ways in which it could be used to reprove the Queen for falling short of the biblical ideal, see Alexandra Walsham, '"A very Deborah?" The myth of Elizabeth I as a providential monarch', in Doran and Freeman, *Myth of Elizabeth*, pp. 143–68.

27 Chamberlain to Carleton, 23 August 1599, N. E. McClure (ed.), *Letters of John Chamberlain* (Philadelphia, 1939), I, p. 83.

28 Examination of Richard Pearne, 15 August 1599, TNA, SP12/272, fo. 78, calendared in *CSPDom 1598–1601*, pp. 295–6.

29 The dossier on Myriell's case is in LPL, MS 3470, fos 208–15. The Thomas Myriell who published several printed sermons and compiled the musical collection 'Tristitiae Remedium' (BL, Additional MS 29372–7) is now thought to be a younger man of the same name; see Pamela Willetts, 'The identity of Thomas Myriell', *Music & Letters*, 53 (1972), 431–3.

30 Bodl, MS Rawlinson, C79. The manuscript can be assigned to Coventry as the majority of the sermons are ascribed to Dr Hinton (William Hinton, vicar of St Michael's and Archdeacon of Coventry). The copyist, who signs himself 'Richard Willes of the Citie',

may be the Richard Wills whose son Samuel, born and educated in Coventry, was later rector of Birmingham and one of the ejected ministers in 1662: see A. G. Matthews, *Calamy Revised* (Oxford, 1934), p. 534.

31 BL, Sloane MS 2023, fo. 60[v].

32 Jeremy L. Smith, *Thomas East and Music Publishing in Renaissance England* (Oxford, 2003), p. 103.

33 Scott-Warren, 'Harington's gossip', p. 226.

34 Peter Wentworth, *A Pithie Exhortation to her Maiestie for Establishing her Successor to the Crowne Whereunto is added a Discourse Containing the Authors Opinion of the True and Lawfull Successor to Her Maiestie* ([Edinburgh,] 1598), p. 2 (1st pag.). Whyte to Sidney, 3 and 17 October 1599, *HMC De L'Isle & Dudley*, II, pp. 398, 403.

35 Harington, *Supplie or Addicion*, p. 171.

36 Wentworth, *Pithie Exhortation*, pp 14–15 (1st pag.). See Chapter 3 in this volume.

37 Patrick Collinson, 'Biblical rhetoric: the English nation and national sentiment in the prophetic mode', in Collinson, *This England: Essays on the English Nation and Commonwealth in the Sixteenth Century* (Manchester, 2011), pp. 167–92 (ref. p. 178).

38 Sermon on Psalm 122: 6, preached on 20 March 1602–3, Bodl, MS Rawlinson, C79, fos 174[r–v].

Chapter 9

Hamlet and succession

Richard Dutton

There are those who think that the late long First Folio *Hamlet* is a messy author's expansion of the short, stern early quarto, but they are a minority. — *Adam Gopnik*

Mapping [genetic differences between species of humans] is, in principle, pretty straightforward – no harder, say, than comparing rival editions of *Hamlet*. — *Elizabeth Kolbert*[1]

The question of who was to succeed Elizabeth I – and how – hung over the drama of her reign from its first major work, *Gorboduc, or Ferrex and Porrex*, to the eve of her death. The tragedy composed by Thomas Sackville and Thomas Norton was first performed by the Gentlemen of the Inner Temple in their Great Hall on Twelfth Night 1562. On 18 January it was performed again, at Whitehall, before the Queen, accompanied with a masque. As Henry James and Greg Walker have shown, 'the composite entertainment offered a direct intervention in the political controversy surrounding Elizabeth's marriage plans (or lack of them) and the uncertainty of the succession'.[2] Drawing upon an eye-witness account of the Inner Temple performance preserved among the papers of the courtier and administrator Robert Beale, they demonstrate that these theatricals were specifically understood to back the suit of Robert Dudley (later Earl of Leicester) for Elizabeth's hand, against that of King Eric of Sweden. As the commentator puts it, 'yt was better for the Quene to marye with the L[ord] R[obert] then with the K[ing] of Sweden'.[3]

The play enjoyed a significant afterlife in print and probably in performance. It was printed in octavo in 1565, in a much improved 'authorized' text in 1570, and twice in quarto in 1590. With each reprint the original performance would have receded further from memory, but the general messages remained clear enough: the need to ensure a secure succession as the only remedy against civil war (one version appeared in a collection called *The Serpent of Division*[4]), with the strong suggestion that marriage and the begetting of children was a desirable option. By 1590 marriage was hardly to be contemplated for Elizabeth, and certainly not children. But she steadfastly refused to discuss the succession and resented it when others did. So the resonances of the last recorded performance of *Gorboduc* during her reign must have been very different.

On 7 September 1601 Lord Mountjoy, Lord Deputy of Ireland in succession to the executed Earl of Essex, had members of his entourage perform the play in the Great Hall of Dublin Castle.[5] Dublin and the Pale were virtually the only parts of Ireland where the English writ still ran. Hugh O'Neill, Earl of Tyrone, and Hugh Roe O'Donnell, now in open alliance with Spanish troops, controlled the rest of it after eight years of fighting. The disaster in Ireland perhaps presaged worse to come in England. The aging Queen had ignored all the play's advice. It can only have reinforced the irony that Sackville was not only still alive but one of her principal advisors – now Lord Buckhurst and her Lord Treasurer. As young men he and Norton had voiced the aspirations of many within the Protestant regime. But she had never married and had never settled the succession. And with no agreed successor, civil war seemed only too likely if Spain and Scotland interceded to press their own claims.

Between the early and late performances of *Gorboduc*, Elizabethan drama remained obsessed with issues of succession, of the civil wars and tyrants generated if it was not handled well. The Brute myth was an inexhaustible resource. The Admiral's Men had at least two plays called *The Conquest of Brute*, while William Haughton wrote them a new *Ferrex and Porrex*. The Queen's Men had *King Leir*. Shakespeare, of course, wrote obsessively about the English civil wars of the fifteenth century and the search for stable monarchy from Richard II to Richard III. More recent civil wars in France, as analogues, supplied Marlowe with *The Massacre at Paris*, while Henslowe's *Diary* records what seem to be four plays on the subject. It also records what seem to be four plays on the great Roman civil war between Caesar and Pompey. In the midst of this obsession 'R. Doleman's' *A Conference about the Next Succession* (1594/5) caused a wide stir, though officially banned in England. It mischievously implied that the Infanta of Spain had the strongest claim to the English throne, and made provocative suggestions to the effect that Lord Burghley supported Lady Arbella Stuart, while its dedication to Essex intimated that he had a historic responsibility as Earl Marshal to determine a disputed succession. Of course, history ruled otherwise. But Essex's own futile rebellion on 8 February 1601 could only have reinforced fears about what would actually happen when death finally deposed Elizabeth.

In such an atmosphere these issues hung over many other, less obvious fictions. Shakespeare's romantic comedies replay with ever-greater urgency a wish-fulfilment that Elizabeth had married. The spinsterly Beatrice in *Much*

Ado (*ca* 1598) is belatedly tricked into marrying Benedick, which helps seal the discord within Messina, a city at war without. Rosalind's 'holiday' exile in Arden in *As You Like It* (*ca* 1599) is inextricably linked with the process of restoring her father to his throne and thereby becoming once more its legitimate heir (but not before marrying a tried-and-tested husband). Illyria in *Twelfth Night* (*ca* 1601) is trapped in a loveless, childless stasis, ruled over by a mooning duke and a mourning 'Madonna'; plucky Viola injects fresh life, but the marriages this generates (including her own) are so perfunctory as to be literally incredible. We are left with the inescapable anti-romantic truth that the rain it raineth every day. Shakespeare never wrote in this mode again and had already begun the great change towards tragedy, where his theme more often than not is regime change – from republic to empire in Rome, or the obliteration of the royal line in Denmark, Britain and (almost) Scotland.

All these plays were licensed and (where necessary) censored by Edmund Tilney, who as Master of the Revels oversaw court and London theatricals through the last half of Elizabeth's reign and into James's. Tilney established his literary credentials by publishing *The Flower of Friendshippe*, a humanist text in the mode of Castiglione's *Book of the Courtier*, extolling the virtues of marriage. It was dedicated to his distant cousin, the Queen, and was immediately popular, going through three editions in 1568; four subsequent editions appeared, the last in 1587. His advice, like Sackville's, had been ignored. As he licensed Shakespeare's plays for performance, and weighed up their suitability for presentation at court, there can be little doubt that he appreciated their coded anxiety, and perhaps helped to channel them appropriately.

HAMLET

Hamlet, of all plays, is deeply informed by succession anxieties. The play begins with a new king and replays obsessively the tale of how he came to the throne by murdering his brother; it depicts an attempt by Laertes, seeking to avenge his father, which could easily have ended with the overthrow of Claudius; but it ends instead with Claudius's death by other means and replacement by young Fortinbras of Norway, passing over the also dead Hamlet, 'Th' expectation, and *Rose* of the *faire* state'.[6] It is a sustained demonstration of how *not* to do it.

A good deal of this is inherent in the material that the Elizabethans inherited from Saxo Grammaticus and François de Belleforest, which I discuss below, and this doubtless helps to explain why they revisited it. But the figure of Fortinbras is new and distinctive in the only Elizabethan version to have survived, Shakespeare's play. Fortinbras complicates succession issues radically by translating what had been an intra-family revenge plot into one of regime change. In what follows, therefore, I shall be concentrating on his role in the play as a marker of what the play had to say in its own time about the succession question.

But I am getting ahead of myself. When I say 'the play', I am glossing over the fact that this is not just one text, but three – a first quarto (Q1) published in 1603; a second (Q2), some copies of which are dated 1604 and others 1605; and a version in the 1623 folio (F) of Shakespeare's *Comedies, Histories and Tragedies*. Long editorial tradition, which has only recently begun to change, treated all of these texts as deriving ultimately from a single Shakespearean original, which suffered various forms of abuse as it was transmitted to posterity. It was considered legitimate, therefore, to conflate them in a putative reconstruction of that original.[7] And these assumptions linger in the general consciousness (see the epigraph by Adam Gopnik). I strongly doubt that explanation of the origins of the three texts. I believe each version represents (inadequately, perhaps, in the case of Q1) the play at different stages of development, during which it underwent at least two significant revisions. Each version therefore needs to be treated as a text in its own right, especially to tease out the differences evident between them on the matter of succession.

The issue of the relationship between the three texts is reviewed – and, to my mind resolved – in masterly fashion by Roslyn Knutson, in one of the most liberating documents ever written on the play. Concentrating on the passages in the different versions about the boy actors (only in Q1 and F – there is no equivalent in Q2), advanced to explain why the players are travelling, she concludes:

> the manuscript Shakespeare wrote in 1599–1600 was altered in a process of deletions and additions that produced Q1, Q2, and F (more or less directly, at different times, for different reasons)...the question is not *whether* Shakespeare's manuscript was revised but *when* and *in what ways*. I suggest the following textual history: a passage very like the 'humour of the children' passage existed in the *Hamlet* that was staged at the Globe in 1600; that passage was cut by 1604 and its place filled with the line about an inhibition, caused by an innovation; at a still later date (*circa* 1606), the 'little eyases' passage was added in the place formerly occupied by the 'humour of the children' passage in the *Hamlet* of 1600.[8]

The superficial resemblance between the references in Q1 and F to the boy actors long fuelled the assumption that both passages derived from one mother-text. 'Gilderstone' in Q1 explains that the players are on the road because 'noveltie carries it away, / For the principall publike audience that / Came to them, are turned to private playes, / And to the humour of children'. 'Rosincrance', in a much longer passage in F, tells Hamlet that 'there is Sir an ayrie of Children, little Yases, that crye out on the top of question'.[9] There is a big difference between 'noveltie' being the reason for drawing away audiences and 'crye[ing] out on the top of question', making a scandalous noise like fledgling hawks. Knutson convincingly suggests that the former relates to the reopening of the indoor boy theatres – Paul's and the Children of the Queen's Chapel – in 1599/1600, after ten years of inactivity; while the latter refers to the notoriety of the Children of the Blackfriars around 1606–8, as they staged scandal after scandal – Daniel's *Philotas*; Chapman, Jonson and Marston's *Eastward Ho!*; Day's *The Isle of Gulls*; Chapman's *Byron* plays; and others.[10] Shakespeare was here joining Thomas Heywood who, in *An Apology for Actors*, similarly decried this dangerous policy.[11] Two senior figures from the adult theatres admonished the Blackfriars management for their provocative policies, which potentially threatened all their livelihoods.

Significantly, both of these dates miss the 1601 to which conflationists most commonly assign the supposed original play. That assignment is largely because it was thought that the 'little Yases' passage referred to the so-called War of the Theatres, which reached its height in that year with Jonson's *Poetaster* for the Children of the Chapel and Dekker's *Satiromastix*, a shared project of the Lord Chamberlain's Men and Paul's Boys.[12] It was also assigned that date because it was assumed that the passage in Q2, which replaces the passages about boy players in both other versions (*Rosencraus*: 'I thinke their inhibition, comes by meanes of the late innovasion' (TLN 1379–80), referred to the Essex rebellion and so was written after it. In both of these assumptions, I shall argue, the conflationists were wrong.

What I want to add to Knutson's analysis is a different mechanism to explain how and why the play was revised as it was, and especially how Q2 came into being, and at such gargantuan length. Q1 is only 2,154 lines long, notably short by comparison with most of Shakespeare's tragedies and histories.[13] Q2 *Hamlet* accurately proclaims itself to be 'Newly imprinted and enlarged to almost as much againe as it was, according to the true and perfect Coppie'. At 3,668 lines it is the longest text in the Shakespeare canon. My explanation for this dramatic 'enlargement' is that Q2 was prepared for performance in the one venue in early seventeenth-century England where length was no object: the court, and in this case specifically the court of James I. I have no space here to elaborate on this theory, which I have recently outlined elsewhere.[14] But the fact of revision of texts for court performance is clearly spelled out in Henslowe's *Diary*, where revisions several times elicited payments amounting to half the costs of a new play, suggesting significant labour.[15] And there is a good deal of circumstantial evidence that the outcome was – in some cases at least – the creation of versions of plays that would, without cuts, take markedly longer to perform than the versions used on the commercial stage. If we need to ask why the actors would go to this trouble and cost for the £10 fee they received for court performances, we need only remember that the actors concerned were those who, by the court's authority, had privileged performing rights in the lucrative London region. This was a mutually beneficial arrangement, and the whole process was overseen by the man who managed the Revels season at court, the Master of the Revels, Edmund Tilney. Thomas Heywood speaks of the visits made by the actors to Tilney's quarters in the former Priory of St John in Clerkenwell, 'the office of the Revels, where our Court playes have been in late daies yearely rehersed, perfected, and corrected before they come to the publike view of the Prince and the Nobility'.[16]

Q1 and succession

Q1 *Hamlet* is, in Knutson's analysis, clearly an Elizabethan play, written around the time *Julius Caesar* contemplated the horrors of regime change and *As You Like It* conjured a pastoral comedy from the same concerns. It was entered in the Stationers' Register on 26 July 1602 and so certainly antedated the Queen's death.[17] What relationship the text printed in 1603 had with any earlier *Hamlet* plays there is no way of knowing, but a play certainly existed by 1589, when Thomas Nashe satirically evoked 'English Seneca', who 'will afford you whole Hamlets, I should say handfuls of tragical speeches'.[18] This may have been the same *Hamlet* that Philip Henslowe records having received a single performance at Newington Butts in June 1594, and again the one that Thomas Lodge saw which caused him to write in 1596 about the 'ghost which cried so miserably at the Theatre, like an oyster-wife, *Hamlet, revenge*'.[19]

Knowing no more than these traces, however, we cannot know one thing which I have suggested is critical to Shakespeare's version of *Hamlet* as a succession play: who added the figure of Fortinbras? In the earliest tellings of the Hamlet legend, to be found in Saxo Grammaticus's twelfth-century *Historiae Danicae*, there is no parallel to Fortinbras, because Amleth overcomes Feng (the ur-Claudius) and then is acclaimed king himself. And in this respect the French prose version that Shakespeare himself probably read, that by François de Belleforest in his *Histoires Tragiques* (first published 1570), followed Saxo. The death of Hamlet in pursuing revenge for his father's murder, and with it the extinction of the Danish royal line, leaving a vacuum filled by Fortinbras, first appears in print in Shakespeare's versions of the play.

I describe the addition of Fortinbras to the plot as 'critical', because it is the one narrative change which allows the succession issues in the play to map suggestively onto those of England as the reign of Elizabeth neared its end. The Tudor dynasty was bound to die with her. The search was not just for a new prince but for a new line of princes. And there was every chance that this would not emerge from within the kingdom but would come – perhaps be imposed – from abroad. A victorious, living Hamlet at the end of the play thus made no suggestive sense at all. As Susan Doran and Paulina Kewes explain in Chapter 1, there was no shortage of claimants to the English throne which Elizabeth would leave vacant, including the heirs of Edward Seymour, Earl of Hertford through the Suffolk line, Lady Arbella Stuart and the Spanish

Infanta. But the most credible claim on grounds of bloodline was always that of Elizabeth's 'cousin of Scotland', James VI.

The ultimate role of Fortinbras in all three versions of Shakespeare's *Hamlet* is to pick up the pieces when Hamlet himself dies, to assume the throne of Denmark, and implicitly in the not-too-distant future – when the aged king, his uncle, dies – to assume also the throne of Norway. It is little remarked that Denmark–Norway enjoyed a personal union of the crowns between 1536 and 1814, with a single king reigning over two politically distinct countries. There were other instances of this in Shakespeare's day, but it spoke directly to the situation of James VI of Scotland, whose queen was from Denmark. When James finally did succeed to the English throne, he belatedly emulated his brother-in-law, Christian IV of Denmark–Norway, in bearing two crowns, those of a northern and a southern kingdom. Fortinbras in the play of *Hamlet* (Fortenbrasse in Q1) foreshadows that outcome.

It is difficult to believe that contemporary audiences of Q1 did not see what we might call this wish-fulfilment element in the dramatic retelling of the old tale, though it is not heavily underscored. The familiar path of Fortenbrasse's career is sketched in: he plans to avenge his father's death at the hands of old Hamlet by attacking Denmark; following an embassy from the Danish king to old Norway he is ordered not to do this, and chooses instead to use his troops against the Poles; we briefly see him for the first time on Danish soil, seeking the pass he has negotiated through the country (TLN 2735–43; 4.4.1–8); finally he appears at Elsinore after the deaths of the Queen, Leartes, the King and Hamlet. And he stakes his claim almost as an afterthought:

> I have some rights of memory to this kingdome,
> Which now to claime my leisure doth invite mee: (TLN 3885–7; 5.2.389–90)

It is a functional solution, hardly a metaphysical one.

Q2 and succession: 'inhibition' and 'innovasion'

The Q2 text, by contrast, invests the whole issue of succession with metaphysical circumstance, a good deal of it focused on Fortenbrasse (as he here remains). I suggest that this can best be explained by the circumstances of its composition, which I further suggest were dictated by the expectation of presenting the play at the court of Fortenbrasse himself, James I. As I have already argued, the extreme length of the text is best explained by court presentation. To pin this to the court of James I, we need to consider its likely dating, which again is best deduced from the text's explanation of why the players are travelling. In this version we hear nothing of 'noveltie', 'the humour of children' or of 'little yases'. We are, rather, confronted with a terse account which contains a famous crux.

Rosencraus explains: 'I thinke their inhibition, comes by the meanes of the late innovasion' (Q2, TLN 1379–80; 2.2.332–3). 'Inhibition' and 'innovasion' have both been subjected to extreme scrutiny. The former seems to refer to a ban on playing, and there have been numerous attempts to identify this as a topical allusion to one in the real Elizabethan/Jacobean world.[20] Many of the conflationists, convinced that the references to the boy actors in both Q1 and F pointed to the War of the Theatres in 1601, wanted to construe 'innovasion' as an 'uprising' of some sort, which would most likely point to the Essex rebellion of February in that year. It seemed logical, therefore, to try to find an 'inhibition' in the same time frame, though in fact nothing we know of fits that bill. But if, as I argue, Q2 dates from a court revision of 1603/4, the strongest and most logical connotation of 'innovasion' would be something like 'new regime'.

In fact this suggestion was first made as long ago as 1785 by John Monck Mason, who found such a usage in the Shirley play, *The Coronation*. The king, Demetrius, has been deposed in favour of someone masquerading as his elder brother, and two gentlemen discuss the outcome:

> PHILOCLES: The new King has possession.
> LISANDER: And is like
> To keep't, we are alone, what dost thinke of
> This innovation? ist not a fine Jigge?[21]

As Mason suggested, this probably means 'the late *change* of government', for which of course in *Hamlet* the accession of James I would constitute a real-life equivalent.[22] For many years, however, the primacy usually accorded the folio text – where both the inhibition/innovation and the 'little Yases' passages appear, misleadingly pointing to 1601 – made Mason's suggestion unthinkable. Yet in that context we have a perfect accompanying 'inhibition'.

The London theatres closed on 19 March 1603 in anticipation of Elizabeth's death. They may well not have reopened that year. Although the Lords of the realm proclaimed James king immediately after the old Queen died, there was anxiety as people waited to see if his accession was contested. Plague broke out in April and was certainly bad enough by 19 May to have closed the theatres, since the King's Men's new patent contains a proviso about their licence to play only 'when the infection of the plague shall decrease'.[23] And it apparently did not do that until Easter 1604. It is also noteworthy that Philip Henslowe recorded on 5 May 1603: 'we leafte of playe now at the kynges cominge'.[24] James had reached Cecil's estate at Theobalds on his way south from Scotland on 3 May and entered London on the 7th. It would be natural to try to forestall major disturbances. Between the change of monarchs and the plague there were clearly overlapping 'inhibitions'.

So if the company played Q2 during the Revels season of 1603/4 it would have been immediately intelligible that the players in *Hamlet* were touring because of an 'inhibition' that followed an 'innovasion'. Their King's Men counterparts who played them had been doing just that earlier in the year, as the title-page of Q1 tells us: 'As it hath beene diverse times acted by his Highnesse servants in the Cittie of London: as also in the two Universities of Cambridge and Oxford, and else-where'. This wry piece of in-joking was probably all the more pointed in that the King's Men almost certainly had to travel further to perform than they normally did to perform at court, a consequence of the court seeking to avoid the worst of the plague. Their first performance that Revels season was at the Earl of Pembroke's estate at Wilton, a journey so exceptional that John Heminge was paid £30 'for the paynes and expences of himself and the rest of the company in comming from Mortelake in the countie of Surrie unto the courte aforesaid and there p'senting before his ma[jestie] one playe'.[25] But that apart, all bar one of their other court performances that season were at Hampton Court, the furthest flung of the royal palaces regularly in use, some eleven miles upstream from London.[26]

Do any other circumstances give us reason to suppose that *Hamlet* was performed at court in 1603/4? Ordinarily we would have little chance of answering that, because so few of the records of the *titles* of plays performed at court have survived. But by the sheerest good luck we know what was performed there the following Revels season, 1604/5.[27] That Christmastide the King's Men performed eleven times in all, and the plays were *Othello* (opening the season on All Saints, 1 November), *Merry Wives, Measure for Measure* (St Stephen's Day, 26 December), *The Comedy of Errors, Love's Labour's Lost, Henry V, Every Man Out of His Humour, Every Man In His Humour* (Candlemas, 2 February), *The Spanish Maze* (an anonymous, lost play), and *The Merchant of Venice* twice, repeated by the King's command (Shrove Sunday and Tuesday, 10 and 12 February). The number of performances is staggering – almost twice as many as in the company's busiest Elizabethan season (1596/7), and three times the number in a usual year. And they had performed exactly the same number of plays in 1603/4. That is, over two seasons they performed 22 times – perhaps 20 plays, allowing for repetitions.

The royal demand for drama – indeed *fresh* drama – was a concern even of the King's ministers. As early as January 1605 Sir Walter Cope, one of Sir Robert Cecil's agents, reported to him: 'I have sent and bene all thys morning huntyng for players jugglers and such kynde of creaturs...Burbage is come, and says ther ys no new [King's Men's] playe that the Queene hath not seene, but they have revyved an olde one cawled *Loves Labore Lost*, which for wytt and mirthe he sayes will please her exceedingly'.[28]

The next remarkable fact, other than the sheer volume, is how many of the 1604/5 plays were by Shakespeare – eight, including the repetition. It is as if, faced with the need to impress the new royals, the King's Men pulled out the family silver, the repertory of their star 'ordinarie poet'.[29] They would have had guidance on this from Tilney, who made the final decisions about what went on, but probably also from the one new, sharing member of the company when they reformed as the King's Men. Laurence Fletcher had spent several years in Edinburgh with a troupe of players and entertained the then James VI of Scotland. His knowledge of the King and Queen and their tastes must have been invaluable. At all events, if 1604/5 is any guide at all, it is a fair guess that a *further* six or seven Shakespeare plays had been performed in 1603/4. If popularity or reputation is anything to go by it is reasonable to suppose that these would have included *Richard III*, *Henry IV Part I*, *Romeo and Juliet*, *A Midsummer Night's Dream* – and *Hamlet*.

Let us suppose, then, that Edmund Tilney, drawing on his unrivalled knowledge of the drama of the day and contemplating the need to cater for a greatly expanded Revels season, suggested to the King's Men that *Hamlet* was a play ripe for revision and a court performance. How might Shakespeare have set about it? John Kerrigan has given the best account of the revision of early modern play-texts in his essay 'Revision, adaptation, and the Fool in *King Lear*'.[30]

> The available evidence strongly suggests that when, in the early seventeenth century, one man of the theatre overhauled another's play, he cut, inserted and substituted sizeable pieces of text without altering the details of his precursor's dialogue. Revising authors, by contrast, though they sometimes worked just with large textual fractions, tended to tinker, introducing small additions, small cuts and indifferent single-word substitutions. A survey of rewritten plays reveals two kinds of textual variation then, one rarely authorial in origin, the other characteristically so. (p. 196)

We cannot know how exactly Shakespeare behaved in making the revision that produced Q2 *Hamlet*, since what he revised would have been the manuscript that ultimately lay behind Q1, not Q1 itself. But Shakespeare seems characteristically to have been a 'tinkering' reviser, what Kerrigan also dubbed a 'fidgeting authorial reviser' (p. 209). A classic demonstration of this would be the differences between the first quarto and folio texts of *Richard III*, which can best be accounted for by a thorough, 'tinkering' re-write.[31] The theatres were, as we have seen, closed for most of 1603. If Shakespeare did not tour with the rest of the company during this period, he would have had plenty of time to conduct a thorough, 'tinkering' revision of *Hamlet* before the first Revels season of the new reign.

If I am right about this, Q2 (and indeed F) are both Jacobean texts, revised when the outcome of the succession was a *fait accompli* and it was possible to review events with some equanimity. Q1 is an Elizabethan play, as fraught with anxieties about regime change as *Gorboduc* or *King Leir*. But it contains none of the particularities on the issue that we find in Q2 or F: nothing alluding to the Essex rebellion (which, on my dating, had not happened when it was written), nothing about Hamlet's sense of having been cheated of the throne, nothing about an 'inhibition' or an 'innovasion', little about the workings of providence, little to underscore the parallels/contrasts between Hamlet and Fortenbrasse. These are all part of the Q2 revision.

When Shakespeare revised the play it is apparent, for example, that he approached it with classical precedents in mind. It is evident even in the naming of the characters. Q1 had set the precedent of mixing names of a Danish or Anglo-Saxon derivation (Hamlet himself, Gertred, Voltemar) with Roman ones (Horatio, Marcellus) and Greek (Leartes), and the oddly unexplained Corambis, which nevertheless *sounds* classical.[32] But Shakespeare tilts the balance further towards the classical in Q2 by renaming Corambis Polonius, which perhaps has something to do with the play's interest in Poland but is unequivocally Latin in form. Much more significantly, however, he gives the king the name of Claudius – the Roman emperor who married his own niece, Agrippina, the mother of his eventual successor, Nero. The incest theme and the uncle/stepfather role make this instantly appropriate, as we might expect an educated courtly audience to appreciate.[33] There is little doubt but that King James, sternly tutored in his youth by George Buchanan, would have known about Claudius as one whom Erasmus dubbed, in *The Education of a Christian Prince*, a type of the bad ruler. More generally the naming of Claudius focuses us on the fact that Elsinore is reliving the internecine (and sexually excessive) power struggles of imperial Rome.

This is further underlined by the first substantial interpolation in the revised text (TLN 124+1 to 124+18; 1.1.108–25). The passage includes Horatio's recitation of the portents said (in Plutarch and elsewhere) to have occurred before the assassination of Julius Caesar:

> In the most high and palmy state of Rome.
> A little ere the mightiest *Julius* fell
> The graves stood tennantlesse, and the sheeted dead
> Did squeake and gibber in the Roman streets
> As stares with traines of fier, and dewes of blood
> Disasters in the sun…(+6 to +11)

It is commonly observed that Shakespeare had something of *Julius Caesar* in mind – written no more than a year earlier than Q1 *Hamlet* – when he has Corambis recall, 'My lord, I did act *Julius Caesar*, I was killed in the Capitoll' (TLN 1958–9), foreshadowing his own death. But Horatio's Q2 passage takes us far beyond Polonius's personal fate.

Disturbance in the macrocosm often mirrors disturbance in the microcosm in Shakespeare's plays at moments of regime change (e.g. *King Lear*, *Macbeth*). At such moments the affairs of men are closely in touch with otherworldly forces. Of course the Ghost flags something of this in all versions of *Hamlet*. But nothing in Q1 matches this broader reference to the definitive self-made ruler who was never quite a king, but might have been. The assassination of Julius Caesar prompted the archetypal historical example of a succession by civil war, as Rome pivoted between its republican past and (as it proved) imperial future. Horatio's words similarly look in two directions. He identifies the Ghost as 'prologue to the *Omen* coming on' (TLN 124+16; 1.1.123). But it is actually the tale of a murderous regime change that has *already* secretly happened that the Ghost unfolds, prologue to his own poisoning. This will preoccupy the play at least until 'The Mousetrap', if not until Hamlet's confrontation with his mother. If the Ghost is indeed an omen of *further* regime change, it is a very early and indirect one. All these dimensions may be implicit in Q1, but it is Q2 that realizes them.

As Q2 is the first text to discuss 'innovasion', it is also the first to raise the question of how Claudius succeeded to the throne rather than (young) Hamlet. The answer, of course, is that Denmark historically had an elective monarchy, albeit one that tended to make its selection within the same royal family. A court whose Queen was sister of the King of Denmark might be expected to know this. It is never an issue in Q1. The closest we get to it is Hamlet's complaint 'Why I want preferment', to which Rossencraft replies 'I thinke not so my lord' (Q1, TLN 979–80). This reappears in Q2 in much fuller, 'tinkered' form, and in a different place:

> Sir I lacke advancement.
> ROSENCRAUS: How can that be when you have the the voyce of the king himselfe for your succession in Denmarke (TLN 2210–12).

This reiterates what Claudius had publicly said on his first appearance, repeatedly claiming Hamlet as his son: 'for let the world take note / You are the most imediate to our throne' (TLN 290–1; 1.2.108–9). The voice of the reigning monarch was obviously expected to weigh heavily in the choice of his successor.

Q2 Hamlet does not, therefore, challenge Claudius's right to the throne until he knows that he only acquired it by murder. When he tells Rosencraus that he 'lacke[s] advancement' he wraps his resentment in the language of any ambitious courtier. But when he unburdens himself to his mother in her bedroom he denounces Claudius as 'a vice of Kings, / A cut-purse of the Empire' who 'stole' the crown (Q2, TLN 2477–9; 3.4.98–9), and he later complains to Horatio how he 'Pop't in betweene th'election and my hopes' (Q2, TLN 3569; 5.2.65). None of this is in Q1, indicating how much more fully Q2 considers the rights and wrongs of succession, and the mechanisms that affect it, even in a constitution like this, which was alien to the English.

Another marked omission in Q1 *Hamlet* had been the lack of any reference to revolt or rebellion. In itself this does not prove that this version antedates the Essex rebellion, since *any* reference to that would surely have been censored in the months after the event.[34] But it is suggestive. Q1 shows Leartes returning alone, 'like a most desperate gamster' (TLN 2891; 4.5.145). Q2 by contrast depicts Laertes returning from Paris 'in a riotous head' (TLN 2841; 4.5.102) and expressly marks it as a 'rebellion [which] lookes so gyant like' (2866) in which Claudius's throne is at stake. He calls for his Swiss mercenary guard (2836; 4.5.98) and the messenger reports that 'the rabble' cry 'choose we, *Laertes* shall be King' (2846). The messenger characterizes this as 'Antiquity forgot, custome not knowne' (2844), an abandonment of the social practices by which kingship has been established and reverenced over the years. When Q2 was performed this could hardly have been received without stirring memories of Essex, whose memory and earldom were rehabilitated under James. The Earl of Southampton, Essex's principal supporter during the rebellion, had been imprisoned for life but was freed on James's accession and restored in honour at court.

In short, Q1 *Hamlet* is not about rebellion at all; and it is only rather perfunctorily about succession – the extinction of the Danish royal family and the transfer of the throne to 'Fortenbrasse' are shown but hardly analysed. In this, the revenge play mirrors the comedies of *ca* 1598–1601, where the anxieties about succession are contained within conventional generic formulae. Q2 *Hamlet* is quite markedly and openly about both rebellion and succession; it also picks up Q1's brief reference to the 'divinitie' which 'doth wall a King' (TLN 2868), making it Claudius's last defence when his Swissers fail and showing how it more generally 'shapes our ends, / Rough hew them how we will' (TLN 3509–10; 5.2.10–11). That is, luxuriating in its greater length, Q2 *Hamlet* contrives to be a reflection on the inscrutable processes by which a throne passes from king to king, about how it evades the threat of rebellion, and follows divine will in (eventually) effecting succession on a fitting heir. An evil king may rule for a time: he may even, ironically, take *Gorboduc* to heart, both marrying and settling the succession, illegitimately wrapped for a time in the 'divinitie' which guards a legitimate monarch. 'T'expectation, and Rose of the faire state' may never achieve Tamburlaine's 'perfect bliss and sole felicity, / The sweet fruition of an earthly crown'.[35] But a proper outcome should never ultimately be in doubt.

The most marked development in Q2 furthering this theme is the enhancement of the role of Fortenbrasse, and most particularly the development of what in modern texts is 4.4, where his army appears, crossing Denmark on its way to Poland. In Q2, Hamlet – *en route* to England with Rosencraus and Guyldensterne – observes the scene, questions a Norwegian captain about the campaign and, incredulous that anyone could go to war for such a small cause, is prompted to another soliloquy: 'How all occasions doe informe against me, / And spur my dull revenge' (TLN 2743+26–7; 4.4.33–4). So a man who veers between rashness and indecision to the point of perplexity observes and reflects upon a man of resolute steadfastness, even where the object hardly warrants it. The capriciousness of Hamlet's condition is underscored by the fact that the next passage of his life is dictated by the improbably romantic intervention of the pirates. Fortenbrasse, by contrast, determines his own fate. And steadfastness eventually wins the day. The dying Hamlet can only 'prophecie th'ellection lights / On *Fortinbrasse*, he has my dying voyce' (TLN 3844; 5.2.355–6; not in Q1), but Fortenbrasse behaves as though he does not intend to wait for any election. Where in Q1 it is his 'leisure' which invites him to claim his 'rights of memory in this kingdome', in Q2 it is his 'vantage'. Fate has made him the right man in the right place; and he has an army to answer any doubters.

This was surely just what James I wanted to hear after his long wait in the wings. Q2 was a version 'augmented' for his first Revels season in his new kingdom, a meditation on the role he was born to play: he is Fortinbras, uniting the kingdoms of England and Scotland, as his dramatic counterpart does those of Norway and Denmark. When his King's Men set out to entertain him, they came to Elsinore (or, very probably, Hampton Court) not driven out by the 'humour of children' or the 'little Yases', but to give proper thanks for their own good fortune in the wake of James's miraculously peaceful succession. In uniting the two crowns he had created a new empire of Great Britain, and this imperial theme of sovereign territories bound together under a single authority was to run throughout Shakespeare's Jacobean plays (*King Lear*, *Antony and Cleopatra*, *The Winter's Tale* and *The Tempest* being only the most obvious examples).

The folio Hamlet, *and after*

Q2 was, however, Fortenbrasse's textual high-water mark in the evolution of *Hamlet*. When Shakespeare revised it to produce the folio text, which (with Knutson) I would date at 1606/8, he did so, in Kerrigan's categorization, as if he were revising someone else's play: 'he cut, inserted and substituted sizeable pieces of text without altering the details of his precursor's dialogue'. So there is relatively little of the 'fidgeting' which characterizes the much more complex transformation of Q1 into Q2. But one major cut and one major insertion stand out. The cut is the whole sixty lines of act 4, scene 4, in which Hamlet observes Fortinbras (as he finally becomes); and the insertion is the 'little Yases' passage (TLN1384–408, 2.2.337–62) by which we may date the revision.[36] The Q2 determination to parallel Fortinbras and Hamlet, and to contrast their fortunes, is relaxed. The succession question is now less topical, and the scandals of the Children of the Blackfriars who 'crye out on the top of the question' (TLN 1387, 2.2.340) steal some of its thunder in the Folio version.

There is evidence, moreover, that Fortinbras's role continued to diminish in public performances of the play over the next half century and more. Q2 was followed by three further quartos that substantially reprinted it, the last in 1637. But in 1676 Sir William Davenant's abridgement of *Hamlet* (often called *The Players' Hamlet*) was published. Based on the 1637 quarto, it nevertheless contained this note 'To the Reader' after the title page:

> This Play being too long to be conveniently Acted, such places as might be least prejudicial to the Plot or Sense, are left out upon the Stage: but that we may no way wrong the incomparable Author, are here inserted according to the Original Copy with this Mark ".

This represented the text as Davenant had worked on it for Thomas Betterton, who first played the lead in 1661, so it may be an entirely Restoration creation. But Davenant was the most significant bridge between pre-Civil War theatre and Restoration practice, and it is not unlikely that the text represented something approximating the play as it had been staged in the 1630s – if indeed not significantly earlier.[37] Q2 (and indeed F) were always 'too long to be conveniently Acted' – except, as I have argued, at court.[38]

When we analyse what Davenant left out as 'least prejudicial to the Plot or Sense' the first thing that strikes us is that '[t]he omissions include nearly all references to Fortinbras before his final entrance (including Hamlet's 'How all occasions do inform against me' soliloquy in act 4, scene 4.)'.[39] Indeed his name and Polish expedition are not voiced until the closing moments of the play, although his father, 'old Fortinbras', is mentioned three times, which would doubtless flag the bare outcome to familiar audiences. It is indeed as if the motivation which had prompted Shakespeare or some earlier Elizabethan to add Fortinbras to the Saxo/Belleforest story had all but disappeared. And the motivation to make him as prominent as he is in Q2 had certainly retreated. He is reduced to the minimal function, even less than in Q1, of filling a gap left by the annihilation of the Danish royal family. Nothing even gives us reason to suppose that the thrones of Denmark and of Norway will eventually merge in his person, since the Norwegian context is left so obscure.[40] By the Restoration, succession is not the key theme in *Hamlet* that it had been for the Elizabethans and early Jacobeans. Other dimensions had begun to assert themselves.

NOTES

1 Adam Gopnik, 'The corrections: abridgment, enrichment, and the nature of art', *The New Yorker*, 22 October 2007, pp. 66–76, at p. 70; Elizabeth Kolbert, 'Sleeping with the enemy', *The New Yorker*, 15 and 22 August 2011, pp. 64–75, at p. 72.

2 Henry James and Greg Walker, 'The politics of *Gorboduc*', *English Historical Review*, 110 (1995), 109–21, at p. 109.

3 James and Walker, 'The politics of *Gorboduc*', pp. 112–13. See also Marie Axton, *The Queen's Two Bodies: Drama and the Elizabethan Succession* (London, 1977), and Norman Jones and Paul Whitfield White, '*Gorboduc* and royal marriage politics: an Elizabethan playgoer's report of the premiere performance', *English Literary Renaissance*, 26 (1996), 3–16.

4 As the 1590 title page proclaims, 'Wherein is contemed the true History *or Mappe of* Romes *overthrowe*, governed by Avuarice, Envye, and Pride, the decaye of Empires be they never so sure … *England* take heede, such chaunce to thee may come'.

5 See Chris Morash, *A History of Irish Theatre, 1601–2000* (Cambridge, 2002), pp. 2–3.

6 Q2 TLN 1808 (3.1.152). The textual complications of *Hamlet* are part of my theme, so it is essential that I quote from the original versions. To help make that manageable I have used Bernice W. Kliman and Paul Bertram (eds), *The Three-Text 'Hamlet': Parallel Texts and the First and Second Quartos and First Folio*, 2nd edn (New York and London, 2003). The through-line numbering system (TLN) was devised for Charlton Hinman's *Norton Facsimile: The First Folio of Shakespeare*, 1st edn (New York, 1968). Kliman and Bertram have used it as the basis of their own line-numbering, relating both the quarto texts (Q1, 1603; Q2, 1604/5) to the folio where correspondences exist. They also give the corresponding act/scene/line numbering from Blakemore Evans (ed.), *The Riverside Shakespeare*, 1st edn (Boston, 1974), to give readers an approximate sense of where to find things in a modern text. I do likewise. Further explanations will be given as necessary.

7 This would be true of any edition before about 1985, and is still commonly found. A classic example of an edition following these principles is Harold Jenkins's Arden 2 *Hamlet* (London, 1982). He scorns Q1, fixes Q2 as the most authoritative copy text, but justifies adding to it, almost exclusively from F (see pp. 74–5). This approach allows him to offer a single date for the play: 'as it has come down to us it belongs to 1601' (p. 13).

8 Roslyn Lander Knutson, '*Hamlet* and company commerce', in her *Playing Companies and Commerce in Shakespeare's Time* (Cambridge, 2001), pp. 103–26, at pp. 112–13.

9 TLN 1386–91; 2.2.339–44. *The Three-Text Hamlet* follows the traditional assumption that the 'yases' passage is a version of the 'humour of the children' passage in Q1, which both Knutson and I would deny. But the TLN faithfully guides the reader to both.

10 The Children of the Queen's Chapel had been reformed in 1604 as the Children of the Queen's Revels (i.e. Queen Anne's). By 1606 they had been stripped of the royal association, presumably because of the scandals. In 1608 their licence was withdrawn altogether. See Richard Dutton, 'The Revels Office and the boy companies, 1600–1613: new perspectives', *English Literary Renaissance*, 32 (2002), 324–51.

11 The Heywood passage (written *ca* 1608/9) is: 'Now to speake of some abuse lately crept into the quality, as an inveighing against the State, the Court, the Law, the Citty, and their governments, with the particularizing of private mens humors (yet alive) Noble-men, & others. I know it distastes many; neither do I any way approve it, nor dare I by any meanes excuse it. The liberty which some arrogate to themselves, committing their bitternesse, and liberall invectives against all estates, to the mouthes of Children, supposing their juniority to be a priviledge for any rayling, be it never so violent, I could advise all such, to curbe and limit this presumed liberty within the

bands of discretion and government'. *An Apology for Actors* (London, 1612), sig. G3ᵛ.

12 See, for example, Jenkins's edition, p. 473; and Joseph Loewenstein, 'Plays agonistic and competitive: the textual approach to Elsinore', *Renaissance Drama* 19 (1988), 63–96.

13 Line-length counts are notoriously unreliable, because people's opinions differ on whether to include stage directions, how to handle prose passages, and so on. For some consistency I have used those offered by Lukas Erne in his *Shakespeare as Literary Dramatist* (Cambridge, 2003). His figures for the so-called 'bad' quartos, like Q1 *Hamlet* appear on p. 194; those for folio and 'good' quarto texts on p. 141.

14 Richard Dutton, 'A Jacobean *Merry Wives?*', *Ben Jonson Journal*, 18 (2011), 1–18.

15 See Roslyn L. Knutson, 'Henslowe's diary and the economics of play revision for revival, 1592–1603', *Theatre Research International*, 10 (1985), 1–18.

16 *An Apology for Actors*, sig. E1ᵛ. The title page of *Love's Labour's Lost* (1598) proclaims it to be *Newly corrected and augmented by W. Shakespere* as well as being *As it was presented before her Highnes this last Christmas*, as if the two facts are linked. Leaving aside the special case of Ben Jonson, who self-consciously wrote and published for a readership as well as performance, no one wrote more plays that have survived in markedly long versions than Shakespeare (some advertised as 'augmented', like the 1599 second quarto of *Romeo and Juliet*, some as 'enlarged' like Q2 *Hamlet*). By the same token, on the admittedly very limited evidence of what plays were actually performed at court during Shakespeare's career, no one else had remotely as many plays performed there.

17 This is consonant with Gabriel Harvey's famous reference to *Hamlet* – along with *Venus and Adonis* and *The Rape of Lucrece* – 'hav[ing] it in them, to please the wiser sort' (cited in Jenkins's edition, p. 4). Other features of that note seem to date it after 1598 and before February 1601, something that causes perplexity to conflationists who want to date the original play later in 1601, after the Essex rebellion.

18 Preface to Robert Greene's *Menaphon*, in *The Works of Thomas Nashe*, ed. R. B. McKerrow, 5 vols (Oxford, 1904–10), vol. 3, p. 315.

19 R. A. Foakes and R. T. Rickert (eds), *Henslowe's Diary* (Cambridge, 1961), p. 21; Thomas Lodge, *Wit's Misery* (London, 1596), p. 56.

20 Knutson gives an excellent review of how critical fashions on this have changed. See '*Hamlet* and company commerce', pp. 115–18.

21 James Shirley, *The Coronation* (London, 1640), H3ʳ. The 1640 quarto credits Fletcher as author and it was reprinted in the second Beaumont and Fletcher folio (1679), where Mason found it. But modern scholarship gives the play to Shirley.

22 John Monck Mason, *Comments on the Last Edition of Shakespeare's Plays* (London, 1785), p. 381.

23 Cited in Andrew Gurr, *The Shakespeare Company* (Cambridge, 2004), p. 254. Shakespeare's company, formerly the Lord Chamberlain's Men, became the King's Men with this new patent.

24 Foakes and Rickert (eds), *Henslowe's Diary*, p. 209.

25 Cited in E. K. Chambers, *The Elizabethan Stage*, 4 vols (Oxford, 1923), vol, 4, p. 168. Hereafter cited parenthetically as *ES*.

26 The only exception was their last performance, at Whitehall – James's preferred residence – on Shrove Sunday.

27 For most years only the Chamber Accounts have survived, recording payments but not titles, but for 1604–5 the Audit Office Accounts (part of the Revels Accounts) have also survived, and they do give us titles. See *ES*, vol. 4, pp. 171–2; see also pp. 136ff for Chambers's thorough review of claims that these might be forgeries.

28 Quoted in *ES*, vol. 4, p. 139. Chambers discusses the trickiness of dating the letter and of squaring Cope's report of what seems to have been a special performance of *Love's Labour's Lost* at a private house with the record of it having been performed at court earlier that month.

29 They did something similar in 1612–13, the Revels season which included the wedding of Princess Elizabeth to the Elector Palatine, when we again have titles. The King's Men were called on to perform 20 plays and eight of them (nine if we include *Cardenio*) were by Shakespeare.

30 In Gary Taylor and Michael Warren (eds), *The Division of the Kingdoms: Shakespeare's Two Versions of 'King Lear'* (Oxford, 1983), pp. 195–239.

31 See, for example, *Richard III*, ed. Anthony Hammond, The Arden Shakespeare (London, 1981), p. 2, for a description of the issues.

32 There are also two with Italianate names, Francisco and Montano (who would unaccountably become Reynaldo in Q2). 'Cornelia' as he appears at TLN 213 could be classical, but it also had a modern Dutch usage. Horatio would be Horatius in true Latin, but was clearly marked out as 'more an antike Roman, Then a Dane' (TLN 3826–7) even in the earliest version. Laertes, the proper and Q2 form, was the father of Odysseus. It is a curiously eclectic mix.

33 The name Claudius is only marked in the stage direction at the head of 1.2 and its first speech prefix. Oddly, it is never voiced. It was widely thought that Claudius was poisoned by Agrippina, so the climax of the play in which Gertrude inadvertently drinks the poison and then Hamlet forces Claudius to drink from the same cup is an ironic twist, made much more pointed by the king's name.

34 *Some* references were censored significantly later. Daniel's *Philotas* was examined by the Privy Council in 1604 expressly because it was felt to shadow the Essex rebellion, and there is good reason to suppose that Chapman's *Byron* plays (1607–8) got into trouble because they 'glanced' at Essex. He remained a dangerous figure to discuss, despite his rehabilitation by James.

35 *Tamburlaine, Part 1*, 2.7.28–9, in E. D. Pendry and J. C. Maxwell (eds), *Christopher Marlowe: Complete Plays and Poems* (London, 1976).

36 F as we have it rather clumsily offers *both* the 'Inhibition [which] comes by meanes of the late Innovation' *and* the popularity of the 'little Yases' ('tyrannically clapt') to explain why the players are travelling.

37 Mary Edmond spells out why Davenant's 'importance as a champion of continuity can hardly be overestimated' in *Rare Sir William Davenant: Poet Laureate, Playwright, Civil War General, Restoration Theatre Manager* (Manchester, 1987), p. 141. It is probably not coincidental that 1637, the year of the Q5 text, was also a year when we *know* that *Hamlet* was performed at court (24 January; see J. Q. Adams, *The Dramatic Records of Sir Henry Herbert* (New Haven, CT, 1917), p. 76). Revivals, reprints and court performances seem commonly to have occurred together by the 1630s, if not earlier.

38 It is worth noting in this regard that Davenant started with what is essentially the Q2 text, and did not revert to anything resembling Q1. This is often overlooked by those who like to argue that Q1 is a clumsily reproduced acting version of a text close to Q2.

39 Erne, *Shakespeare as Literary Dramatist*, p. 167.

40 By this date, intriguingly, it is neither his 'leisure' (Q1) nor his 'vantage' (Q2, F), but his 'interest' which invites him to claim his 'rights of memory' in Denmark.

Chapter 10

The poetics of succession, 1587–1605: the Stuart claim

Richard A. McCabe

According to Bishop John Leslie's *Historie of Scotland* (1578), the young James VI modelled himself upon the legendary King Arthur, 'heiring of not ane in ancient antiquitie amang all his predecessprs, to quhom he wald be sa conforme'.[1] As the once and *future* 'King of Britain', Arthur held a peculiar fascination for the man who hoped to reunite the island by succeeding to the English throne. But all of that depended on the goodwill of the incumbent, on the would-be Arthur's relentless courtship of England's Eliza. So relentless was it that readers of Spenser's 1590 *Faerie Queene* might have been forgiven for seeing in the young Prince Arthur's perpetually frustrated pursuit of the titular heroine an allegorical representation of James's lifelong quest for Elizabeth's recognition. But a reader so minded would have been hard put to determine whether that representation was sympathetic or parodic. The elements of Sir Thopas in the prince's make-up undercut his heroic character.[2] He rides out of the third and final book of the first edition on a false trail, belatedly discovering that the lady 'royally clad … in cloth of gold' whom he has pursued into a trackless forest is not in fact the fairy queen (III. v. 4–9). It is a bitter blow to all his hopes:

> Oft did he wish, that Lady faire mote bee
> His faery Queene, for whom he did complaine:
> Or that his Faery Queene were such, as shee. (III. iv. 54)[3]

The qualification in the final line might also prompt readers' speculation: James never met Elizabeth but pursued his twenty-year courtship through letters and emissaries. Their correspondence is accordingly riddled with misunderstandings and disagreements, latent threats and vague promises.[4] It has been argued that James 'always writes *as a monarch*', but in this case he does not.[5] From 1586 he was, effectively, Elizabeth's pensioner, a client financially dependent on someone who could, if she chose, secure or undo his future.[6] When Elizabeth failed to respond to one of his courtly sonnets in 1586, for example, the nineteen-year-old King wrote again in the incongruous manner of an eager lover to 'satisfy [his] unrestful and longing spirit':

> Madame, I did send you before some verse. Since then Dame Cynthia has oft re-newed her horns and innumerable times supped with her sister Thetis…I doubt not ye have read how Cupid's dart is fiery called because of the sudden ensnaring and restless burning; thereafter what can I else judge but that either ye had not received it…or else that ye judge it not to be of me because it is *incerto authore*. For the which cause I have insert[ed] my name to the end of this sonnet here enclosed.[7]

This letter and accompanying sonnet have received much attention: commentators have examined the sexual politics of the Petrarchan diction, teased out the potentially 'incestuous' overtones of the sentiments, and noted the preference for signature over anonymity.[8] But *'incerto authore'* is fundamental to the problem in a sense that James never intended. It is not the uncertainty of the authorship but the instability of the authorial persona that lies at the heart of the matter. James addresses Elizabeth variously as 'mighty princess', 'madame', 'sister', 'cousin' and even 'mother', desperately attempting to gain some purchase on their complex relationship. The most remarkable feature of his letters is their inconsistency of tone, veering from the embarrassingly amorous (as above) to the obsequiously filial. They suggest a writer acutely aware that the great prize may yet elude his grasp. There may have been no succession 'crisis', in any formal sense, in England, but there were multiple crises in the mind of the man who styled himself heir apparent in Scotland but was acknowledged only as a pretender south of the border.[9] There his claims were advanced most forcefully in manuscript circulation, often *'incerto authore'*.

Overtly Spenser's epic is a poem about a reigning queen, but its central fable concerns the coming of a king, the development of Arthur from prince into monarch. In the ninth canto of the second book the young hero, ignorant of his own fate, reads an anonymous manuscript that identifies the issue uncompromisingly:

> After him Uther, which *Pendragon* hight,
>   Succeeding There abruptly it did end,
> Without full point, or other Cesure right,
> As if the rest some wicked hand did rend,
> Or th'Author selfe could not at last attend
> To finish it… (II. x. 68)

The 'abrupt' orthography of the second line brilliantly captures the anxious urgency of the succession debate with its related fears of 'wicked' censorship and authorial disablement. Yet viewed as an episode in his ongoing quest, Arthur's reading of the 'Briton Moniments' strongly implies that his pursuit of Gloriana is in some undefined, and perhaps indefinable, way allegorically cognate with his succession to the Briton crown. And since 'Briton' was a key term for James and his supporters, he had good reason to read Spenser as closely as subsequent events reveal that he did.

APPROPRIATING ARTHUR

As David Allan has demonstrated, hopes of the coming union of Britain occasioned a rehabilitation of the Arthurian myth in sixteenth-century Scotland.[10] Traditionally it was regarded as politically dangerous for representing Scotland as a client state anciently conquered by the legendary King, and possibly destined to be conquered again in accordance with Galfridian prophecy. In the early 1540s, however, during the abortive negotiations for the marriage of the future Edward VI to the future Mary Queen of Scots, the Arthurian narrative was adopted by James Henryson and others in order to promote Protestant union between the two countries. The problem at that stage, from the Scottish viewpoint, was the predominant Anglo-centrism of the unionist debate, since even Henryson was acting on behalf of Protector Somerset. By contrast, the Arthurian revival in the person of James VI afforded the more palatable prospect that the future Arthur would be Scottish, but that in turn raised fears of a counter 'conquest' that James's English supporters, such as Peter Wentworth, were at pains to allay.[11] Whereas Buchanan characteristically dismissed the validity of Merlin's vague prophecies, that very vagueness supplied grist to the mills of those who sought to underpin the Stuart claim with what Lady Macbeth terms 'metaphysical aid' (I. iii. 29–30). Hence Sir John Harington's recourse to 'Welsh prophecies' to lend support to the claims of the 'cradle king':

> For earst in Wales this prophecie was found:
> A King of Brittish blood in Cradell crownd,
> With Lyon markt, shall joine all Brutus ground,
> Restore the Crosse, and make this ile renown'd.[12]

As the Norman kings were the first to realise, such 'prophecy' offered a means of transforming pseudo-historical narrative into dynastic validation. *The Whole Prophesie of Scotland*, published in Edinburgh in 1603 as James set out for England, is merely one case in point.[13] In many ways it set the political stage for Shakespeare's 'Scottish play'.

From the twelfth century onwards, so far as matters of state were concerned, 'Arthur' embodied an imperial concept, and it was that concept that lent 'historicity' to the man, as the strength of the reaction to Polydore Vergil's dismissal of Geoffrey of Monmouth's *Historia* demonstrates.[14] Similarly, Spenser's 'Letter to Ralegh' makes it clear that the Arthur of *The Faerie Queene* is essentially conceptual, operating in a narrative only tangentially linked to the traditional stories. It might therefore be expected that Spenser's Merlin would translate that concept into political doctrine when he too reaches the point at which the issue of the succession becomes unavoidable: 'Thenceforth eternall union shall be made / Betweene the nations different afore' (III. iii. 49). Read in the context of Scottish polemic, of James's insistence on the manifold blessings of peaceful 'union' that his coming would deliver, these lines might look like the prelude to a formal endorsement. But Spenser's Merlin stubbornly refuses to describe the world after Elizabeth, even though it is one 'that secretly he saw':

> But yet the end is not. There *Merlin* stayd,
>   As overcomen of the spirites powre,
> Or other ghastly spectacle dismayd,
> That secretly he saw, yet note discoure ... (III. iii. 50)

On one level, of course, 'Merlin' is simply obeying the Treasons Act (13 Eliz c. 1) that forbade public discourse of the succession, but the level of anxiety, not to say hysteria, built into Spenser's account – notable in the wizard's 'halfe extatick stoure' and the marked distress of his listeners – does not augur well for a peaceful transition of power. He smiles at the conclusion, it is true, but very enigmatically. The contrast with James's supporters is striking. Writing in 1595, Walter Quin, an official propagandist for James, presented the name 'Charles James Stuart' as an anagram for 'Claimes Arthur's Seat' and glossed accordingly:

> A peerless pearle, and prince Claimes Arthur's Seat ...
> To winne his right his courage voide of dredde
> With GOD and mans assistance he shall bend;
> And under foote as Conquerour shall tredde
> The pride of such as shall with him contend.
>   So to *King Arthur's Seat* attain he shall
>   Whereto by name and claime the Heavens him call.[15]

Writing in a similar vein to affirm the succession in 1604 in *A Prophesie of Cadwallader, Last King of the Britaines*, Sir William Herbert has Henry VII's supposed ancestor predict the coming of James who 'shall three in one, and one in three unite'.[16]

Just one year after the composition of Quin's poem, the second part of *The Faerie Queene* was banned in Scotland on the grounds that, as the English ambassador Robert Bowes reported to Lord Burghley on 12 November, the King had 'conceaved great offence against Edward Spence [*sic*] publishing in prynte in the second book p[ar]t of the Fairy Queene and ix*th* chapter some dishonourable effects (as the k. deemeth thereof) against himself and his mother deceassed'.[17] Bowes's wording is of great interest. Technically, Spenser does not appear to mention James at all in the ninth canto of book five, but Bowes makes it clear that the King found himself there. He objected to 'dishonourable effects…against himself and his mother deceassed'. The order of priority is also significant. Being 'deceased', Mary could hardly be hurt by anything Spenser says, but her son most definitely could. The implication that James found in *The Faerie Queene* was that Duessa's son could never be Gloriana's heir. Those opposed to James's succession had long argued that Mary's condemnation for treason disqualified her son from succeeding under the terms of the popular Bond of Association of 1584, even though the official Act for the Queen's Surety of 1585 excluded only those complicit in the crime.[18] Whereas Wentworth supplied both versions and favoured the latter, Persons's *Conference* (1594/5) insisted on the former and James took the threat very seriously.[19] As a result, he was in a state of particularly acute anxiety in the mid-1590s.[20] Any derogatory references to his mother were seen as attacks upon himself. In 1595, for example, he demanded the punishment of William Leonard for speaking words 'to the dishonour of the King and Queen of Scotland, as also of his mother'. Leonard had alleged that Mary 'was a whore' and embarrassingly cited in evidence Buchanan's *Ane Detection of the Doings of Marie Quene of Scottes* (1571) – a work published in England with the full approval of Elizabeth (to whom it was dedicated) and the Privy Council.[21] In Spenser's case the implied insult was doubtless aggravated by its Arthurian context. Complaining of Mary's incarceration in 1571 in *A Treatise concerning the Defence of the Honour of…Marie Queene of Scotlande*, Bishop Leslie appealed to Arthurian chivalry to shame his English readers, and her execution was subsequently denounced by her supporters as an infamous violation of the same traditions.[22] But Spenser presents matters very differently. In the passage of *The Faerie Queene* that so offended James, Prince Arthur himself deserts Duessa's cause in the light of the evidence advanced at her trial:

> All which when as the Prince had heard and seene,
>   His former fancies ruth he gan repent,
>   And from her partie eftsoones was drawen cleene. (V. ix. 49)

This boxes James into an Arthurian corner. Whereas he could not be seen in England to countenance Mary's plots against Elizabeth, he could not be seen in Scotland to countenance her execution. While assuring Leicester privately that he would be mad to prefer his mother to his title, he feared the public 'dishonour' of her fate. Writing privately to Elizabeth on 26 January 1587 he asked, 'what thing, madame, can greatlier touch me in honour that [am] a king and a son than that my nearest neighbour, being in straitest [friend] ship with me, shall rigorously put to death a free sovereign prince and my natural mother…?'[23] Spenser's presentation of the matter exacerbates James' difficulty: if he saw himself in Prince Arthur, or remembered his 'Arthurian' ancestry as he read the offending canto, he found himself made complicit in his mother's execution – as indeed he was to the extent that he would never have endangered his claim to the throne in order to save her life.[24] The canto must have seemed calculated to maximize the 'dishonour' and disgrace that James so feared. If he is to be read as Arthur he condemns his mother and disowns 'her partie' (which would include all her Catholic sympathisers in England) on the grounds of her criminality. But if he is not Arthur he is merely Duessa's son with no claim to Arthurian inheritance – and the 1590 *Faerie Queene* has much to say of the despicable nature of witches' sons with aspirations above their station (III. viii. 1–13).

The contrast with the account of the execution that first appeared in the 1596 edition of William Warner's *Albions England* is telling. From the outset Warner professes to ameliorate his account of Mary's fall 'in Reverence of her Sonne', an employment of *excusatio* all the more likely to commend itself to Scottish eyes for its refusal to make any adverse determination on the essential justice of Mary's claim to the succession:

> Thus, from Seventh *Henries* Daughter, she her Title did advance.
> But howsoere by blood, or by our Lawes, she here could clame,
> T'is sure, too soone, and treacherously, she did preferre the same,
> And first and last unto our Queene her selfe a Foe did Frame.

Whatever the validity of the claim, it was wrongly pursued by a woman who is shown to have been largely the dupe of Catholic conspirators intent on advancing their own nefarious ends through her. But if Mary was a 'Foe', James is 'so firme a frend' to England that Warner hesitates to offend him by recalling the details of his mother's crimes against his father and himself. She would gladly have 'betrayed' the 'Infant-King', it is alleged, to restore herself to the Scottish throne. Her actions were dangerous not only to Elizabeth but to James who remains 'an happie Prince in all…Precelling his Progenitours, a Iusticer upright'.[25] Here might well be a worthy king in waiting – and one who, as the contrast with Mary suggests, is content to wait. While Warner, unlike Spenser, does not expressly invoke an Arthurian context for these events, it is implicit in James's unquestioned descent through Mary from Henry VII, the creator of the 'Tudor myth' that Warner elsewhere endorses.

HIS MOTHER'S SON

At the heart of the problems arising from his mother's execution lay James's uncomfortable recognition that the most compelling arguments for his right to the succession had been honed by her Catholic supporters. In the early

1580s the prospect that the adolescent James might convert to Catholicism under the influence of his cousin Esmé Stuart, or enter into joint sovereignty with Mary, increasingly led his mother's supporters to couple his name with hers in the matter of the English succession.[26] Most notable in this regard is Bishop Leslie's *A Treatise towching the Right, Title, and Interest of the Most excellent Princesse Marie, Queene of Scotland, And of the most noble king Iames, her Graces sonne, to the succession of the Croune of England* (1584). In keeping with his title Leslie is careful to use the plural throughout, addressing Mary and James as 'his undoubted Sovereignes' (sig. B1r). The verso of the title-page bears dual portraits of James and Mary with verses which implicitly suggest that Mary has provided England with the heir that Elizabeth failed to supply:

Encrease of blesse expected long
  In Britain was begonne:
When suche a mother dyd bring foorth
  With so good happe a sonne.
Through princelie grace and pietie
  Great is the mothers fame,
The king her sonne doth yield muche hope
  To imitate the same.

Leslie's readers might well recall Elizabeth's alleged remarks on hearing of James's birth, 'the Queen of Scots has a fair son and I am but of barren stock'.[27] The issue is driven home in the 'Preface' in which it is stated that 'all politike Princes wanting issue of their own bodies to succede them, have ever had a speciall care and foresight (for avoyding of civil dissention) that the people allwayes myght knowe the true and certain heyr apparent of the Croune' (fo. 10v). Elizabeth is being asked to recognize James as, effectively, her 'son' – she was already, as he often reminded her, his godmother (and eventually godmother to his own son, Prince Henry). He would later style himself 'son to the present queen' when discussing the succession with Robert Cecil.[28] That self-representation was greatly facilitated by Leslie's insistence, from the title-page onwards, on the 'British' context of the succession debate.[29] In the eyes of his opponents James was disqualified from succeeding as an alien-born, but in Leslie's account his birth occasions 'encrease of blisse' not in Scotland but 'in Britain'. The bishop's preface ends with a poem by 'T. V. Englishman' addressed to 'the Nobilitie and people of England and Scotland' collectively apostrophized as 'You Britaines' (fo. 12v). The term 'England', Leslie explains, was a relatively late invention. Originally there were only 'Britianes of the South' and 'Britaines of the Northe', and so it would be again (fo. 65r). Paradoxically, then, James was already 'English' because he was 'British', but he would create 'Britain' because he was Scottish!

But Mary's execution in 1587 marked a watershed in 'British' politics. Fearful of a Protestant succession Leslie and Persons turned against the Stuart cause, while Puritans such as Peter Wentworth rehabilitated the late Queen's claim in order to promote her son, refining many of the arguments that Leslie had developed.[30] But while Wentworth, like Warner, tended to distance James from Mary while simultaneously insisting upon the claim he inherited through her, Stuart apologists of the later 1590s (including James himself in *Basilikon Doron*) increasingly rehabilitated Mary's reputation to stress, as Leslie had done, the closeness of mother and son – a development that culminated in James's reburial of his mother alongside Elizabeth in Westminster Abbey.[31] According to Sir John Harington's *Tract on the Succession to the Crown* (1602), for example, in becoming King of Britain James would achieve what his mother might have achieved had her destiny allowed her to wed Edward VI and become Queen of England.[32] Thus Mary's alternative history adumbrates her son's future or, to put it another way, he inherits the glorious future that she was cruelly denied. Similarly, in a poem contributed to John Johnston's *Inscriptiones Regum Scotorum* (1602), Andrew Melville has Mary bequeath the 'sceptres' of Scotland and England to James ['Tibi debita Nate / Sceptra dedi'] who thereby recoups her losses in both kingdoms and initiates a golden age ['aurea regna'].[33] In *A Trewe Description of the Nobill Race of the Stewards* that appeared the following year, James is presented as legitimate heir to both Mary and Elizabeth, 'mother' and 'cousin'. A new mythology was in the making, one that stressed continuity and accord over conflict, even if that entailed supplanting history with romance. Richard Mulcaster's account of Elizabeth's last moments is indicative of this trend:

> Nor when she died, did she forget hers here,
> As many mothers doe forget their babes,
> But left us such a King whose vertues might
> Abridge the griefe which lack of her might breed.

'This', he concludes, was 'her lives last act', thereby consigning to oblivion the thirty-year controversy about Elizabeth's stubborn refusal to nominate an heir. And what she had given the nation, according to Mulcaster, was simultaneously 'one of our English blood' and 'the greatest King that Brittish soyle hath seene'.[34]

GARLAND AND CROWN

It was, perhaps, the greatest irony of James's accession that the term 'Britain', the key term of the union debate, should prove to be so divisive.[35] The flood of publications triggered by his journey south celebrated his British blood and Arthurian ancestry to such an extent that it must have seemed as if poetic metaphor had for once translated into political reality, as if the *praxis* of poetry had been demonstrated beyond all doubt. All of James's previous attempts at seeming 'English' were intended as preludes to becoming 'British', and the Venetian ambassador's assertion that he intended to 'abandon the titles of England and Scotland, and to call himself King of Great Britain…like that famous and ancient King Arthur' doubtless captures the mood of the moment quite accurately.[36] Samuel Daniel's *Panegyricke Congratulatory* (1603) represents the union as a fait accompli:

> Now thou art all *Great-Britaine* and no more,
> No Scot, no English now, nor no debate;
> No borders but the Ocean and the shore:
> No wall of *Adrian* serves to separate
> Our mutuall love, nor our obedience,
> Being Subïects all to one imperiall Prince.[37]

As would soon become clear, however, Daniel's 'our' was authorial rather than properly collective. With an eye to future patronage, he was responding to James's own propaganda rather than expressing a common aspiration. As a printed author, the King was arguably his own best publicist. His authorial and regal personae were carefully honed to promote one another, to relate, if not to fuse, two mutually supportive forms of 'authority'. James's first speech to the English Parliament was the culmination of a self-presentational campaign that began with the publication in 1584 of *The Essayes of a Prentice in the Divine Art of Poesie*. But for James, the 'divine art of poesie' and divine right of kings were closely allied, and their relationship was exemplified in the person, and persona, of the biblical David. The *Essayes* incorporate translations from the Psalms, just as James's political works draw heavily on Davidic texts to support their controversially absolutist (and certainly anti-Buchananist) theories of sovereignty. As James saw it, the 'garland' was complimentary to the 'crown'. The self-styled 'prentice' of the *Essayes* lays down with the authority of a master the 'Reulis and Cautelis to be observit and eschewit in Scottis *Poesie*' and warns fellow poets to eschew dangerous political matters on the grounds that 'they are to grave materis, for a Poet to mell in' – while broaching such matters himself in *Ane Metaphoricall Invention of a Tragedie Called Phoenix*, which tackles the vexed problem (north and south of the border) of Esmé Stuart.[38] The royal prentice arrogates to himself a licence he would deny to subject masters. His supposed anonymity is transparent 'for *Cæsars* works shall justly *Cæsar* crown', as 'R. H' (probably Robert Hudson) remarks in the second commendatory sonnet.[39] But of which 'crown' does Hudson speak? The 'laurell' crown or garland would seem the most obvious one, but it would be naïve to suppose that the *Essayes* were intended purely for a Scottish readership. As Jane Rickard observes, 'most of *Essays of a Prentice* reveals at least a degree of Anglicisation: tellingly, given English concerns about Esmé Stuart, particular care seems to have been taken with anglicising the poem in which he is defended'.[40] 'For *Cæsars* works shall justly *Cæsar* crown' might mean different things in England and Scotland. As every classically educated reader knew, the 'crown' that Caesar desired was one he did not have, and one that many Romans were determined he would never have. Was it possible that James's 'works' could help him to win the English 'crown', that poetic authority could build political authority? What for instance, were the political implications of incorporating poems by 'K. of Scots' into an anthology so specifically entitled *Englands Parnassus* (1600), particularly when the first passage is a quotation from James's translation of Du Bartas's prophetic *Uranie* (lines 85–92), and it is directly followed by a passage from Spenser's *Teares of the Muses* (559–70) recalling a time when only 'Princes and high Priests' wrote verse and the art was held in 'soveraigne dignitie'?[41]

As public discussion of the succession was officially banned in England, it is important to ask to what extent overt praise of James as a poet constitutes oblique endorsement as a future king; to what extent, in other words, the conferral of a laurel crown anticipated, or implied, that of a kingly diadem. When the *Poetical Exercises* appeared in 1591, for example, William Fowler's commendatory sonnet subtly employed spatial metaphor to elide poetic fame and political power: 'Where', he asks, 'shall the pillars which your praise proclame / Or Trophees stand, of that exspected crowne?'[42] What were English readers to make of that 'exspected crowne'? Suppression of open discussion bred a hermeneutics of suspicion than infected everyone from Elizabeth and James, who maintained an active surveillance of the presses in both countries, to lowly subjects who scoured the literature for clues as to which way the wind was blowing. The atmosphere of secrecy nourished conspiracy theory: even Thomas Wilson, an otherwise hard-headed commentator who favoured James's claim and deplored the prohibition on public discussion, suggested that secret documents had been drawn up by Elizabeth and parliament nominating James 'and sealed up in [3] bales, and delivered to the king of France and 2 others, they haveing taken oath not to open itt until the Queen's death'.[43] In a climate such as this it is hardly surprising that the allusive possibilities of poetics were seen to afford an outlet for stifled political expression, just as the multiple *personae* adopted by the royal author invited plurality of response.

The English poet Henry Constable, who supported James' succession in the belief that he would eventually convert to Catholicism, supplied the *Poeticall Exercises* with a commendatory sonnet complementary to Fowler's suggesting that James, despite his avowed preference for things spiritual over earthly, cannot escape the 'fame' for which he is destined: 'with all thy speed from fame thou canst not flee / But more thow flyest the more it followes thee'.[44] Who could believe that only literary fame was involved? Sir John Harington, another of James's English supporters, reprinted the Constable sonnet in the commentary to his translation of the *Orlando Furioso* (a copy of which he presented to James) overtly to illustrate Ariosto's distinction in the thirty-fourth canto between true and false fame.[45] Constable reprinted it again in his *Diana* of 1594, together with a poem asserting that he longed to 'kisse' the hands that wielded the Scottish 'scepter' and kneel before 'thy altar throne':

> Yet prince of hope suppose not for all this
> That I thy place and not thy guifts adore
> Thy sceptre no thy pen I honoure more
> More deare to me then crowne thy garland is.[46]

This is an elegant disclaimer, certainly, yet the connotations of the phrase 'prince of hope' would be lost on few, particularly as it leads to a comparison with James's exemplar, King David. The structure of Constable's sequence is equally significant. The second part of the work, which consists of seven sonnets, brackets James with Elizabeth. The first three sonnets are addressed to her and the final four to James, beginning with the sonnet that hails him as 'prince of hope'. But nothing in the succession debate is ever quite that clear, or even that oblique. Amongst the ladies praised in the concluding section of *Diana* is James's closest genealogical rival for the crown, Lady Arbella Stuart, to whom two sonnets are directed. While the location of these sonnets outside the section reserved for monarchs might indicate a sort of relegation to commoner status, Arbella is addressed as the 'onely hope of oure age' and the final sonnet of the collection dedicates the poet's Muses 'to the divine protection of the Ladie Arbella'.[47] Constable's strategy affords an epitome of James's dilemma: every group of potential supporters had at least one rival claimant to whom they might transfer their allegiance. Many Catholics held out great hopes for Arbella, and as late as May 1602 James himself feared that she would 'declare herself Catholic' in a last ditch attempt to block his succession.[48]

In another respect, however, Constable's approach was entirely in accord with James's policy. The Anglo-Scottish alliance of 1586 was intended to secure his recognition as Elizabeth's heir but made him only her pensioner, a client to the English crown publicly dependent on handouts from Whitehall. Thereafter it became all the more important to insist on the sovereignty he already possessed, so his second collection of poetry was published as *His Majesties Poeticall Exercises at Vacant Houres* (1591). Yet it would be quite wrong to suppose, as Jonathan Goldberg and others have done, that James's royal persona was in any sense fixed, let alone absolute.[49] In England James needed to be, if not quite all things to all men, as many things to as many men as possible. The voice that addresses us in the prefatory materials is not authoritarian but defensive and circumspect – on both aesthetic and political matters. James can turn from speaking in self-deprecating *propria persona* (as fictive, one might think, as his other personae) to appropriating the prophetical voice of Du Bartas: 'But ô thou holie Pilote great / Will guide me safe and sound

/ Unto the port of my desire'.[50] This is an admirably spiritual aspiration as Constable noted, but the exact location of James's 'port' is perhaps best indicated by the incorporation into the collection of *The Lepanto of James the sixt, King of Scotland*, a work that had previously circulated in manuscript and given rise to suspicion about James's commitment to the Protestant cause. In this regard 'The Authors Preface to the Reader' must be accounted a masterpiece amongst paratexts in its attempt to manipulate readerly response. 'It falles out often', James explains,

> that the effects of mens actions comes cleane contrarie to the intent of the Authour. The same finde I by experience (beloved Reader) in my Poëme of LEPANTO: For although till now, it have not bene imprinted, yet being set out to the Publick view of many, by a great sort of stoln copies...it hath for lack of a Præface, bene in some things misconstrued by sundry...the special thing misliked in it, is, that I should seeme, far contrary to my Degree and Religion, like a Mercenary Poët, to penne a worke, ex professo, in praise of a forraine papist bastard [Don John of Austria].

Epic had long been regarded (*pace* Lucan) as an imperial genre, written about kings for kings by court poets hoping to gain royal favour or patronage. For James to appear 'like a hireling' courting the favour of Spain might prove fatal to his reputation in England.[51] But James was playing a many-handed game. So long as Elizabeth refused to acknowledge him as her heir he needed to keep all potential allies in play, including potential Catholic allies.[52] If the original *Lepanto* of 1585 is ambiguous it is studiously so, and subtly attuned to the circumstances of the year in which it was written. Rickard emphasizes James's desire to 'control' readers' responses, but I would argue, rather, that he was cultivating diversity of response through studied ambiguity.[53] By reproducing the 1585 text without substantial revision in 1591 he made it possible for Catholics such as Constable to read it against the grain of the preface, and when it appeared on the continent that same year in Du Bartas's French translation the preface was omitted. To someone in James's position the cultivation of ambiguity brought distinct advantages, none the least of which was plausible deniability. Despite official protestations to the contrary, James's attitude to Catholicism was deliberately opaque, and anyone privy to the diplomatic correspondence of the period prior to 1588 might well have entertained doubts as to his outlook. But once he had (as he imagined) secured his objectives through tough negotiation, and the Armada had conspicuously failed, his publications sought to give an impression of unwavering solidarity with the Protestant cause. It is my contention in this chapter that the elaborate re-contextualization of *Lepanto* in the *Poeticall Exercises* forms part of this strategy.[54]

James's most immediate response to the Armada was the issuing of two meditative works: *Ane Fruitfull Meditatioun*...(on Revelation) (1588) and *Ane Meditatioun*...(on Chronicles) (1589).[55] Both works speak of danger to the 'ile' rather than England and proceed as though the Armada was directed primarily against James, an effect greatly enhanced when they were republished in Anglicized versions in 1603. Elizabeth scarcely merits a mention. Indeed by styling James 'cheif defender of the treuth', the title page of *Ane Fruitfull Meditatioun* almost, but not quite, appropriates Elizabeth's title of 'Defender of the Faith'. When the work was republished soon after the succession, part of the subtitle was altered to read, 'chiefe defender of the trueth *Iames* by the grace of God King of *England, Scotland, France* and *Ireland*, defender of the faith'. The gambit of 1588 is the checkmate of 1603. *Ane Meditatioun* also points the reader to the succession by beginning with the suggestion that James had foretold the defeat of the Armada and closing with 'His Maiesties awin Sonnet' celebrating that defeat: 'They forward came in monstruous array / Baith sea and land beset us every quhair'. The effect was, once again, greatly enforced when the poem was republished in Anglicized form in 1603 and the 'us' of the sonnet could be read as both collective and royal. By republishing these two 'prophetic' works on the occasion of his succession, James made it seem not just that he was both prophet and king, but prophet to his own kingship – an ideal that resonates powerfully with Shakespeare's treatment of the Stuart succession through prophecy in *Macbeth*.

In the late 1580s, however, there was one great problem with all of this: the *Lepanto* of 1585 was already in manuscript circulation, and the poem could be read as celebrating the victory of another great Spanish Armada in not entirely anti-Catholic terms. As the preface to the version printed in the *Poeticall Exercises* makes clear, the discrepancy was not lost on James's critics. His solution was ingenious but is not very well understood. One needs to read the preface very carefully. 'The nature then of this Poëme', he explains,

> is an argument à minore ad majus, largely intreated by a Poetike comparison, beeing to the writing hereof mooved, by the stirring uppe of the league and cruell persecution of the Protestants in all countries, at the very first raging wherof, I compiled this Poëme, at the exhortation to the persecuted in the hinmost eight lines thereof doth plainely testifie, being both begun and ended in the same Summer, wherein the league was published in France.

James claims, in other words, that he has used the events of 1571 as what Spenser might term 'a continued Allegory, or darke conceit' for those of 1585, moving from the lesser issue of Lepanto to the greater matter of the Catholic League (hence 'à minore ad majus') by sustained 'Poetike comparison'. A Spanish victory over the Turks is used to predict a Protestant victory over the Spanish. There were, of course, precedents in anti-Catholic propaganda for comparing the Spaniards to Turks, but seldom in the context of a Christian victory over the infidel celebrated alike on the continent and in England.[56] Reading the preface, one is reminded of the rhetorical summersaults James undertook in trying to convince Elizabeth that his quotation of the ominous Virgilian line, 'flectere si nequeo superos Archeronta movebo' ['if I cannot move heaven I shall move hell'] was not intended as a threat. She pretended to be happier with his 'gloss' than his 'text' and he doubtless hoped the same of his Protestant English readers in 1591.[57] It is, I think, unprecedented in the literary tradition for an epic hero to be described in an authorial preface as anything resembling 'a forraine papist bastard', but the power of paratexts is not be underestimated. With James's 'Poetike comparison' in mind, a post-Armada reader might even see in the miraculous turning of the wind against the Turks at Lepanto an adumbration, perhaps again 'prophetic', of the Armada victory:

> Before the chocke, ô miracle,
>   It turnd into their face,
> Which Christians joyfull as a seale
>   And token did receave,
> That God of Hosts had promis'd them
>   They victorie should have. (lines 567–72)

By happy accident it was precisely this miraculous detail that 'His Maiesties awin Sonnet' on the Armada had commemorated. Taken together then, *Ane Fruitfull Meditatioun*, *Ane Meditatioun* and the *Lepanto* (which was also re-printed in London in 1603) presented English readers with a king-in-waiting who had stood shoulder to shoulder with them against the Armada and praised Spain only to undermine it. The fact that *Lepanto* was entered in the Stationers' Register on 17 August 1589, presumably with a view to London publication, tends to corroborate the point.

From the mid-1590s onwards James was relentless in advancing the presentation of his claim to the succession, both in his oversight of the English press and in the attention he paid to an English readership. But Elizabeth was watching the Scottish press as carefully as he watched the English. When Andrew Melville published *Principis Scoti-Britannorum natalia* in celebration of Prince Henry's birth in 1594, her ambassador, Robert Bowes, pointed out to James 'that the poet, by naming him King of all Britain in possession, cannot but breed offence to her Majesty, considering her portion is the greatest part of Britain and his the less'. James replied rather unconvincingly that he had not read Melville's poem even though he had authorized it for publication but, in any case, 'being descended as he was, he could not but make claim to the crown of England after the decease of her Majesty, who was well pleased to promise to him that upon his good behaviour towards her she would never hurt or impeach his title or right therein.' Even more disingenuously, he observed 'that poets and scholars oftentimes and without good discretion publish "conceiptes" occupying ther heads and pleasing their minds, notwithstanding their actions therein little profited' – and this from the man who called for the prosecution of Barnaby Rich in 1595 and Spenser in 1596![58] Poetry could be subtly resonant when James employed it and inconsequential when he disclaimed it; that was the advantage of poetics. Melville and James disagreed on many matters, but the poem's 'Scoti-Britannic' vision closely coincided with the King's own, as the heavy emphasis on hereditary succession, overtly addressed to the Scots but evidently directed to the English, in the closing paragraphs of *The True Law of Free Monarchies* (1598) bears witness.

Basilikon Doron is certainly more problematical. It has been argued that the work, privately published in only seven copies in 1599 with the publisher 'sworne for secrecie', was neither intended for public readership nor directed to an English audience.[59] This was certainly what James was to claim in the preface of 1603 when the work re-appeared in Edinburgh and London within a few days of Elizabeth's death. But his claims are in many respects inconsistent. While the holograph is in Middle Scots, the seven printed copies are Anglicized – although none of the recipients was English and the work goes out of its way to disclaim any attention to English politics. News of the secret publication leaked very quickly. Andrew Melville read a copy within months and predictably found it objectionable on religious grounds, but English supporters such as Sir John Harington hailed it as a guarantee of James's moral character.[60] It is therefore hard to resist the suspicion that *Basilikon Doron* was intended from the outset as an open secret, consciously endowed with the allure of an occult classic with a view to disclosure when the moment was right. James was accounted 'one of the most secret princes of the world' (in Sir Henry Wotton's phrase), and his diplomatic and private correspondence is enmeshed in webs of intrigue, subterfuge and cipher.[61] *Basilikon Doron* allowed him to use that reputation to his advantage. The first three paragraphs of the preface he added in 1603 use the word 'secret' or its derivatives no fewer than nine times in expounding Luke 12: 2–3, 'nothing is covered, that shal not be revealed'. And, despite making assurance doubly sure by disclaiming any intention to avenge his mother or harass 'Puritan' clerics, James could feel confident in having this particular 'secret' found out. What follows the preface is no discreditable Machiavellian tract urging his heir to practise *realpolitik*, but an essay on the distinction between Christian kingship and amoral 'tyranny' written in the ancient tradition of the *consilium principis*. 'Since it was first written in secret', James concludes, 'and is now published, not of ambition, but of a kinde of necessitie, it must be taken of all men, for the trew image of my very minde, and forme of the rule, which I have prescribed to my selfe and mine'.[62] The great 'secret' revealed in 1603 – in possibly as many as 14,000 copies – was that James was a good man, and therefore a good king! It is surely one of the best pieces of political propaganda ever engineered, expertly exploiting the work's publishing history to promote its impact.

CONCLUSION

The 1603 edition of *Basilikon Doron* is best regarded as the tract designed to set the keynote for the literature of the accession. James began in the *Essayes* by presenting himself as a 'prentice' poet who could instruct in aesthetics and politics like a master; he ended in *Basilikon Doron* as a professed master of the kingly art of instructing a 'prentice' prince in the dual arts of kingship and poetry.[63] His own writings provide the subtext for much of the celebratory literature of 1603–4 as poets hastened to reiterate in the key of triumph what he had written in the key of expectation.[64] The *Essayes* had promised that '*Cæsars* works shall justly *Cæsar* crown', and Henry Petowe responded in *England's Cæsar: His Maiesties most Royall Coronation* (1603) by asserting that,

> Within the Table of Æternitie,
> In leaves outwearing Brasse shall Fame write downe,
> With Quilles of Steele the lasting memory,
> Of Englands *Cæsar*, and great *Cæsars* Crowne. (sig. B1ʳ)

In *Ave Cæsar. God save the King* (1603) Samuel Rowlands hailed 'our famous Kingly *Poet*' (sig. Biiiᵛ) and stressed the continuity of the Tudor and Stuart lines from the uniting of York and Lancaster in Henry VII:

> A glorious Arbour from this roote hath sprong,
> Of sweetest Roses, crown'd with Diadames:
> From Prince to Prince, the branch hath run along,
> And now the noble Flower is cald *King James*. (sig. Biiiiʳ)

In his first address to parliament on 19 March 1604 James would make exactly the same point, and with good reason. The poetics of succession characteristically rely upon the fabrication of myths of continuity and on the presentation of change as 'natural' progression, political fulfilment or providential design. So while English poets commemorated James's Tudor blood, Irish bards hailed his descent from ancient Gaelic kings.[65] The poetics of exclusion contrarily demand images of disjunction, regression and loss – hence Spenser's self-consciously 'abrupt' conclusion to the 'Briton Moniments' and Merlin's prophecies, suggesting that there is no evident successor to Eliza. But James desired to develop the poetics of continuity still further in the direction of full political union. Bruce Galloway casts doubt on Francis Bacon's assertion that the new King was in too much of a hurry to promote the union, but that is to overlook the crucial role that the notion of 'Britain' played, as we have seen, in his campaign from the outset.[66] The throne, James believed, was his by right, but union afforded its greatest public advantage: union, or so he imagined, was what was in it for others. Standing before parliament and professing once again to disclose 'the secrets of [his] heart', James recalled a time when there had been no single nation south of the Scottish border but 'seven little Kingdomes, besides Wales'. Union was therefore to be seen as part of an unfolding providential design that culminated in him, and might now be expressed in a sort of prose poem:

> These two countries being separated neither by Sea, nor great River, Mountaine, nor other strength of nature, but onely by little brookes, or demolished little walles, so as rather they were divided in apprehension, than in effect; And now in the end and fulnesse of time united, the right and title of both in my Person…whereby it is now become like a little World within it selfe, being intrenched and fortified round about with a naturall, and yet admirable pond or ditch, whereby all the former feares of this Nation are now quite cut off.[67]

One notices the clever syntax: two countries 'is' become one 'nation'. But James was soon to discover the limits of poetry, the inability of the kingly poet or poet king to shape policy in the image of his rhetoric and make life imitate art. Reality is harder to hide in person than in persona: James could 'english' his orthography but not his accent, and the 'apprehension' that differentiated England from Scotland was not to be dispelled so easily. The coming years would witness vigorous hostility to the Scots in England as the legal and constitutional implications of the proposed 'union' became apparent. James had gained the English throne but 'Arthurs seate' would forever elude him. The poetic fiction that helped to promote his success would ultimately define his failure.

NOTES

1 John Lesley, *Historie of Scotland*, ed. E. G. Cody and W. Murison, trans. J. Dalrymple, 2 vols (Edinburgh, 1888–95), vol. 2, p. 128.

2 See Richard A. McCabe, 'Parody, sympathy and self: a response to Donald Cheney', *Connotations*, 13: 1–2 (2003–4), 5–22.

3 All quotations are from Edmund Spenser, *The Faerie Queene*, ed. A. C. Hamilton (London, 2001).

4 See Susan Doran, 'Loving and affectionate cousins? The relationship between Elizabeth I and James VI of Scotland 1586–1603', in Susan Doran and Glenn Richardson (eds), *Tudor England and its Neighbours* (Basingstoke, 2005), pp. 203–34; Susan Doran, 'James VI and the English succession', in Ralph Houlbrooke (ed.), *James VI and I: Ideas, Authority and Government* (Aldershot, 2006), pp. 25–42.

5 Peter C. Herman, '"Best of poets, best of kings": King James VI and I and the scene of monarchic verse', in Daniel Fischlin and Mark Fortier (eds), *Royal Subjects: Essays on the Writings of James VI and I* (Detroit, MI, 2002), pp. 61–103 (p. 61).

6 For the disappointments of the Anglo-Scottish treaty, see Maurice Lee, *Great Britain's Solomon: James VI and I in His Three Kingdoms* (Urbana, IL, 1990), pp. 64–5.

7 G. P. V. Akrigg (ed.), *Letters of King James VI & I* (Berkeley, CA, 1984), p. 71.

8 See Herman, 'Best of poets', pp. 62–72.

9 See Helen Georgia Stafford, *James VI of Scotland and the Throne of England* (New York and London, 1940).

10 David Allan, '"Arthur redivivus": politics and patriotism in Reformation Scotland', *Arthurian Literature*, 15 (1997), 185–204. See also Roger A. Mason, 'Scotland, Elizabethan England, and the idea of Britain', *Transactions of the Royal Historical Society*, 14 (2004), 279–93.

11 Peter Wentworth, *A Pithie Exhortation to her Maiestie for Establishing her Successor to the Crowne Whereunto is added a Discourse Containing the Authors Opinion of the True and Lawfull Successor to Her Maiestie* ([Edinburgh,] 1598), pp. 76–9 (2nd pag.).

12 Sir John Harington, *A Treatise on the Succession to the Crown (AD 1602)*, ed. C. R. Markham (London, 1880), p. 121. See Alan Stewart, *The Cradle King: A Life of James VI and I* (London, 2003), pp. 33–50.

13 See J. A. H. Murray (ed.), *The Romance and Prophecies of Thomas of Ercildoune*, Early English Text Society, o.s. 61 (London, 1875), pp. xxx–xlii.

14 See T. D. Kendrick, *British Antiquity* (London, 1950), pp. 37–44.

15 Walter Quin, *Sertum Poeticum, in Honorem Iacobi Sexti Serenissimi, ac Potentissimi Scotorum Regis* (Edinburgh, 1600), sig. B3^r. The poem was written in 1595.

16 Sir William Herbert, *A Prophesie of Cadwallader, Last King of the Britaines* (London, 1604), sig. B2^v.

17 Frederick Ives Carpenter, *A Research Guide to Edmund Spenser* (Chicago, IL, 1923), pp. 41–2.

18 See Patrick Collinson, 'The Elizabethan exclusion crisis and the Elizabethan polity', *Proceedings of the British Academy*, 84 (1994), 51–92.

19 Wentworth, *Pithie Exhortation*, pp. 16–28 (2nd pag.); R. Doleman [Robert Persons], *A Conference about the Next Succession to the Crowne of Ingland* ([Antwerp], 1594 [1595]), p. 117. For the Catholic dimension see Joel Hurstfield, 'The succession struggle in late Elizabethan England', in S. T. Bindoff, Joel Hurstfield and C. H. Williams (eds), *Elizabethan Government and Society: Essays Presented to Sir John Neale* (London, 1961), pp. 369–96.

20 Susan Doran, 'Revenge her foul and most unnatural murder? The impact of Mary Stewart's execution on Anglo-Scottish relations', *History*, 85 (2000), 589–612.

21 J. E. Phillips, *Images of a Queen: Mary Stuart in Sixteenth-Century Literature* (Berkeley, CA, 1964), pp. 200–1.

22 See Richard A. McCabe, 'The masks of Duessa: Spenser, Mary Queen of Scots, and James VI', *English Literary Renaissance*, 17 (1987), 224–42; Phillips, *Images of a Queen*, p. 165.

23 Akrigg (ed.), *Letters of King James*, pp. 77, 80.

24 See Robert S. Rait and Annie I. Cameron (eds), *King James's Secret: Negotiations between Elizabeth and James VI relating to the Execution of Mary Queen of Scots, from the Warrender Papers* (London, 1927).

25 William Warner, *Albions England* (1596), pp. 244–5, 247.

26 Akrigg (ed.), *Letters of King James*, pp. 44–5, 55–6.

27 See Wallace MacCaffrey, *Elizabeth I* (London, 1993), p. 89.

28 Akrigg (ed.), *Letters of King James*, p. 186.

29 See Christopher Highley, *Catholics Writing the Nation in Early Modern Britain and Ireland* (Oxford, 2008), pp. 105–6.

30 See esp. Wentworth, *Pithie Exhortation*, p. 76 (2nd pag.).

31 King James VI and I, *Selected Writings*, ed. Neil Rhodes, Jennifer Richards and Joseph Marshall (Aldershot, 2003), pp. 221–2. Hereafter King James, *Selected Writings*.

32 Harington, *A Treatise on the Succession to the Crown*, pp. 10–17.

33 *Inscriptiones Regum Scotorum* (Amsterdam, 1603), pp. 58–9.

34 Richard Mulcaster, *The Translation of Certaine Latine Verses Written upon her Maiesties Death* (London, 1603), sigs B1ᵛ–B2ʳ.

35 See Bruce Galloway, *The Union of England and Scotland 1603–1608* (Edinburgh, 1986), pp. 35–8; Glenn Burgess, 'Becoming English? Becoming British? The political thought of James VI & I before and after 1603', in Jean-Christophe Mayer (ed.), *The Succession Struggle in Late Elizabethan England: Politics, Polemics and Cultural Representations* (Montpellier, 2004), pp. 143–75.

36 *CSPVen 1603–7*, p. 5 (17 April 1603).

37 Samuel Daniel, *Complete Works*, ed. A. B. Grosart, 5 vols (London, 1885–96), vol. 1, p. 143.

38 King James, *Select Writings*, p. 35.

39 *Ibid.*, p. 22.

40 Jane Rickard, *Authorship and Authority: the Writings of James VI and I* (Manchester, 2007), p. 41.

41 *Englands Parnassus* (London, 1600), sig. Q4ʳ⁻ᵛ.

42 James Craigie (ed.), *The Poems of James VI of Scotland* 2 vols (Edinburgh, 1955–58), vol. I, p. 103.

43 Thomas Wilson, *The State of England, anno dom. 1600*, Camden Miscellany, 16 (London, 1936), p. 9.

44 Craigie (ed.), *Poems*, p. 102. For James's cultivation of religious verse, see James Doleman, 'The accession of King James I and English religious poetry', *Studies in English Literature*, 34 (1994), 19–40.

45 Sir John Harington (trans.), *Ludovico Ariosto's 'Orlando Furioso'*, ed. Robert McNulty (Oxford, 1972), p. 399.

46 Joan Grundy (ed.), *The Poems of Henry Constable* (Liverpool, 1960), p. 140.

47 *Ibid.*, pp. 149, 179.

48 Akrigg (ed.), *Letters of King James*, p. 191.

49 Jonathan Goldberg, *James I and the Politics of Literature: Jonson, Shakespeare, Donne, and their Contemporaries* (Baltimore, 1983), pp. 17–28.

50 King James, *Selected Writings*, p. 50.

51 *Ibid.*, pp. 94–5.

52 For this aspect of James's policy, see David Harris Willson, *King James VI and I* (London, 1956), pp. 142–9.

53 Rickard, *Authorship and Authority*, p. 38.

54 For *Lepanto* generally, see Daniel Fischlin, '"Like a mercenary poet": the politics and poetics of James VI's *Lepanto*', in Sally Mapstone (ed.), *Older Scots Literature* (Edinburgh, 2005), pp. 540–59.

55 *Ane Fruitfull Meditatioun contening ane plane and facill epositioun of ye 7.8.9. and 10 versis of the 20 Chap. of the Revelatioun in forme of ane sermone. Set doun be ye maist christiane King and synceir professour, and cheif defender of the trueth, IAMES the 6 King of Scottis* (1588) and *Ane Meditatioun upon the xxv, xxvi, xxvii, xxviii, and xxix verses of the xv chapt. of the first buke of the Chronicles of the Kingis* (1589). For a fuller account of these works, see Rickard, *Authorship and Authority*, pp. 76–82.

56 See Raphael Holinshed, *Chronicles of England, Scotland, and Ireland*, 6 vols (London, 1808), vol. 4, p. 262.

57 Akrigg (ed.), *Letters of King James*, p. 130; Leah S. Marcus, Janel Mueller and Mary Beth Rose (eds), *Elizabeth I: Collected Works* (Chicago, IL, 2000), p. 383.

58 *CSPScot*, 11, p. 431. See T. M. Cranfill, 'Barnaby Rich and King James', *ELH* 16 (1949), 65–75.

59 King James, *Selected Writings*, p. 203. See Jenny Wormald, 'James VI and I, *Basilikon Doron*, and the *Trew Law of Free Monarchies*: the Scottish context and the English translation', in Linda Levy Peck (ed.), *The Mental World of the Jacobean Court* (Cambridge, 1991), pp. 36–54 (pp. 49–50).

60 Harington, *A Treatise on the Succession to the Crown*, p. 86.

61 See Willson, *James VI and I*, p. 136.

62 King James, *Select Writings*, pp. 203, 204–5, 210, 218. See James Doleman, '"A king of thine own heart": the English reception of King James VI and I's *Basilikon Doron*', *The Seventeenth Century*, 9 (1994), 1–9.

63 King James, *Select Writings*, p. 252.

64 On the royal iconography, see Graham Parry, *The Golden Age Restor'd: The Culture of the Stuart Court* (Manchester, 1981), pp. 1–39.

65 For the bards, see Richard A. McCabe, *Spenser's Monstrous Regiment: Elizabethan Ireland and the Poetics of Difference*, 2nd edn (Oxford, 2005), pp. 52–3. Compare Thomas Greene, *A Poets Vision and a Princes Glorie* (London, 1603), sigs B4ᵛ–C1ʳ.

66 Galloway, *The Union of England and Scotland*, p. 15.

67 King James, *Selected Writings*, pp. 296, 298.

Part V

Britain and beyond

Chapter 11

Polemic and prejudice: a Scottish king for an English throne

Susan Doran

The execution of Mary Stuart in February 1587 left her son King James VI of Scotland as the claimant with the best title to the English succession. His great advantages comprised his lineage, legitimacy, gender and religion. None of his potential competitors could tick all these boxes. Yet despite his obvious advantages over potential competitors, James was all too aware that a peaceful succession might still elude him. English history taught that the monarch's bloodline was not always followed in matters of succession (the accession of Richard III rather than Edward V) and that a man with a weak title could take the throne (Henry VII). Furthermore, James correctly realised that two major obstacles stood in the way of his claim: prejudices surrounding his Scottish birth; and the general perception of him in England as untrustworthy. In this chapter I explore these drawbacks in turn, examining how each one kept the succession issue alive in the long 1590s. Additionally, I reveal how discussions about James's Scottish identity had repercussions on the sense of nationhood developing in England during this period.

JAMES VI: A FOREIGNER

In polemical literature, the Stuarts' foreign birth had always been at the centre of attempts to delegitimize their right to the English crown. As already seen, during the succession debates of the 1560s, the Protestant opponents of Mary Stuart usually presented legal, rather than religious, objections to her claim to be Elizabeth's heir, all of which were based on the Scottish Queen's foreign birth. Both English common law and a statute of Edward III, they asserted,

---

For suggestions and advice I would like to thank Paulina Kewes and Richard Proudfoot.

prohibited any foreigner from inheriting the crown, while Henry VIII's will had excluded the Stuart offspring of his elder sister Margaret on the grounds of their status as foreigners.[1] These legal impediments, inherited by James, were reviewed again in *A Conference about the Next Succession*, even though Robert Persons (under the pseudonym Doleman) was implicitly promoting the election of another foreign candidate, the Infanta of Spain.[2] For James's supporters, the legal objections repeated in *A Conference* were thought sufficiently weighty to warrant full and detailed replies, and so, to counter them, pro-Stuart polemicists of the 1590s did not just assert the hereditary principle but also tried to demonstrate that James's dynastic claim was legal according to English custom and statute.

Their arguments were not original but followed closely the pro-Stuart tracts of the 1560s and John Leslie's treatises in support of the Stuart title, the latest one published in English in 1584.[3] Following Leslie, James VI's propagandist Alexander Dickson explained in 1598 why the common law did not apply to the crown, and offered as precedents the historical examples of Stephen of Blois and Henry of Anjou who had become kings, even though born outside the allegiance of the English monarchy. As for the statute of 25 Edward III (1351), Dickson like Leslie maintained that it was not intended to apply to the 'enfants du roi'. Dickson also agreed with Leslie that Henry's will was a forgery but maintained that, even were it not, the document would have no validity since monarchs did not possess the right to donate the crown away from a legitimate heir and thereby defy the principle of the divine right of kings.[4] Dickson clearly judged that English law and Henry's will – both matters associated with James's foreign birth – were crucially important in the succession debates, for he placed them as the first and second of four 'bars' made in the 'libels' against James's accession and he devoted considerable space to rebutting them.[5]

While Dickson's tract remained in manuscript, John Colville's *Palinod*, which went over exactly the same points, though more briefly, was printed in Edinburgh in 1600.[6] Yet, some advocates of James still did not think this sufficient to end doubts about the legal situation, and consequently the manuscript tracts of both Sir John Harington (in 1602) and Sir Thomas Craig (January 1603) restated the arguments to contest the objections arising from the King's foreign birth and the will of Henry VIII.[7] Harington's polemic was in English and circulated amongst close friends; Craig's more learned treatise in Latin was presented to James.

Peter Wentworth's pro-Stuart tract, published posthumously in 1598/9, explains why these concerns remained pressing. He openly admitted that Edward III's statute was held to be a strong legal impediment to James's claim on two grounds: first, that the historical precedents of Stephen and Henry II did not hold water, as their accessions had predated the statute; second and more important, that when Elizabeth had consulted English judges and sergeants at law about the statute a few years previously, they had pronounced that the *'enfants du roi'* only extended to the first degree, and hence did not comprehend James. Although Wentworth tried to argue away these legal technicalities with a few of his own, he evidently believed that the judges' opinion was quite widely held in England.[8] So did Thomas Wilson. In 1600 he reported that Arbella Stuart had support as a successor because of her English birth, 'the want whereof, if our Lawyers opinions be corant, is the cause of his [James's] exclusion'.[9]

In their tracts, Dickson and Harington ignored these new objections but Craig dealt with them head-on. Providing both legal and historical evidence, he devoted nine chapters of his long and erudite treatise to cover every conceivable argument against a Scottish accession. His overall case concerning Edward III's statute was twofold: it dealt solely with private property; and its wording only excluded from the crown those who lived 'beyond the sea' and therefore exempted the Scots. Countering the claim that the historical examples of foreign kings in England predated Edward III, Craig reminded readers that Richard II, John of Gaunt (the father of Henry IV) and Lionel Duke of York (the ancestor of Edward IV) had all been born overseas yet had either ruled themselves or transmitted their right to their heirs.[10] Had Elizabeth not died so soon after Craig's delivery of his manuscript, it would very likely have been more widely disseminated since it answered not only Persons but also those doubts referred to by Wentworth. Craig was a respected jurist, so his analysis carried considerable clout.

Although official censorship and Elizabeth's disapproval limited the circulation of succession tracts in England, we can see from the comments of Wentworth and Wilson that the legal issues surrounding James's foreign birth were in the public domain. Furthermore, the general issue of his foreign birth informed other media. Many English dramatists expressed anxiety about foreign domination, while both *The Troublesome Raigne of King John* (*ca* 1591), now attributed to George Peele, and Shakespeare's adaptation, *King John* (*ca* 1596), directly engaged with the question of the foreign-born Arthur's right to the English throne.[11] The latter play opens with the announcement that Philip of France was seeking to uphold Arthur's 'most lawful claim' to England and closes with a rousing speech containing the lines:

> This England never did, nor never shall
> Lie at the proud foot of a conqueror
> But when it first did help to wound itself.[12]

The speaker here is the Bastard of Faulconbridge, the English-born son of Richard Lionheart (invented by Peele in Shakespeare's source play), who displays characteristics throughout the drama that suggest he would make a far better king than either of the two claimants born in wedlock: surely this is another instance of the contemporary relevance of the play, given that Lord Beauchamp, the main English competitor of James, was legally a bastard!

JAMES VI: A SCOT

James's foreign birth, therefore, proved a live issue right until his accession. But the King was not just foreign; he was also Scottish, which added another dimension to the debate about the desirability of his succession. In the 1590s, Persons brought James's national identity to the foreground when he delineated several 'great inconueniences' that would result from a Scottish king sitting on an English throne in order to demonstrate that Englishmen had far more to fear from a Scottish than a Spanish monarch. Because of Scotland's poverty, explained Persons, a dynastic union with that kingdom (unlike an alliance with Spain) would bring England no economic advantage but, on the contrary, would drain the realm of its 'commodities and riches'. Furthermore, since history had manifestly demonstrated 'the auersion and natural alienation of that people, from the Inglish', the union between the two realms could not last and would end in 'slaughter, bloodshed, and infinyt losses and charges of Ingland'. In the meantime, there was the danger of foreign oppression, as James would necessarily have to rely for his authority on 'his owne nation, and allied frends', namely the French, Danes and 'the vnciuil [Gaelic]part of Ireland'. The results, warned Persons, would be just as calamitous for the English as they had been when Canute advanced his Danes and William the Conqueror his Normans.[13] How much better it would be, argued Persons, for England to be subject to the distant 'great and mightie' power of Spain than be 'under a little prince or King' of a neighbouring realm.[14] Finally, disagreeing with 'the fauourers' of James who pointed to similarities between England and Scotland especially in matters of religion, Persons asserted that the two realms had little in common and were even disunited in their religion, for the Presbyterianism of the Kirk was 'different or rather opposite to that forme which in Ingland is mainteyned'.[15]

Persons's arguments fell on fertile ground, because ethnic prejudices against the Scots were commonplace in Elizabethan England.[16] Sixteenth-century Scottish Highlanders – or Redshanks, as they were called – were generally portrayed as wild, rude and unruly, a separate people with an alien, even uncivilized, culture, who were often described as closer to the Irish than the English in their dress and language.[17] The sixteenth-century migration of Scots into Ulster, as well as current reports reaching England of aid offered by the Highlands and Islands to Irish rebels, confirmed this impression of a natural affinity between the two peoples. James himself admitted – or so it was said – that he could not stay his subjects' aid to the Irish because there was 'suche a love betwene his people and them'.[18]

Another general prejudice held by the English was that the ancestors of contemporary Scots were thought to be unusually barbaric. Although, of course, he knew better, William Camden was aware that ordinary people mistakenly believed that the Scots were cannibals, a misunderstanding that had arisen, he explained, because the 'vulgar sort' did not realise that St Jerome – the source for this piece of information – was referring merely to the 'Attacotti', not the whole Scottish nation.[19] The Picts, commonly associated with the Scots, were likewise held to be barbaric: Holinshed's *Chronicles* described them as a 'wild and sauage people' who 'persecuted' their more civilized southern neighbour;[20] while Theodor de Bry's three engravings of Picts in Thomas Harriot's *A Briefe and True Report of... Virginia* (1590) reinforced the stereotype, especially the first plate which showed a Pictish warrior brandishing the head of an enemy with another at his feet.[21]

Although Lowland Scots – of whom James was one – were recognized as closer to the English in culture, the Elizabethan stereotype of them too was overwhelmingly negative.[22] In chronicles, Scots were usually shown as unchivalrous or untrustworthy, such as when Holinshed's *Chronicles* recorded how William Wallace took 'pleasure to behold' the humiliation he inflicted on some 'religious', and how Scottish soldiers skinned the corpse of Sir Hugh Cressingham 'for the malice' which they bore toward him.[23] In popular culture the Scots were commonly identified with ruffianly pirates and 'cruell' reivers, an association that was seemingly borne out by direct experiences, judging from complaints to the Privy Council.[24] The tale of the depredations and death of the pirate Sir Andrew Barton appeared in various chronicles as well as in at least one ballad that had been orally transmitted before its printing in 1630. Similarly, 'John Armstrong's last good-night' – which contained the line 'Scotland is so full of treachery' – related the story of how that particular notorious Scottish reiver was killed at the court of James V.[25]

Scottish kings and nobles, not just their unruly subjects, were equally objects of popular prejudice; their treachery and cowardice were common tropes in print and drama. Chronicles made great play of how Scottish kings and nobles owed and offered fealty to the king of England but then perfidiously denounced or denied it whenever they chose. Chronicles (Stow's even more than Holinshed's) also offered many occasions when the Scots avoided fighting, sped over the border after a raid into England, or fled from the field of battle.[26] In drama, Scottish kings and lords tended to be disloyal, duplicitous and cowardly. In George Peele's *Edward I* (published in 1593) John Baliol and 'these treacherous Scottes' betrayed the English King in throwing off his suzerainty and refusing to give homage, once he took the throne.[27] Likewise, in *Edward III* (1596), which Shakespeare may have co-written, Montague tells the English nobles:

> The treacherous [Scottish] king no sooner was informed
> Of your withdrawing of your army back,
> But straight, forgetting of his former oath,
> He made invasion of the bordering towns.[28]

In the next scene, the Scottish King retreats hastily before an English advance and the Countess of Salisbury sneers at 'The confident and boist'rous boasting Scot' who

> Turned hence against the blasting north-east wind
> Upon the bare report and name of arms.[29]

In two very different plays – the anonymous comedy *The Pinner of Wakefield* and Robert Greene's generic hybrid *The Scottish History of James the Fourth* (published in 1599 and 1598 respectively) – Scottish kings were dark figures, despite the plays' light tone. In the former, King James of Scotland is first met warring hard on the borders, where he threatens to slaughter the young son of a married Englishwoman if she does not comply with his lustful desires.[30] In the latter, the eponymous James IV is first ready to betray his new English bride, because of his lust for the Scottish beauty, Ida, and is later persuaded by the sycophant, Ateukin, to murder her. Furthermore, playgoers were told through a speech of Bohun, a disgruntled Scot, in the Induction that the corrupt and unruly court depicted in the play was 'much like our court of Scotland this day'.[31] Indeed so common were negative representations of the stage Scot that London 'comediens' performing in Edinburgh felt no qualms about putting on a play that did 'scorne the King and people of this lande', while, just before Elizabeth's death, her putative heir James was the subject of satire on the English stage.[32]

Additionally, Scots appeared regularly in chronicles as the ancient enemy who (with the exception of Bannockburn) had been regularly trounced on the battlefield. Elizabethan chronicles were littered with examples of English victories over the Scots, triumphs that displayed the justice of the English cause as well as the superiority of their martial skills. To take but one example: according to Holinshed's *Chronicles*, the Scottish army at Flodden enjoyed an advantageous position and possessed superior numbers, but the English soldiers won a magnificent victory largely because they were 'kindled with desire to fight' so that 'they might shew what earnest wils they had to be reuenged; not onelie of new receiued wrongs, but also of ancient iniuries'.[33] Although Holinshed allowed that James IV and his noblemen had fought valiantly at Flodden, more usually, the Scots were presented as cowardly and their defeats as ignominious. Stow made no mention of Scottish valour at Flodden but merely noted that 17,000 Scots were slain there in contrast to the 5,000 or so English soldiers.

Persons, then, was exploiting deeply rooted anti-Scottish sentiment in *A*

Conference. But he was also repeating arguments made earlier by Protestants who had opposed Mary Stuart's accession. One English polemicist had then declared that it would be dishonourable if the Scots, who owed homage to England, should now come to rule over their realm, and he also claimed that the Scots would 'force us to lyve in the same sort of servitude and bondage that those of other Contreys doth lyve' under the government of strangers'.[34] There was nothing new in Persons's assault on James's title on the grounds of his Scottishness; and therein lay its potency.

JAMES VI: ENGLISHMAN OR BRITON?

In order to counter Persons and to sidestep the anti-Scottish feeling within English culture, James's adherents deployed a variety of rhetorical strategies. First, they all tried to present the Stuart monarchs as English, not aliens, in lineage and consequently as pro-English in sympathy. Mary, argued Leslie, was 'no stranger to England'; being descended from the 'Royal blood of the Realme', she had 'come so many ways of English blood'.[35] With an English-born father, explained Wentworth, James was still more English: 'he who is so often, and by both his parents descended of English blood, wil in England becom English and a favourer cheiflie of Englishmen'.[36] The same trick had been played when Philip of Spain married Mary I, and he was cast in pageant, pamphlet, poem and printed genealogy as an honorary Englishman because of his descent from Edward III.[37]

Second, James constructed an image of himself as English, not only in his lineage, but also in his language and culture. Although he promoted Scottish poetry at his court, his own poems published in England were in the English tongue, and extracts from them came to be included in *England's Parnassus*, a celebration of the best of English poetry.[38] When his first-born son was baptized, James took the opportunity to parade the English character and sophistication of his court before the English ambassadors. Moreover, William Fowler's narrative of the celebrations (targeting an English readership) describes a tournament which included masques as well as fighting, and a feast where women sat next to men (as occurred in England but not Scotland), all of which would have seemed familiar to readers of accounts of Elizabethan tilts and entertainments.[39] Meanwhile, in *Basilikon Doron*, James distanced himself from the Celtic peoples of the Highlands and Islands when he expressed his intention to 'reforme and civilize' the 'best inclined' of them and root out 'the barbarous and stubborne sort'.[40]

Third, polemicists favouring a Stuart succession made much of the fact that James had been born on the island of Britain. Because Britons, they claimed, shared a common heritage, history and culture, the Scottish King (unlike the Infanta of Spain) was not really a foreigner at all. And, contrary to Persons's view, the two British realms of England and Scotland shared a 'vnitie of true religion, vnitie of language, likenes of discipline and manners'.[41] James's accession, therefore, would not result in a foreign yoke, as Persons had alleged, but would bring together two similar nations in one people on one island. In the words of one anonymous pro-Stuart writer, 'yt seemeth most meett that since both the Countries are but one Island they should be also under one dominion'.[42] In adopting this line of argument, he and other writers opened up discussions about the nature of 'Britishness' and stimulated questions about national identity that were to be raised again in the union debates of 1604–7.

Within England, the sense of a Britain as a geo-political entity had a long, if contested, history, and stories of Brut's foundation of Britain and Arthur's heroic conquests over the island flourished in the late Elizabethan period.[43] Furthermore, during the 1590s, a number of English writers defended the historicity of these kings even though George Buchanan in 1582, like Polydore Vergil before him, had exposed them as the fabrications of Geoffrey of Monmouth.[44] Of course national pride was partly at stake in these exchanges, as English patriots were loath to lose such noble national heroes, but Richard Harvey's attack on Buchanan and defence of Brutus as a historical figure in *Philadelphus* could well have been written to encourage a more positive attitude towards a Scottish accession. A defence of Brutus was an unusual topic for Harvey to tackle; his patron and dedicatee was the Earl of Essex, who was at that time developing ties with James VI, and the work was published in 1593, a time when the succession was on the political agenda.[45]

The myth of a historically united British kingdom was also valuable in that it could help prove that James was not technically – even legally – an alien. In his succession tract, Harington maintained that because Scotland was 'taken and holden as subject to England by way of homage', James could be deemed no foreigner; and Harington speculated that 'the subjection of Scotland by way of homage to the Crowne of England' was possibly the result of it being 'accompted of old but one dominion or Allegiance'.[46] Repeating Wentworth, Harington also referred to the judicial decision made in 1571 that a Scot accused of rape was not 'to be accompted in England for a stranger, but rather a subiect', because of England's suzerainty over Scotland.[47]

In Scotland, these arguments and the Brutus myth understandably carried far less sway just because of their association with Anglocentric imperialism.[48] Furthermore, many intellectual Scots imagined their civilisation (or at least that of the Lowlands) as cultured and independent.[49] James himself took pride in his Celtic forebears and traced his ancestry back not to Brut but, through Banquo, to the equally mythical Fergus I of Ireland.[50] So did his the Presbyterian divine and poet Andrew Melville who, in an unpublished and unfinished epic poem that looked forward to a British union, ignored Brut and described James as '*Maxime Fergusidum*' (Greatest of the sons of

Fergus).[51] Craig went further and explicitly rejected the Brutus myth, and not simply because it was an ahistorical fable but rather because England's right to demand homage from the Scottish king derived from it. For the same reason, Craig dismissed Arthur as a 'fabulous' figure and declared the stories that the King had subdued Scotland and demanded homage from the Scots to be 'monstrous Lies' spread by English writers for their own political ends.[52] Craig even questioned whether the island of Britain had ever existed as a geo-political entity. During Roman times, he wrote, 'it is certain that the antient Writers did by the Name of Britain, understand only that part which was inhabited by the Britains, and inclos'd within Severns's Wall as a Roman Province'.[53] Before then, Britain seemed to be divided into many towns, tribes and provinces: 'If in Kent alone there were four Kings, how many must we allow to all Britain?'[54]

Nonetheless, some Scots – including James when it suited him – were prepared to play the Arthurian card in order to promote the King's claim to the English succession. The Irish poet Walter Quin was rewarded well in 1595 after he presented James with a 'treatise of poesie' celebrating his claim 'by heavinlie providence' to Arthur's seat and anagrammatizing his full name (Charles James Stuart) to 'Claimes Arthur's Seat' and 'Ceass Letts, I am Arthur'. It was James's destiny, wrote Quin, 'to clayme my seat and throne, / My kingdomes severed to rejoyne in one'. Five years later, James ensured that Quin's 'litle bowke of annagrames' was reissued.[55]

Of course, even James's strongest supporters could not deny that Scotland and England had spent many years warring against each other. But some of them tried to turn this historical fact to their political advantage by arguing that dynastic union would bring eternal peace to the two realms in much the same way as Henry VII's marriage to Elizabeth of York had ended the discord between the two warring houses of Lancaster and York.[56] On the frontispiece of Leslie's 1584 tract was the rhyme

> All Britaine Yle (dissentions over past)
> In peace & faith, will growe to one at last.

To reinforce the point, Concordia was depicted between two soldiers in the border at the bottom. At the same time within his text Leslie was keen to point out the benefits of a dynastic union that 'after so long warres, they wolde now at last agree, and ioyne together in one true league of frendshippe and amitie'.[57] Wentworth, likewise, admitted that 'These two Realms could never hitherto agree because they were still kept as two' and that for war to end between them 'it is absolutelie necessarie, that they be vnited in one'.[58]

Craig, however, took a different tack. He made a case that the two realms had always been natural allies when united against a common – and irreligious – foe. Past Anglo-Scottish wars, he wrote, were the result of the English kings' illegitimate and unreasonable demand for homage and not a natural antipathy between the two peoples. Before then, in the eleventh century, the Christian Scots had helped England against the heathen Danes at great cost to themselves; more recently, during the reigns of Henry VIII and Edward VI, Protestant Scots had worked for union, only to be foiled by the 'fierce prelate', Cardinal Beaton, and the French whose friendship 'had cost us so much Blood'; finally, under Elizabeth, once Protestants took over the government of Scotland, 'continual peace' had reigned between the two realms. Returning to Scottish unionist arguments of the 1540s, Craig saw James's future succession in providential terms, as the union of two Protestant realms against Catholics, and he dismissed claims that the differences between the two Churches were significant and a cause of disunity.[59] Implicitly, so did Melville, when he celebrated the birth in February 1594 of James's first child, Prince Henry, with a Latin poem – *Principis Scoti-Britannorum Natalia* – which looked forward to the union of two peoples who together would destroy the power of Catholic Rome and Spain: '*Gloria nunc quibus / Quantisque surget Scoto-Britannica / Rebus?*' (To what great heights will Scoto-Britannic glory now rise?), he asked.[60]

All pro-Stuart polemicists countered Persons by pointing to the practical benefits that England would gain from union with Scotland: the northern back door would be permanently locked against the French or any other potential enemy; money could be saved on defending the northern border; Irish rebels would no longer rely on aid from the Scots; indeed both nations could send troops there to suppress rebellion. And most important of all, the peace between the two realms would result in an increase in the dominion and power of England.[61] With its increase in land and population, a newly united Britain would count far more internationally than did England alone.

JAMES VI'S REPUTATION IN ENGLAND

James VI's nationality was his main disadvantage in his bid to succeed Elizabeth, but it was not the only one. Another handicap was the general perception of him as weak and untrustworthy, characteristics that understandably created uncertainty and anxieties about his fitness to rule over England. The English government – especially Burghley and Robert Cecil – consistently received negative reports about James from a variety of sources: the many 'Advices from Scotland' which described the political state of the country; the regular dispatches detailing James's statements and behaviour that frequently arrived from ambassadors and agents based in Edinburgh; and the rumours passed on by spies and intelligencers on the continent about James's exchanges with Catholics and foreign powers. Gossip and speculation about the King's clandestine activities co-existed with genuine news items, and it was not easy to discern which, if any, information was accurate. Nonetheless, there was sufficient consistency in the material transmitted to the English court to stimulate concern about James's susceptibility to favourites, his difficulties in asserting royal authority, his unreliability in religion and his tendency to be economical with the truth. It is sometimes stated that the English were ignorant about their new king in 1603, but in reality their ignorance stemmed not from a total lack of information about the King but rather from James's own secretiveness and double-dealings, which fed rumour and uncertainty.

Doubts about James's abilities as a ruler stemmed primarily from what observers perceived to be his failure to control both his Presbyterian ministers and factional nobility. Elizabeth and Bishop Bancroft were scathing about the King's powerlessness in relation to the Kirk (at least, until 1597).[62] Equally, Elizabeth frequently accused James of weakness in failing to stand up to the Scottish nobility and especially in 'winking at' the Catholic Earls' open practice of their religion. Part of the problem here, it was thought, was James's propensity to be swayed by intimates, or, as William Bowes expressed it in May 1599, 'the fatall facillitye of this k[ing]' to be influenced by the members of his chamber.[63] The mysterious Gowrie conspiracy of August 1600 – though foiled – reignited concerns about the King's authority and political acumen. After all, even according to the official version, the Earl of Gowrie and his accomplices had successfully tricked the King into riding unawares into a trap and nearly murdered him. Their motives, moreover, seemed factional since no satisfactory explanation was given for their treason.[64]

However, rather than just weak, James was for the most part considered to be untrustworthy and duplicitous. His secret communications with the Earl of Tyrone were thought a case in point. In January 1598, Cecil complained: 'Her Majesty has been informed out of Ireland that Tyrone hath much bragged to have written to the Scottish King, and that her Majesty knoweth he hath had it. Of all which, he never advertised the Queen'.[65] Suspicions were also aroused when James received at his court James McSorley, who 'had maintained open Rebellion in Ireland', less than a month after his victory over an English army and capture of Olderfleet. To Cecil's mind, the King was 'thereby comforting and upholding with his countenance the rebellion in Irlande', all in contravention of the treaty of alliance between the two realms and James's promise to assist Elizabeth against her rebels.[66]

Cecil and his father also suspected that James had deliberately turned a blind eye to the activities of the Catholic Earls and Jesuits at his court, because either he secretly shared their religion or else he was using them as conduits in his negotiations with Rome and Spain. This conclusion seemed confirmed by the 1592 affair of the 'Spanish Blanks', although James hotly denied involvement, declaring that all such accusations were 'falslye and malitiouslye invented'.[67] Many in England, however, were not convinced. In April 1594 Tobie Matthew, Dean of Durham, warned Burghley not to believe any of James's statements, as he was 'a great dissembler, by all men's judgment that know him best'.[68]

The reports of double agents from within the exiled Catholic community and testimonies from priests captured in England seemed to verify Matthew's judgement. Throughout the 1590s they revealed James's communications with Rome and the Spanish King, and passed on rumours that he intended either to convert to Catholicism or to offer a degree of religious toleration in England, all in order to secure international Catholic aid for his pursuit of the English throne. Given that James was said to be building up a party amongst English 'Puritans' as well, it would be surprising if Cecil and other recipients of such reports did not judge him guilty of religious cynicism as well as deception.[69] Even worse, during 1598 and 1599, Cecil had reason to suspect that James was laying plans to invade England with the aid of foreign allies – both Catholic and Protestant – and impose his rule by conquest. Spies were issuing warnings that James intended 'to gather grapes befor they be rype' and 'to cut the grass under her Majestie's feet'.[70] More reliable information, gleaned from the Secretary's agents in Scotland, seemed to corroborate these alarmist rumours, when they told of James's overtures to his German and Danish in-laws and plans to levy an army of his own. That Cecil took these reports seriously is suggested by his instructions in July 1599 that Attorney General Coke should question one Weyman, amongst other matters, '[w]hat reasons he hath to persuade that the Scot entendeth a conquest'.[71]

It is difficult to know how far members of the wider political community had access to similar information about James. Certainly, well-informed and politically engaged people were regular recipients of the gossip and rumour that reached the court. Furthermore, some of them may have read for themselves materials that would result in a similar questioning of James's trustworthiness, especially in regard to the Protestant Church and 'godly' religion. In circulation in 1598 and 1599 were a couple of libellous pamphlets, written by two warring members of the exiled Catholic community, that disclosed the nature of James's negotiations in Spain and made public Catholic hopes for his conversion. The first, by the Jesuit William Crichton (whose involvement in the 'Spanish Blanks' affair was already quite extensively known), accused his long-time enemy John Cecil (a Catholic priest and emissary of the Scottish Catholic earls) of writing a libel against James and handing it over to Philip II. According to Crichton, John Cecil had called James 'an impious and dishonourable Prince' and 'an obstinate heretick', whereas in reality the King was ripe for future conversion and a present protector of all Catholics who were not traitors. Crichton's pamphlet circulated only in manuscript, but it was immediately noticed.[72] John Cecil's rebuttal, which went into print the following year, did nothing to rescue James's reputation amongst Protestants, for he claimed that he had recommended James's 'cause, person and conversion' to the Pope.[73] Both Crichton and Cecil's works, therefore, confirmed that many Catholics believed James to be sympathetic to their religion and as a result had been pressing his cause in Spain and Rome. Indeed John Cecil criticized Crichton on this very point, namely bringing James's 'actions to publique examination that might better have bene past ouer with sylence'.[74]

James's 1599 treatise for his son, *Basilikon Doron* may also have alarmed some English Protestants. Although the King had only allowed seven copies to be printed, a bowdlerized version was 'vented and set foorth to the publicke view of the world'; and, according to James, it contained 'some sentences therein [which] should seeme to furnishe groundes to men, to doubt of my sinceritie in that Religion, which I haue euer constantly professed'.[75] Because of his 'sharp and bitter wordes' against the Puritans, explained James, some Protestants had mistakenly thought he was critical of all preachers, especially those who objected to the surplice and other 'outward badges of Popishe errours'.[76] We cannot know how many of James's future subjects in England had read *Basilikon Doron* before his accession, but a number definitely knew of its existence and contents.[77] One reader, moreover, in noting down some passages from the book, underlined those quotations that expressed criticisms of the Scottish Reformation and Scottish ministers.[78] All too aware of the rumours spreading in England about his dislike of the Kirk and toleration of Catholics, James felt the need to contradict 'such malitiouse calumnnyes and iniust imputacons'. He consequently asked one of his agents in England to assure English Protestants that he would 'not only mainteyne and continew ye profession of ye Gospell there, but withall not suffer or permitt any other Religion to be professed and avowed within the bounds of the kingdome'.[79]

This was not all that James attempted in order to enhance his reputation in England. As seen earlier in this chapter, he and his friends encouraged or organized the publication in England of his poetry and descriptions of celebratory events at his court.[80] Also aimed at an English readership was his version of the Gowrie conspiracy. Originally printed by Robert Waldegrave in Edinburgh, it was soon afterwards reprinted in London by Valentine Simmes. While it is possible that Robert Cecil was behind this piece of propaganda, as George Nicolson had sent him a copy of the Edinburgh pamphlet, it is more likely that either Simmes received the pamphlet directly from Waldegrave or else the Earl of Essex was the patron.[81] Cecil had not yet been won over to the Scottish King's cause, and *The Earle of Gowries Conspiracie* contains many elements that were designed to recommend James to his future English subjects. Early in the text, James respects his subjects' right to their own treasure, expresses hostility to Catholic priests and is initially suspicious of the conspirator Master Alexander Ruthven. Once taken prisoner and under threat of death James is fearless and resourceful; when freed, he immediately offers thanks to God for his deliverance 'assuring himself that God had preserved him from so despaired a peril, for the persisting of some greater worke be had to his glorie, and for procuring by him the weale of his people'. Finally, the text makes much of James's general popularity in Scotland. The bell-ringing, bonfires and large crowds that gathered to greet him over the following week bear 'testimony of the subiectes hearty affection and ioy for his maiesties deliverie'.[82]

It is hard to know how successful James was in demonstrating to the English that he would make a good king. Whatever historians now conclude about his performance as king of Scotland, his future English subjects possessed strong evidence that he was devious, duplicitous and capable of treachery. Indeed his character seemed all too close to that of the stereotypical Scot they encountered in literature and history. Nonetheless, by the turn of the century, more positive descriptions of James were beginning to circulate, such as Sir Henry Wotton's complimentary appraisal in June 1602 where he praised the King's *'bonta natural tirando al modesto'* (natural goodness verging on modesty), his learning, especially in theology, and his readiness to take counsel. Also approving was Wotton's comment that James was far less under the control of his ministers than he had been in the past, and was *'piu sul grave sul severo'* (more serious and severe) with his magnates. Wotton did offer the familiar criticism that James was *'tenuto per un di piu secreti Principi del mondo'* (held to be one of the most secret Princes in the world) in his handling of state affairs, but this was not stressed, nor even perhaps intended as disapproving.[83] Wotton's account was based on personal experience, but – by then anyway – many others too were focusing on positive qualities they could detect in the man who was most likely to succeed their ageing Queen. Robert Cecil had of course been converted from an enemy into an ally.

CONCLUSION

Given all this hostility, how then did James VI become Elizabeth's unchallenged successor in March 1603? Well, as Alexander Courtney and Thomas M. McCoog, SJ, have shown in Chapters 7 and 13 respectively, James's peaceful accession owed much to Cecil's *volte face* after the Essex rising and Philip III's decision not to pursue the Infanta's spurious claim. Paulina Kewes's argument (in Chapter 3) that Persons's *A Conference* played into James's hands by winning over godly Protestant support is also pertinent. Furthermore, by March 1603, there was simply no credible alternative that the English could rally around. Arbella Stuart lost potential political support after her foolhardy bid at the beginning of 1603 to elope with a grandson of Katherine Grey.[84] On the Suffolk side, death in 1600 removed from the frame Thomas Seymour, Katherine Grey's younger son, who unlike his elder brother could claim to be legitimate. Huntingdon was also dead, and neither Edward Seymour, Lord Beauchamp, nor William Stanley, sixth Earl of Derby, showed the remotest sign of interest in fighting James for the throne.[85]

James's accession was naturally greeted with sermons, treatises and poems that heralded the benefits expected to flow from dynastic union with Scotland.[86] However, ambivalence about a Scottish succession was still evident and neatly summed up in the perspicacious words of the Venetian envoy: 'The heretics partly desire him and partly they reject him as a stranger'.[87] Furthermore, issues raised in the 1590s succession tracts about the advantages and disadvantages of a Scottish monarch immediately resurfaced. Only two days after Elizabeth's death, Sir Robert Cotton produced a short discourse that reprised the theme of England and Scotland being 'of one discent in bloud, of one language and ioyntlie by the mayne Seas separated from other nations, the Religion all the same, and so the church policy nowe and of old'. At the same time, Cotton implicitly recognized at least one problem with the new dynastic union; a new name for James's inheritance was needed to prevent one of his kingdoms feeling subservient to the other, as might well happen 'if either name should conteyne or proceade the other'.[88] When deciding that no name 'ariseth any fitter then Brittain, either in its capacity or regall practice', Cotton noticeably ignored its derivation from the disputed Brutus, and looked instead to its usage by Aristotle and under the Romans.[89]

Once James presented proposals for a more perfect union between his two realms, issues surrounding 'Britishness' and the separate identities of England and Scotland came fully under the spotlight, but once again they had already been rehearsed in late-Elizabethan succession literature. Take John Hayward's 1604 tract, where the benefits of union were there listed as 'the extinguishing of warres betweene the two nations' and 'the enlargement both of dominion and power'.[90] He argued that greater constitutional union was possible because the two kingdoms had once been one and consequently now shared common features:

> the fundamentall lawes (as they are termed) of both kingdomes and Crownes doe well agree. In other lawes of gouernment they hold good conformitie, as hauing heretofore bin vnder one scepter; but now by long seuerance the lawes of either nation are like a shooe worne long vpon one foote, and thereby made rather vnseemely than vnseruiceable for the other.[91]

Union of hearts, claimed Hayward, was also achievable because the English and Scots were so alike in habits and language: 'For they are both of one climate, not onely annexed entirely together, but separated from all the world'.[92] Those against the union, similarly, drew upon arguments that had long been in the public domain. Henry Spelman, for instance, contended that the two realms were so different in laws, manners and language that they needed at least seven years to get used to each other before any changes were introduced. The Scots, he argued, were more similar in language and customs to the Irish than to the English; and their laws were continental and thus different from English common law.[93]

So, even though new constitutional principles and issues arose during the parliamentary debates on union, the underlying arguments were fundamentally the same as those expressed in the 1590s. The British question did not appear out of the blue in late 1603, for the dilemma of the late-Elizabethan succession had been instrumental in reopening and reinvigorating discussions about union and 'Britishness'. I would argue, then, that the succession should be counted alongside the Reformation and the 'timeless desire to believe that the past can be recaptured' amongst those forces that fostered senses of national identity in late-Elizabethan and early-Stuart England.[94]

NOTES

1 [John Leslie], *A Defence of… the Princesse Marie Quene of Scotlande…1569* (London, 1569); NLS, Advocates' MS 6.1.19, fos 97–103[v], an undated tract that was probably written in the 1570s; CUL, Dd.ix.14, fos 53–60[v]; CUL, Ii.iv.33, fos 42[v]–46.

2 R. Doleman [Robert Persons], *A Conference about the Next Succession to the Crowne of Ingland* ([Antwerp], 1594 [1595]), pp. 111–17. For the debates, see Chapter 2 of this volume.

3 John Leslie, *A Treatise Towching the Right, Title, and Interest of the Most Excellent Princess Marie, Queene of Scotland, and of the Most Noble King Iames* (Rouen, 1584). For Leslie, see Chapter 2 in this volume.

4 Alexander Dickson, 'Of the right of the Crowne efter Hir Majesty', NLS, Advocates' MS 31.4.8, especially fos 53[r]–62[v]. For Dickson, see Susan Doran 'Three late-Elizabethan succession tracts', in Jean-Christophe Mayer (ed.), *The Succession Struggle in Late Elizabethan England: Politics, Polemics and Cultural Representations* (Montpellier, 2004), pp. 91–117.

5 The remainder, which were also raised in *A Conference*, were the Act of Attainder against Mary, and the superiority of the hereditary right of the House of Lancaster over that of York.

6 *The Palinod of Iohn Coluill* (Edinburgh, 1600).

7 Sir John Harington, *A Treatise on the Succession to the Crown (AD 1602)*, ed. C. R. Markham (London, 1880), pp. 34, 55–6; Thomas Craig, *The Right of Succession to the Kingdom of England* (London, 1703), pp. 246–304.

8 Peter Wentworth, *A Pithie Exhortation to her Maiestie for Establishing her Successor to the Crowne Whereunto is added a Discourse Containing the Authors Opinion of the True and Lawfull Successor to Her Maiestie* ([Edinburgh,] 1598), pp. 8–11 (2nd pag.).

9 Thomas Wilson, *The State of England, Anno Dom. 1600*, Camden Miscellany, 16 (2nd series, 1936), p. 2.

10 Craig, *Right of Succession*, pp. 246–304.

11 Paulina Kewes, 'History plays and the royal succession', in Paulina Kewes, Ian W. Archer and Felicity Heal (eds), *The Oxford Handbook of Holinshed's Chronicles* (Oxford, 2013), pp. 493–509 (esp. pp. 499–504); for Peele's play, see Brian Vickers, 'The *Troublesome Raigne*, George Peele, and the date of *King John*', in Brian Boyd (ed.), *Words That Count: Essays on Early Modern Authorship in Honor of MacDonald P Jackson* (Cranbury, NJ,

2004), pp. 78–116. For Shakespeare's play, see Robert Lane, '"The sequence of posterity": Shakespeare's King John and the succession controversy', *Studies in Philology*, 92 (1995), 460–81, especially 468–72, and Willy Maley, '"And bloody England into England gone": empire, monarchy and nation in *King John*', in Willy Maley and Margaret Tudeau-Clayton (eds), *This England That Shakespeare* (Farnham, 2010), pp. 49–61 (esp. pp. 56–7). John is referred to in many succession tracts: Harington, *A Treatise on the Succession to the Crown*, p. 59; John Hayward, *An Answer to the First Part of a Certain Conference Concerning Succession, Published Not Long Since under the Name of R. Dolman* (London, 1603), sigs S2ᵛ–S3; Craig, *Right of Succession*, pp. 179, 281–2.

12 Act 5.7, lines 112–5, *The Arden Shakespeare: Complete Works*, ed. Richard Proudfoot *et al.*, p. 631.

13 Doleman [Persons], *A Conference*, pp. 118–23.These arguments are summarized in the anonymous tract CUL, Ii.iv.33, fos 52ᵛ–3ᵛ.

14 Doleman [Persons], *A Conference*, p. 193.

15 *Ibid.*, p. 123.

16 Christopher Highley contends that racialism informs *A Conference* in *Catholics Writing the Nation in Early Modern Britain and Ireland* (Oxford, 2008), p. 98. See also Roger Mason, 'Scotland', in *Oxford Handbook of Holinshed's Chronicles*, pp. 648–62.

17 William Harrison, *The Description of England*, ed. Georges Edelen (Washington, DC, and New York, 1994), pp. 417–18; John Stow, *The Chronicles of England* (London, 1580), p. 9; William Camden, *Britain, or A chorographicall description of the most flourishing kingdomes, England, Scotland, and Ireland, and the ilands adjoining*…trans. Philemon Holland, 2nd edn (London, 1637), pp. 5, 126. See also Christopher Highley, *Shakespeare, Spenser, and the Crisis in Ireland* (Cambridge, 1997), pp. 68, 69.

18 8 July 1598, TNA, SP52/62, fo. 49ᵛ.

19 Camden, *Britain*, p. 127. Book 3 of William Warner's *Albions England* (1597) had earlier made the same allegation. For the roots of this prejudice, see Arthur H. Williamson, 'Scots, Indians and empire: the Scottish politics of civilization 1519–1609', *Past and Present*, 150 (1996), 46–83 (esp. pp. 47–52).

20 Raphael Holinshed, *The Chronicles of England, Scotlande, and Irelande* (London, 1587), vol. 2, p. 72 (online edition p. 71).

21 Andrew Hadfield, 'Bruited abroad: John White and Thomas Harriot's colonial representations of ancient Britain', in David J. Baker and Willy Maley (eds), *British Identities and English Renaissance Literature* (Cambridge, 2002), pp. 159–77 (esp. pp.166–73). See also Lucas de Heere's drawings (1575) of Scottish Highlanders, Wild Irish and Picts, in T. D. Kendrick, *British Antiquity* (London, 1950), p. 124.

22 According to Camden, the Lowlands were once part of Northumberland and their inhabitants had thus been Anglicized.

23 Raphael Holinshed, *The Chronicles of England, Scotland, and Ireland* (London, 1587), vol. 3, pp. 303, 305.

24 BL, Cotton MS Caligula, Dii, fo. 348ᵛ.

25 Another ballad referred to the murder of Lord Russell in 1585. See the English Broadside Ballad Archive produced by the University of California at Santa Barbara, Department of English. Though printed after 1682, 'Johnny Armstrong's last goodnight' is thought to have been composed soon after 1528.

26 Stow, *Chronicles*, p. 366.

27 George Peele, *The Famous Chronicle of King Edward the First* (London, 1593), sig. I.

28 *King Edward III*, ed. Giorgio Melchiori (Cambridge, 1998), I.i.124–7.

29 *Ibid.*, II.i.79–80.

30 According to Henslowe's *Diary*, *George a Greene the Pinner of Wakefield* was performed before 1594, entered in the Stationers' Register in April 1595, and printed in 1599.

31 Robert Greene, *The Scottish History of James the Fourth*, ed. Norman Sanders (London, 1970), lines 104–5. The play was adapted from Cinthio's *Hecatommithi* and, according to Ruth Hudson, virtually every incident in the play 'that connects it with the Scotland of 1590 is Greene's addition'. See her 'Greene's James IV and contemporary allusions to Scotland', *PMLA* 47 (1932), 652–67 (esp. p. 663).

32 15 April 1598, TNA, SP52/62, fo. 19ᵛ. That the London comedians were playing in Edinburgh can be deduced from an entry in *The Register of the Privy Council of Scotland 1599–1604*, ed. David Masson (Edinburgh, 1884), pp. 41–2. For the 1603 satire, see Dorothea Townshend, *The Life and Letters of the Great Earl of Cork* (London, 1904), p. 35.

33 Holinshed, *Chronicles* (1587), vol. 3, book 6, p. 828. The description of Flodden takes up a few pages (pp. 826–9), whereas only a short paragraph is devoted to Bannockburn (p. 322).

34 NLS, Advocates' MS 6.1.19, fo. 96.

35 Leslie, *Treatise*, fo. 20ᵛ.

36 Wentworth, *Pithie Exhortation*, pp. 53, 73, 76 (2nd pag.).

37 Alexander Samson, 'Changing places: the marriage and royal entry of Philip, prince of Austria and Mary Tudor, July–August 1554', *The Sixteenth Century Journal*, 36 (2005), 761–84.

38 Robert Allott, *Englands Parnassus* (London, 1600). In 1587 James contributed the only sonnet that was written in English (as well as Latin) to a volume of Latin and Greek verse commemorating the death of Sir Philip Sidney. Jane Rickard, *Authorship and Authority: The Writings of James VI and I* (Manchester, 2007), pp. 39, 41, 44, 62. For a different slant on James's poetry, see Peter C. Herman, *Royal Poetry* (Ithaca, NY, and London, 2010), pp. 166–7, 176.

39 William Fowler, *A True Reportarie* (London, 1594). See also, Michael Lynch, 'The reassertion of princely power in Scotland: the reigns of Mary Queen of Scots and King James VI', in Martin Gosman, Alasdair A. MacDonald and Arie Johan Vanderjagt (eds), *Princes and Princely Culture, 1450–1650*, vol. 1 (Leiden, 2003), p. 26; Rick Bowers, 'James VI, Prince Henry, and *A True Reportarie* of baptism at Stirling 1594', *Renaissance and Reformation*, 29 (2005), 3–22.

40 James Craigie (ed.), *The Basilicon Doron of King James VI*, 2 vols (Edinburgh, 1944), vol. I, p. 71. See also notes 75 and 76.

41 Wentworth, *Pithie Exhortation*, pp. 68–71 (2nd pag.).

42 CUL, Ii.iv.33, fo. 38ᵛ.

43 Stow, *Chronicle*, pp. 16–17; Warner, *Albions England*, Book 2, pp. 62, 300, and Book 3, p. 90; Richard Hakluyt, *The Principal Nauigations, Voyages, Traffiques and Discoueries of*

the English Nation, pp. 2–3; William Segar, *Honor Military, and Ciuill*, 2nd edn (London, 1602), p. 55; William Fulbecke *et al*, *The Misfortunes of Arthur* (London, 1588); Thomas Churchyard, *Worthiness of Wales* (London, 1587); and a lost play, *The Life and Death of King Arthur*, by Philip Hathwaye. In Derrick Spradlin, 'Imperial anxiety in Thomas Hughes's *The Misfortunes of Arthur*', *Early Modern Literary Studies*, 10 (2005), 1–20 (at p. 1), it is argued that 'the late English Renaissance era saw a sharp decrease from previous centuries in the number of texts using the Arthurian legend for its plot'.

44 For example, Holinshed, *Chronicles* (1587), vol. 1, p. 7; Llodowick Lloyd's *The Consent of Time* (1590), p. 710; Kendrick, *British Antiquity*, pp. 121–5.

45 Richard Harvey, *Philadelphus, or a Defence of Brutes, and the Brutans History* (London, 1593). For the significance of 1593, see Chapter 3 of this volume. For Essex's relationship with James, see Chapter 6.

46 Harington, *A Treatise on the Succession to the Crown*, p. 61.

47 Wentworth, *Pithie Exhortation*, p. 11 (2nd pag.); Harington, *A Treatise on the Succession to the Crown*, p. 24. Mortimer Levine claims the 1571 ruling was 'hardly sound legally' and 'carried little weight in law', in 'A more than ordinary case of "rape", 13 and 14 Elizabeth', *The American Journal of Legal History*, 7 (1963), 159–64 (esp. pp. 161, 162).

48 Roger A. Mason, 'The Scottish Reformation and the origins of Anglo-British Imperialism', in his *Scots and Britons: Scottish Political Thought and the Union of 1603* (Cambridge, 1994), pp. 161–86.

49 Williamson, 'Scots, Indians and empire', esp. pp. 52, 72.

50 Michael J. Enright, 'King James and his island: an archaic kingship belief?', *Scottish Historical Review*, 55 (1976), 29–40.

51 George Buchanan, *The Political Poetry*, ed. and trans. P. J. McGinnis and A. H. Williamson, Scottish History Society 5th series VIII (Edinburgh, 1995), line 10. See also their 'Politics, prophecy, poetry: the Melvillian moment, 1589–96, and its aftermath', *Scottish Historical Review*, 89 (2010), 1–18.

52 Sir Thomas Craig, *Scotland's Soveraignty Asserted* (London, 1695), pp. 20, 34, 66, 72, 109, 113.

53 *Ibid.*, p. 127.

54 *Ibid.*, p. 24.

55 4 and 5 December 1595, TNA, SP52/57, fos 78ᵛ and *CSPScot*, 12, pp. 80–2. TNA, SP52/66, fo. 111. See also Graham Parry, 'Ancient Britons and early Stuarts', in Robin Headlam Wells, Glenn Burgess and Rowland Wymer (eds), *Neo-Historicism: Studies in Renaissance Literature, History and Politics* (Cambridge, 2000), p. 156. See Chapters 6 and 10 in this volume.

56 Harington, *A Treatise on the Succession to the Crown*, p. 18. The proclamation of 1603 referred to this marriage which had brought to an end the 'bloody and Civil Warres'.

57 Leslie, *A Treatise*, fo. 67ᵛ.

58 Wentworth, *Pithie Exhortation*, pp. 68–9 (2nd pag.).

59 Craig, *Right of Succession*, pp. 270, 348–9, 353.

60 Buchanan, *Political Poetry*, lines 34–6, pp. 276–81.

61 Wentworth, *Pithie Exhortation*, pp. 81–2 (2nd pag.); CUL, Ii.iv.33, fo. 38ᵛ.

62 See, for example, 5 January 1597, Elizabeth to James VI, University of Edinburgh, Laing MS III, pp. 45–6. For Bancroft, see NLS, 6.1.13, fos 46–55, and Chapter 5 in this volume.

63 BL, Cotton MS Caligula, Dii, fos 401, 381 and 386 and BL, Harley MS 4648, fo. 428.

64 *The Earle of Gowries Conspiracie against the Kings Maiestie of Scotland* (London, 1600).

65 4 January 1598, BL, Harley MS 4648, p. 384.

66 27 April 1598, note in margin of TNA, SP52/62, fo. 22ᵛ. For James's intentions, see Chapter 12 in this volume.

67 20 April 1594 letter from James to Colville and Edward Bruce, NLS, Advocates' MS 33.1.7 (vol. 21), no. 2. To dissociate himself from the 'traiterous practises' uncovered in 1593, James had Bruce prepare a report for Cecil and John Davidson compile *A Discouerie of the Vnnatural and Traiterous Conspiracie* (Edinburgh, 1593). The latter was also printed by Robert Field in London. For the affair, see T. G. Law, 'The Spanish blanks and Catholic earls, 1592–94', in *Collected Essays and Reviews*, ed. P. Hume Brown (Edinburgh, 1904), pp. 244–76. For Davidson, see Chapter 3 in this volume.

68 John Strype, *Annals of the Reformation* 3rd edn, 4 vols (Oxford, 1824), vol. 4, pp. 281–2.

69 Nick Myers, 'The gossip of history: the question of the succession in the State Papers (Domestic and Foreign)', in Jean-Christophe Mayer (ed.), *The Succession Struggle in Late Elizabethan England: Politics, Polemics and Cultural Representations* (Montpellier, 2004), pp. 52–9.

70 28 April/8 May and 18/28 August 1599, TNA, SP77/6, fos 12ᵛ and 34ᵛ.

71 13 July 1599, Hatfield House, CP 71/52.

72 T. G. Law (ed.), *Documents Illustrating Catholic Policy in the Reign of James VI 1596–98*, Miscellany of the Scottish History Society, 15 (Edinburgh, 1893), pp. 42–56 (esp. p. 43). John Petit informed the government about Crichton's 'litle pamflet' on 22 January 1598, TNA, SP77/5, fo. 256.

73 John Cecil, *A Discoverye of the Errors Committed* (Paris, 1599), especially sig. Cii. John Cecil was actually a double agent.

74 *Ibid.*, sig. Hiii.

75 *Basilicon Doron*, II, pp. 16–14, 21; Rickard, *Authorship and Authority*, pp. 113–6. The unauthorized version called *The King's Testament* probably came out in 1602 and was probably based on notes taken by Andrew Melville.

76 *Basilicon Doron*, I, pp. 13, 14, 16–17. *Basilicon Doron*, II, pp. 14–15.

77 In September 1602, Nicolson reported that the book was due to be reprinted following advice taken in England, *CSPScot* 13(ii), p. 1050. 15 October 1602, TNA, SP12/285, fo. 59ᵛ, John Chamberlain claimed the book 'had gon abrode subiect to many constructions and much depraved by many copies'. Sir Robert Cotton referred to it knowledgeably in his treatise dated 26 March 1603, TNA, SP14/1, fo. 11ᵛ.

78 For example, James's comment that the Scottish ministers fashioned for themselves a 'democratick frame of government'. BL, Additional MS 48049, fos 311–4. The catalogue dates the manuscript *ca* 1600.

79 BL, Stowe MS 156, fos 44b–45 and Hatfield House, CP 197.8 (*HMC Sal*, XIV, p. 264).

No date appears on the manuscript; the Stowe version is catalogued under 1600–1; the Cecil manuscript is catalogued under 1602–3.

80 See additionally, Anon., *The Ioyfull Receiuing of Iames the Sixt of that Name King of Scotland, and Queene Anne His Wife* (London, 1590).

81 W. Craig Ferguson, *Valentine Simmes, Stationer* (Birmingham, 1959).

82 *The Earle of Gowries Conspiracie*, especially sigs A2ᵛ, A3, C2ᵛ, C3.

83 Logan Pearsall Smith (ed.), *The Life and Letters of Sir Henry Wotton*, 2 vols (Oxford 1907), vol. I, pp. 314–15.

84 For the Arbella Stuart affair, see *HMC Sal*, XIV, pp. 247–9, 252–3. According to Giovanni Carlo Scaramelli, James's partisans were spreading prejudicial reports 'in order to destroy public sympathy for Arabella'. *CSPVen 1592–1603*, p. 554. Earlier support for Arbella can be detected in BL, Stowe MS 1555, fos 18–38.

85 Seymour could be considered legitimate as he had been born after his parents had publicly avowed their marriage. See *ODNB* articles on all these men.

86 Brian P. Levack, 'Towards a more perfect union: England, Scotland and the constitution', in Barbara P. Malament (ed.), *After the Refomation* (Manchester, 1980), pp. 57–8; Jenny Wormald, 'The union of 1603', in Mason, *Scots and Britons*, pp. 17–40 (esp. pp. 17–19).

87 *CSPVen 1592–1603*, p. 562. For further examples of ambivalence, see Judith M. Richards, 'The English accession of James VI: "national" identity, gender and the personal monarchy of England', *English Historical Review*, 117 (2002), 513–35 (esp. pp. 513–19). David Cressy provides examples of rash seditious words spoken against the intrusion of a Scottish monarch, '*Dangerous Talk: Scandalous, Seditious, and Treasonable Speech in Pre-Modern England* (Oxford, 2010), pp. 91–2.

88 In fact, one argument against using the name 'Britain' was that 'England's 'priority and precedence' over Scotland in James's style would thereby be lost. Huntington Library MS HM102, fo. 16ᵛ.

89 TNA, SP14/1, fo. 11ᵛ. For Cotton, see Kevin Sharpe, *Sir Robert Cotton, 1586–1631* (Oxford, 1979), pp. 114–15 and Jenny Wormald, 'The creation of Britain: multiple kingdoms or core and colonies', *Transactions of the Royal Historical Society*, 6th series, 2 (1992), 178–9. Cotton's proposal was of course rejected in parliament.

90 John Hayward, *A Treatise of Union of the Two Realmes of England and Scotland* (London, 1604), p. 3.

91 *Ibid.*, p. 14.

92 *Ibid.*, p. 31.

93 B. P. Levack (ed.), *The Jacobean Union: Six Tracts of 1604*, ser. 4, Scottish History Society, 21 (1985).

94 For the quotation, see Philip Schwyzer, *Literature, Nationalism, and Memory in Early Modern England and Wales* (Cambridge, 2004), p. 10.

Chapter 12

Brinkmanship and bad luck: Ireland, the Nine Years' War and the succession

Rory Rapple

The years from 1594 to 1603 in Ireland were marked by conflict above all else. A stop–start struggle, dubbed the Nine Years' War, pitted the crown administration and its allies in Ireland against confederated Irish forces led by Hugh O'Neill, Earl of Tyrone, and 'Red' Hugh O'Donnell. Tyrone's eventual defeat, which came after a long period of military and political success, had momentous ramifications for Ireland, breaking the control that indigenous Irish influences had hitherto maintained over the country's politics. These events provide the striking backdrop against which the question of the succession unfolded in Elizabethan Ireland. But that backdrop is distracting. The Nine Years' War has taken on such historiographical importance that treatments of the period can become overly teleological. Furthermore, anyone studying the Irish dimension of the succession has to work against the grain of much of the primary material, since treason legislation exerts the same inhibiting effect on discussion of the succession in Irish state correspondence as it does elsewhere. Even so, in Ireland as in England, few of the politically aware during the 1590s could shun what Robert Cecil termed 'lively apparitions of anticipation'.[1] This was particularly the case because the political fates of England and Ireland in the 1590s were more intertwined than they had been at any time since the reign of Henry VI.

CONTENDING HISTORIOGRAPHIES

The late Elizabethan succession question has not received much attention in Irish historiography. A good deal of attention, however, has been given

The author would like to thank the Institute for Scholarship in the Liberal Arts at the University of Notre Dame for its support of the research informing this chapter.

to the importance of the Nine Years' War as the catalyst in a longer process whereby Irish ambitions became increasingly integrated with, and beholden to, those of the continental Catholic powers. This process in turn resulted in the broadening of Irish political, social and intellectual horizons. Yet this was not inevitable. The Nine Years' War started out in 1594 as a regional demonstration in Ireland's northern province, Ulster. By the summer of 1595 it had prompted a total repudiation of Elizabethan rule in Gaelic Ulster. The revolt then spread throughout Ireland with serious implications for the course of the ongoing Anglo-Spanish war. From an early stage, the confederates rejected an opportunity to arrive at a favourable domestic settlement with the crown administration, opting rather to ally themselves with Spain. The tipping-point in the conflict came in 1596, when the 'chances of complete victory…appeared bright'. From that point on, the confederates intensified hostilities and increased the use of extreme national and religious rhetoric.[2] It was then anticipated that the Spaniards would lead an armada to Ireland.[3] Possible rearrangements of Ireland's ancient constitution were rehearsed: an offer of the Irish crown to Archduke Albert of the Netherlands was mooted. Some even suggested that Pope Clement VIII might make Tyrone king of an autonomous Ireland.

The history of this and the confederates' other continental contacts has provided the enduring historiographical focus in Ireland as investigated by J. J. Silke, Thomas O'Connor, E. Garcia Hernan, O. Rosaro-Morales, Mary-Ann Lyons and Hiram Morgan, among others.[4] Perhaps more could be done, however, to reintegrate English, even British concerns into this already cosmopolitan approach so the matter of the Elizabethan succession can be put in as central a place in Irish historiography as it enjoys in English historiography.[5] The common designation of the Irish insurgency of 1594–1603 as the 'Nine Years' War' may have impaired our capacity for such an understanding, as it precludes the possibility of evaluating the war as either a hard, open-ended negotiation or, crucially, an exercise in brinksmanship in anticipation of Elizabeth's death.[6] This separation of the Irish conflict from contemporaries' awareness of English dynastic concerns has left us with a major blind-spot when seeking a full understanding of the motivations of the Irish rebels, the communities loyal to the crown, and those who toiled in the very engine room of the regime itself. The significance of the succession has until now largely been winnowed out.

The career of Elizabeth's last Lord Deputy of Ireland, Charles Blount Lord Mountjoy, provides a good illustration of how pressures felt at the centre of the factionalized political world of the English court could spread out in a dangerous way to affect the crown administration in Ireland during this period. The extent of Mountjoy's former implication in Essex's gambles on the succession came to light during the arraignments and trials of Essex and his followers after the abortive rising of 8 February 1601. Two of Essex's intimates, Henry Cuffe and Sir Charles Danvers, attested that Mountjoy, prior to his own departure for Ireland to be invested as the new Lord Deputy, had confessed to them that he had sent personal messages to James VI of Scotland the previous summer. Mountjoy had offered this confidence in autumn 1599 while Essex was in confinement. According to Danvers, Mountjoy had urged that James should forcefully display his intent to be the next king, perhaps by making a show of strength along the border. Once the King had shown his hand, Mountjoy would then lead a force of about 5,000 men extracted from the royal army in Ireland to (in Danvers's words) 'assist that enterprise which, with the party that my Lord of Essex would be able to make, [would be]…sufficient to bring that to pass which was intended'.[7]

The aim was to force Elizabeth to name James as her heir and also to eliminate Essex's enemies at court. Once Mountjoy took up office in Ireland, however, he divested himself of these prior commitments and became less amenable to his erstwhile fellow conspirators. Mountjoy made sure that his messenger returning to Ireland from the Scottish King was thrown in gaol, and when Essex and Southampton contacted Mountjoy in July 1600, suggesting that he should 'proceed on to the accomplishment of the former design', they were stonewalled. Personal visits by both Southampton and Danvers made no difference; Mountjoy expressed affection and counselled patience, but ultimately distanced himself from the Essex faction. He sought to couch his earlier involvement in terms of a patriotic bid for national stability: he had just wanted 'to do his country good by the establishment of the succession'.[8] Danvers hoped that further leverage could be exerted over the Queen by asking Mountjoy to write an anti-Cecilian letter to Essex lamenting the 'ill government' of the time and suggesting that 'bad instruments' around the Queen should be removed, a letter which might then be leaked to Elizabeth in hope of manipulating the political debate, but Mountjoy demurred.[9] Later on, Mountjoy must have realized how tremendously fortunate he had been. His journey from inconsequential office to defender of England's western flank in an Anglo-Spanish war allowed him to escape the fall-out from Essex's destruction. Danvers and Cuffe would not be so lucky.

COMPETING BRINKMANSHIPS

The uncertain effect of succession politics also percolated down to the crown's Irish subjects. The 'recusancy revolt' of spring 1603 by English-Irish townsmen was one instance of communal miscalculation under the shadow of the succession.[10] Having consistently held aloof from Tyrone's long rebellion despite heavy pressure from the insurgents, the English-Irish townsmen of the chartered towns of Munster, the Irish midlands and the southeastern coast embarked on a month-long assertion of municipal autonomy on 11 April 1603. A deferred symptom of the late Elizabethan succession question, it occurred *after* Elizabeth's death and Tyrone's submission. The revolt tried to send a message to the incoming King that while his accession was welcome to his loyal municipal Irish subjects, he would have to pay an entry fine – allowing them to renew their royal charters and permitting the public practice of the Catholic faith – before they could show him abundant love. Their timing was unfortunate. Attempting to open negotiations with James at the very point at which he had safely attained his ambition to become king of England, and also at a time when a stronger Irish insurgency had been crushed, was politically naïve, but symptomatic nonetheless. Once Mountjoy turned against them, their capitulation was prompt.[11]

Bids to manage political risk were located within a rapidly changing international environment. With the conclusion of the Treaty of Vervins between Henry IV and Philip II in 1598, European powers seemed to be entering a period of *détente*. Robert Cecil and Elizabeth were eager to be part of this cooling down of hostilities once particular conditions relating to the United Provinces were met. In England some were willing to put a positive gloss on Philip II's grant of the sovereignty of the Netherlands to his daughter Isabella (with the assumption that Albert of Austria, her husband-to-be would take up the reins of power also). The Edict of Nantes opened up the possibility of religious toleration for militant confessional minorities.[12] In short, the assumptions, information and possible ends that governed the Irish rebels' and especially Tyrone's diplomatic strategy during the Nine Years' War existed in a more subtle international context than some contemporary, uncompromisingly Catholic rhetoric might suggest. Perhaps the chief utility of extreme Catholic political propaganda was as an instrument to aid solidarity among those normally ill-inclined to work together within the Irish polity.[13] Politically complex, Ireland was naturally teeming with conflicting allegiances. The rebel confederacy was in some ways designed as a discrete *détente*, formed in the knowledge that collective bargaining in a time of flux strengthened each supporter's hand.

Anticipation of the Queen's death had been burgeoning. This was especially the case during the 1590s when occasional, often inaccurate, rumours about her ill-health became more common.[14] These in turn prompted a *fin de siècle* atmosphere and a search among the political elite for solidarities, based on baronial, confessional or popular consensuses.[15] The example of Essex is particularly instructive here. Why else did he, in Northumberland's words, 'promise papists freedom in religion, puritans the sway of the commonwealth, soldiers other men's lands and houses' and tell James VI that he was doing it all for him.[16] James himself allowed Catholics, most notably Clement VIII (as Thomas M. McCoog, SJ, demonstrates in Chapter 13) to feel resolutely optimistic about a future toleration of Catholicism. Essex even fraternized with Catholics, favouring what might be termed a proto-Jacobean approach to the issue of toleration over the Elizabethan stance.[17] With the convert Henry IV on the French throne and James VI (married to another convert to Catholicism) presiding over Scotland the future seemed to promise an end to anti-Catholic severity.

In Ireland rumours about James's possible conversion emerged as early as the beginning of the 1590s, a revival perhaps of the suspicions generated in the early 1580s. Charles Egerton, the constable of Carrickfergus – merely a few hours from Kintyre – had heard reports in October 1593 that 'the King of Scots ha[d] revolted to papistry'. The following year a Dublin merchant, Richard Nugent, reported to Irish councillors that he had been told by an Irish *émigré* in Madrid that Anne of Denmark was about 'to procure all the forces she could … under the leading of some noble man' to help the insurgents – Tyrone, O'Donnell, Maguire and O'Rourke, 'who had combined together and thereupon received the sacrament to make war and to rebel against her Majesty' and that Anne's pregnancy meant that James 'would deny her nothing'.[18] So, in Ireland, as elsewhere, hope and fear were breaking in.

CONQUESTS AND CONTRACTS

Whoever Ireland's sovereign would be, the country was a peculiar polity with a distinct tradition of constitutional and political thinking. At first glance the main social distinction was between two ethnic identities – the Gaelic-Irish and the English-Irish – each of which contained a wide degree of political and cultural diversity. The former (the *Gaeil*) traced their existence to a single progenitor, a king from northern Spain *Míl* (or in Latin, Milesius) who arrived in Ireland at some time in the mists of prehistory, a commonplace since perhaps the seventh century A.D. The second ethnic group (the *Gaill*) traced their origins to the late-twelfth-century English invasion of Ireland and the widespread colonization that ensued. But by the mid-sixteenth century the distinction between the English-Irish and Gaelic-Irish hid a multitude of peculiarities. Gaelic-Irish magnates (and the clans they sprang from) comprehended varying degrees of political and cultural Anglicization (a marker that did not necessarily correlate with amenability to crown policy). The English-Irish community was highly variegated, comprehending a number of groups, first, a caste of substantial landowners in the prosperous Pale who modelled themselves on Home-County political and cultural ideals; second, an English-Irish aristocracy that included not only the loyal and Anglicized Earl of Ormond but the thoroughly Gaelicized Lower MacWilliam Burkes of Mayo; third, figures like the Viscounts Baltinglass, members of a martial petty nobility hardened by life on the frontiers of the Pale; as well as fourth, urbane and mercantile townsmen from Dublin and other chartered towns of the country who maintained strong trading links with the Continent. Despite this diversity all identified themselves as English-Irish.

It was significant that the two most prominent claimants to the English throne between 1587 and 1603, the Infanta Isabella and James VI, were from Spain and Scotland respectively: each country held a distinct place in Gaelic-Irish historical thinking. In the late 1590s the Milesian myth was far from a mere antiquarian fancy without real political resonance. It was treated with solemnity and could be diplomatically useful, as when Alonso Cobos, Philip II's envoy, prefaced a meeting with O'Neill and O'Donnell in May 1596 with a speech which mentioned 'how their first original came out of Biscay'.[19] While Spain was the Irish people's *fons et origo*, Ireland, in turn, was Scotland's progenitor. The latter country's very name, so the Irish story went, had been bestowed on it by Niall of the Nine hostages – the eponymous founder of the royal dynasty of Tara and, also, obliquely, the progenitor of the O'Neill clan. Scotland's genesis was founded on Irish dominion over the Picts and subsequent colonization by the Dál Riata.[20] It may be significant that the leading poetic champion of James's claim to be king of Great Britain was Walter Quin, a Dubliner of Gaelic-Irish descent. Quin was presented to the King in 1595, and on New Year's Day 1596 proffered him an oration extolling his title to the English throne. Quin's 'blended' ethnicity and ability to adapt to a royal allegiance at variance with the one under whose sovereignty he had been born is emblematic of the fluidity and adaptability of Irish political allegiances at this time.[21] Quin, although he may not have known it, was at the beginning of a long poetic tradition of Gaelic-Irish praise for the Stuarts.[22]

Of course there were other possible foci of loyalty for those disaffected with Elizabethan rule in Ireland. In 1555 Pope Paul IV had inaugurated Philip of Spain as king of Ireland alongside his wife Mary, and some, especially among the English-Irish, may have believed this to be an enduring title or, at least, the best reversionary title following Elizabeth's excommunication.[23] But none of these dynastic claims seems to have commanded unanimous political appeal. This may well have been because sixteenth-century Irish thought on monarchical right seemed to put greater priority on factors other than dynasty and blood. The traditional indigenous understanding of Ireland's ancient constitution prioritized contractual thinking above all else. In 1155 Pope Adrian IV, in his desire to reform the Irish Church along Western European lines and yield revenue to the papacy, had granted Ireland as a fiefdom to Henry II, the Angevin king of England, by means of the bull *Laudabiliter*. Centuries later, different strata of Irish society came to emphasize different elements of this transaction.[24] While English-Irish magnates could take pride in being papally mandated *conquistadores* in the spirit of Giraldus Cambrensis's redaction of the bull in his *Expugnatio Hibernica*, the English-Irish communities in the towns and the English Pale tended to take a view that complemented their concerns with their own 'culture war', glimpsing in *Laudabiliter* their right to uphold the English way of life and promote English laws over and against rude Gaelic-Irish customs that had no papal imprimatur.[25] The Gaelic-Irish, by contrast, had a tradition of pointing to what they perceived to be the conditional nature of the papal contract: for the grant to be valid, it was argued, both the Church's prosperity and, even more fundamentally, ongoing indigenous consent should have been secured. However, the Church lay in ruins and there had been a consistent lack of just English treatment of the Irish over centuries.

The most systematic scrutiny of the implications of *Laudabiliter* attempted during the Nine Years' War would be found in Peter Lombard's *De Hibernia insula commentarius*, composed in 1600. Lombard, a professor at Louvain, was himself an English-Irish townsman. The *Commentarius*, a remarkable amalgam of English-Irish and Gaelic-Irish political tropes, was prepared in the hope of convincing Clement VIII that the insurgency was in fact a Catholic crusade. The corollary to this hope was the prospect that Clement, using his temporal power, of which *Laudabiliter* was such an outstanding example, might loosen the constitutional hold the Elizabethan regime exerted over Ireland and excommunicate all Catholics who remained loyal to the Queen against O'Neill. Lombard embraced many arguments to make his point, but inexorably he returned to *Laudabiliter* and demonstrated, in predictable ways, that the English had breached the terms of the papal contract and the indigenous Irish had never wholly accepted English overlordship. Furthermore, he suggested, debate about the licitness of English overlordship was academic, having been short-circuited by the Anglican schism, definitively so by Elizabeth's excommunication. According to Lombard, the onus was now on Clement to transfer the sovereignty of Ireland to a Habsburg prince.[26] This analysis allowed for no 'succession question': Elizabeth's demise would have no significance as she had long forfeited all rights to be considered Ireland's monarch.

We should be cautious before we accept that an ardour for *translatio imperii* might have been the primary motivation behind the Irish insurgency. While it can be tempting to consider Ireland's polity in the ideal terms of contract law, in reality, it was supremely messy. Not only did the Irish polity have historical problems with regnal solidarity, but it also had difficulties mustering solidarity *tout court*. Certainly the sixteenth century is littered with apparently unilateral Irish diplomatic initiatives which aimed to translate the *imperium* of the whole, or part of, Ireland to a new prince.[27] Dynastic loyalty in each case was secondary to a desire to attain military help, political leverage, religious alliance or bargaining power. Most significantly, while each of these appeals in some way purported to be universal in scope, they were all in fact regional or partial; none of the offers could by any means be deemed to be representative of a unanimous Irish seigneurial initiative to institute a *translatio imperii*. It is not that dynastic loyalty did not matter, but rather that in the sixteenth century it seemed that any dynasty would do.

One intellectual relatively unconcerned with this constitutionalist focus was Richard Stanihurst, the scion of one of Dublin's most illustrious municipal families, who along with Lombard stands as one of sixteenth-century English Ireland's most impressive thinkers. After fleeing England in 1582 (following a period in custody occasioned by the fall of his patron the eleventh Earl of Kildare) he joined the English-speaking *émigré* population in the Habsburg territories. From 1592 to 1596 he was an *habitué* of the Spanish court, close to both Sir Francis Englefield and Robert Persons. A. J. Loomie and Colm Lennon have both argued that Stanihurst collaborated on *A Conference about the Next Succession,* ascribed to 'Robert Doleman' on the title page.[28] If so, Stanihurst did not leave the issue there, going on to write an *ad hominem* refutation of James's claim to the English throne entitled *Beware of the Northern Gate / Cave a porta septenrionali* published in 1598.[29] Unfortunately, no copy is extant.

Stanihurst identified strongly with the Habsburg interest *vis-à-vis* the succession and it is clear this meant more to him than the Irish insurgency. He held the traditional view that English-Irish culture had to impose discipline on the Gaelic Irish and preferred to think of the country's politics, constitution and culture in a similar vein. Not until 1601 – and even then only grudgingly – did he assent to doing diplomatic work for Tyrone. His personal disdain for both the Stuart dynasty and Gaelic Ireland was in tension with his hopes for a future in which England would be an off-shoot of the Habsburg Empire, and Ireland, with a resurgent and pre-eminent Catholic English-Irish population, would be in turn an off-shoot of England – a reprise of the reign of Philip and Mary. Part of the appeal for Stanihurst may have been that Spanish state servants, like highbrow Palesmen, cast a stark cultural difference between the Gaelic-Irish, *los salvajes* and the English-Irish civil population, *los civiles.*[30]

THE TAKING OF SIDES IN AN AVOIDABLE WAR

Of course, according to the crown's view of Irish constitutional reality, all contractual bric-a-brac had been swept away by Henry VIII's 1541 Act of Kingly Title. Passed by acclamation in the Irish Parliament in the presence of many Gaelic-Irish magnates, the act had not only aimed to remove England's papal mandate but also pledged the King to a policy of correcting the long-standing disenfranchisement and abuse of the Gaelic-Irish. The Gaelic-Irish were to participate in and have unimpeded access to English law and government. Constitutional views based on *Laudabiliter,* despite their resilience, were not so compelling as to void the panoply of political deals that the 1541 Act facilitated, whether transactions of political legitimation arising out of 'surrender and regrant' or the bestowal of English offices on Irishmen. In spite of recurring troubles, a functioning Tudor administration endured in Ireland. It continued to extend its reach by means of agreements with English-Irish and Gaelic-Irish potentates to fulfil the stated aim of establishing the touted benefits of the king's law from shore to shore.[31] Despite substantial tumults (especially the first and second Desmond rebellions and the coincidental insurgencies in Leinster) and persistent low-level violence, by the time of Sir John Perrot's viceroyalty (1584–88) many of the political elite, whether Gaelic, Gaelicized or English-Irish, received benefits from the crown without voicing political-theological scruples. But given Elizabeth's broadly negligent approach to Irish affairs, the array of day-to-day actions and legislation that accrued as expressions of the royal will depended greatly on the viceroy and numerous crown officers and their interaction with the brute political realities that obtained at any given time. As a result, petitioning, cajoling, bribing and violent acting out were the tried and tested means of achieving advantage in Ireland: a pattern of behaviour as current in Ulster as in any other part of the country.

The 'composition' of Ulster embarked on by both Lord Deputy Sir John Perrot and the Gaelic lords of that province made the crown government's political contact with the region more comprehensive than ever. The inching forward of a reform programme which aimed to mould the highly militarized seigneurial, indeed tribal, political realities of Gaelic Ulster into a process of 'shiring' was powered by the vying ambitions of a range of political actors, Gaelic-Irish lords, freeholders and English officers, each ready to take advantage of Perrot's engagement with the province. The implementation of any crown policy in Ireland threw up apparent paradoxes, but the inconsistencies that attended the 'composition of Ulster' might have corrected themselves given the right circumstances. However, the replacement in 1588 of Sir John Perrot as Lord Deputy by Sir William Fitzwilliam, a quietist, negligent and corrupt figure, ensured that tendencies towards resolution in the province were scotched. Fitzwilliam appointed impulsive English captains to the sheriffdoms in the Gaelic lordships and also implemented the partition of Monaghan (the MacMahon lordship). The Deputy's apparent pandering to subaltern political interests in Gaelic Ireland and the heedless brutality of the partition's implementation were the epitome of a nightmarish spectacle for the lords of Ulster and did not bode well. Furthermore, Fitzwilliam's tacit collaboration in the rise of Hugh O'Neill, Earl of Tyrone, a collaboration facilitated by bribery and graft, created a figure committed to securing seigneurial hegemony in Ulster no matter how beholden he had once been to the crown.[32]

So reform government broke down in Ulster. Simultaneously the Gaelic lords of the western part of the Province and northern Connacht – Red Hugh O'Donnell, Hugh Maguire and Brian O'Rourke *inter alia,* each of whom had been sheltering papal bishops – asserted themselves in the face of the

Connacht President Sir Richard Bingham's unrelenting exploitation of that region. In mid-Ulster and further east, Tyrone gradually but unremittingly set himself to the continued assertion of his ancestral rights as 'the O'Neill' against a crown administration which was attempting to clip his wings. He had been driven to this, it seems, by regional crown officers pursuing their own sectional interests at his expense. Consequently he seemed to be asserting that he would brook no breach of the proper bounds of his power and authority.[33]

Despite the tensions and hostilities, Tyrone continued to play the courtier in his communications with the crown and its officers. Elizabeth and her ministers had long regarded Tyrone, rescued from near extinction by the crown in the 1560s, to be the finest example of an anglicized Gaelic-Irishman. Despite their disappointment, Tyrone never relinquished the proper courtly tone in his dealings with Elizabeth, although he often posed as a spurned retainer.[34] Ultimately, his ability to play this role convincingly enabled both him and Red Hugh O'Donnell to combine as a scintillating negotiating team, with Tyrone as the supposed sober influence on his 'mad-dog' son-in-law. Although he could flaunt his connections to Spain, or threaten individuals committed to remaining loyal to Elizabeth, or demonstrate his association with demands that were fundamentally inimical to any idea of a royal prerogative, he never relinquished this courtly register; indeed, crown officers believed at times that he used the threat of returning to quiet allegiance to gain leverage and mastery within the confederacy. [35]

Given the Queen's advanced age, aristocratic politics in Ireland (as in England) mattered to a greater extent than ever before. Functional loyalty to Elizabeth and the established administration was the persistent, if somewhat sullen, norm among the Irish aristocracy, and in many respects a court interest existed in Ireland without there being a court. The archetype for this approach was Thomas Butler, tenth Earl of Ormond, at once tremendously close to the Queen and a fierce defender of his liberties and privileges against the attempts of her Irish administration to mitigate them. In truth, despite occasional disaffection many Irish aristocrats showed surprising steadfastness to the regime during the Nine Years' War, for example Donough O'Brien Earl of Thomond, Ulick Burke third Earl of Clanricard, and Henry Fitzgerald twelfth Earl of Kildare, the latter of whom died from wounds sustained while fighting the rebels.[36]

To counter this loyal seigneurial party, Tyrone and the confederates pursued a policy of supporting rival claimants often of spurious legitimacy to destabilize loyal peers and create local interests docile to the confederate agenda: for example in Desmond, James FitzThomas the *sugán earl*, in south Connacht, Redmond Burke who posed as a competing Earl of Clanricard, in the Midlands, Onie McRory O'More who re-asserted Gaelic hegemony there, and, to some degree, Florence McCarthy Reagh who claimed to be 'The MacCarthy Mór'.[37]

Sir Richard Bingham, that seasoned practitioner of Irish government, drily described this erection of a parallel peerage as Tyrone's taking up of 'the office of a King, raising and putting down in these Irish titles whom he pleaseth'. Tyrone further insisted that all the confederates' grievances be subject to his central bargaining. His reach in domestic politics combined with his international diplomatic politics had resulted in a largely unprecedented coherence in Irish politics.[38]

Why did Tyrone ramp up the stakes so vertiginously? Hiram Morgan has correctly concluded that generalizing the conflict was the only way he could attain maximum security for his power and liberties in Ulster against the forces of governmental modernization. That said, Tyrone was not against modernization in principle as long as it was suitably seigneurial and he was in control of the military–fiscal administration in his own sphere of influence, broadly understood. His consistent willingness to deal with English captains and administrators indicates as much. It is more than plausible that Tyrone, like Essex, saw Elizabeth's demise and the consequent dynastic handover as a sort of finishing line, the point at which he could turn his liabilities into assets and assert his indispensability by handing Ireland over to the new monarch from a position of strength in order to take his place within a military–fiscal state which respected his dominance over Ulster and Gaelic-Ireland – a sensitive geographical and cultural frontier relative to both England and Scotland. In short, Tyrone's rebellion may have been more about having the power to deliver Ireland to a new monarch than about deliverance of Ulster or Ireland from the cosh of interventionist crown government. By raising the stakes Tyrone, the consummate negotiator, could extend the stand-off until Elizabeth's death and then lead his confederates into obedience, in return for the ceding of key compromises to his associates and *de facto* acknowledgement of his primacy in Ireland.[39] Not 'Ewtopia', perhaps, but a substantial victory.[40]

THE NINE YEARS' WAR AND THE SUCCESSION

Significantly, by 1598 the Dublin administration had placed Tyrone's dynastic strategy, especially his links to the King of Scotland, under scrutiny. Gunpowder and other resources from Scottish merchants in Kintyre and Glasgow were still entering Ulster ports despite James's 1595 proclamation forbidding his subjects to assist Tyrone or O'Donnell. As far as the Irish Secretary of State Sir Geoffrey Fenton was concerned (and he cited the testimony of his network of spies well ensconced within the rebel camp), insurgent/Jacobean contacts were especially intimate, going beyond links with established Irish agents in Scotland or the fortuitous actions of the Earls of Huntly and Erroll. Fenton became sure that James was actively, if surreptitiously, aiding Tyrone.

Fenton's correspondence with Sir Robert Cecil on the subject of this Scottish threat in Ireland indicates that he assumed his patron shared his paltry respect for James. Indeed, Fenton may later have had cause to regret his frankness as his career went into serious decline after the Jacobean succession. In early January 1598, however, Fenton reported that his spies had discovered that Tyrone was in receipt of correspondence from the King. These allegations complemented testimony from Captain William Warren that Tyrone had received craftsmen from the King of Scotland to cast heavy artillery for him.[41] Fenton was not alone in his worries. Tyrone's former mentor, the Earl of Ormond, was similarly vexed. He told Elizabeth that the King was reaching out to both the Irish confederates and to Spain. By March Ormond could claim that he had got his hands on a copy of a letter from James to Tyrone, as well as corroborating evidence from a Captain Atherton in Carrickfergus. He sent all this material to the Privy Council.[42] The authenticity of the document is impossible to gauge as (perhaps significantly) no copy remains in the archive. How did Ormond get the letter in the first place? Might Tyrone have sent him a copy? If so, this would resemble O'Neill's apparent betrayal of the integrity of his correspondence with Philip II in 1596. On that occasion, Tyrone had handed over a letter from the Spanish King to the Dublin government on condition that he would get it back – at once a threatening gesture displaying how well connected he was and a disarming demonstration of enduring loyalty to Elizabeth. The Scottish letter, as we shall see, would also have a bewildering afterlife.

Continuing speculation about O'Neill's intimacy with both Spain and Scotland cast a shadow over the diplomatic initiative attempted between Thomas Jones, Bishop of Meath, and Tyrone and O'Donnell in early April 1598. On that occasion O'Neill admitted to his interlocutors that the Spaniards had agreed to supply an army, and Jones was also concerned about rumours he had heard that the Scottish King had sent Tyrone 'letters of good encouragement'. At around the same time, Ormond stated that he believed that James VI was so enthused at the likelihood of O'Neill receiving Spanish aid that he too promised to send him men and munitions. This led to Ormond fearing for the 'overthrow of the whole kingdom'.[43] By the next month, Fenton had openly alleged to Cecil that he could not 'but think that the King [of Scotland] [wa]s a secret supporter of these Irish rebels'. Fenton believed that Spanish money would be used by the confederates to pay for Scottish men and matériel.[44] Subsequent intelligence alleged that the copy of the aforementioned letter from James to Tyrone which Ormond had sent to the Privy Council had been, in turn, forwarded to the King who, piqued at the disclosure, had sent the letter back to Tyrone in anger. The same sources reported that Tyrone had assured the King that the letter had been stolen from him. Nonetheless Fenton, true to his *idée fixe*, asserted that, despite this tiff, James was still committed to doing O'Neill any favour within his power.[45]

In late June, Fenton received word that Tyrone's sons were in the custody of James McSorley of the Ulster-based Scottish Clan Iain Mac Donnell, and on the verge of being handed over to James VI as pledges 'upon some compact made between his highness and Tyrone'.[46] At this point Fenton put his cards on the table to an unprecedented degree:

> I find still that the meaning of that King is to bear up the rebellion and underhand to hold her Majesty entangled here to the end to draw her to serve some turn of his, which he thinketh he cannot bring to pass by other means ... [the King of Scots] runneth on with his practices to keep Ireland in sedition, of which I have had so many strong presumptions as I have no reason to rest any longer in doubt thereof.[47]

The 'turn' to which Fenton was delicately alluding was obviously the exertion of pressure on the succession question. Furthermore, the rumour was abroad, fuelled perhaps by awareness of the wider diplomatic context in the immediate aftermath of Vervins, that England was on the point of arriving at a peace with Spain. Tyrone, according to Fenton, was utterly prepared for this new dispensation.

It seems James was perturbed by these rumours. Three days after the confederates' crushing victory at the Battle of the Yellow Ford on 14 August, the King sent a regal, but cantankerous, letter to the Lords Justice Adam Loftus and Robert Gardener complaining about the rumours concerning his links with Tyrone. He asked the Irish Council for a copy of the notorious letter so that he could confirm or deny whether it actually was a letter he had sent Tyrone. He also informed them that another proclamation was at the printing press forbidding Scottish aid for the Irish rebels.[48] The Lords Justice somewhat cheekily noted James's 'princely justifications' but added that a ship from Scotland full of munitions for the rebels was in Lough Foyle. Hardy Irish perennials like Ormond, Fenton, Adam Loftus and Robert Gardener believed the King was treating the confederates as if they were his party in Ireland – that, in spite, and maybe even because, of their continued Spanish intrigues the rebels were advancing his agenda. Furthermore, there are indications that the rank and file among the rebels believed the same thing. Bingham, now knight marshal of Ireland, declared in January 1599 that the confederates themselves had been 'made to believe that they ha[d] the assistance of the King of Scotland'. With characteristic deviousness, he recommended that a regiment or two of Scots should be employed against the rebels, because they would be crestfallen 'to hear that their friends were waged against them'.[49]

The advent of Essex as Lord Lieutenant, in spring 1599, himself an advocate of James's claim, brought a new complexion to affairs. With few friends in the Irish administration (Fenton, in particular, was no admirer) and with an army of 16,000 foot and 1,400 horsemen to bolster his martial reputation, Essex seemed like the best chance to provide fresh leadership and regain lost ground. But his expedition was not merely a martial endeavour. Many indications (largely ignored) suggest that the new Lord Lieutenant was pushing his own Irish-based political programme based on the acquisition of a discrete aristocratic clientele designed to compete with Tyrone's biddable network of magnates and lords. The keystone of Essex's political plan was shrewdly chosen given the persistent allure of factional politics in the sister-kingdom. That keystone was William Fitzgerald, the thirteenth Earl of Kildare, who after his brother's death in the field fighting the rebels in 1597 had acceded to that most venerable title in Ireland. Fitzgerald's relationship with Essex was symbiotic. Having gone to court in the spring of 1598, Kildare, along with eighteen leaders of the Pale gentry, had sought Essex out and joined his expedition, making it a remarkable display of English-Irish chivalry serving alongside 'the flower of the English forces', a notion appealing to any sentimentally inclined English-Irish aristocrat.[50]

Essex must have known that a friendly and dependent Earl of Kildare not only would be indispensable in any future appeals to doubtful rebels with ancestral ties to the Geraldine faction but also was an invaluable member of his portfolio of grandees in the Elizabethan realms, peers whose allegiance could be subsequently handed over to James at the appropriate time. Essex, it seems, was not only attempting to outmanoeuvre Tyrone's usurpation of 'the office of a King' but also trying to assert his own pre-eminence as a British and Irish kingmaker over Tyrone's pretensions in that regard. Tragically for Essex and his strategy, the ship carrying Kildare and those gentlemen of the Pale sank taking all hands with it, unable to withstand a severe storm in the Irish Sea. With it sank Essex's hopes of erecting an indigenous Irish political consensus beholden to him. This may explain the baffling character of Essex's viceroyalty. It became an improvisation.

Essex was pursuing his own Irish agenda, but his was but one among many pursued at the same time. The complexity of the situation can be appreciated when we consider intelligence Essex received in July 1599 about James VI's intentions. Essex's informant was an intimate of Tyrone's, Richard Weston. The letter, catalogued as an attachment to correspondence from Fenton to Robert Cecil, poses a number of questions. Weston recorded that a 'gent from the king of Scots' had lately brought Tyrone a message from his master 'letting him understand that [James] was one that wished him well' and furthermore that Tyrone 'should not want anything that he might help him withal'. James also offered to 'write to his sister of England for a peace to him and to all his country', apologized for not sending an actual letter of goodwill to Tyrone 'for fear of a great bruit in England', and enquired after details of Essex's proceedings as Lord Lieutenant. One of Tyrone's councillors, Weston reported, urged the Earl that James was in the best position to make peace for him, but Weston assured Essex that he had countered this advice with the opinion that no one 'could deal better with Tyrone nor for him than [the Lord Lieutenant]'. Tyrone toasted the King, but wrote a careful response, fearing it was a 'fetch' to draw him out.

Weston's dispatch seems like a signal to Essex, the disclosure of the wider circumstances in which Tyrone might seek a permanent peace: an endgame facilitated by the King of Scots and an initiative in which the Lord Lieutenant might assist. On the other hand, we might ask why this letter, addressed to Essex, was forwarded to Cecil by Fenton so soon after its composition. Perhaps a patient plan to bring about Essex's self-destruction was already afoot. James's supposed appeal on Tyrone's behalf could be characterized as intimidatory or as an attempt to claim pre-emptively the responsibilities of British monarchy. Either way, in the late summer and early autumn of 1599, Essex, Tyrone and James could all be perceived as being pretty much on the same side.[51] This may help explain the defining episode of Essex's viceroyalty – his personal interview with Tyrone on 7 September 1599 at Bellaclinthe which contravened Essex's own explicit criteria about how parleys were to be carried out, leaving him open to charges worse than incompetence. Francis Bacon later summed up Essex's supposed folly: 'the secrecy of that parley, as it gave to [Essex] the more liberty of Treason, so it may give any man the more liberty of surmise'.[52] Many took that liberty.

After Essex's execution, Bacon's 1601 *Declaration of the Practises & Treasons Attempted by Robert late Earle of Essex* published a dossier of these surmises along with circumstantial evidence to prove that Essex 'carried into Ireland a heart corrupted in his allegiance' and 'an intent…to pleasure and gratify the Rebel with a dishonourable peace, and *to contract with him for his own greatness*' [my italics].[53] To this end Bacon first outlined the allegations of James Knowd, an associate of Thomas Lee, who had stated that after Essex's first arrival in Ireland Tyrone had sent one of his own creations, Onie McRory O'More, a letter asking him to 'frame his course' in 'light of the secret agreement between the earl of Essex' and himself. One of Onie's associates allegedly told Knowd that the terms of the 'agreement' included a *quid pro quo* arrangement which outlined 'that the earl of Essex had agreed to take [Tyrone's] part and that they [the Irish rebels] should aid him towards the conquest of England'. Knowd also alleged that he himself had brought Essex a message from Tyrone prior to Bellaclinthe promising that 'if the earl of Essex would follow Tyrone's plot, he [Tyrone] would make the earl of Essex the greatest man that ever was in England and further that if the Earl would have conference with him, Tyrone would deliver his eldest son in pledge for his assurance'. Essex, Bacon noted, went to the parley without a third party in spite of this incriminating invitation because 'being only true to his own ends [he] easily dispensed with all such considerations'. Essex's only protection was that he made doubly sure that no one would be able to hear what passed between them.

Bacon then scrutinized the speculation that had done the rounds in Ireland after Essex's sudden return to Court. These were third-hand allegations based on a certain Thomas Wood's account of a conversation with Lord Fitzmaurice, Baron of Lixnaw. According to these, Tyrone had written to another of his creations, the *sugán* Earl of Desmond that it had been agreed 'that Essex should be king of England and that Tyrone should hold of him the honour and state of viceroy of Ireland, and that the proportion of soldiers which Tyrone should bring or send to Essex were 8000 Irish'. According to Bacon's gloss on these statements and others, the 'general and received opinion that went up and down in the mouths both of the better and meaner sort of rebels' was 'that the Earl of Essex was theirs, and they [were] his and that he would never leave the one sword, meaning that of Ireland, till he had gotten the other in England and that he would bring them to serve where they should have other manner of booties than cows'.

The hope of English remuneration and indeed the augmentation of Irish honours with English land and title, it was alleged, was widespread among the rebels. Sir William Warren stated that on the day of Essex's arrival at Court, Tyrone had declared on oath 'that within two or three months [Warren] should see the greatest alterations and strangest that ever he saw in his life or could imagine, and that he, the said Tyrone, hoped ere long to have a good share in England'. Bacon artfully intertwined all this testimony around the confessions of the Earl of Southampton and Sir Christopher Blount which alleged that Essex had considered bringing several thousand troops with him on his return to England from Ireland in September 1599. This created a coherent tale of hubris on the part of both Essex and Tyrone, birds of a feather, both out to usurp what they could by working together.[54] And yet Bacon's account, although lurid in detail was singularly delicate about the wider circumstances in which this speculation took place. Quite simply, there was only one context in which any of these apparently rash actions made any strategic sense and there was one obvious reversionary interest which stood to benefit most from these machinations. Given Elizabeth's continued existence, the most important player in the tragedy, James VI, was perforce absent from Bacon's scene-setting and as a result Bacon's dossier cannot but read like *Macbeth* without the King of Scotland.

The details of the parley at Bellaclinthe have been reconstructed elsewhere on the basis of subsequent statements by Essex.[55] While they amount to an un-minuted negotiation aimed at opening the possibility of a permanent end to hostilities, they do not have any of the glamour that their secret nature allows to be projected upon them. However, among the many different accounts that exist of the interview between Essex and Tyrone (Fynes Moryson's and Sir John Harington's among others), there is one, William Udall's, that reveals much about the character of the gossip and debate that obtained in Ireland during the period from Essex's disgrace to his ultimate self-destruction.

Udall, originally in the employ of the thirteenth Earl of Kildare, liked to pose as a pivotal player in the tortuous high politics of the time; he bragged about his indispensability to Robert Cecil and even claimed to be 'the Queen's spy' in order to secure money on credit, but, in reality, he was a small sprat among big beasts. Hungry for attention, he let his ego and mouth run away with themselves, leading to his interrogation by the Irish Council in May 1601, followed by his deportation and close imprisonment in England.[56] The initial charges levelled against him in Ireland in 1601 pitted him against a rather unimpressive captain Marmaduke Neilson and 'poor' Thomas Bath. Although it was a minor matter, the details of the allegations tell us quite a lot about a world where speculation about dynastic ambition and expectation was rife even in the furthest nooks and crannies of Ireland among relative nobodies.[57] Neilson testified that Udall had been consumed with excitement throughout 1600 and early 1601 about Elizabeth's death. He combined his eager anticipation with 'glances northward' and an unquenchable enthusiasm for the 'happy time' that would ensue with the establishment of the Scottish King 'in the three realms'.[58] Bath then alleged that Udall said that he had heard testimony from a certain Thomas Blunt, who had eavesdropped on the notorious conference at Bellaclinthe from nearby bushes. Udall claimed that Tyrone had initially greeted Essex by welcoming him to Ireland, to which Essex replied suggestively and enigmatically: 'You are too Scottish to bid me welcome'. Was this a reference to Tyrone's supposed intimacy with James VI?[59]

Perhaps it was Elizabeth's stubborn longevity more than anything else that prevented a stabilization of Irish affairs over the nine years between 1594 and 1603. Fynes Moryson's story about the way Mountjoy withheld news of Elizabeth's death from Tyrone until after he had solemnly submitted in March 1603 at Mellifont is well known, yet speaks to a broader and deeper strategic truth. If Elizabeth had died at anytime before the fatal defeat of the confederates at Kinsale on 24 December 1601, Tyrone and O'Donnell with a standing army could have played a confident dynastic game from a position of strength, becoming brokers for Ireland's future with James VI – their secret trump card – in spite of a discombobulated 'loyal' English-Irish community (itching to have a well-timed 'recusancy revolt') and a weary crown administration. Furthermore, the confederates would have played a pivotal part in the affairs of the three kingdoms, because whatever inadequacies the term 'Nine Years' War' labours under when describing the conflict that took place between 1594 and 1603, one thing is clear: because of the politics of the late Elizabethan succession it was, in many ways, England's last war and 'Britain's' first.

NOTES

1   *CJRC* (London, 1861), p. 7.

2   Hiram Morgan, *Tyrone's Rebellion* (Woodbridge, 1999), pp. 208–13; Hiram Morgan 'Hugh O'Neill and the Nine Years War in Tudor Ireland', *Historical Journal*, 36 (1993), 21–37. For specifics on the notion of making Tyrone king, see Bishop of Killaloe to Brian O'Rourke, '3 February' 1596, TNA, SP63/186/38.

3   Enrique Garcia Hernán, *Ireland and Spain in the Reign of Philip II* (Dublin, 2009), pp. 208–11.

4   Particular highlights include J. J. Silke, *Kinsale: The Spanish Intervention in Ireland at the End of the Elizabethan Wars* (Liverpool, 1970); Hiram Morgan (ed.), *The Battle of Kinsale* (Bray, 2004); T. O'Connor and M. Lyons (eds), *The Ulster Earls and Baroque Europe* (Dublin, 2010). This literature has grown in the aftermath of the 400th anniversary of the battle of Kinsale and 'Flight of the earls'.

5   An honourable exception is David Edwards, 'Securing the Jacobean succession: the secret career of James Fullerton of Trinity College, Dublin' in S. Duffy (ed.), *The World of the Gallowglass* (Dublin, 2007), pp. 188–219.

6   One of the earliest uses of the term can be found in Standish Hayes O'Grady's *The Flight of the Eagle* (Dublin, 1908).

7   See the 'Declaration of Sir Charles Danvers', 1 March, 1601 (four days after Essex's execution), *CJRC*, pp. 101–4, and Henry Cuffe and Christopher Blount's testimonies to the Privy Council, *CJRC*, pp. 86, 107–10.

8   For Danvers's account of Mountjoy's view of the succession question, see *CJRC*, p. 102. See also 'Confession of Southampton', *CJRC*, pp. 96–8.

9   This treatment of supposed private letters as public documents was a recurring political strategy of the Essex faction, see Paul E. J. Hammer's *ODNB* article on Robert, second earl of Essex and Alexandra Gajda, 'Debating war and peace in late Elizabethan England', *Historical Journal*, 52 (2009), 851–78.

10 See Anthony Sheehan, 'The recusancy revolt of 1603: a reinterpretation', *Archivium Hibernicum*, 38 (1983), 3–13.

11 For a parallel, see Michael Questier, 'The politics of religious conformity and the accession of James I', *Historical Research*, 71 (1998), 14–30.

12 R. B. Wernham, *The Return of the Armadas* (Oxford, 1994), pp. 210–49; Gajda, 'Debating war and peace'.

13 Morgan, 'Hugh O'Neill', pp. 24–32.

14 8 February 1594, TNA, SP12/247/50; John Chamberlain to Dudley Carleton, 23 August 1599, TNA, SP12/272/68.

15 Paul E. J. Hammer, 'The smiling crocodile: the earl of Essex and late-Elizabethan "popularity"', in Peter Lake and Steven Pincus (eds), *The Politics of the Public Sphere in Early Modern England* (Manchester, 2007), pp. 95–115; Mervyn James, 'At a crossroads of the political culture: the Essex revolt, 1601', in *Society, Politics and Culture: Studies in Early Modern England* (Cambridge, 1986), pp. 416–65.

16 Northumberland to James, *CJRC*, p. 66.

17 See Alexandra Gajda, *The Earl of Essex and Late Elizabethan Political Culture* (Oxford, 2012).

18 Capt. Egerton to L. D. Fitzwilliam, 8 October 1593, TNA, SP63/172/2 XIX; 'Declaration of Richard Nugent ... made to the Lord Chancellor &c', 19 April 1594, TNA, SP63/174/18 VI.

19 Declaration of George Cawell, 24 June 1596, TNA, SP63/190/42i. See also Morgan *Tyrone's Rebellion*, pp. 208–11; for an earlier gesture to this myth in international diplomatic correspondence, see Cornelius O'Bryen to Charles V, 21 July 1534 in *L&P Henry VIII*, viii, 999.

20 Dauvit Broun, 'When did Scotland become Scotland?', *History Today*, 46 (1996), 16–21; Seathrún Céitinn, *Foras Feasa ar Éirinn*, ed. Patrick S. Dinneen, Irish Texts Society 15, 4 vols (1914), vol. I, pp. 206–9; 2, pp. 372–413.

21 Marc Caball, *Poets and Politics: Continuity and Reaction in Irish Poetry, 1558–1625* (Cork, 1998); Peter McQuillan, *Native and Natural: Aspects of the Concepts of 'Right' and 'Freedom' in Irish* (Notre Dame, IN, 2004); Brendan Kane, *The Politics and Culture of Honour in Britain and Ireland, 1541–1641* (Cambridge, 2010). See also Chapters 10 and 11 in this volume.

22 Breandán Ó Buachalla, *Aisling Ghéar: na Stiobhartaigh Agus An t-aos Léinn* (Dublin, 1996).

23 For Paul IV's bull of 7 June, 1555, see BL, Stowe MS 1054, fo. 7.

24 For questions about the authenticity of the version of *Laudabiliter* in Giraldus Cambrensis's *Expugnatio Hibernica* and the 'fantasy life' the document lived afterwards, see Anne J. Duggan, 'The power of documents: the curious case of Laudabiliter', in Brenda Bolton and Christine Meek (eds), *Aspects of Power and Authority in the Middle Ages*, International Medieval Research 14 (Turnhout, 2007), pp. 251–75.

25 For Stanihurst's *hauteur* towards the Gaelic Irish, see Colm Lennon, *Richard Stanihurst, The Dubliner, 1547–1618* (Dublin, 1981), pp.143–60; James Murray *Enforcing the English Reformation in Ireland: Clerical Resistance and Political Conflict in the Diocese of Dublin, 1536–1590* (Cambridge, 2009), pp. 37–98.

26 The reassessment of Lombard's *Commentarius* began with Morgan 'Hugh O'Neill', 29–32. See also Thomas O'Connor, 'A justification for foreign intervention in early-modern Ireland', in T. O'Connor and Mary Ann Lyons (ed.), *Irish Migrants in Europe after Kinsale, 1602–1820* (Dublin, 2003), pp. 14–31; O'Connor's 'Diplomatic preparations for Kinsale', in Enrique Garcia Hernán *et al.* (eds), *Irlanda y la Monarquia Hispánica: Kinsale 1601–2001 – Guerra, Politica, Exilio y Religion* (Madrid, 2002). See also David Finnegan's summation of Lombard's argument in 'The impact of the counter-reformation on the political thinking of Irish Catholics *c.* 1540–1640' (Ph.D. dissertation, University of Cambridge, 2007), pp.100–5. For the most commonly used redaction of the text based on the version in the Barberini Archive, see Peter Lombard, *De Regno Hiberniae, Sanctorum Insula Commentarius* ed. Patrick F. Moran (Dublin, 1868).

27 Cornelius O'Bryen to Charles V, 21 July 1534, *L&P Henry VIII*, vii, 381. On this approach and James Fitzgerald's, see Laurence McCorristine, *The Revolt of Silken Thomas: A Challenge to Henry VIII* (Dublin, 1987); Michael Ó Siocrú, 'Foreign involvement in the revolt of Silken Thomas', in *Proceedings of the Royal Irish Academy* Section C, 96C, no. 2 (1996), 49–66. For Conn O'Neill's approach to James V, see Alison Cathcart, 'James V, king of Scotland – and Ireland?', in Sean Duffy (ed.), *The World of the Gallowglass*

(2007), pp. 124–143. For Shane O'Neill's approach to Charles IX, 25 April 1566, TNA, SP63/17/34; for 'Los principes católicos de Irlanda a Maurice, Arzobispo de Cassel, 4 May, 1570, Archivo General de Simancas, E-Sueltos, Leg 8336, 27, printed in *La Batalla del Mar Oceano: Corpus Documental de las Hostilidades entre Espana e Inglaterra* (5 vols, Madrid, 1988), vol. 1, pp. 47–8.

28 Peter Holmes, 'The authorship and early reception of *A Conference About the Next Succession to the Crown of England*', *Historical Journal*, 23 (1980), 415–29.

29 Lennon, *Stanihurst*, pp. 79–105.

30 For example, Guerau de Spes to Philip II, 14 June 1569, and 'Letter of intelligence to Alba', 17 November 1572, *CSPSpan*, 2, pp. 165, 441, and García Hernán, *Ireland and Spain*, p. 7.

31 Brendan Bradshaw, *The Irish Constitutional Revolution of the Sixteenth Century* (Cambridge, 1979); Ciaran Brady, 'Court, castle and country: the framework of government in Tudor Ireland', in Ciaran Brady and Raymond Gillespie (eds), *Natives and Newcomers: Essays on the Making of Irish Colonial Society, 1534–1641* (Dublin, 1986), pp. 22–49; Ciaran Brady, *The Chief Governors: The Rise and Fall of Reform Government in Tudor Ireland, 1536–88* (Cambridge, 1994).

32 Morgan, *Tyrone's Rebellion*, pp. 55–81.

33 *Ibid.*, pp. 5–135.

34 Sir William Warren to Cecil, 5 December 1599, TNA, SP63/206/74. Tyrone's second statement comes from Bishop Thomas Jones's account of the negotiations the Lord Lieutenant held with O'Neill and O'Donnell in early April 1598 at Dundalk, TNA, SP63/202 part II/9.

35 For Tyrone's assaults on the prerogative, see 'Articles intended to be stood upon by Tyrone' TNA, SP63/206/55. See also Hiram Morgan, 'Faith and fatherland in sixteenth-century Ireland', *History Ireland*, 3:2 (1995), 13–20, and Morgan, *Tyrone's Rebellion*, pp. 85–112.

36 See *Dictionary of Irish Biography*, 'Donough O'Brien 4th earl of Thomond' by Bernadette Cunningham, 'Ulick Burke, 3rd earl of Clanricard and 'Henry Fitzgerald, 12th earl of Kildare' by Terry Clavin; Sir George Carew to Cecil, 29 May, 1602, TNA, SP63/211/37.

37 Morgan, 'Hugh O'Neill', pp. 5–6. See also the *DIB* entries, 'James fitzThomas Fitzgerald', 'Ulick Burke, 3rd earl of Clanricard' and 'Florence MacCarthy Reagh', by Terry Clavin.

38 Bingham to Cecil, 2 January 1598, TNA, SP63/203/1.

39 See Bishop Jones to Burghley, 18 April 1598, TNA, SP63/202 part II/9 for an example of confederate negotiating strategy.

40 Cecil famously scribbled 'Ewtopia' on his copy of the November 1599 rebel demands; see TNA, SP63/206/55.

41 Fenton to Cecil, 3 January 1598, TNA, SP63/202 part I/3.

42 Ormond to the Queen, 24 January 1598, TNA, SP63/202 part I/34; Ormond to the Privy Council, 1 March 1598, TNA, SP63/202 part I/65.

43 Thomas Jones, Bishop of Meath, to Burghley, 18 April 1598, TNA, SP63/202 part II/9; Ormond to Cecil, 18 April 1598, TNA, SP63/202 part II/8.

44 Fenton to Cecil, 7 May 1598, TNA, SP63/202 part II/28.

45 Intelligence sent to Fenton, 21 June 1598, TNA, SP63/202 part II/82.

46 Fenton to Cecil, 22 June 1598, *ibid.*

47 Fenton to Cecil, 25 June 1598, TNA, SP63/202 part II/83.

48 James VI to Lords Justice Loftus and Gardener, 17 August 1598, TNA, SP63/202 part III/143

49 Bingham to Cecil, 2 January 1599, TNA, SP63/203/1. Bingham died two weeks later.

50 For Essex's forces, see Francis Bacon, *A Declaration of the Practises & Treasons Attempted and Committed by Robert Late Earle of Essex* (London, 1601). Ciaran Brady first brought my attention to Fitzgerald's involvement. Its significance is further attested to by the fact that the death of Kildare and 'eighteen of the chiefs of Meath and Fingall' is the first event mentioned in the relatively voluminous entry for 1599 in the Annals of the Four Masters, *Annála Ríoghachta Eireann*, ed. J. O'Donovan (Dublin, 1998) VI 2092–3.

51 'Advertisement from the North of Ireland, being a letter from Richard Weston to the earl of Essex', 20 July 1599, TNA, SP63/205/118i.

52 Bacon (1601), sig. C2^v.

53 *Ibid.*, sig. B3^v.

54 *Ibid.*, sigs B3^r–C3^v.

55 Hiram Morgan, 'Hugh O'Neill', *DIB*.

56 For Udall, see P. R. Harris, 'The reports of William Udall, informer, 1605–12', *Recusant History*, 8 (1965), 252–84.

57 For Neilson's role in frustrating plans to bring about a political settlement with various O'Neills of Clandeboy, see Christopher Carleill's irritated comments in undated 1592, TNA, SP63/167/66. 'Information given by Marmaduke Nealson', 30 April 1590, TNA, SP12/231/92.

58 'Marmaduke Neilson's declaration upon his oath…the 7th of May, 1601', TNA, SP63/208 part 2/55ii. For Udall's fate, see Mountjoy and Council to the Privy Council, TNA, SP63/208 part II/55, and for his later protests, see 11 June 1601, *HMC Sal*, XI, p. 537.

59 Udall's Walter-Mitty-like qualities are underlined by Bath's rehearsal of Udall's claim that James VI had written to him personally, accusing him of being the author of *A Conference*. Udall apparently also claimed that Elizabeth had personally commissioned him to write a refutation of the same work.

Chapter 13

A view from abroad: continental powers and the succession

Thomas M. McCoog, SJ

The published proceedings of a 2003 conference commemorating the accession of James VI to the English throne convey the impression that the English succession was a British affair with little or no interest to continental powers.[1] A few contributors, it is true, touched on French, Spanish or Roman involvement, but no one addressed the continental issue *per se*. In this chapter, however, I demonstrate that European monarchs, especially the Catholic ones, did monitor the emerging crisis, often at the insistence of religious exiles who were fearful that this was the last realistic opportunity for the complete restoration of Catholicism. I also explain that their cries went unheeded, and that this was at first because their usual supporters were fighting a war over the succession to the French throne. Only after Spain and France ended their conflict did Philip II turn his attention to England, but then his and his son Philip III's insistence that the Infanta Isabella Clara Eugenia be the Catholic candidate (despite her suspicions of the King's intentions and her general disinterest in the English throne) prevented a unified Catholic front. I show that with assistance from Henry IV, eager to re-establish French influence in a Rome equally eager to escape Spanish hegemony, James consolidated support at the papal court with insinuations and suggestions that he would in fact imitate Henry and become a Catholic, an allure that was especially tempting to Pope Clement VIII. By the time Philip abandoned his sister's candidacy in favour of someone less aligned, it was too late.

FROM PAPAL EXCOMMUNICATION TO THE SPANISH ARMADA

The continental powers considered Mary Queen of Scots the rightful heir to Elizabeth. After Pius V's excommunication of Elizabeth as a heretical usurper in 1570, Mary progressed from rightful heir to rightful queen in the eyes of Catholic rulers. Before and after *Regnans in excelsis* John Leslie, Bishop of Ross and Mary's ambassador at Elizabeth's court, championed her cause with *A Defence of the Honour of the Right Highe, Mightye and Noble Princesse Marie Quene of Scotlande and Dowager of France...*[2] Subsequent editions and Latin, Spanish and French translations stirred up European anger at Mary's treatment and justified enterprises against England. Spain, Rome and the Guise network drafted strategies for the liberation of the imprisoned Mary and, preferably married to a Catholic prince, her immediate succession to the English throne. The active involvement of advisers and confidantes of James VI of Scotland, and their promise of his acceptance of Catholicism, provided Catholic Europe with an orthodox dynasty as a replacement for the heretical Tudors.[3]

The Anglo-Scottish League of 5 July 1586 ended James's involvement with these ventures: James promised to maintain the religious settlement of both kingdoms, and Elizabeth, although refusing to acknowledge him as her heir, granted him an annual subsidy and swore that she would do nothing to prevent his succession.[4] Given Mary's age, a marriage between her and a good Catholic no longer guaranteed a Catholic succession. Who would now succeed or replace Elizabeth? The question had a practical urgency. Philip II refused to sponsor any military intervention that would ultimately benefit the Scottish King. Indeed, he demanded that James be barred from the English throne. Pope Sixtus V's and the Guises' refusal to abandon James resulted in a postponement of the discussion of Mary's heir until she had actually ascended the throne. The Scottish Queen herself advanced Spanish pretensions in her 'phantom will', almost certainly never written but intended as a lure to entice Philip into action. Mary promised to bequeath her claims to the English throne to Philip if her son James had not become a Catholic before her death.[5] William Allen, head of the English Catholics in exile, and Robert Persons, superior of the Jesuit mission to England, demonstrated that Philip was the only legitimate descendant of the House of Lancaster *with the power to implement his right* (my italics) by pointing out errors in Leslie's genealogical tree. Other factors, including Mary's will and the alleged desire of Queen Mary I that her husband succeed her, consolidated Philip's pretensions.[6]

The failure of the Armada in 1588, the assassinations of Henry Duke of Guise, Louis Cardinal of Guise and Henry III in 1588–89, and the emergence of the Protestant Henry of Navarre as the King of France, pushed any future English enterprise to the back burner. There were failed attempts by Allen, Persons, a Scottish Jesuit William Crichton and others to arouse Philip into action.[7] Europe, Protestant and Catholic, concentrated on the religious struggles over the French succession. Spain and the Guises rallied around Charles, Cardinal of Bourbon, as their candidate. With the Cardinal's death on 9 May

1590, Philip advanced the dynastic claims of his daughter, Infanta Isabella Clara Eugenia, as the eldest daughter of Henry III's sister, Elisabeth, the wife of Philip II, despite France's adherence to Salic law.[8] Spanish insistence that Isabella marry a Habsburg cousin, and not a French prince, made her candidacy even less tenable.[9] Meanwhile, three popes briefly sat on the papal throne between the death of Sixtus V (27 August 1590) and the election of Clement VIII (30 January 1592). Taking advantage of the confusion, Henry of Navarre repeated his intention to receive instruction in the Catholic faith. On 25 July 1593 he abjured Calvinism. Clement VIII's absolution and recognition of him as Henry IV on 17 September 1595, transformed an internal religious struggle into a straightforward war between Spain and France with her allies England and Holland.

A CONFERENCE AND ITS IMPACT

The appearance of R. Doleman's *A Conference about the Next Succession to the Crowne of Ingland* refocused attention on the English succession.[10] The author(s) claimed to speak ill of no candidate *in se*. Nothing, Persons insisted, was said against James except his religious views. The Jesuit believed the book would undoubtedly serve God without offending anyone by opening English eyes to the number of available candidates.[11] The Spanish princess was the preferred claimant, but, if she were unwilling or unable to succeed, Doleman advised Philip II to secure the crown for the House of Parma (the Italian Farneses) or the Portuguese House of Braganza, or be prepared to stake his own claim.[12]

Post hoc or, as many believed, *propter hoc* – namely the publication of Doleman's treatise – James took a more active interest in securing wider continental recognition of his right of succession.[13] Through his marriage to Anne of Denmark in 1589, James was related to the royal House of Denmark–Norway, and to many German Lutheran nobles.[14] He could therefore presume their support. James employed various and sundry different agents in his quest for wider recognition. David Edwards's recent lament about a 'particularly glaring lacuna…[specifically] the absence of any systematic examination of the role played by special agents and "intelligencers" in negotiating by stealth the progress of King James's claim to the English and Irish thrones with the key figures of both kingdoms'[15] could be expanded to similar activities on the continent.[16] Many Scots, generally Catholic, travelled the continent on special missions. They and their missions remain shrouded in mystery. Written credentials were rare: the absence of a paper trail allowed James to disown them if the negotiations became public and embarrassing. Of the Scottish agents operating on the continent some represented the more militant Catholic earls, and others, allegedly the King himself. The two often competed.

In 1595 the 'Young Laird of Pury Ogilvie' – that is John Ogilvie of Pury – portrayed James as so sympathetic to Catholics that he merited papal endorsement as Elizabeth's heir. Philip II feigned interest in Catholicism but, according to Pury Ogilvie, was motivated solely by a desire for the acquisition of yet another title for his family. James needed overt papal support lest the Catholic earls, specifically George Gordon, sixth Earl of Huntly, and Francis Hay, ninth Earl of Erroll, hand over Scotland to the King of Spain to the detriment of not only James himself, but of Italy, the papacy and Christendom in general.[17]

Pury Ogilvie found a receptive listener in Innocenzo Malvasia, papal agent in the Spanish Netherlands, whose pro-Scottish and anti-Spanish sentiments became so obvious that Philip II eventually demanded his withdrawal. In a subsequent memorial to Pietro, Cardinal Aldobrandini, Secretary of State, Malvasia stressed James's protection of, and trust in, Catholics. The political situation in Scotland prevented him from doing more. But even stronger political concerns compelled James to favour Catholics whose support he needed to gain the English throne. Someone should be sent to Scotland to negotiate with James; the said agent would let it be known that the pope was prepared to damage his cause through excommunication unless he made some public concessions. Malvasia recommended that the envoy be the King's relative (through the Guise family) Charles (II), Duke of Lorraine, who visited occasionally, and definitely not a Jesuit because James had 'little confidence [in Jesuits], looking on them with suspicion as dependants of the king of Spain'.[18]

James's campaign was having some success in Rome, but Philip, despite numerous memorials flowing from the pens of English Catholics, did nothing. In March 1596 Persons (but more likely Sir Francis Englefield or the Jesuit Joseph Creswell) bemoaned the slow seepage of support for a Spanish candidate because of Philip's inertia and the extraordinary efforts of his opponents. James was making overtures to English Catholics and to the pope. Because France and Scotland tended to behave similarly, James would imitate Henry. Nonetheless, the author argued, there would be no more hope for the eradication of heresy and the reformation of evil government in England under James than France was then experiencing under Henry. The anti-Spanish faction, with encouragement from French cardinals in Rome, Italian nobles and the English government itself (by sowing discontent between Jesuits and secular clergy[19]), spread rumours that Philip aspired to be monarch of the world. They claimed they desired a king nominated by the pope and not by the Spanish King.[20] Persons later contended that France in truth would prefer the Infanta to James, especially if she renounced her own claims to Brittany, Aquitaine, Anjou, Normandy, etc., and also the traditional English claims to the French crown. But Philip must take the initiative. Since the pope should take an active role in the selection, Philip should open papal eyes to the fact that the Infanta was the ideal candidate by expounding reasons for her succession and dispelling fears of Spain's annexation of England. Assurances that Philip was acting for the good of the Catholic faith and not for his own self-aggrandizement, would minimize real opposition.[21]

SPANISH POLICIES IN FLUX 1596–97

Despite continual Spanish military involvement in France and Holland, the success of the Cadiz expedition conducted by Robert Devereux (Earl of Essex) and Charles, Lord Howard of Effingham (later Earl of Nottingham) in 1596 so piqued Philip that he launched his oft-postponed armada in October, but the ships returned to port within a week because of storms.[22] Another armada, which sailed a year later, also failed. A prepared proclamation explained that Philip, prompted by the 'universal outcry of the oppressed Catholics', had undertaken the attack to enforce 'ecclesiastical censures' imposed by the popes. The proclamation said nothing explicit about the deposition of the Queen and the accession of a successor. Parliament and those with legitimate authority would decide the successor most suitable 'for the preservation of the Catholic religion and the tranquillity of the same nations by lightening the burden of the oppressed subjects and establishing peace and concord with the rest of the states and princes of Christianity'.[23]

Instead of a Scottish–Spanish conflict over the succession, someone, perhaps Crichton or another within his circle, suggested an alternative strategy: a Spanish *rapprochement* with James. The author observed the situation objectively. James not only was the closest blood heir, but was actively building up a body of Protestant and Catholic sympathisers within England. Philip, on the other hand, had no support among the English Catholics with the exception of those dependent on the Jesuits. Moreover, James had wide foreign support. Scotland had formed alliances with Holland, certain German princes and Denmark, and James was a blood relative of the Dukes of Lorraine, Florence and Bavaria. Even Henry IV, not a great admirer of James, gave him preference for the sake of curbing Spanish power. Thus, the author concluded, Spain should reach an accord with James so that his accession to the English throne would depend on Philip's assistance.[24]

In 1597 Philip II arranged the marriage between Archduke Albert Habsburg, an Austrian cousin, and his daughter Isabella, and established them as joint sovereigns of the Spanish Netherlands with semi-independent status. On 6 May 1598, four days after the Peace of Vervins ended the war between Spain and France, Philip made over to the Archduke and the Infanta both the northern and the southern Netherlands. They were married by proxy at Ferrara on 15 November 1598 in the presence of Clement VIII.[25] Philip did not see their marriage: he had died on 13 September. Attempts to include the

Dutch and English and to address the English succession and position of Catholics within the Franco-Spanish peace failed.[26]

With proper direction, the Brussels court of Isabella and Albert could have served as a fulcrum for supporters of Spanish claims, and as a launching pad for any necessary military force to enforce them. Catholics and supporters of Spain in general and particularly in England urged Philip III to procrastinate no longer but make a decision. They wanted to know the King's position and awaited a sign.[27] They waited in vain. The clearest sign once again came from Scotland.

A SCOTTISH CONVERSION?

Quasi-authoritative news in 1598 that James's consort Anne of Denmark had become a Roman Catholic corroborated reports of James's tolerance.[28] William Crichton showered lavish praise upon the Scottish King:

> He is wise, he is learned, he is a Mecenas, and with his royall penne hath added immortall honor unto the Muses. I passe over his moderation, his ingenuytie, his moral vertues, which in hopes and blossoms are flowers of fruits to come, when it shall please God to temper his humane perfection with true pietie and religion.

Doleman's book, Crichton contended, had opened the eyes of many by demonstrating that James was the 'righteous and lawfull heyre to the crowne of England'.[29] In the subsequent fall-out over Crichton's comments about Spain, Claudio Acquaviva, Superior General of the Society of Jesus, re-assigned the Scot to Avignon on 2 May 1598 at the expressed wish of Archduke Albert.[30]

The English secular priest John Cecil, a confidant of Persons, a correspondent of William Cecil, Lord Burghley, and an agent of the Catholic earls, whose initial attack on James had prompted Crichton's defence, renewed his offensive in *A Discoverye of the Errors Committed and Iniuryes Done to his Ma. off Scotlande.*[31] *Beware of the Northern Gate*, no copy of which apparently is extant, appeared in Antwerp in late 1598. The English secular priest William Gifford, a Stuart supporter and known opponent of Jesuits, attributed principal authorship to the Irish religious exile Richard Stanyhurst. Interestingly the treatise also argued that Mary Stuart's conviction and execution for treason rendered her son ineligible for the English throne according to the Act for the Queen's Surety.[32] Cecil, Stanyhurst, Persons *et al.* tried to halt the Stuart juggernaut as Frangipani explained the urgency of papal direction, but their pleas for guidance were met with silence in Spain and Rome.[33]

Alarmed by rumours of a peace treaty between England and Spain, and a marriage between Albert's brother Matthias and James's cousin Lady Arbella Stuart, James accelerated his campaign by consolidating his Scottish base and seeking foreign assistance. In November he proposed an oath to his Scottish subjects that they would advance his claims to the English throne without, in any way, jeopardizing Elizabeth's rights. Charles Paget, an English Catholic exile, went to Paris allegedly to push James's claims at the French court. Within England, James, seeing the hand of Sir Robert Cecil in the peace overtures with Spain, turned to the anti-Spanish Earl of Essex.[34]

James's agents pleaded his case in Rome. Sir Edmund Drummond reported authoritatively to William Chisholm, Bishop of Vaison in the south of France, that James would grant liberty of conscience to Catholics in England and Scotland and arrange public disputations on the conflicting claims of Catholics and Protestants. Moreover, he promised to place his oldest son in the custody of Catholics to be raised in that religion. James's wife Anne was already a Catholic and there was a good chance that he would follow her example. Chisholm relayed the information to Cardinal Aldobrandini. The King did not wish to remain a Protestant, but feared the loss of the English throne and possibly of his life if he became a Roman Catholic. Once he had secured the throne James would be able to act more freely. What choice did the papacy have? Other rulers would not accept a Spanish candidate for fear of Spanish expansion; the majority of Englishmen would resist and rebel against a Spanish monarch.[35]

Philippe de Béthune, a new French ambassador to Scotland, arrived in Edinburgh ostensibly to renew the old alliance.[36] He carried advice from James Beaton, Archbishop of Glasgow,[37] that James should more actively advance his cause in Rome.[38] Clement, he asserted, was 'well-affected to the king's title [to the English throne], and jealous of the grandour of Spaine'. From 1601 Béthune advanced James's cause as French ambassador in Rome. James Elphinstone, Scottish Secretary of State, thus recommended that the King establish contact with the pope via Beaton or Chisholm, duly promoted cardinal.[39]

In Paris in late 1599 Henry Constable – poet, courtier and Catholic follower of the Earl of Essex – rallied English Catholics to James's cause with the active support of King Henry IV.[40] Constable defended James's credentials in *A Discoverye of a Counterfecte Conference* … Roman authorities, he urged, should be as patient with James as they had been with Henry.[41] That such a policy paid off could be seen everywhere in France. To bolster James's claims, Constable stressed the numerous Marian and early Elizabethan officials who had advocated the succession of Mary Queen of Scots, and who indeed now considered her a martyr. Sometime in the spring, Constable left Paris for Rome to continue the campaign at the papal court.[42]

James did initiate direct contact with the pope on 24 September 1599, although he later claimed that he had signed the letters unknowingly. Addressing Clement VIII as *'beatissime pater'* [most blessed father] and signing himself '*obsequentissimus filius*' [most obedient son], he requested a red hat for Chisholm.[43] Clement replied to James's overture on 13 April 1600 with elaborate arguments on the necessity of Catholicism without a comment about Chisholm's promotion. Two months later, either Cardinal Aldobrandini or Cardinal Borghese answered in more detail. The author sang James's praises, discoursed on his many virtues, and rejoiced at the news that James considered conversion, but stated that, for unspecified reasons, Chisholm at this time could not be promoted. If, however, James became a Catholic, there was no barrier that could not be overcome.[44]

SPANISH INERTIA

As James discreetly but actively manoeuvred for the throne, Spain remained inactive. Thomas Fitzherbert, English secretary to Philip III, conjectured that an announcement would follow an upcoming meeting between Philip III and Archduke Albert. In a curious letter to William Sterrell,[45] Fitzherbert explained how he and others had told Philip II and Philip III that neither could entertain any hope of being acceptable to the English. Now he asked Sterrell's advice about publicizing the Infanta's claims in order to counteract James's tactics, to form a party within England, and to spur Spain into action.[46] With Essex already spoken for, his rival Sir Robert Cecil seemed a logical candidate. By the end of the year Cecil had asked for portraits of the Archduke and Archduchess.[47]

An unidentified informant, perhaps Sterrell, wrote to Persons in April 1600 that Sir Robert Cecil, Charles Howard, Earl of Nottingham, and Sir Thomas Sackville Lord Buckhurst sought an alternative to James.[48] They had examined the credentials of the Derby line – especially that of the oldest daughter Anne Stanley – but, before they proceeded any further, they wanted to know Philip III's position. These men, according to the informant, were 'persons of considerable power and as "politiques" not ill-affected to the Catholic religion'.[49] Persons recommended encouraging these nobles by reminding them of the dangers and disasters that would result from a Scottish successor. He wondered whether they would accept 'a foreign prince agreeable to his Catholic Majesty' as a husband for the Earl's daughter. A month later the same informant claims: 'if the King of Spain would come to a decision, he would find here [England] many friends, heretics among them; but…this want of decision in the past has kept everyone in suspense'. James VI, of course, had easier access to England, and many would flock to his side. Unless plans were devised now and preparations clearly made, there would be no organized resistance. In July Philip replied cautiously: he would support the Catholics and ensure that Elizabeth's successor was Catholic, an unsatisfactory reply according to Persons:

> The English have to keep two things in view as regards the person they are to rec-
> ognise as King: in the first place the well-being of the kingdom or state, and in the
> second the particular interests and position of those concerned, especially those of
> great influence. Neither the one nor the other, they will say, can they consider with-
> out knowing who the person is.[50]

A specific person and not a generic category must be proclaimed immediately upon the death of Elizabeth. Thereafter, anyone who opposed the person
named could be accused of high treason: 'It is, however, impossible to proclaim publicly an indeterminate person, neither known nor named: and there
will be no time after the death of the Queen to send [a messenger] to know his
Majesty's decision'.[51] Similar Spanish procrastination, some English Catholics
believed, had resulted in the defeat of the Catholic cause in France. Now they
feared that England would suffer similarly.

THE ROMAN RESPONSE

Hesitancy characterized Rome. On the one hand, Clement did not favour
any increase in Spanish predominance, but, on the other, he wanted more
than James's promises. In the summer of 1600, the pope sent three briefs
addressed to the nuncio in Brussels, to the Archpriest and English clergy, and
to English Catholics in general. Their message was pithy: no heretic, real or
suspected despite a legitimate claim to succession, should receive any support
from Catholics.[52] If this was the papal ultimatum as threatened by Beaton, it
was implemented half-heartedly. Many might have inferred the brief to be
directed against James, but the omission of his name held out hope to his
supporters. This ambivalence frustrated Frangipani, who compared the apostolic briefs to syrup after which real medicine should be administered, viz. the
proclamation of a specific Catholic claimant.[53] Persons reluctantly observed
that they must be content with such small measures designed to prevent
Catholics from supporting different candidates. 'Unquiet spirits' still dangled
the prospect of James's conversion, but the pope had made it clear that he
would approve only a known Catholic candidate and not someone who hinted
or promised to become one. Everyone continued to wait for Spain because
Philip III would most likely have to provide the military means for the en-
forcement of his candidate's claims.

On 1 February 1601, the Council of State finally counselled Philip to
promote Isabella's claims. On the 12th the King instructed his ambassador in
Rome, Gonzalo Fernández de Córdoba, Duke of Sessa, to discuss the subject
with the pope. But the monarch's insistence that the decision remain a secret
prevented the formation of a clear policy. At an unspecified later date, Philip
proposed that Isabella and Albert restore Flanders to the Spanish crown, once
they had settled in England, lest it fall into the hands of strangers upon their

death. Philip also promised significant sums of money to secure support within England. Meanwhile, he understood that Robert Cecil, Lord Buckhurst, Charles Howard (Earl of Nottingham) and Sir Thomas Egerton, Chancellor of the Realm, would support the Spanish candidate. In late June Baltazar de Zúñiga, Spanish ambassador to Flanders, still had not raised the subject of the restoration of Flanders with the Archduke and Archduchess.[54]

Disagreement between the Archdukes and Philip may have complicated the situation. Eager to pursue an independent foreign policy and to establish friendly relations with other kingdoms in the region, Isabella and Albert wanted peace with England and perhaps a revival of the old Anglo-Burgundian alliance. Philip, on the other hand, wished to preserve Spanish influence and resented attempts at greater independence from what he considered to be at best a temporarily alienated part of the Spanish patrimony. Isabella and Albert suspected that Philip promoted her title to the English throne as a diversion to hide his goal of reclaiming the Low Countries.[55]

In January 1601 Clement had raised France's possible reaction to a Spanish succession during an audience with Sessa. He claimed France would do anything in its power to prevent the union of England with Flanders. Indeed, Clement believed that France preferred the union of England and Scotland to this encirclement. Proud of his role in Henry IV's reconciliation and fearful of disrupting good relations with the French King, Clement urged caution and secrecy. In March the pope confessed to Sessa that he preferred England and Flanders united in one strong Catholic power, but he refused a public declaration lest that increase the activities of the Scottish and French factions. Once Elizabeth died, Clement would proclaim his support for the Infanta. No woman, Sessa remarked, more carefully avoided arousing the suspicions of her husband than Clement did with Henry![56]

Rome thus avoided any public declaration and monitored James and, especially, Henry's efforts in his behalf. Cardinal Aldobrandini knew that Henry preferred James, so much so that the King promised to work actively for James's immediate conversion.[57] He intended to include someone for this role in the entourage of his ambassador Charles Cauchon, Baron du Tour, in the summer of 1601.[58] Clement recommended that Chisholm be sent, but the nuncio, Innocenzo del Bufalo, delayed Chisholm's departure because many claimed that the Scottish Bishop was so well known in Scotland that his mission would do more harm than good.[59]

JAMES'S VICTORY

The failure of Essex's uprising in February 1601 resulted in a diplomatic realignment detrimental to Spanish interests. Whatever the relations were between Essex and James, the latter did not suffer from association with the disgraced Earl. Essex's elimination left Sir Robert Cecil supreme, unchallenged and fearful of any public disclosure of his correspondence with Spanish officials. Within a month of Essex's execution, Cecil and James began their secret correspondence.[60] With the aid of Cecil, James's candidacy, long ascendant, appeared unstoppable. He had obtained the support of the Scottish nobility, had cultivated English Catholics and Puritans with intimations of promotion of their Church, had established access to the English court, had maintained good relations with the court of Isabella and Albert in Brussels, and had secured the support of Henry IV. Pope Clement VIII, suspicious of James's intended Catholicism, was nonetheless reluctant to abandon him in favour of a Spanish contender. Philip III meanwhile made no public declaration.

The Spanish Council of State again addressed the succession in May 1602. Convinced that Isabella was a better candidate and thus there was no reason for a *rapprochement* with James, the council voted to fund a faction within England. Archduke Albert dismissed these efforts: 'the hope of excluding him [James] from the succession in England can never be fulfilled, not to mention the worry and discomfort that it will arouse among the Catholics of that kingdom who are still asking your [Philip's] assistance'.[61] Instead, Albert advised Philip to support James. Zúñiga, the Spanish ambassador to Flanders, believed James's 'game for the crown of England [wa]s almost won'. James had successfully forced a coalition among the northern countries that would defend his claims, an alliance too formidable for Spain. He too suggested that Spain should assist James to the throne in return for liberty of conscience for the Catholics. Perplexed by these reports, the council asked why Spain should assist or encourage a Protestant heretic after deciding to promote a Catholic candidate.

Papal recommendations that France and Spain find a mutually acceptable Catholic candidate foundered because of Philip III's insistence that Henry had no right to interfere in the case. Rumours circulated that Henry considered making it a three-horse race. In 1599, after his marriage with Queen Margot was dissolved, he could have married Anne Stanley.[62] On the Scottish front, with letters of introduction from Jesuits, Sir James Lindsay visited Rome in the summer of 1602, ostensibly to discuss papal support for James's claims and to prevent any papal recognition of Henry's pretensions or Franco-Spanish agreement on an alternative candidate. In order to obtain the first, he may also have been commissioned to propose James's son and heir as security for the King's promise to convert. Upon his return to Scotland, he carried papal letters to James and Anne. Clement had earlier written to Anne about his joy at the news of her conversion and his subsequent hope that she would play a role in the eventual conversion of her husband.[63] In his letter to James, the pope conveyed his sincere best wishes and true affection; he could wish the King nothing more than that he would convert to Catholicism. He urged that his successor Henry Frederick be raised a Catholic, a request that he repeated in his letter to Anne: 'how like he would be to his forefathers and ancestors...who flourished in every kind of kingly splendour but earned the chief praise for their Catholic faith'.[64]

In February 1603 the Spanish Council of State finally abandoned Isabella in the hope of the identification and promotion of a candidate acceptable to France and Rome. Philip could transfer his rights to the crown – rights greater than any other candidate save the King of Scotland's – to anyone. But to whom? Charles Emmanuel I, Duke of Savoy, perhaps married to Arbella Stuart or Anne Stanley? Rainutio Farnese, Duke of Parma? A son of Edward Somerset, Earl of Worcester, married to Anne Stanley?[65] The council recommended that the King ask English Catholics to name their preferred candidate whom, in return for future favours, Philip would endorse. With Spanish assistance, the new king could defend his claims against James of Scotland and 'easily re-establish the religion entirely in the country, seeing how readily in the past the latter ha[d] changed its faith for that of its Princes'.[66] But it was too late. Or was it?

James's seamless succession to the English throne upon the death of Elizabeth on 24 March 1603 blindsided many. Fears of rival contenders, a disputed succession, proved unfounded. James had done his job well. Now the recipients of James's promises, including English Catholics, expected their realization. The Elizabethan Jesuit John Gerard recounted Catholic hopes at James's succession:

> was it not now time for them to hope that God would say unto them, 'Levate capita vestra quia ecce appropinquat redemptio vestra?' [Lift up your heads because your redemption is at hand (Luke 21:25).] We had now suffered more than a full number of years, not days, of this deluge of persecution pouring down upon us. Was it not now time for us to look out and to long that the earth would begin to dry and afford us some quiet habitation upon it? Were we not now to expect that some gracious bird would bring us an olive branch in sign of peace, which we had looked for and desired so much? True it is that most Catholics had great hope and expectation of this King James, then King of Scotland only. And this hope, as a human help of no small force, did join with God's grace and bring some comfort with it, amidst the many discomforts sustained under the long-continued reign of Queen Elizabeth.[67]

Expectations were not realised; hopes were not fulfilled. Gerard wondered how to describe

> the state of all Catholic minds when all these hopes did vanish away; and as a flash of lightning, giving for the time a pale light unto those that sit in darkness, doth afterwards leave them in more desolation? What grief may we imagine they generally felt, when not only no one of these hopes did bring forth the hoped fruit, nor any promise was performed.[68]

In the summer of 1603 Anthony Dutton and Guy Fawkes travelled to Spain to assure Philip that some English Catholics were still prepared to act if promised aid arrived in time.[69]

CONCLUSIONS

Bella gerant alii, tu felix Austria nube (Let others make war; you, fortunate Austria, marry). Successful marriages had established the Habsburgs as the most powerful European family of the early-modern period. Philip II had inherited the Portuguese empire in 1580, but he had less success with other thrones. Attempts to place his daughter Isabella on the throne of France, failed because of Habsburg stubbornness and Bourbon adaptability. Philip's attempt to ascend to the English throne with the deposition of Elizabeth through an armada failed for military and meteorological reasons. But why was he unable to secure the throne for his daughter? Especially after the publication of Doleman's treatise on the succession, Isabella's claims had some legitimacy, but how realistic were her chances in a post-Armada England? So effective had been the anti-Spanish 'black legend', would she have been acceptable to English subjects? Some Elizabethan Privy Councillors apparently thought so. Catholic exiles urged the formation of a Spanish party through publications and bribes. But would she have been acceptable to continental powers? That was the rub. Despite the occasional whisper of a diplomatic marriage between Arbella Stuart or Anne Stanley and a continental Catholic noble, only the Infanta Isabella and King James attracted serious continental recognition. Through James's marriage he was related to Scandinavian and German Protestant rulers. James could also depend on a certain amount of anti-Habsburg sentiment. Of the Catholic powers Henry IV, James's blood relative, may not have liked an Anglo-Scottish union, but he preferred it to the Habsburg encirclement that would follow an Anglo-Burgundian union. Any increase of Habsburg power also troubled Clement VIII, proud of his success with the reconciliation of Henry and still hopeful of something similar with James, a hope cultivated by anti-Spanish, pro-French Roman officials, and exploited by James himself as he dangled promises and assurances before credulous papal eyes. France's struggle to restore the kingdom's former influence within the papacy and Catholic world provided Clement with a proper equilibrium against Spanish dominance.[70]

British religious exiles considered the succession as the last opportunity for the complete restoration of Catholicism. Submitting proposals and memorials, they disagreed among themselves over candidates and strategies. Persons insisted on a Catholic, for the future of Catholicism in the isles depended on him or her and not on a tenuous promise. Crichton, however, believed that James would keep his promise. James himself carefully and cleverly exploited anti-

Habsburg and anti-Spanish fears and sentiment, and cultivated his French connections. James also provided England with a dynasty, whereas Isabella's and Albert's lack of children might result in yet another succession crisis. Spain and Rome dilly-dallied so long over affairs in France that they conceded James an advantage. James too had his distractions, notably the Catholic earls, but he used them to good effect. After the Peace of Vervins Henry IV was strong enough and influential enough in Rome to prevent Spain's unilateral decision on a Catholic candidate. Philip's initial insistence on Isabella, despite her scepticism over his motives and her unwillingness to stand, prevented agreement among Rome, Spain and France. By the time Philip III was willing to consider other 'neutral' candidates it was too late. Now, as convincingly demonstrated by Albert Loomie, SJ, 'the frustration over his [Philip's] previous miscalculations would stimulate for the next two years a conscientious effort on behalf of toleration in England...[which had been] one of the persistent reasons for his diplomacy against the Stuart succession'.[71]

NOTES

1 Jean-Christophe Mayer (ed.), *The Succession Struggle in Late Elizabethan England: Politics, Polemics and Cultural Representations* (Montpellier, 2004).

2 John Leslie, *A Defence of the Honour of the Right Highe, Mightye and Noble Princesse Marie Quene of Scotlande and Dowager of France with a declaration as well of her right, title & intereste to the succession of the crowne of Englande* (London [*vere* Rheims], 1569).

3 See Thomas M. McCoog, SJ, *The Society of Jesus in Ireland, Scotland, and England 1541–1588. 'Our Way of Proceeding'?* (Leiden, 1996), pp. 178–213.

4 See Susan Doran, 'Loving and affectionate cousins? The relationship between Elizabeth I and James VI of Scotland 1586–1603', in Susan Doran and Glenn Richardson (eds), *Tudor England and its Neighbours* (Basingstoke, 2005), pp. 203–34 (pp. 223–6).

5 De Lamar Jensen, 'The phantom will of Mary Queen of Scots', *Scotia*, 4 (1980), 1–15; *idem.*, *Diplomacy and Dogmatism: Bernardino de Mendoza and the French Catholic League* (Cambridge, MA, 1964), pp. 83–5.

6 Leo Hicks, SJ (ed.), *Letters and Memorials of Father Robert Persons, S.J.* (London, 1942), pp. 295–303. See also Allen to Philip II, Rome, 19 March 1587, in Thomas Francis Knox (ed.), *The Letters and Memorials of William Cardinal Allen (1532–1594)* (London, 1882), pp. 272–5.

7 For Crichton's projects, see Francisco de Borja Medina, SJ, 'Intrigues of a Scottish Jesuit at the Spanish Court: William Crichton's mission to Madrid (1590–1592)', in Thomas M. McCoog, SJ (ed.), *The Reckoned Expense: Edmund Campion and the Early English Jesuits*, 2nd edn (Rome, 2007), pp. 311–18. See Allen's memorials on a possible marriage between Arbella Stuart and Rainutio Farnese, Prince of Parma, in Penelope Renold (ed.), *Letters of William Allen and Richard Barret 1572–1598* (London, 1967), pp. 209–16. Allen refused to get involved until he had secured Philip's approval. On the differences and tensions between Crichton and Persons regarding the succession, see Thomas M. McCoog, SJ, 'Harmony disrupted: Robert Parsons, S.J., William Crichton, S.J., and the question of Queen Elizabeth's successor, 1581–1603', in Thomas M.

McCoog, SJ, *'And touching our society': fashioning Jesuit identity in Elizabethan England* (Toronto, 2013), pp. 283–447.

8 See Stuart Carroll, *Martyrs and Murderers: The Guise Family and the Making of Europe* (Oxford, 2009), pp. 298–9.

9 R. J. Knecht, *The French Wars of Religion 1559–1598* (London, 1989), pp. 74–5. See also Mark Holt, *The French Wars of Religion 1562–1629* (Cambridge, 1995), pp. 148–9.

10 R. Doleman [Robert Persons?], *A Conference about the Next Succession to the Crowne of Ingland* ([Antwerp], 1594 [1595]. I am less inclined than many to attribute authorship to Persons; I prefer editorship.

11 Persons to Claudio Acquaviva [Jesuit superior general], Madrid June 4 and 16, 1594, Archivum Romanum Societatis Iesu (ARSI), Hisp. 136, fos 362^r–363^v.

12 Doleman, *A Conference*, pp. 263–4.

13 See Susan Doran, 'James VI and the English succession', in Ralph Houlbrooke (ed.), *James VI and I. Ideas, Authority and Government*, (Aldershot, 2006), pp. 25–42. I agree with Dr Doran that the succession was of less importance in the 1580s but, because of the activities of Spain and the Catholic earls, became increasingly more important in the early 1590s. The appearance of Doleman's treatise moved it to a higher gear.

14 See D. Harris Willson, *King James VI and I* (London, 1956), pp. 85–95; W. B. Patterson, *King James VI and I and the Reunion of Christendom* (Cambridge, 1997), p. 89; Doran, 'James VI', p. 32.

15 'Securing the Jacobean succession: the secret career of James Fullerton of Trinity College, Dublin', in Seán Duffy (ed.), *The World of the Galloglass: Kings, Warlords and Warriors in Ireland and Scotland, 1200–1600* (Dublin, 2007), p. 188. I thank Dr Paul E. J. Hammer for this reference. See also Helen Georgia Stafford, *James VI of Scotland and the Throne of England* (New York and London, 1940), pp. 234–5; Doran, 'James VI', pp. 32–3.

16 Crichton to James Tyrie, Brussels, 10 February, 1595, BL, Lansdowne MS 96, fos 91^r–92^v; same to same, Antwerp, 18 June 1595, *CSPScot*, 11, pp. 611–13, 613–15.

17 For various memoranda regarding these negotiations, see *CSPScot*, 11, pp. 225–7, 227–9, 230–3 and 'Summa de los Memoriales', in T. G. Law (ed.), *Documents Illustrating Catholic Policy in the Reign of James VI 1596–98*, Miscellany of the Scottish History Society, 15 (Edinburgh, 1893), pp. 21–40.

18 Biblioteca Apostolica Vaticana (BAV), Ottob. lat. 2510, fos. 270^r–76^v. This report, inexplicably without the first part, was published in Alphons Bellesheim, *History of the Catholic Church of Scotland*, 4 vols (Edinburgh/London, 1887–90), vol. 3, pp. 460–73.

19 Peter Lake and Michael Questier situate the succession issue within the intramural Catholic conflict regarding the archpriest in Chapter 4 of this volume.

20 Valladolid, Archivum Collegium Sancti Albani, Series II, vol. 1, num. 25.

21 Persons to Don Juan de Idiáquez, Valladolid, 2 September 1596, Archivum Britannicum Societatis Iesu (ABSI), 46/12/3 [this is a collection of transcripts]. Leading English Catholics including Englefield and Jane Dormer, Duchess of Feria, favoured the Spanish Princess and urged Philip to treat this matter with the pope. Although the authors of the memorial delineated reasons for their preference of Isabella, from the pope 'must necessarily emanate the light and guidance which will lead the Catholics' (*CSPSpan*, 4, pp. 636–7). Another memorial detailing reasons in favour of the princess

can be found in Archives of the Archdiocese of Westminster, VI, 81.

22 See Albert J. Loomie, SJ, 'The Armadas and the Catholics of England', *Catholic Historical Review*, 59 (1973), 394–8.

23 Albert J. Loomie, SJ, 'Philip II's Armada proclamation of 1597', *Recusant History*, 12 (1974), 216–25.

24 'Considerations addressed to the Spanish minister, Pegna, on the subject of invading England, 1597', in M.A. Tierney (ed.), *Dodd's Church History of England*, 5 vols (London, 1839–43), vol. 3, pp. lxvii–lxx.

25 For the exact arrangements between the Netherlands and Spain, see John Lynch, *Spain 1516–1598: From Nation State to World Empire* (Oxford, 1991), pp. 470–2.

26 Most likely this is the context for the undated 'A discourse concerning a successor to Queen Elizabeth', in Jean-Christophe Mayer (ed.), *Breaking the Silence on the Succession* (Montpellier, 2003), pp. 125–56. See also Susan Doran, 'Three late-Elizabethan succession tracts', in Mayer, *Succession Struggle*, pp. 91–117.

27 Persons to Philip II, Rome, 28 May 1598, ABSI, 46/12/5; same to Philip III, Rome, 10 November 1598, ABSI, 46/12/5.

28 Crichton to [Acquaviva or George Duras, his assistant], Louvain, 3 February 1598, ARSI, Germ. 178, fo. 40$^{r–v}$.

29 'An Apologie and Defence of the King of Scotland', in Law, *Documents*, pp. 41–64.

30 Acquaviva to Crichton, 2 May 1598, ARSI, Fl. Belg. 1/II, pp. 678–79. In his exceptional study of Archduke Albert, Luc Duerloo argues that 'the Conference went largely unheeded at the Spanish court' (*Dynasty and Piety* [Farnham, 2012], p. 70). Philip III only became interested in his sister's claims once attempts at a peace treaty with England have failed. Perhaps, but as the case of Crichton demonstrates, Philip did not want anyone to disparage those claims.

31 John Cecil, *A Discoverye of the Errors Committed and Iniuryes Done to his Ma. off Scotlande* (n.p., n.d. [Paris, 1599]). See McCoog, 'Harmony disrupted', in McCoog, *'And touching our society'*, pp. 306–12.

32 27 Eliz. I c.1. See Gifford to James Younger, 9 October 1598, BAV, Lat. 6227, fo. 140^r, and Albert J. Loomie, SJ, 'Richard Stanyhurst in Spain: two unknown letters of August 1593', *Huntington Library Quarterly*, 28 (1965), 149–50.

33 Ottavio Mirto Frangipani, papal nuncio in Brussels, to Pietro, Cardinal Aldobrandini, Brussels, 20 March 1599, in Leon Van der Essen and Armand Louant (eds), *Correspondance d'Ottavio Mirto Frangipani, Premier Nonce de Flandre (1596–1606)*, 3 vols in 4 parts (Rome: Academia Belgica, 1924–42), vol. 3(i), pp. 28–30.

34 Doran, 'Loving and affectionate cousins', pp. 223–6; Willson, *King James VI and I*, pp. 142–8; Patterson, *James and Reunion*, pp. 39–42; Pauline Croft, *King James* (Basingstoke, 2003), pp. 44–5.

35 Chisholm to Aldobrandini, Vaison, 23 January 1599, Archivio Segreto Vaticano (ASV), Segr. Stato Francia 42, p. 527.

36 His instructions from Henry IV are dated 13/23 May 1599, *CSPScot*, 13(i), pp. 467–74.

37 Beaton had been Mary's agent in Paris. In late 1597/early 1598 James named him ambassador to France, apparently in the hope of reviving the 'auld alliance' and establishing a conduit with Rome. See Stafford, *James VI of Scotland*, pp. 226–7.

38 According to John Colville, who put a more sinister interpretation on these events, Beaton insisted that this was James's last chance. If he did not accept the papal offer and side publicly against Elizabeth, Clement would never recognize his claim to the English crown (Colville to Cecil, 21 August 1599, *CSPScot*, 13(i), pp. 531–3).

39 'A true relation of the service done by me, in procuring the letter to the pope from his majesty', published in David Calderwood, *History of the Kirk of Scotland*, ed. T. Thomson, 8 vols (Edinburgh, 1842–49), vol. 5, pp. 740–2. See also Alan Stewart, *The Cradle King: A Life of James VI & I* (London, 2003), p. 228; Gasparo Silingardi to Pietro, Cardinal Aldobrandini, Paris, 10 November 1599; same to same, Paris, 22 November 1599; same to same, Paris, 22 December 1599, in Bertrand Haan (ed.), *Correspondance du Nonce en France Gasparo Silingardi Evêque de Modène (1599–1601)* (Rome, 2002), pp. 367, 369, 377.

40 George Wickes, 'Henry Constable, poet and courtier, 1562–1613', *Biographical Studies [=Recusant History]*, 2 (1953–4), 282–6.

41 [Henry Constable], *Discoverye of a Counterfecte Conference* (Collen [*vere* Paris] 1600), pp. 90–1.

42 Wickes, 'Henry Constable', 285–6. See also Gasparo Silingardi to Pietro, Cardinal Aldobrandini, Paris, 14 March 1600, in Haan (ed.), *Correspondance du Nonce Gasparo Silingardi*, p. 408.

43 The mysterious letter of 24 September 1599, and a summary of the *mandata* which he sent to the two dukes and the pope, can be found in *CSPScot*, 13(ii), pp. 1144–8 and Calderwood, *History*, vol. 5, pp. 742–4. See also Stafford, *James VI of Scotland*, pp. 235–9.

44 Clement VIII to James, Rome, 13 April 1600, *CSPScot*, 13(ii), pp. 1145–8; [Aldobrandi or Borghese?] to James, Rome, 1 June 1600, *CSPScot*, 13(ii), pp. 1148–9.

45 On him, see Patrick Martin and John Finnis, 'The identity of "Anthony Rivers"', *Recusant History*, 26 (2002), 39–74.

46 Fitzherbert to Sterrell, Madrid 1 March 1599, TNA, SP12/270/47.

47 Leo Hicks, SJ, claimed that Cecil had a sincere interest in the Infanta's cause ('Sir Robert Cecil, Father Persons and the succession 1600–1601', *Archivum Historicum Societatis Iesu*, 24 [1955], 112). Joel Hurstfield dismissed the allegations with a claim that mere curiosity prompted the request in Joel Hurstfield, 'The succession struggle in late Elizabethan England', in S. T. Bindoff, Joel Hurstfield and C. H. Williams (eds), *Elizabethan Government and Society: Essays Presented to Sir John Neale* (London, 1961), pp. 369–96 (pp. 376–7). Subsequent research by Albert J. Loomie, S.J., especially 'Philip III and the Stuart succession in England, 1600–1603', *Revue Belge de Philologie et d'Histoire*, 43 (1965), 492–514, has, I think, demonstrated sufficiently the plausibility of Hicks's interpretation. For further discussion, see Chapter 6 in this volume.

48 The convoluted process whereby these letters were deciphered, translated and re-ciphered is explained by Hicks ('Cecil, Persons and the succession', pp. 112–13). See also Francis Edwards, SJ, *The Succession, Bye and Main Plots of 1601–1603* (Dublin, 2006), pp. 75–6.

49 Cited and translated in Hicks, 'Cecil, Persons and the succession', p. 113.

50 *Ibid.*, p. 119.

51 *Ibid.*, p. 121.

52 Clement VIII to Frangipani, Rome, 12 July 1600, in Tierney/Dodd, *Church History*, 3, pp. lxx–lxxi; same to Blackwell and the English clergy, Rome, 12 July 1600; same to English Catholics, Rome, 12 July 1600, in Van der Essen and Louant (eds), *Correspondance de Frangipani*, vol. 3(ii), pp. 784–6, 782–3. Papal instructions to the nuncio regarding the apostolic briefs and dated 20 July can be found in Persons's letter of 20 July 1600, ABSI, Anglia II, 62 (published in Tierney/Dodd, *Church History*, 3, pp. lxxi–lxxii).

53 See Frangipani to Persons, Brussels 19 August 1600, in Van der Essen and Louant (eds), *Correspondance de Frangipani*, vol. 3(i), p. 169.

54 Hicks, 'Cecil, Persons and the succession', pp. 129–30; Loomie, 'Philip III and the Stuart succession, 492–7; Duerloo, *Dynasty and Piety*, pp. 70–1.

55 Loomie, 'Philip III and the Stuart succession', pp. 502–3; Duerloo, *Dynasty and Piety*, pp. 77–8.

56 Hicks, 'Cecil, Persons and the succession', p. 132; Loomie, 'Philip III and the Stuart succession', p. 503. Alain Talon highlights Clement's affection for Henry and *vice versa* in 'Henry IV and the Papacy after the League', in Alison Forrestal and Eric Nelson (eds), *Politics and Religion in Early Bourbon France* (Basingstoke, 2009), pp. 30–1.

57 Aldobrandini's instructions to Bishop Innocenzo del Bufalo, nuncio in France, July 1601, ASV, Segreteria di Stato, Francia 291, fos 15^{r-v}.

58 See Vincenzo Urgarino, secretary of the nuncio, to del Bufalo, Paris, 2 July 1602; and del Bufalo to Aldobrandini, Paris, 30 July 1602, in Bernard Barbiche (ed.), *Correspondance du Nonce en France Innocenzo del Bufalo, Evèque de Camerino (1601–1604)* (Rome, 1964), pp. 311–12, 326.

59 Aldobrandini to del Bufalo, Rome, 20 July 1602; del Bufalo to Aldobrandini, Paris, 30 December 1602, in Barbiche (ed.), *Correspondance du Innocenzo del Bufalo*, pp. 322, 401–2.

60 Hicks, 'Cecil, Persons and the succession', 134–9; see also Chapter 7 in this volume.

61 Cited in Loomie, 'Philip III and the Stuart succession', p. 508.

62 *Ibid.*, pp. 507–9.

63 Clement VIII to Queen Anne, Rome, 16 July 1602, *CSPScot*, 13(ii), p. 1150.

64 Clement VIII to King James, Rome, 9 August 1602, same to Queen Anne, Rome, 9 August 1602, ASV, Armadio XLIV, vol. 46, fos 228^v–229^r; 229^{r-v} (printed in *CSPScot*, 13(ii), pp. 1151–2).

65 This may have been his son and heir Henry Somerset. The consideration of a son of Worcester is most interesting, in the context of the identification of the elusive 'Anthony Rivers' with William Sterrell, secretary to the earl. See Patrick Martin and John Finnis, 'The secret sharers: "Anthony Rivers" and the Appellant controversy, 1601–2', *Huntington Library Quarterly*, 69 (2006), 195–237. Persons had suggested him as a candidate in 1600. See the report of the council, 11 July 1600, *CSPSpan*, 4, p. 664.

66 Report of the council, 1 February 1603, *CSPSpan*, 4, pp. 719–29; report of the council, 2 March 1603, *CSPSpan*, 4, pp. 729–37. See also Loomie, 'Philip III and the Stuart succession', pp. 511–14.

67 John Gerard, SJ, *The Condition of Catholics under James I. Father Gerard's Narrative of the*

Gunpowder Plot, ed. John Morris, SJ (London, 1871), pp. 20–1.

68 Gerard, *Condition of Catholics*, p. 25.

69 See Albert J. Loomie, SJ, 'Guy Fawkes in Spain: the "Spanish treason" in Spanish documents', *BIHR Special Supplement*, 9 (1971).

70 See Tallon, 'Henry IV', pp. 32–3.

71 Loomie, 'Philip III and the Stuart succession', p. 514.

Chapter 14

States, monarchs and dynastic transitions: the political thought of John Hayward

R. Malcolm Smuts

For some time, historians of early Stuart politics have sought to develop a British perspective by giving due weight to Scottish and Irish participation in the multiple kingdom ruled from Westminster. But with a certain literal mindedness, they have applied a three-kingdoms approach mainly to the period after 1603, although for many years previously Stuart claims to succeed Elizabeth had made Scottish politics a matter of vital concern to English statesmen. Since incursions by warlike Scots also exacerbated English problems in Ireland, a triadic relationship between the three kingdoms had already developed by at least the 1580s. It was increasingly clear that the long-term stability of each kingdom required a solution embracing all of them. The unsettled English succession had become a British problem.

James's arrival in London, just weeks after the rebel Earl of Tyrone's submission secured English control over Ireland, did not so much introduce radically new issues onto the English agenda as provide an occasion to resolve long-standing questions. Fully to understand Jacobean debates over Anglo-Scottish union and relationships between the prerogative and common law, we must connect them to late Elizabethan anxieties about England's future under a foreign-born king. We need to ask how ideas about the English polity evolved in response to the wider British and European dimensions of the succession problem, both before and immediately following Elizabeth's death.

This chapter seeks to address these issues with respect to one thinker, the civil lawyer and historian Sir John Hayward. Hayward has previously attracted scholarly attention chiefly as author of *The First Part Life and Raigne of King Henry the IIII*, a history of the deposition of Richard II published in 1599 and dedicated to Robert Devereux, Earl of Essex. This tract landed Hayward in serious trouble after Essex's fall from favour in August 1599, resulting in his imprisonment and interrogation by the Attorney General Edward Coke and the Lord Chief Justice Sir John Popham, on suspicion that he intended his history as a seditious reflection on his own time. His troubles deepened when Essex rebelled in February 1601, shortly after several of his followers paid Shakespeare's company to stage a play about Richard's fall.[1]

Modern scholars have mostly focused on Hayward's historiography – especially his use of Tacitus to create a more analytical style of historical narrative – and the question of whether he really intended to justify a rebellion such as Essex's.[2] They have therefore paid relatively little attention to a continuation of his work on Henry IV, which reached print only in 1991, and several tracts he published after his release from the Tower between 1603 and 1606: a reply to Robert Persons's *A Conference about the Next Succession*, a treatise supporting James's proposals for Anglo-Scottish union, and a work defending absolute royal authority over the Church.[3] What can this cluster of writings tell us not only about the evolution of Hayward's thought between 1599 and the early seventeenth century but also about wider intellectual currents of the period?

Superficially the early Jacobean tracts look very different from *Henry IIII*. Although Hayward continued to quote Tacitus and other classical writers, in the early years of the new reign he temporarily abandoned the genre of history in favour of close philosophical and legal analysis.[4] If we look carefully, however, common features emerge. Hayward remained preoccupied with sources of political instability that weakened what he often calls 'the state'. This fashionable word had a range of meanings in English and European discourse of the period and in Hayward's own writings: in different contexts it might refer to a government, to ceremonial dignity or to a condition, in phrases such as 'the state of England'. But the dominant meaning resembled the definition given by the French philosopher Pierre de Charron: 'rule, dominion or a certain order in commanding and obeying … the bond of society.'[5] 'The state' meant government less in the sense of institutional structures than as having a capacity to exact obedience and secure civic peace.

Hayward always thought of the state as authority over people with differing languages and customs that must be exercised in geographically dispersed locations. Even when writing under Elizabeth about the Middle Ages, he explored how political upheavals in the heart of England interacted with Scottish and French raids along the kingdom's frontiers and with Irish and Welsh rebellions. This pluralistic concept of the state is linked to a second major preoccupation, Hayward's concern for the practical implications of political ideas or, as he puts it in the preface to *Henry IIII*, 'what events have followed what counsel'.[6] Although interested in philosophical arguments, he was never simply content to explore them abstractly. He always wanted to know what happened when an idea gave rise to a programme of action, and thus entered into the chain of secular causation that determined political outcomes. His fascination with the interplay between ideas and historical processes affecting state authority provides a key to his outlook.

HENRY IIII, LATE ELIZABETHAN POLITICS AND THE PROBLEM OF MISRULE

At the most basic level, *Henry IIII* tells the story of the violent overthrow of a flawed monarch. The central issue it raises is therefore whether subjects have the right to depose a bad king by force and select a replacement seemingly better equipped to govern. Since the Scots had deposed their Queen in 1567 and the English had later executed that Queen and explored mechanisms for altering the succession, the question had considerable contemporary relevance.[7] In two lengthy passages Hayward lays out the justifications of Henry's partisans for removing Richard and a set of counter-arguments by Thomas Merk, bishop of Carlisle, upholding the divine right of kings and the absolute duty of obedience.[8] But although given due weight, this clash of ideas does not dominate the narrative. Hayward had a broader purpose than simply exploring arguments over resistance theory; he also wanted to explain how Richard destroyed his authority, how and why Henry came to lead the rebellion against him and what happened to both Henry and England after power changed hands. The daring topicality of the book had at least as much to do with its handling of these topics as with its airing of arguments justifying rebellion.

Elizabeth famously told the antiquarian John Lambarde, 'I am Richard II, know ye not that?'[9] Although it is not clear exactly what she had in mind, others also made the comparison. As early as 1580 Lord Henry Howard had paralleled the two monarchs in a manuscript urging the Queen to marry the Duke of Anjou and conceive an heir. If she did not do so, he warned, 'there will not lack a Henry Bolingbroke presumptuously to undertake the usurpation of the royal dignity'.[10] Hayward gestured toward a similar conclusion in a ringing aphorism on his book's first page, which Coke singled out for its seditious implications: 'neither armies nor strongholds are so great defences to a prince as the multitude of children' (p. 67).

But as Hayward tells it, Richard's main difficulties lay elsewhere. In part he suffered from being a young king, who had to escape the dominance of nobles grown accustomed to ruling England during his minority, a situation seemingly very unlike Elizabeth's, though similar to that of James VI. The most serious problem, however, was that Richard repeatedly fell prey to bad advice from social upstarts who picked quarrels with noblemen to increase their own fame. Richard listened to them because his weakness and timidity made him easy to manipulate, and his addiction to 'pleasure and sloth' allowed 'the chiefest affairs of state' to be governed 'according to private respects'

(p. 106). The King's favourites 'extenuated or depraved' the achievements of any peers who served him well, so that they earned displeasure rather than reward. Richard's inability to disguise his thoughts let nobles know when he disliked them, so that they took pre-emptive action (p. 88). This led to a series of upheavals and reversals of fortune, in which the King alternately lost power and then regained it, punishing his opponents with execution or banishment. Richard's base followers proved vindictively arrogant in victory but cowardly and indecisive in adversity, like the King himself. Their misrule not only caused rebellions but weakened England's border defences, encouraging Scottish and French incursions.

This narrative follows the chroniclers Hall and Holinshed, who had also stressed Richard's dependence on unpopular favourites. But Hayward embellished the story with vignettes modelled after Tacitus's descriptions of sycophantic Roman courtiers who played upon the fears and jealousies of emperors such as Domitian, Tiberius and Nero. The first English translator of Tacitus, Henry Savile, had called attention to these passages in the notes to his 1591 edition of *The Histories* and *The Agricola*, which Hayward sometimes paraphrases closely.[11] As Lisa Richardson has shown, Tacitus's portrayal of Domitian provided a particular model for Hayward's account of Richard.[12] By describing Richard's misrule in this way, Hayward also implicitly echoed unflattering contemporary portrayals of Elizabethan court politics. As early as 1572 the *Treatise of Treasons*, written by a Catholic supporter of Mary Queen of Scots, argued that a group of low-born Machiavellians exploited Elizabeth's fears of Catholic conspiracy to poison her mind against her natural counsellors, the virtuous nobility, and erect a corrupt tyranny. A series of Catholic polemics reiterated this charge.[13] More recently Essex and his entourage had also come to view Elizabeth's court as a place where clever low-born men manoeuvred to destroy virtuous nobles by exploiting the jealousies and suspicions of the aging woman on the throne. The writings of Tacitus, filtered through Savile's notes and the informal commentaries of other scholars in Essex's circle, such as Francis Bacon, Henry Cuffe and the Spanish exile Antonio Perez, provided an intellectual underpinning to these complaints. By paraphrasing Tacitus and exaggerating the low birth of Richard's favourites, Hayward went out of his way to invite comparisons between his narrative and contemporary criticism of the Queen.[14]

He further extended the implied parallel by allusions to recent events, such as Scottish border raids, that some people attributed to Elizabeth's mishandling of James VI. Hayward's description of Richard's problems in Ireland comes even closer to long-standing complaints about the Queen: 'many succours had been sent into these several [Irish] countries but scatteringly and dropping, and never so many at once as to furnish the wars fully' (p. 107). Elizabeth's Irish servitors had grumbled for years about her penury in funding military expeditions and half-hearted support for systematic reform, which in their view allowed problems to fester and grow into the ultimate catastrophe of Tyrone's rebellion.

Although these parallels would have seemed obvious to well-informed readers of Hayward's book, it would have been very awkward to prosecute him for them. For he would naturally have denied intending disrespectful allusions to the Queen, placing her attorneys in the embarrassing position of having to show in detail how his portrait of Richard's misrule reflected what people were privately saying about Elizabeth. Coke did single out descriptions of the resentment aroused by Richard's levies of taxation, prompting Hayward to insert an explicit defence of the crown's right to tax for legitimate public needs in the preface to his second edition. But such fiscal issues were peripheral to the main reasons Hayward's book was so provocative. Since these could not be aired in a public trial, Coke and Popham had to look for other ways to convict Hayward of sedition, by accusing him of saying things that he had never intended. This may explain why the case against him eventually collapsed.

Throughout the early pages of *Henry IIII* the story of Richard's shortcomings alternates with an account of the early career of Henry, Earl of Derby, as the future King was then known. Hayward portrays the young Henry as an exemplary character, not only physically attractive and highly capable but also courageous, modest, just and merciful. Richardson suggests that the model here was Tacitus's favourable account of Agricola.[15] When banished by Richard, Henry calmly departs for France and when offered the opportunity to lead a rebellion against a King who has confiscated his property and chased him from his country, he initially declines, preferring a retired life in exile to dangerous ambition. In Hayward's account the origins of the rebellion that topples Richard initially have nothing to do with Henry. They derive instead from the universal hatred that Richard's actions have inspired. People looked to Henry only because his royal blood and stellar reputation made him seem the obvious alternative to the King. Men who had already resolved to use force against Richard therefore secretly wrote to him, urging him to return to England. But their pleas had no effect until seconded by the arguments of Thomas Arundel Archbishop of Canterbury, whom Richard had also banished. Arundel visited Henry and persuaded him – rather easily, it must be said – that he really had no choice but to lead a rebellion, since Richard would inevitably learn of the rebels' letters to him. This would arouse the King's deadly enmity, causing him to order Henry's assassination (pp. 112–17).

This narrative is modelled closely on a passage from Savile's *The Ende of Nero and Beginning of Galba*, written to fill a gap in Tacitus's *Histories*, in which the minor Roman commander Vindex used an identical argument to persuade Galba, the Governor of Gaul, to rebel. But whereas Savile portrays Galba as a timid leader soon overtaken by events and Vindex as a hero, Hayward alters the moral equation. Although not fully discussed, Arundel's motives appear more self-interested than principled, while Henry is a reluctant rebel who acts to protect his own life. If this does not entirely exonerate him from responsibility for Richard's fate, it does attenuate his guilt. But it also removes any impression that concern for the public good motivated him to take arms. Only after he has marched on London does Henry appeal to a concept of the common welfare, by telling his supporters: 'your name is in suspense, whether to be termed rebels or subjects, until you have made manifest that your allegiance was bound rather to the state of the realm than the person of the prince' (pp. 119–21). It is clear that this is an *ex post facto* rationalization.[16]

On one level Hayward probably intended his account of why Henry rebelled to reflect advice given to Essex by hot-headed followers such as Henry Cuffe, who warned the Earl that since his court enemies sought his life he must strike first. Precisely such calculations triggered Essex's rebellion two years later, and already in 1599 his circle may have discussed circumstances in which the use of force against powerful enemies might be construed as legitimate self-defence.[17] But Hayward's portrayal of Henry also sharpens the lesson provided by the rebellion's aftermath. The issue becomes not simply whether subjects may rightfully depose a tyrant, but what will happen when a deeply flawed king is violently replaced by a man who seems to possess all the virtues of an ideal ruler. The remainder of the book gives the answer: not only will the new monarch face multiple challenges to his authority that inflict calamitous damage on his kingdom, but also his own character will change for the worse as the pressures of office cause him to take on the unpleasant traits of the man he has replaced.[18]

Once deposed and imprisoned, Richard begins to attract pity, while dissatisfaction with Henry mounts because he cannot satisfy the greed of people who supported him in hopes of reward. The weakness of his title invites malcontents to conspire against him, foremost among them the Abbot of Westminster. A man of learning and zeal and former counsellor of Richard,[19] the Abbot recalled hearing Henry say years earlier 'that princes had too little and religious men too much'. Fearing the new King would foment lay attacks on ecclesiastical wealth, the Abbot encouraged discontented nobles to plot against Henry (pp. 154–5). The conspirators' initial plan to assassinate the King leaked, and their subsequent divisions, hesitations and cowardice doomed their rebellion. But before the uprising collapsed a priest in the rebel camp set fire to the city of Chichester and in the aftermath Henry executed several nobles, many 'knights and gentlemen, and a great number of mean and base persons'. His previously merciful disposition had altered into 'a hard and haughty dealing in revenging his own injury, or rather maintaining the injury that he had done' (p. 162). Richard was murdered a short time later, if not by Henry's direct order then at least under circumstances that 'made [him] a party in the punishment. For King Henry, perceiving that the lords had so far prevailed with their late stratagem that if their stomach had been answerable to their strength…they might have driven him to a hard hazard caused King Richard to be put to death' (p. 164). Although he does not comment on the irony, Hayward describes Henry sanctioning Richard's murder for much the same reason that Arundel had predicted Richard would order Henry's assassination. The protagonists have effectively swapped roles, as if cold political logic had rendered their differences in character irrelevant.

Around the edges of this story of English conspiracies and rebellions Hayward weaves an account of problems with foreign kings and distant provinces of the monarchy. Charles VI of France, whose daughter had married Richard, prepared to invade England, while English subjects in Aquitaine and Bordeaux resisted French attacks less stoutly because they resented their legitimate king's deposition. Even greater problems arose in Wales, whose inhabitants took advantage of England's unsettled condition to revolt under the leadership of Owen Glendor (p. 169). The Scots also raided across the border, provoking Henry to retaliate by invading Scotland and terrorising its inhabitants in a campaign that left 'the air infested with stink, the ground imbrued with corruption and blood, the country wasted' (p. 173). Hayward's published narrative of the first year of Henry's reign ends here, with bloodshed and mayhem spreading through Britain.

The unpublished continuation of the history, found among Hayward's papers after his death in 1628, also stressed the dialectical relation between England's internal problems and troubles along its Welsh, Irish and Scottish peripheries, in ways reminiscent of the 1590s. Hayward's Glendor resembled the great Elizabethan rebel Tyrone in recognising the importance of military discipline and in the way he turned his raw Welsh forces into a competent army by 'arming and training his followers' (p. 190). Like most sixteenth-century Irish armies, his soldiers also fell back when confronted with large English forces and tried to wear down their enemy with guerrilla tactics. Henry's Welsh campaign paralleled Essex's experiences as commander of the English army in Ireland in 1599. The King showed his qualities as a general by pursuing Glendor's forces resolutely and rallying his soldiers by 'bearing his part deeply in their hardest adventures', as Essex also endeavoured to do (p. 194). But like the Earl, Henry failed to make headway and returned home with his reputation diminished, showing 'that a fugitive and fleeting enemy in places of advantage is not to be pursued with a main army but with standing camps to be wasted at seasons and by degrees' (pp. 208–9).[20] Essex, backed by the Irish Council, had made a similar argument against Elizabeth's demands that he pursue Tyrone into Ulster, to no avail. Hayward implicitly rejects the Queen's desire for a quick decisive military victory as unrealistic. He also implicitly criticises severe treatment of the Irish, commenting that 'doubtless that prince maketh war to his great disadvantage who vexeth a people that hath nothing to lose' (p. 198).

During the Welsh campaign a second war began with Scotland, inspired by the 'merciless ... hatred ... hereditary between the two nations' (p. 215). English forces under the Earl of Northumberland and his son, Henry 'Hotspur' Percy, defeated the Scots. But instead of consolidating this victory King Henry broke off the campaign, 'not upon distrust of success' but because he feared that his subjects would contrast the Percies' victories with his failure in Wales (p. 218). Here again Hayward seems to echo Essex's complaints that the Queen had sabotaged his Irish campaign to discredit him. But this time the advice of low-born favourites has nothing to do with the decision to squander the achievement of English armies. Henry recognises that he has failed to reward the Percies adequately for their help in placing him on the throne, giving them reasons for disloyalty. 'Being guided by the most powerful of passions, fear', he refuses even to listen to those who defended Northumberland and Hotspur, 'so much greater was his hate to suspected friends than it was to known and ancient enemies' (p. 220). Royal antipathy to noble virtue cannot be ascribed here to evil counsel and royal weakness; it is a natural feature of the political world.

But so too is the tendency of proud nobles to rebel when provoked by royal ingratitude. The Percies conclude an alliance with Glendor and endeavour to overthrow Henry and divide his dominions. Although their revolt ultimately collapses, it exacts a heavy toll, not only on the opposing armies but also on civilians, as Henry's soldiers pillage and slaughter, while 'rascally people' take advantage of the confusion to rob and spoil (p. 249). Hayward's whole narrative emphasises the confluence of problems – Celtic rebellion, Scottish invasion and English civil war – that ensued once the title to the throne fell into dispute. For Englishmen worried about the aftermath of Elizabeth's long-anticipated death, as they followed news from Ireland and heard rumours of Spanish invasions, the story would have carried a pointed warning. Further comments by Hayward echoed other contemporary anxieties. Richard's subjects displayed a spirit of 'wasteful excess (a certain argument of a sick state)', especially in their extravagant clothing (pp. 222–3). Essex and his admirers had similarly complained about the wasteful vanities of their society, which consumed money that should have supported the war with Spain. Early fifteenth-century London also resembled the Elizabethan metropolis in its religious discords and rash of seditious libels. Hayward again expressed his dislike of severity in commenting on the failed efforts of Henry's government to suppress Lollardy by burning heretics at the stake and by executing a few authors of seditious libels.

The continuation of Hayward's history ends abruptly in the midst of yet another war, this time against the French, during Henry's fourth year on the throne. Read impartially and in its entirety, the narrative leaves no doubt that Richard's deposition harmed England. Although Hayward repeatedly echoes the critical views of Elizabeth prevalent within Essex's circle, he makes clear that any efforts to solve these problems by force will only make matters worse. By weakening royal legitimacy, rebellion opens the floodgates to noble factionalism, clerical conspiracies, rebellion by subject peoples such as the Welsh and Irish, and invasions by foreign powers. Henry's story also refutes the idea advanced by writers such as George Buchanan that virtue ultimately matters more than birth in determining fitness to rule. Hayward not only portrayed a world in which genuine virtue was in short supply, whatever men pretended; his narrative also showed that even a virtuous man would become a vicious tyrant if he seized the throne without a clear title. This would have provided another warning for Essex, whose outlook revolved around an intense belief in personal virtue and honour.[21]

HEREDITARY MONARCHY, CUSTOM AND THE COMMON LAW OF THE WORLD

Five eventful years intervened before the publication of Hayward's next tract on public affairs, *An Answer to the First Part of a Certaine Conference, Concerning Succession*.[22] This work continued to look back to the politics of the recent past by rebutting the arguments of a notorious 1595 treatise, now generally attributed to the Jesuit Robert Persons, disputing James's title to the English throne.[23] But in it Hayward also analysed the relationship between hereditary kingship, custom and law in ways that raised fundamental questions about the nature of the polity created by James's succession. Hayward virtually ignores Persons's attempts to discredit James's hereditary claim, focusing instead on a second strand of the Jesuit writer's argument, concerning the rights of kings under natural law.

Persons argued that although the law of nature leads people to recognise the need for settled government, it does not prescribe the form such government should take, since the variety of polities that have existed historically shows that none can claim universal validity.[24] Although in a hereditary monarchy the next heir should normally succeed, his title can never be absolute and ultimately matters less than the public good, the true purpose for which government exists. Hereditary rulers have repeatedly been deposed throughout history. Persons proceeds to examine the basic rights and duties of kings through an antiquarian analysis of coronation oaths and rituals. He contends that since kings invariably swore to observe the fundamental laws of their kingdoms before receiving their crowns, and normally went through some kind of acclamation ceremony, their power had originally been limited and conditional. Although the people had delegated authority to kings, they retained the right to withdraw their allegiance from a monarch of obvious incapacity or depravity if the public interest so required. The single most important purpose of government is to uphold religion. 'Want of religion' therefore disqualifies an individual from ruling and it is damnable for a subject to support the succession of a prince whose religion differs from his own.[25]

Against these arguments Hayward argued that the Fall had so clouded human understanding of natural law that no polity reproduced it exactly. The variety of historical laws and institutions therefore proved nothing about the laws of nature. He then distinguished between the primary law of nature, deriving directly from God and a 'secondary law of nature, which is the received custom, successively of all…[or] most nations' (sig. A4ᵛ). The two are connected because all good custom derives from human awareness of natural justice. But not all customs are good, so we must always be prepared to correct particular usages by recourse to the wider judgement of mankind. In many ways Hayward here followed a well-trodden path. A few years earlier Richard Hooker had invoked a comparable argument to justify the survival of medieval rituals within the English Church.[26] Edward Coke had similarly celebrated custom as a reflection of God's will, in the Preface to his *Third Reports*, published the year before Hayward's tract. Coke argued that beneath the superficial diversity of national law codes there lay an underlying uniformity that must derive from a divine source.

> For as in nature we see the infinite distinction of things proceed from some unity, as many flowers from one root, many rivers from one fountain…so without question *lex orta est cum mente divina*, and this admirable unity and consent in such diversity of things proceeds from God the fountain and founder of all good laws and constitutions.[27]

But whereas Hooker and Coke deployed these arguments to defend the usages of England's Church and common law courts, Hayward's concept of universal custom led to a more cosmopolitan and flexible outlook. He acknowledged that 'the particular custom of every nation is at this day the most usual and assured law between the Prince and the people' (p. 22), but this did *not* mean that title to the English throne depended solely on English custom. Instead, Hayward appealed to the 'common law or custom of the world', determined by the three criteria of 'antiquity, continuance and generality' (sig. B1ᵛ). He expected to find that national laws and customs, including those of his own country, would sometimes differ from 'the common law of the world' because human imperfection made this inevitable. In such cases the laws of one country must yield to more universal practice.

This argument reflected Hayward's training as a civil, rather than a common lawyer, especially the Roman concept of the *ius gentium* or law of nations. It allowed him to spar with Persons while simultaneously taking pot shots at Coke, as he set about elevating James's natural-law authority over English custom. Hayward began by examining whether a survey of historical custom indicated that hereditary monarchy had a universal natural basis. He challenged Persons's claim that European monarchies had originally been elective and limited: 'It is evident that in the first heroical ages the people were not governed by any positive law but their kings did both judge and command by their word, by their will, by their absolute power' (p. 31). Many monarchies owed their foundation to conquest or had been resettled through conquest. In such kingdoms any liberties enjoyed by the people must derive from voluntary royal concessions, since the right of conquest conferred absolute power. More recently some monarchies had become elective. But experience showed that elections bred faction and conflict, so most of these had reverted to a system of hereditary succession, in practice if not always in principle. Of the Holy Roman Empire, he writes, 'of late it hath been settled in one family', while in Denmark, Sweden, Hungary and Bohemia the people 'do challenge to themselves a right of election but they accept their king by propinquity of blood' (pp. 17–18). Similarly the Romans expelled the Tarquins but then re-established monarchy under Augustus. During the Republic the Roman state had 'never enjoyed ten years free from sedition', whereas under the Emperors Rome's power and prosperity reached their zenith (sig. Cr^v, p. 38). Even republics and democracies often functioned as monarchies, as had often happened in republican Rome, as well as in Athens under Pericles and in Florence under Lorenzo de Medici. Beneath the outward diversity of political forms, history revealed a marked preference for hereditary monarchy.

If ancient monarchs ruled arbitrarily, there can never have been an original delegation of power from the people to kings. Consequently, coronation oaths can have no binding legal force, since it is a maxim of the civil law that courts will not enforce promises made voluntarily, rather than as conditions to a contractual agreement (sig. M2^r). Kings are obligated to rule justly, but to God rather than their people. If they violate their oaths God alone must hold them accountable. In any case, in true monarchies coronations have never been necessary to the exercise of royal authority. Under English law 'so soon as the king departeth out of life, the royalty is presently transferred to the next successor…All writs go forth in his name; all course of justice is exercised; all offices are held by his authority; all states, all persons are bound to bear to him allegiance' (sig. O3^v). Although usurpers such as Henry IV and Edward IV tried to buttress weak titles by seeking popular acclamation during coronations, their opportunism created no valid custom (sig. N2^v).

Not only have most nations demonstrated a marked preference for hereditary monarchy; in addition, polities that departed from the norm have repeatedly suffered from calamities related to disputed successions:

> Where one claimeth the Crown by succession and another possesseth it by title of election there not a disunion only of the people, not a division in arms, but a cruel throat-cutting, a most immortal and merciless butchery doth usually ensue. It is somewhat inconvenient (I grant) to be governed by a prince either impotent or evil, but it is a greater inconvenience, by making a breach into this high point of state, to open a way to all manner of ambitions, perjuries, cruelties and spoil…This I have manifested before by the examples of King Edward and King Richard, both surnamed the Second. (sig. O1ʳ)

Hayward invokes his earlier history to support the more philosophical analysis in which he is now engaged. Even bad princes keep the peace and enforce justice for most of their subjects, he argues. 'But when the people do break into tumult then all course of justice is stopped; then is either assistance made, or resistance weakened for foreign invasion' (sig. N3ᵛ). Persons's arguments subvert the fundamental purposes of government – securing civic peace, administering justice and restraining wrongdoing – by encouraging civil wars and weakening royal authority in its everyday operation. If impiety, tyranny and incapacity justify the removal of kings, 'what action of state can be so ordered that either blind ignorance or malice will not easily strain it to one of these heads? Every execution of justice, every demand of tribute or supply shall be claimed tyranny; every unfortunate event shall be exclaimed insufficiency; every kind of religion shall by them of another sect be proclaimed impiety' (sig. K1ᵛ–K2ʳ). If a prince depends on the 'pleasure' of his subjects, how will he resist the multitude's fickle passions (sig. T1ᵛ)? The implicit lesson of the latter part of *Henry IIII* is here spelled out: any act or idea that calls into question royal legitimacy will weaken the social fabric, since sinful people will exploit every available excuse to satisfy their passion and self-interest.

In making religion the primary criterion for choosing rulers, Persons has compounded the problem. 'For seeing that there are many different professions of religion, not only in the world, but in almost every nation of the world', chaos will ensue if each sect feels entitled violently to set up a king who shares its opinions (sig. V3ᵛ). This will debase not only civic life but religion itself. Hayward's dislike of religious coercion and suspicion of ambitious clergy resurface as he develops the point. 'It is far more moderate and safe to use the ordinary means both of maintaining and propagating the truth, and to commit the success thereof to God', lest by offering 'violence against any religion…we provoke thereby the professors to do the like against ours' (sig. V3ᵛ). Persons and his colleagues will not recognise this truth because they belong to an order founded by a soldier that is committed to spreading violence (sig. H1ᵛ, pp. 34, 41).

If Hayward had left matters at this level, most English readers would have welcomed his treatise. But he extended his argument through a provocative excursus into the history of legal custom that explicitly elevated royal authority above law. Since kings existed before the emergence of the first legal codes, he argued, and governed 'without either restraint or direction but only of the law of nature', all laws and political institutions must derive from their decrees. Far from limiting royal power, laws were created to make it more effective: 'when any people were subdued by arms, laws were laid like logs upon their necks, to keep them in more sure subjection' (p. 33). English history illustrated the point perfectly, through the way in which each successive conqueror had altered the laws:

> When the Romans had reduced the best part of this island into the form of a province, as they permitted liberty of law to no other country under their obedience, so here they planted the practice of their laws…Again when the Saxons had forced this realm and parted it into seven kingdoms, they erected so many sets of law, of which only two were of continuance, the Mercian law and the West Saxon law. After these the Danes became victorious and by these new lords new laws were also imposed, which bare the name of Danelaw. Out of these three laws, partly moderated, partly supplied, King Edward the Confessor composed that body of law, which afterwards was called Saint Edward's laws. Lastly the Normans brought the land under their power, by whom Saint Edward's laws were abrogated and not only new laws but new language brought into use, insomuch as all pleas were formed in French. (p. 33)

The main target here was undoubtedly Coke, who had argued the previous year that the Romans, Saxons, Danes and Normans had all preserved an English law of immemorial antiquity.[28] Hayward went on to argue, a page later, that in England and all other places 'Parliaments…have been erected by kings'; before the reign of Henry I English kings 'did never call the common people to counsel' (p. 34). Rather than merely vindicating James's right to succeed Elizabeth, he had developed a case that hereditary kingship carried with it an absolute natural-law authority transcending the customs and institutions of any particular kingdom that extended claims the King himself had made in *Trew Law* and *Basilikon Doron*.

Hayward's *Treatise of Union* extended this conclusion by arguing that the common law must be modified to serve the enlarged state that James's hereditary right had created. In the preface Hayward presented himself as 'an honest citizen' intent on fulfilling his duty to promote 'the good of the state'.[29] In particular, he wished to foster unity and combat divisions threatening to weaken the bonds of community among James's subjects. The establishment of a 'state of Union' within the old English monarchy, he argued, has 'altogether appeased the cruel and inveterate not only butcheries but hate between the English and Welsh'. By contrast the absence of a full and complete union has rendered all policies, 'whether of clemency, or of justice, or of arms, if not unprofitable, yet insufficient, to repress the riotous rebellions of Ireland'.[30] The long history of Anglo-Scots warfare further showed how division produces bloodshed and destruction. A mere confederation under a single crown will not overcome these ills because 'in a people rather confederated than united is seldom seen, either a conformity in will or a joint readiness in power' to pursue common objectives. A 'diversity of interest' will always generate 'disdains [and] distrusts', weakening the state from within (p. 6). 'For if people reduced under one government be not therein united; if they be set together and not into one, they are like sand without lime, subject to dissipation by every wind' (p. 7).

Hayward asserted that the 'benefits' of a more 'perfect Union of diverse states' can be secured only by 'incorporating the people into one politic body' and 'knitting their minds in one contentment and desire'. Both objectives require a 'common government and command' through obedience to a single head, 'for these two points of commanding and obeying are the very soul of a commonwealth' (pp. 8–9). But since 'laws are the instrument and mean both of obedience and rule, it followeth that there is no firm connection in one form of government…where the people are not bound together by one common law' (p. 10). English and Scottish law must therefore be combined into a single system. As he drives home this argument Hayward takes another swipe at Coke's belief in the common law's immemorial antiquity, saying that he 'will not now spend time upon this opinion, partly because it is not commonly received' but also because he has already refuted it. It is a 'hyperbolical' position 'now out of season, as never suitable but with artless times' (p. 11).

While it is not advisable to revise laws frequently for frivolous reasons, Hayward concedes, 'yet on the other side, I am as far from allowing a strict and severe tenacity of laws, which (being another extreme) is many times more either hurtful or unprofitable than the light change of them'. Indeed, 'sometimes [an] entire alteration of government' is necessary, as in the age of Augustus when, Tacitus records, 'certain wise men' rightly declared 'that there was no other means to appease the disorders of the state but by reducing it under the principality of one'. Provided that legal change is not too great or too sudden, it can be implemented without inconvenience (pp. 12–13). Fortunately, reducing English and Scottish law 'into one body' will not be difficult because 'the fundamental laws (as they are termed) of both kingdoms and crowns do well agree'. Although differing in specific points they are not fundamentally 'contrary', so that the maxims of each system may be introduced into the other without significant disruption. Hayward cautions that this process should take place gradually to avoid stirring 'humours' in the body politic, much as Augustus quietly refashioned republican institutions into a monarchical state (p. 14). James must also take care to leave the administration of the government of each of his kingdoms in the hands of its natives, until the spirit of unity takes root. But over time the ancient rivalries and divisions will disappear, as shown by the fact that Welsh natives now bear high authority in the English state, without provoking envy or even much notice (p. 19). The final reform needed to promote Anglo-Scottish unity is a change in name, for two people can never 'be perfectly knit in affection and will, so long as they stand divided in those names, whereby one of them hath lately been very odious to the other' (p. 35).

In 1606 Hayward once more argued for the importance of a single personal source of unifying authority in the state, in *A Reporte of a Discourse Concerning Supreme Power in Affaires of Religion*.[31] This was probably intended as a contribution to the Oath of Allegiance controversy, an international pamphlet war provoked by a loyalty oath enacted in the wake of the Gunpowder Plot, in which the King took a keen interest. Hayward began with another analysis of 'the proper qualities of sovereign or majestical power', arguing on Bodinian grounds that this power must be absolute and perpetual. Since 'there is nothing in a commonwealth of so high nature, nothing so important as is religion', sovereign power must include control over matters of faith. Catholic attempts to distinguish between secular and spiritual authority are unconvincing, because experience shows that people's spiritual beliefs determine their political conduct. 'If the conscience of a people be commanded by a stranger, if their souls be subjected to a foreign power…it is but a weak, but a dead dominion, which the natural prince shall hold over their bodies'. Hayward provides another historical excursion on the terrible political crimes inspired by superstitious religious beliefs, the priestly functions of rulers and political power of priests in ancient societies, and the role of Christian emperors in governing the early Church. The emperors made a fatal mistake, he contends, by allowing the bishops of Rome to claim pre-eminent authority over spiritual affairs, contrary to early Christian practice. This settled ecclesiastical authority in a place distant from the imperial capital, Constantinople, allowing the papacy to gain sway over the common people, and ultimately to remove 'the western part of the Empire from' the Emperor's authority (p. 33). The new empire that arose in Germany was then repeatedly undermined by rebellions stirred up by Rome. European kingdoms will remain weakened, Hayward argues, until the spiritual authority usurped by the popes is restored to its rightful possessors, the sovereign kings of Europe.

CONCLUSIONS

The differences in content and manner of presentation between *Henry IIII* and Hayward's early Jacobean tracts reflect his response both to a changed political environment and to the different outlooks of the two men whose patronage he sought to attract, Essex and James I. *Henry IIII* not only explored subjects of topical importance in the late 1590s; it also examined closely the impact of personalities and personal conflicts on high politics, taking up themes such as the corrosive effects of royal jealousy on relationships between kings and great peers. In doing so it spoke directly to the obsession with personal virtue and honour of Essex and his followers. By contrast, Hayward's early Jacobean treatises approach politics from a more impersonal vantage point calculated to appeal to a king who disliked Tacitus and mistrusted efforts to scrutinise the motivations and personality quirks of monarchs, but who enjoyed philosophical arguments and displays of erudition, especially when they supported royal authority. In making this adjustment Hayward altered the angle from which he approached the problem of relating political ideas to concrete historical circumstances. In *Henry IIII* maxims and theories emerge from the narrative, as Hayward extracts lessons from his story or recapitulates the theoretical arguments of his protagonists. Conversely, the Jacobean treatises normally begin with abstract arguments and proceed to illustrate them with concrete historical examples.

But despite these dissimilarities Hayward's fundamental attitudes remain essentially consistent and we can see how the philosophical positions of his early seventeenth-century writings reflect concerns already evident in *Henry IIII*. He distrusted efforts to bring about political change on the basis of religious or moral principles, because he did not believe that people were fundamentally moral. Although they may claim to act from concern for true religion or the common good, in actuality they rarely do so. The real motivational forces of political life are personal ambition, religious intolerance and ethnic or national antagonisms that lead different communities to commit crimes against each other. In any society these forces will create centrifugal tendencies that can easily rend the social fabric into pieces. For that reason, polities need a single unquestionable source of supreme personal authority to enforce civic peace. Hayward did not believe in arbitrary and coercive governance, as his comments on topics such as the persecution of Lollardy and Henry IV's wars against the Welsh demonstrate. But he believed firmly that royal authority should be absolute in principle, to remove any loophole that unscrupulous people might exploit to foment discord.

These convictions reflect a pessimistic theological outlook that Hayward shared with many of his contemporaries, which his reading of Tacitus presumably reinforced. But his outlook also reflected his responses to the political problems of his age: the Nine Years' War in Ireland; the disastrous infighting at court that precipitated Essex's rebellion; the anxieties over Spanish invasions and Catholic rebellions that overshadowed Elizabeth's late reign; and the promise of a way out of these difficulties that James's arrival seemed to offer. It would take us well beyond the bounds of a short essay to assess the degree to which his views were typical of broader currents of thought. But it should already be clear that he had staked out alternative positions to the celebration of republican virtue found in writers such as Buchanan, as well as to the 'common law mind' of Sir Edward Coke and others who opposed James's plans for British Union in the name of English custom. Hayward never mentioned Coke by name in his treatises, just as Coke never referred to Hayward in the prefaces to his law reports, but they must have read each other's arguments and it looks very much as if they were sparring with each other. If Coke was responding to Hayward, this sheds light on the famously insular and ahistorical character of his thought. It suggests that he argued as he did, not because he was incapable of seeing English common law within a wide comparative perspective but because he knew where such a comparative analysis might lead and wanted to forestall it from the outset.[32] English insularity was less a habit of mind than a response to historical developments and intellectual arguments that threatened to undermine rules and institutions in which Coke had a deep personal stake.

Hayward shows us the opposite side of the coin: an English thinker who welcomed change both because he believed in it and because he glimpsed an opportunity to win royal patronage by advocating a more unitary state. His thought and Coke's represent radically different responses to the challenge of settling English politics, within its British context, after the turbulence and uncertainty of the previous twenty years. Persons, who published a treatise attacking Coke in 1606, staked out a third position, equally hostile to the other two, that might well repay closer investigation. The work of New English administrators and lawyers such as Edmund Spenser and Sir John Davies also needs to be brought into the comparison. In these troubled and uncertain years, English political thinkers never had the luxury of focusing simply on England, even when they were striving to insulate their native realm from Scottish, Irish and European ideas. We need more comparative work on the diversity of their responses to the complex situation growing out of the issue of the succession, which threatened to render hallowed structures of authority fluid and susceptible to change, in ways that made concepts such as custom, natural law and the state deeply problematic.

NOTES

1   For a summary, see the excellent introduction to John Manning (ed.), *The First and Second Parts of John Hayward's The Life and Raigne of King Henrie IIII*, CS 42 (4th series, 1991), esp. pp. 17–33.

2   See, S. L. Goldberg, 'Sir John Hayward, "Politic Historian"', *Review of English Studies*, NS 6 (1955), 233–54; F. J. Levy, *Tudor Historical Thought* (San Marino, 1967), pp. 259–69 and 'Hayward, Daniel and the beginnings of politic history in England', *Huntington Library Quarterly*, 50 (1987), 1–34; D. R. Woolf, *The Idea of History in Early Stuart England* (Toronto, 1990), pp. 106–15; and Lisa Richardson, 'Sir John Hayward and Elizabethan Historiography' (Ph.D., University of Cambridge, 1999) and 'Plagiarism and imitation in Renaissance historiography', in Paulina Kewes (ed.), *Plagiarism in Early Modern England* (Basingstoke, 2003), pp. 106–18.

3 Alzada Tipton, '"Lively patterns…for affayres of State": Sir John Hayward's *Life and Reign of Henry IIII* and the Earl of Essex', *The Sixteenth Century Journal*, 33 (2002), 769–94, is a partial exception, although Tipton concentrates on whether Hayward meant to justify rebellion. Rebecca Lemon, *Treason by Words: Literature, Law and Rebellion in Shakespeare's England* (Ithaca, NY, 2006), pp. 46–48, also briefly considers Hayward's reply to Persons, although again from the perspective of debates about resistance theory. Brian Levack, *The Civil Lawyers in England 1603–1641* (Oxford, 1973), discusses Hayward's Jacobean tracts in passing, e.g. pp. 89–90, 113–15, 138–9. None of these works fully anticipates the analysis developed here.

4 He returned to the genre with *The Lives of the III. Normans, Kings of England* (1613) and two posthumously published works, *The Life and Raigne of King Edward the Sixth* (1630) and *Annals of the First Four Years of the Reign of Queen Elizabeth*, which did not appear in its entirety until 1840. See Barrett L. Beer, *The Life and Raigne of King Edward the Sixth* (Kent, 1993), Introduction, pp. 6–10.

5 Quotation from the English translation by Samuel Lennard, *Of Wisdome: Three Books Written in French* (London, 1608), pp. 189–90.

6 Manning, *Hayward*, p. 62. Lemon, *Treason by Words*, ch. 2, makes a similar argument with respect to *Henry IIII*.

7 Howard Nenner, *The Right to be King: The Succession to the Crown of England, 1603–1714* (Chapel Hill, NC, 1995), ch. 1.

8 Manning, *Hayward*, pp. 134–8 and 142–9. All parenthetical references in the text are from this edition.

9 The authenticity of this statement has been called into question by Jonathan Bate, 'Was Shakespeare an Essex Man?', *Proceedings of the British Academy*, 162 (2009), 249–86, but convincingly re-established by Jason Scott-Warren, 'Was Queen Elizabeth I Richard II?: the authenticity of Lambarde's "conversation"', *Review of English Studies*, forthcoming.

10 Lloyd E. Berry, (ed.), *John Stubb's* Gaping Gulf *with Letters and Other Relevant Documents* (Charlottesville, VA, 1968), pp. 164–5. Berry's printed text of Northampton's reply to Stubbs (pp. 153–94) derives from a collation of the three extant manuscript copies: BL, Additional MS 48027, fos 197–215; BL, Harley MS 180, fos 75–147 and BL, Cotton MS Titus, C:xviii.

11 Malcolm Smuts, 'Court-centred politics and the uses of Roman historians, *c.* 1590–1630', in Kevin Sharpe and Peter Lake (eds), *Culture and Politics in Early Stuart England* (Basingstoke, 1994), pp. 21–43, esp. 28–30.

12 Richardson, 'Plagiarism'.

13 On this, see Simon Adams, *Leicester and the Court: Essays on Elizabethan Politics* (Manchester, 2002), ch. 3.

14 Manning noted these tendencies, for example pp. 70, n. 9 and 72, n. 15.

15 Richardson, 'Plagiarism'.

16 I disagree here with Lemon, *Treason by Words*, p. 30, that 'Bolingbroke agrees to seek the English crown out of loyalty to a faltering state'. Henry explicitly declines an invitation to act on behalf of the English people, saying the enterprise is too dangerous (p. 115). Only when persuaded that inaction is even more perilous does he agree to rebel (p. 117).

17 Paul E. J. Hammer, 'Shakespeare's *Richard II*, the play of 7 February 1601 and the Essex rising', *Shakespeare Quarterly*, 59 (2008), 1–35.

18 Richardson, 'Plagiarism', observes that from this point Henry begins to take on the characteristics of Tacitus's Domitian, while Richard assumes those of sympathetic figures like Germanicus.

19 Hayward does not supply the Abbot's name.

20 In Hayward's account the strategy of harrying the Welsh by 'standing camps' is eventually carried out successfully by the King's eldest son, Prince Henry (p. 254).

21 Paul E. J. Hammer, *The Polarisation of Elizabethan Politics: The Political Career of Robert Devereux, 2nd Earl of Essex, 1585–1597* (Cambridge, 1999), pp. 19–22.

22 John Hayward, *An Answer to the First Part of a Certaine Conference, Concerning Succession, Published Not Long Since under the Name of R. Dolman* (London, 1603). In the interim Hayward had anonymously published a religious meditation, *The Sanctuarie of a Troubled Soule Written by I. H.* (London, 1601).

23 R. Doleman [Robert Persons], *A Conference about the Next Succession to the Crowne of Ingland* ([Antwerp], 1594 [1595]); Peter Holmes, 'The authorship and early reception of *A Conference About the Next Succession to the Crown of England*', *Historical Journal*, 23 (1980), 415–29. See Chapter 3 in this volume.

24 Doleman [Persons], *A Conference*, pp. 3–4.

25 *Ibid.*, sig. B3, p. 80, sig. B4ᵛ.

26 Ronald Bayne (ed.), *Laws of Ecclesiastical Polity* (London, 1907), vol. 1, p. 176 (book 8, ch. 3).

27 Edward Coke, *Third Reports*, published as *Le Tierce Part des Reportes del Edward Coke* (London, 1602), sig. Cii.

28 [Edward Coke], *Le Second Part des Reports del Edward Coke* (London, 1602), preface, n.p.: 'If the ancient laws of this noble island had not excelled all others, it could not be but some of the several conquerors and governors thereof, that is to say the Romans, Saxons, Danes or Normans, especially the Romans…would have altered or changed the same.'

29 John Hayward, *A Treatise of Union of the Two Realmes of England and Scotland* (London, 1604), Preface, n.p.

30 *Ibid.*, p. 3.

31 Sir John Hayward, *A Reporte of a Discourse Concerning Supreme Power in Affaires of Religion. Manifesting that this Power is a Right of Regalitie, Inseparably Annexed to the Soveraignty of Every State: and that It is a Thing Both Extreamely Dangerous and Contrarie to the Use of All Auncient Empires and Commonwealths to Acknowledge the Same in a Forraine Prince* (London, 1606).

32 Cf. J. G. A. Pocock, *The Ancient Constitution and the Common Law: A Study of English Historical Thought in the Seventeenth Century* (Cambridge, 1957, 1987), chs 2–3.

Afterword

Blair Worden

In 1980, at Oxford University, I set an examination question which asked candidates to assess the place of the issue of the royal succession in Tudor politics. To some of my colleagues the question seemed dishearteningly old-fashioned. The content of examination papers determines the content of undergraduate study. If Oxford's examiners persisted with stale topics of political history, it was asked, how could the university keep pace with the most striking and animated feature of current historiography, the development of social history and of sociological perspectives? Two assumptions peeped through that objection. The first was that the study of kings and queens, or of the narrow elites they headed, ignores the wider dimensions of society and the lives of most of humanity. The second was that conflicts over the occupancy of thrones, which involve only events and contingencies, belong to the mere surface of historical explanation. They cannot illuminate long-term developments of social or economic organization or ideas, over which rulers may have little control, and which call for methods of study more enterprising and more strenuous than those centring on the personalities of princes.

As the editors of this book remark in their introductory chapter, 'no longer does the study of kings and queens appear dated'. First, events and their attendant contingencies have regained their reputability. Since in Elizabethan minds the 45-year-long problem of the succession turned from first to last on past contingencies and on speculation about future ones, no subject could more readily lend itself to an emphasis upon the contingent. Second, as again the editors indicate, the study of political history has broadened. It has not done so, in this book at least, through the kinds of adjustment to which it might have been expected to look for reprieve in 1980. There is nothing in these pages about the *longue durée*; no hint of the perspectives which an anthropologist might bring to the rules and rituals of linear succession; little or nothing about the social and mental premises that, across a range of European countries, each with its distinctive record of contingency, sustained principles of hereditary power that affront modern generations.

Instead the political history written in this book draws nourishment from a series of other developments in the study of sixteenth- and seventeenth-century history, none of which I can claim to have envisaged in setting that question in 1980. First, the perception of 'high politics' as an elite sport has retreated before our growing awareness of the extent of political involvement, commitment, understanding and opinion to be found beyond the privileged landed class. If, as so often seemed so likely to so many people, civil war or invasion or a change of religion were to follow the death of Queen Elizabeth, it would be not only an elite whose lives and values and interests were at stake. Second, there has been the study of domestic lives and emotions, especially female ones. That preoccupation, which at first seemed a reaction against high politics and high society, has not only found some of its fullest evidence among them: it has reminded us that under hereditary monarchy the fate of nations, even of continents, rests on as private and as contingent an aspect of human existence as there is – the circumstances and consequences of sexual encounter. Biology governed politics as it did everyday life. Third, there has been the recovery of the British dimension of English politics, which Victorian and Edwardian historians took for granted but which was subsequently obscured. If the course of a nation's or a continent's history was at the mercy of dynastic contrivance and chance, then so was the political configuration of an archipelago. Fourth, there has been the diminution of the Protestant dominance in the study of the religious history of the era. This book brings to the succession question insights gained from the broadening of interest in both British and Catholic history.

Another development, which permeates the volume, is the opening of frontiers between political history and two neighbouring academic disciplines. In 1980 one might have predicted those disciplines to be sociology and anthropology, which favour the study of structures rather than of events. Instead they are literature and political science, fields which have taken events on board – though for a while the loudest literary criticism, sooner than study them, preferred a history without tears, where insulated theories and language waived the exertions of scholarly recovery. Movement between history and both literature and political science had begun well before 1980, but it has become far more frequent since. In literature and political science alike an 'internalist' approach to texts, which concentrates on their timeless meanings, has made compromises with, or in some cases yielded to, contextual ones. In both cases generic categories of writing have been loosened; canonical texts have been obliged to mix with smaller fry; and the concern of Renaissance authors to address contemporary political issues has been acknowledged. No contributor to this volume supposes that poetry and drama, which have for so long counted as 'literature', can be read in just the same way as sermons, or historical prose works, or the records of parliamentary or conciliar debates, or polemical tracts, which have not. Each of those genres had its own formal properties and conventions. Yet the chapters in this volume repeatedly show purposes of persuasion cutting across them. It is when the genres are set beside each other that the pervasiveness and intensity of fears about the Elizabethan succession become evident. The urgency of the treatments of the subject in *Gorboduc*, in Sidney's *Arcadia*, in Spenser's poems, or in entertainments performed before the Queen, becomes perceptible only when those compositions are read alongside other kinds of texts produced by the same contexts.

Our inherited conception of 'political theory', no less than of 'literature', is anachronistic. Unless we make an exception of Sir Thomas Smith or Richard Hooker, the Elizabethan age produced no 'canonical' author in the genre. Yet the purpose of political writers was not to claim a place in the evolution of political thought, but to influence events. The succession problem raised awkward questions of constitutional and legal, and hence of political, theory. Most societies at most times manage to avoid such issues. They prefer conceptual incoherence, which can accommodate or obscure a range of potentially conflicting perspectives. But the infertility of the Tudors, and the momentous religious divisions which revolved around it, exposed a series of uncertainties which had to be faced: about the origins and rules of a hereditary succession that some thought unimpeachable, others not; about the rights and responsibilities of parliament, or the nobility, or councillors, or learned counsel; about the place of statute, or the common law, or the royal nomination of heirs; about the legitimacy of rule by a foreigner or 'stranger'; and about whether sanctions of divine providence, or *salus populi*, or reason of state, or religious allegiance, might trump other considerations. In ideal circumstances, perhaps, claims of linear descent, national consent, royal nomination, native birth and religious orthodoxy would complement each other. In Elizabeth's reign they collided. A century later the collisions over the succession in the Exclusion Crisis, and then in the debates that followed the Revolution of 1688, would be cause and symptom of a polarization between two conceptions of political authority, one Tory, one Whig, even if most people tried to steer between them.[1] If a smooth succession had not been achieved in 1603 – for in a subject that turns on contingency, counterfactual questions press at every turn – perhaps there would have been a comparable polarization then.

The essays in this book bring home the opportunism with which, in the absence of clear rules, Elizabethan parties interpreted unclear ones to their individual advantages. They also demonstrate the insecurity of each of the claims to the succession. No one exploited the insecurity so effectively as the author of that nimble plea for a Catholic and Spanish-led succession, *A Conference about the Next Succession to the Crowne of Ingland* (1594/95). Of the contributors who discuss the tract in these pages, most agree that its author was Robert Persons, or Parsons, who might almost be called the presiding spirit of this book. The tract transformed the controversy over the succession and galvanized the international diplomatic endeavours which centred on it. In the next century the succession crisis of Charles II's reign, when the tract was reprinted, would produce the composition or first publication of a series of canonical or near-canonical works of political thought, by Robert Filmer, John Locke, Algernon Sidney, Henry Neville and James Tyrrell, all of whom have been better known to historians of political thought than Persons. Locke and Sidney reached conclusions about resistance to tyranny and the deposition of rulers which were in line with those of *A Conference*; and Sidney's discussion of hereditary and elective monarchy in his *Discourses concerning Government* surely takes a lead from the tract. Yet whereas *A Conference* lit up debate, Locke's and Sidney's treatises remained unpublished in the crisis they addressed and had no identifiable effects upon it.

A Conference has characteristics which may seem weaknesses if the tract is assessed apart from its context, or weighed for logical rigour, but which within that context were strengths. The artful inconsistencies, the apparent breaches of relevance, the abrupt shift from secular premises to religious ones, the alterations of perspective introduced by the dialogue form, the genuflections to conventional opinion which is simultaneously menaced, the disjunction between the tone of sweet reasonableness and the explosive implications of the content, are potent polemical weapons. They combine to unsettle the preconceptions of hostile or suspicious readers and to inject new thoughts or doubts into their minds. Admittedly the work earned as much hostility and suspicion as enthusiasm among its author's co-religionists, and was eventually thwarted by changes in the international context that had inspired it.[2] The treatise nonetheless outlived its time, thanks particularly to its assertions, which were on the face of it irrelevant to the issue of the succession, about the proper limits to the authority of monarchs. That is why John Hayward attacked it even when the succession of James I had signalled its author's defeat. It is also why it resurfaced not only in the Exclusion Crisis but less than a year before the execution of Charles I, when it was reproduced by a printer close to the new model army.[3]

A Conference also went beyond its ostensible subject-matter in reminding its audience that monarchy is but one of the forms of government available to nations. The author was far from arguing for the displacement of kingship. He even accepted the hereditary principle, albeit with disturbing caveats. Yet his insistence that monarchy is a choice rather than an obligation, and that if it is chosen it should be limited and conditional and subject to dismissal, touched nerves in Protestant thinking. By the 1590s Protestants had mostly disowned the doctrines of resistance which the bolder of them had espoused under Queen Mary. Yet the apparent shift towards royal absolutism caused extensive unease. In Sidney's *Arcadia*, a work written around the time of Elizabeth's projected marriage to the King of France's brother the Duke of Anjou (1579–81), the Arcadians' dependence on the peaceful hereditary descent of a monarchy on whose 'will' there are no constraints exposes 'the great dissipations monarchal governments are subject unto'. The 'ill-ordered weakness' of a state where 'public matters had ever been privately governed', and where the subjects 'had not experience to rule', proves fatal – or would do but for a *deus ex machina* – on the apparent death of their ruler, who leaves a disastrously unresolved succession question behind him. There follows a trauma of national disintegration of the kind widely forecast to occur on the death of Elizabeth I. 'The ruinous renting of all estates … brought Arcadia to feel the pangs of uttermost peril' and to expect that the nation would 'either run itself upon the rock of self-division or be overthrown by the stormy wind of foreign force.'[4]

Did the peril of the unresolved Elizabethan succession induce other reflections on the 'dissipations' of 'monarchal government'? In these chapters, as the book's editors remark, 'there is not a republican in sight'.[5] Republican rule, however admirable or interesting some might have found it as an ideal, was far too remote from the laws and customs and experience that sanctioned the English monarchy to become a realistic aspiration. Sidney, who studied the 'good laws and customs' of republican Venice and urged his young brother Robert to do the same, nevertheless explained to him: 'we can hardly proportion [them] to ourselves, because they are quite of a contrary government'.[6] Besides, there would hardly be leisure, even if there were a broad appetite, for so radical an innovation on the Queen's death, which by common expectation would start a race for the throne. On the demise of Arcadia's ruler 'the discoursing sort of men' propose that 'the state' be 'altered and governed no more by a prince'. Yet their ideal is 'a matter more in imagination than practice'. They are brushed aside by the 'active' politicians,[7] who scramble to enthrone their various candidates, as the author of *A Conference* expected the rival parties to do on the Queen's death.

Was there such a 'discoursing sort of men' among Sidney's contemporaries? If so, they have left no written record. Yet historians, who live on what was written down (or what has survived of it), can never know what was only spoken. Equally they cannot recover unrecorded thoughts of readers. Fulke Greville felt the need to warn his readers against the 'praise' of aristocracy and democracy to be found in books – books of other times or places – and to advise them 'rather upon life then pictures [to] looke, / Where practise sees what everie state can beare'.[8] But was there a further reason why England could not 'bear' a republic, and why republican rule could exist only in the 'imagination'? In 1591 another of Sidney's associates, Henry Savile, writing with the predicament of his own country in mind, echoed the Roman historian Tacitus in explaining that the erosion of the virtue of the republic had destroyed Rome's capacity to 'bea[r] a free commonwealth'.[9] That had been Tacitus's own reason for accepting, even as he regretted, the passing of republican liberty. Across the sea in the Netherlands, as the Dutch struggled for independence from the Spanish monarchy, observers judged them 'too corrupt', too 'forlorn of the virtues of former times', to sustain a non-monarchical alternative.[10] In England there was no republican past to recall and no republican future to envisage. There was, however, a keen sense of the social sickness of the time and of its inhabitants. Greville, who was dismayed by the advance of absolutism, also lamented that the principle of hereditary kingship, which he believed to have replaced an elective system, resigns 'True worth to Chance'.[11] Yet he urged frail humanity to bow to those symptoms of its shortcomings. In such assessments we glimpse the retreat of the Ciceronian idea of civic virtue and the advance of Tacitean resignation.

Savile's work on Tacitus was suited to, and may indeed have helped to create, the Tacitean mood of the Queen's late years. Earlier in the reign, when the authority of the monarchy had been impaired by the crown's lurches of religious profession and by the successive previous occupancies of the throne by a boy and two inexperienced women, Elizabeth had been hectored by MPs and preachers and pamphleteers and been bluntly told of the perils awaiting her immortal soul if she failed to provide for a successor. By the 1590s such presumption was rare. Now she stuck more easily to her argument that the nomination of a successor, both by creating a potentially hostile reversionary interest and by provoking opposition to it among rival claimants, would raise more problems than it solved. There was another change. The controversies aroused by the projected Anjou match, or by the proposals of 1584–85 for an interregnum to follow the Queen's death until the nation's leaders had found a successor, produced formal debates among a wide range of councillors and other politicians, which conveniently bequeathed a series of position papers to historians. There is less of such evidence for the late years, when the membership of the Privy Council contracted[12] and when the intrigues and manoeuvres of the court become ever harder to penetrate and look ever more Tacitean.

The frequent inscrutability of the evidence may be one reason why the succession question in the late-Elizabethan period has received less than its historical due. Although the execution of Mary Queen of Scots had removed the most acute and alarming of the prospects raised by the issue, the contributions to this volume bear out its editors' central claim: that the issue itself remained an inescapable component of the political scene. Its significance can be measured by the contrast between the late-Elizabethan years and the reign of James I. Those ills of the late-Elizabethan polity, other than the succession question, which contemporaries bemoaned – the corruption, the faction, the ruthlessness and bitterness and suspicion, the strain on public finances – were not remedied under James, under whom the complaints persisted. Yet the atmosphere of intense strain and impending doom was at least partially lifted. That was partly because of the diminution of international tension brought by the peace between England and Spain in 1604 and the truce between Spain and the Dutch from 1609. It was partly because of the union of the English and Scottish crowns, which, whatever problems it raised, closed England's 'back door' to potential invaders. But it was also because of the smooth succession of a king with male heirs.

That unexpected outcome surely had consequences for the Church as well as for the state. Elizabethan Protestants feared that their faith, being the religion of the establishment but having too few roots beneath it, would fall with it if an invasion or rebellion succeeded or when the Queen should die. They argued that the nation would never commit itself to the new religion so long as a Catholic successor was a serious prospect. The entrenchment of English Protestantism by the earlier seventeenth century has been convincingly related to the rising quality, standing and impact of the ministry, and to the growth of the Church of England's ecclesiological and theological assurance. Perhaps we should add to those explanations the new security acquired by the Protestant ascendancy in 1603.

A Conference took it for granted that 'some war' would follow Elizabeth's death, though its author issued none of the dire or lurid prophecies of havoc and slaughter that had been made not only by a long succession of Protestants but also, in 1584, by the Catholic apologist William Allen.[13] Instead, the author – perhaps remembering the swift resolution of the crisis of 1553 – suggested that the present conflict would be resolved without 'any great or mayne battel'. His unruffled prediction belonged to an accomplished strategy of self-presentation, which gave his voice a sophisticated cosmopolitanism superior to the 'vulgar' and xenophobic passions that had blighted the succession controversy.[14] In the event there was no war. Whether the 'Main' plot to depose James in the months after his accession was a serious threat to him cannot be certainly determined, for that episode too is shrouded in Tacitean obscurity. But the sole military challenge to his occupancy of his new throne was a farcical one, the 'lunatic political adventure' of the Catholic Sir Robert Basset, who 'pretended some right to the crown' and raised his standard on the unpromising soil of Lundy Island.[15]

Why had so many and such enduring fears about the country's prospects on the Queen's death been gainsaid? English and Protestant historians have tended to give English and Protestant answers, which centre on the adroit management of the issue by Robert Cecil and on his negotiations with James VI. Cecil's role, which has attracted able scrutiny, is plainly a large part of the story. Yet his attitude to the succession remains a problematical subject. If the Earl of Essex had not embarked on his suicidal uprising in 1601, and if the confrontation between him and Cecil had persisted until the end of the reign, would the two men have plumped for rival candidates for the throne? Were there, as contemporary reports suggested, the makings of a Spanish party, centring on Cecil, which would put national unity or security before religious allegiance (as many Protestants had done in 1553), and used negotiations for the succession of the Infanta as a means to end the war with Spain?

One difficulty is to tell how much the politicians knew, or supposed they knew, about the calculations of foreign powers, in particular about the relations of the Spanish crown with the Infanta and with her husband the Archduke Albert in Flanders. Did they think of the couple as an arm of the Spanish monarchy, or rather, as it seems they should have done, as a semi-autonomous, peaceable, accommodating force, which might deflect Madrid's purposes and the zeal of the Counter-Reformation? Around the time of the proposed Anjou match, statesmen had asked whether the Duke's ambitions in Flanders might be used either to neutralize the French threat or to provide England with a new counterweight to Spain. Similar kinds of reckoning would surely be visible in the Queen's last years if only the Tacitean shroud could be penetrated.

As Catholic historians have shown, in work deployed and refined in this volume, it was to developments on the Continent, not in England, that the chances of a Spanish-led succession succumbed in the very last years of Elizabeth: to a *rapprochement* between France and Spain, and to misgivings on the parts of both Philip III and the Infanta herself.[16] It looks as if James VI, a 'stranger' but a Protestant one, became the only plausible candidate, at least if it is true that Arbella Stuart discredited such chances as she may have had herself by her personal conduct early in 1603. In that case Elizabeth, whom so many blamed for the succession problem, helped to solve it, in the final intervention of contingency, by living just as long as she did.

NOTES

1 Howard Nenner, *The Right to be King: The Succession to the Crown of England, 1603–1714* (Basingstoke, 1995).

2 Peter Holmes, 'The authorship and early reception of *A Conference About the Next Succession to the Crown of England*', *Historical Journal*, 23 (1980), 415–29.

3 BL, Thomason Tracts, E521[1]; cf. e.g. E425[6], E538[27]; see too *A Treatise concerning the Broken Succession of the Crown of England* (1655).

4 Sir Philip Sidney, *The Countess of Pembroke's Arcadia (The Old Arcadia)*, ed. Jean Robertson (Oxford, 1973), pp. 320, 351, 354, 360.

5 These days that is a refreshing change. I have discussed the recent enthusiasm for the term 'republican' in my 'Liberty for export: "republicanism" in England, 1500–1800', in Gaby Mahlberg and Dirk Wieman (eds), *European Contexts for English Republicanism* (Aldershot, 2013), pp. 13–32.

6 Albert Feuillerat (ed.), *The Prose Works of Sir Philip Sidney*, 4 vols (Cambridge, 1912–1926), vol. 3, p. 127.

7 Sidney, *Countess of Pembroke's Arcadia*, pp. 320–1; Blair Worden, *The Sound of Virtue: Philip Sidney's* Arcadia *and Elizabethan Politics* (New Haven, CT, and London, 1996), ch. 11 and p. 237. Cf. Sir John Harington's reference to the 'fantastic humors' of people who prophesy 'that like to the Low Countries wee should be governed by States': John Harington, *A Tract on the Succession to the Crown (A.D. 1602)*, ed. Clements R. Markham (London, 1880), p. 16.

8 Fulke Greville, Lord Brooke, *The Remains*, ed. G. A. Wilkes (Oxford, 1965), p. 182; cf. pp. 156, 184, 196.

9 Tacitus, *The Ende of Nero and the Beginning of Galba*, prefaced to *Fower Bookes of the Histories Of Cornelius Tacitus. The Life of Agricola*, trans. Henry Savile (Oxford, 1591), p. 2. Cf. Ben Jonson, *Sejanus his Fall*, ed. Philip J. Ayres (Manchester, 1990), act 1, lines 85–104, 400–4.

10 Martin van Gelderen, *The Political Thought of the Dutch Revolt, 1555–1590* (Cambridge, 1992), pp. 171–2, 276ff.

11 Greville, *Remains*, p. 43.

12 John Guy (ed.), *The Reign of Elizabeth I. Court and Culture in the Last Decade* (Cambridge, 1995), pp. 4, 92–3.

13 William Allen, *A True, Sincere, and Modest Defence of English Catholiques* (Menston, 1971), p. 192.

14 R. Doleman [Robert Persons], *A Conference about the Next Succession to the Crowne of Ingland* ([Antwerp], 1594 [1595]), pp. 108, 197, 258–62 (2nd pag.).

15 Hugh Trevor-Roper, *Catholics, Anglicans and Puritans* (London, 1987), pp. 22–3.

16 The essays demonstrate the durability of Albert J. Loomie's article, 'Philip III and the Stuart succession in England, 1600–1603', *Revue Belge de Philologie et d'Histoire*, 43 (1965), 492–514.

Select bibliography

UNPUBLISHED WORKS

Beckett, Margaret J., 'The political works of John Lesley, Bishop of Ross (1527–96)' (Ph.D. thesis, University of St Andrews, 2002).

Courtney, Alexander, 'The accession of James VI to the English throne, 1601–1603' (M. Phil. thesis, University of Cambridge, 2004).

Domínguez, Freddy Cristóbal, '"We must fight with paper and pens": Spanish Elizabethan polemics, 1585–1598' (Ph.D. thesis, University of Princeton, 2011).

PUBLISHED WORKS

Adams, Simon, *Leicester and the Court: Essays on Elizabethan Politics* (Manchester, 2002).

Alford, Stephen, *The Early Elizabethan Polity: William Cecil and the British Succession Crisis* (Cambridge, 1998).

——, 'A politics of emergency in the reign of Elizabeth I', in Glenn Burgess and Matthew Festenstein (eds), *English Radicalism, 1550–1850* (Cambridge, 2007), pp. 17–36.

Allen, Paul C., *Philip III and the Pax Hispanica, 1598–1621: The Failure of Grand Strategy* (New Haven, CT, and London, 2000).

Axton, Marie, 'The influence of Edmund Plowden's succession treatise', *Huntington Library Quarterly*, 37 (1973–74), 209–26.

——, *The Queen's Two Bodies: Drama and the Elizabethan Succession* (London, 1977).

Basing, Patricia, 'Robert Beale and the Queen of Scots', *British Library Journal*, 20 (1994), 65–82.

Bowler, Gerald, '"An axe or an acte": the Parliament of 1572 and resistance theory in early Elizabethan England', *Canadian Journal of History*, 19 (1984), 349–59.

Burgess, Glenn, 'Becoming English? Becoming British? The political thought of James VI & I before and after 1603', in Jean-Christophe Mayer (ed.), *The Succession Struggle in Late Elizabethan England: Politics, Polemics and Cultural Representations* (Montpellier, 2004), pp. 143–75.

Clancy, Thomas H., SJ, 'Notes on Persons's "memorial for the reformation of England" (1596)', *Recusant History*, 5 (1959), 17–34.

——, 'A political pamphlet: *The Treatise of Treasons*, 1572', in G. J. Eberle (ed.), *Loyola Studies in the Humanities* (New Orleans, 1962), pp. 15–30.

Clucas, Stephen, '"This paradoxall Restitution Iudaicall": The Apocalyptic correspondence of John Dee and Roger Edwardes', *Studies in History and Philosophy of Science*, 43 (2012), 509–18.

Collinson, Patrick, *De Republica Anglorum: Or, History with the Politics Put Back: Inaugural Lecture delivered 9 November 1989* (Cambridge, 1990).

——, 'The Elizabethan exclusion crisis and the Elizabethan polity', *Proceedings of the British Academy*, 84 (1994), 51–92.

——, 'The monarchical republic of Queen Elizabeth I', *Bulletin of the John Rylands University Library of Manchester*, 69 (1987), 394–424, repr. in Patrick Collinson, *Elizabethan Essays* (London, 1994), pp. 31–56, and in John Guy (ed.), *The Tudor Monarchy* (London, 1997), pp. 110–34.

——, 'The religious factor', in Jean-Christophe Mayer (ed.), *The Succession Struggle in Late Elizabethan England: Politics, Polemics and Cultural Representations* (Montpellier, 2004), pp. 243–73.

——, *Richard Bancroft and Elizabethan Anti-Puritanism* (Cambridge, 2013).

Cressy, David, 'Binding the nation: the Bonds of Association, 1584 and 1696', in Delloyd J. Guth and John W. McKenna (eds), *Tudor Rule and Revolution: Essays for G. R. Elton from his American Friends* (Cambridge, 1982), pp. 217–34.

Doelman, James, 'The accession of King James I and English religious poetry', *Studies in English Literature*, 34 (1994), 19–40.

——, '"A king of thine own heart": the English reception of King James VI and I's *Basilikon Doron*', *The Seventeenth Century*, 9 (1994), 1–9.

Donaldson, Gordon, 'The attitude of Whitgift and Bancroft to the Scottish Church', *Transactions of the Royal Historical Society*, 4th series, 24 (1942), 95–115.

Doran, Susan, *Monarchy and Matrimony: The Courtships of Elizabeth I* (London, 1996).

——, 'Revenge her foul and most unnatural murder? The impact of Mary Stewart's execution on Anglo-Scottish relations', *History*, 85 (2000), 589–612.

——, 'Three late-Elizabethan succession tracts', in Jean-Christophe Mayer (ed.), *The Succession Struggle in Late Elizabethan England: Politics, Polemics and Cultural Representations* (Montpellier, 2004), pp. 100–17.

——, 'Loving and affectionate cousins? The relationship between Elizabeth I and James VI of Scotland 1586–1603', in Susan Doran and Glenn Richardson (eds), *Tudor England and Its Neighbours.* (Basingstoke, 2005), pp. 203–34.

——, 'James VI and the English succession', in Ralph Houlbrooke (ed.), *James VI and I: Ideas, Authority, and Government* (Aldershot, 2006), pp. 25–42.

Duggan, Anne J., 'The power of documents: the curious case of Laudabiliter', in Brenda Bolton and Christine Meek (eds), *Aspects of Power and Authority in the Middle Ages*, International Medieval Research 14 (Turnhout, 2007), pp. 251–75.

Edwards, David, 'Securing the Jacobean succession: the secret career of James Fullerton of Trinity College, Dublin', in S. Duffy (ed.), *The World of the Galloglass: Kings, Warlords and Warriors in Ireland and Scotland, 1200–1600* (Dublin, 2007) pp. 188–219.

Edwards, Francis, SJ, *The Succession, Bye and Main Plots of 1601–1603* (Dublin, 2006).

Gajda, Alexandra, 'Debating war and peace in late Elizabethan England', *Historical Journal*, 52 (2009), 851–78.

——, *The Earl of Essex and Late Elizabethan Political Culture* (Oxford, 2012).

Galloway, Bruce, *The Union of England and Scotland 1603–1608* (Edinburgh, 1986).

Goodare, Julian, 'James VI's English subsidy', in Julian Goodare and Michael Lynch (eds), *The Reign of James VI* (East Linton, 2000), pp. 110–25.

——, 'The Scottish Presbyterian movement in 1596', *Canadian Journal of History*, 45 (2010), pp. 21–48.

Grant, Ruth, 'The Brig o' Dee Affair, the sixth Earl of Huntly and the politics of the Counter-Reformation', in Julian Goodare and Michael Lynch (eds), *The Reign of James VI* (East Lothian, 2000), pp. 93–109.

Graves, Michael A. R., *Thomas Norton: The Parliament Man* (Oxford, 1994).

Guy, John, *My Heart is my Own: The Life of Mary Queen of Scots* (London, 2004).

——, (ed.), *The Reign of Elizabeth I: Court and Culture in the Last Decade* (Cambridge, 1995).

Hadfield, Andrew, '*Spenser and the Stuart succession*', *Literature and History*, 13 (2004), 9–24.

Hammer, Paul E. J., *The Polarisation of Elizabethan Politics: The Political Career of Robert Devereux, 2nd Earl of Essex, 1585–1597* (Cambridge, 1999).

——, 'The smiling crocodile: the earl of Essex and late-Elizabethan "popularity"', in Peter Lake and Steven Pincus (eds) *The Politics of the Public Sphere in Early Modern England* (Manchester, 2007), pp. 95–115.

——, 'Shakespeare's *Richard II*, the play of 7 February 1601, and the Essex rising', *Shakespeare Quarterly*, 59 (2008), 1–35.

Herman, Peter C., '"Best of poets, best of kings": King James VI and I and the scene of monarchic verse', in Daniel Fischlin and Mark Fortier (eds), *Royal Subjects: Essays on the Writings of James VI and I* (Detroit, 2002), pp. 61–103.

——, *Royal Poetry* (Ithaca, NY, and London, 2010).

Hicks, Leo, SJ, 'Sir Robert Cecil, Father Persons and the succession, 1600–1601', *Archivum Historicum Societatis Iesu*, 24 (1955), 95–139.

Highley, Christopher, *Catholics Writing the Nation in Early Modern Britain and Ireland* (Oxford, 2008).

Holmes, Peter, 'The authorship and early reception of *A Conference About the Next Succession to the Crown of England*', *Historical Journal*, 23 (1980), 415–29.

——, *Resistance and Compromise: The Political Thought of the Elizabethan Catholics* (Cambridge, 1982).

Houliston, Victor, *Catholic Resistance in Elizabethan England: Robert Persons's Jesuit Polemic, 1580–1610* (Aldershot, 2007).

Hurstfield, Joel, 'The succession struggle in late Elizabethan England', in S. T. Bindoff, Joel Hurstfield and C. H. Williams (eds), *Elizabethan Government and Society: Essays Presented to Sir John Neale* (London, 1961), pp. 369–96, reprinted in his *Freedom, Corruption and Government in Elizabethan England* (London, 1973), pp. 104–34.

Ives, Eric, 'Tudor dynastic problems revisited', *Historical Research*, 81 (2008), 255–79.

James, Henry and Greg Walker, 'The politics of *Gorboduc*', *English Historical Review*, 110 (1995), 109–21.

Jenkins, Gladys, 'The archpriest controversy and the printers, 1601–3', *The*

Library, 5th series, 2: 2–3 (1948 for 1947), 180–6.

Jensen, De Lamar, 'The phantom will of Mary Queen of Scots', *Scotia*, 4 (1980), 1–15.

Jones, Norman and Paul Whitfield White, '*Gorboduc* and royal marriage politics: an Elizabethan playgoer's report of the premiere performance', *English Literary Renaissance*, 26 (1996), 3–17.

Kewes, Paulina, 'The exclusion crisis of 1553 and the Elizabethan succession', in Susan Doran and Thomas S. Freeman (eds), *Mary Tudor: Old and New Perspectives* (Basingstoke, 2011), pp. 49–61.

——, 'Henry Savile's Tacitus and the politics of Roman history in late Elizabethan England', *Huntington Library Quarterly*, 74 (2011), 515–51.

——, '"A fit memoriall for the times to come...": admonition and topical application in Mary Sidney's *Antonius* and Samuel Daniel's *Cleopatra*', *Review of English Studies*, 63 (2012), 243–64.

——, 'History plays and the royal succession', in Paulina Kewes, Ian W. Archer and Felicity Heal (eds), *The Oxford Handbook of Holinshed's Chronicles* (Oxford, 2013), pp. 493–509.

Knowles, Ronald, 'The political contexts of deposition and election in *Edward II*', *Medieval and Renaissance Drama in England*, 14 (2001), 105–21.

Kurland, Stuart M., '*Hamlet* and the Scottish succession?', *Studies in English Literature*, 34 (1994), 279–300.

Lake, Peter, 'The King, (the Queen) and the Jesuit: James Stuart's *True Law of Free Monarchies* in context/s', *Transactions of the Royal Historical Society*, 6th series, 14 (2004), 243–60.

——, '"The monarchical republic of Elizabeth I" revisited (by its victims) as a conspiracy', in Barry Coward and Julian Swann (eds), *Conspiracies and Conspiracy Theory in Early Modern Europe: From the Waldensians to the French Revolution* (Aldershot, 2004), pp. 87–111.

——, 'The monarchical republic of Queen Elizabeth I (and the fall of Archbishop Grindal) revisited', in John F. McDiarmid (ed.), *The Monarchical Republic of Early Modern England: Essays in Response to Patrick Collinson* (Aldershot, 2007), pp. 129–48.

—— and Michael Questier, 'Puritans, papists, and the "public sphere" in early modern England: The Edmund Campion affair in context', *Journal of Modern History*, 72 (2000), 587–627.

Lane, Robert, '"The sequence of posterity": Shakespeare's *King John* and the succession controversy', *Studies in Philology*, 92 (1995), 460–81.

Law, T. G., 'The Spanish blanks and Catholic earls, 1592–94', in T. G. Law,

Collected Essays and Reviews, ed. P. Hume Brown (Edinburgh, 1904), pp. 244–76.

Levack, Brian, 'Towards a more perfect union: England, Scotland and the constitution', in Barbara P. Malament (ed.), *After the Refomation* (Manchester, 1980), pp. 57–74.

Levine, Mortimer, 'A "letter" on the Elizabethan succession question, 1566', *Huntington Library Quarterly*, 19 (1955), 13–38.

——, *The Early Elizabethan Succession Question, 1558–1568* (Stanford, CA, 1966).

——, *Tudor Dynastic Problems, 1460–1571* (London, 1973).

Lockie, D. M., 'The political career of the Bishop of Ross, 1568–80: the background to a contemporary life of Mary Stuart', *University of Birmingham Historical Journal*, 4/2 (1954), 98–145.

Loomie, Albert J., SJ, *The Spanish Elizabethans: The English Exiles at the Court of Philip II* (New York, 1963).

——, 'Philip III and the Stuart succession in England, 1600–1603', *Revue Belge de Philologie et d'Histoire*, 43 (1965), 492–514.

——, 'The Armadas and the Catholics of England', *Catholic Historical Review*, 59 (1973), 394–8.

——, 'Philip II's Armada proclamation of 1597', *Recusant History*, 12 (1974), 216–25.

Lowers, James K., *Mirrors for Rebels: A Study of Polemical Literature relating to the Northern Rebellion, 1569* (Berkeley and Los Angeles, CA, 1953).

Lyell, James P. R., 'A tract on James VI's succession to the English throne', *English Historical Review*, 51 (1936), 289–301.

Lynch, Michael, 'The reassertion of princely power in Scotland: the reigns of Mary Queen of Scots and King James VI', in Martin Gosman, Alasdair A. MacDonald and Arie Johan Vanderjagt (eds), *Princes and Princely Culture, 1450–1650* (Leiden, 2003), vol. I, pp. 199–238.

McCabe, Richard A., 'The masks of Duessa: Spenser, Mary Queen of Scots, and James VI', *English Literary Renaissance*, 17 (1987), 224–42.

MacCaffrey, Wallace T., *Elizabeth I: War and Politics, 1588–1603* (Princeton, NJ, 1992).

McCoog, Thomas M., SJ, *The Society of Jesus in Ireland, Scotland, and England, 1541–1588:'Our Way of Proceeding?'* (Leiden, 1996).

——, '"Pray to the Lord of the Harvest": Jesuit missions to Scotland in the sixteenth century', *Innes Review*, 53 (2002), 127–88.

——, 'Harmony disrupted: Robert Parsons, SJ, William Crichton, SJ and the question of Queen Elizabeth's successor, 1581–1603', *Archivum Historicum Societatis Iesu*, 73 (2004), 149–220.

—— (ed.), *The Reckoned Expense: Edmund Campion and the Early English Jesuits*, 2nd edn (Rome, 2007).

——, *The Society of Jesus in Ireland, Scotland, and England: 1589–1597: Building the Faith of Saint Peter upon the King of Spain's Monarchy* (Farnham and Rome, 2012).

McDiarmaid, John F. (ed.), *The Monarchical Republic of Early Modern England: Essays in Response to Patrick Collinson* (Aldershot, 2007).

MacDonald, Alan R., 'The Parliament of 1592: a crisis averted?', in Keith M. Brown and Alastair J. Mann (eds), *The History of the Scottish Parliament, vol. 2. Parliament and Politics in Scotland 1567–1707* (Edinburgh, 2005), pp. 57–81.

McGinnis, P. J., and A. H. Williamson, 'Politics, prophecy, poetry: the Melvillian moment, 1589–96, and its aftermath', *Scottish Historical Review*, 89 (2010), 1–18.

McLaren, Anne, 'The quest for a king: gender, marriage, and succession in Elizabethan England', *Journal of British Studies*, 41 (2002), 259–90.

Manning, Roger, 'The prosecution of Sir Michael Blount, Lieutenant of the Tower of London, 1595', *Bulletin of the Institute of Historical Research*, 67 (1984), 216–24.

Martin, A. Lynn, *Henry III and the Jesuit Politicians* (Geneva, 1973).

Martin, Patrick, and John Finnis, 'The identity of "Anthony Rivers"', *Recusant History*, 26 (2002), 39–74.

—— and ——, 'The secret sharers: "Anthony Rivers" and the Appellant controversy, 1601–2', *Huntington Library Quarterly*, 69 (2006), 195–237.

Mason, Roger A., 'The Scottish Reformation and the origins of Anglo-British Imperialism', in his *Scots and Britons: Scottish Political Thought and the Union of 1603* (Cambridge, 1994), pp. 161–86.

——, 'Scotland, Elizabethan England, and the idea of Britain', *Transactions of the Royal Historical Society*, 14 (2004), 279–93.

——, 'Scotland', in Paulina Kewes, Ian W. Archer and Felicity Heal (eds), *The Oxford Handbook of Holinshed's Chronicles* (Oxford, 2013), pp. 648–62.

Mayer, Jean-Christophe (ed.), *The Succession Struggle in Late Elizabethan England: Politics, Polemics and Cultural Representations* (Montpellier, 2004).

——, *Shakespeare's Hybrid Faith: History, Religion, and the Stage* (Basingstoke,

2006).

Medina, Francisco De Borja, 'Intrigues of a Scottish Jesuit at the Spanish court: unpublished letters of William Crichton to Claudio Acquaviva (Madrid 1590–1592)', in Thomas M. McCoog, SJ (ed.), *The Reckoned Expense: Edmund Campion and the Early English Jesuits*, 2nd edn (Rome, 2007), pp. 277–325.

Meyer, A. O., *England and the Catholic Church under Queen Elizabeth* (with an Introduction by John Bossy) (London, 1967).

Milward, Peter, *Religious Controversies of the Elizabethan Age: A Survey of Printed Sources* (Ilkley, 1977).

Morgan, Hiram, 'Hugh O'Neill and the Nine Years War in Tudor Ireland', *Historical Journal*, 36 (1993), 21–37.

——, *Tyrone's Rebellion* (Woodbridge, 1999).

—— (ed.), *The Battle of Kinsale* (Bray, 2004).

Morrill, John, *'Uneasy Lies the Head that Wears a Crown': Dynastic Crises in Tudor and Stewart Britain 1504–1746*, The Stenton Lecture 2003 (Reading, 2005).

Murray, James, *Enforcing the English Reformation in Ireland: Clerical Resistance and Political Conflict in the Diocese of Dublin, 1536–1590* (Cambridge, 2009).

Neale, J. E., 'Peter Wentworth: II', *English Historical Review*, 39 (1924), 175–205.

——, *Elizabeth I and Her Parliaments*, 3 vols (London, 1953–58).

Nenner, Howard, *The Right to be King: The Succession to the Crown of England, 1603–1714* (Chapel Hill, NC, 1995).

Newton, Diana, *The Making of the Jacobean Regime: James VI and I and the Government of England, 1603–1605* (Woodbridge, 2005).

O'Connor, Thomas, 'Diplomatic preparations for Kinsale', in Enrique Garcia Hernán *et al*, (eds), *Irlanda y la Monarquia Hispánica: Kinsale 1601–2001 – Guerra, Politica, Exilio y Religion* (Madrid, 2002), pp. 137–150.

——, 'A justification for foreign intervention in early-modern Ireland', in T. O'Connor and Mary Ann Lyons (eds), *Irish Migrants in Europe after Kinsale, 1602–1820* (Dublin, 2003), pp. 14–31.

—— and M. Lyons (eds), *The Ulster Earls and Baroque Europe* (Dublin, 2010).

Ó Siocrú, Michael, 'Foreign involvement in the revolt of Silken Thomas', in *Proceedings of the Royal Irish Academy*, Section C, 96C, no. 2 (1996), 49–66.

Parmelee, Lisa Ferraro, *Good Newes from Fraunce: French Anti-League Propaganda in Late Elizabethan England* (Rochester, NY, 1996).

Parmiter, Geoffrey De C., 'Edmund Plowden as advocate for Mary Queen of Scots: some remarks upon certain Elizabethan succession tracts', *The Innes Review*, 30 (1979), 35–53.

Parry, Glyn, *The Arch-conjuror of England: John Dee* (New Haven, CT, and London, 2011).

——, 'The monarchical republic and magic: William Cecil and the exclusion of Mary Queen of Scots', *Reformation*, 17 (2012), 29–47.

Phillips, James E., 'Buchanan and the Sidney circle', *Huntington Library Quarterly*, 12 (1948–49), 23–55.

——, *Images of a Queen: Mary Stuart in Sixteenth-Century Literature* (Berkeley, CA, 1964).

Pollen, J. H., *The Institution of the Archpriest Blackwell* (London, 1916).

Pritchard, Arnold, *Catholic Loyalism in Elizabethan England* (London, 1979).

Questier, Michael, 'The politics of religious conformity and the accession of James I', *Historical Research*, 71 (1998), 14–30.

——, *Catholicism and Community in Early Modern England: Politics, Aristocratic Patronage and Religion, c.1550–1640* (Cambridge, 2006).

Read, Conyers, 'William Cecil and Elizabethan public relations', in S. T. Bindoff *et al.* (eds), *Elizabethan Government and Society: Essays Presented to Sir John Neale* (London, 1961), pp. 21–55.

Richards, Judith M., 'The English accession of James VI: "national" identity, gender and the personal monarchy of England', *English Historical Review*, 117 (2002), 513–35.

Scarisbrick, J. J., 'Robert Persons' plans for the "true" reformation of England', in N. McKendrick (ed.), *Historical Perspectives: Studies in English Thought and Society in Honour of J. H. Plumb* (London, 1974), pp. 19–42.

Scott-Warren, Jason, 'Harington's gossip', in Susan Doran and Thomas S. Freeman (eds), *The Myth of Elizabeth*, (Basingstoke, 2003), pp. 221–41.

Shagan, Ethan H. (ed.), *Catholics and the 'Protestant Nation': Religious Politics and Identity in Early Modern England* (Manchester, 2005).

Shapiro, James, *1599: A Year in the Life of William Shakespeare* (London, 2005).

Shearman, Francis, 'The Spanish Blanks', *Innes Review*, 3 (1952), 81–103.

Sheehan, Anthony, 'The recusancy revolt of 1603: a reinterpretation', *Archivium Hibernicum*, 38 (1983), 3–13.

Silke, J. J., *Kinsale: The Spanish Intervention in Ireland at the End of the Elizabethan Wars* (Liverpool, 1970).

Smith, Victoria, 'The Elizabethan succession question in Roger Edwardes's "Castra Regia" (1569) and "Cista Pacis Anglie" (1576)', *Historical Research*, forthcoming.

Smuts, R. Malcolm, 'Organized Violence in the Elizabethan Monarchical Republic', *History*, forthcoming.

Stafford, Helen Georgia, *James VI of Scotland and the Throne of England* (New York and London, 1940).

Tallon, Alain, 'Henri IV and the Papacy after the League', in Alison Forrestal and Eric Nelson (eds), *Politics and Religion in Early Bourbon France* (Basingstoke, 2009), pp. 21–41.

Torre, Victoria de la, '"We few of an infinite multitude": John Hales, parliament, and the gendered politics of the early Elizabethan succession', *Albion*, 33 (2001), 557–82.

Tyacke, Nicholas, 'Puritan politicians and King James VI and I, 1587–1604', in Thomas Cogswell, Richard Cust, and Peter Lake (eds), *Politics, Religion and Popularity in Early Stuart Britain: Essays in Honour of Conrad Russell* (Cambridge, 2002), pp. 21–44.

Walsham, Alexandra, *Church Papists: Catholicism, Conformity and Confessional Polemic in Early Modern England* (Woodbridge, 1993).

Wernham, Richard B., *The Return of the Armadas: The Last Years of Elizabeth's War against Spain* (Oxford, 1994).

Wormald, Jenny, 'The creation of Britain: multiple kingdoms or core and colonies', *Transactions of the Royal Historical Society*, 6th series, 2 (1992), 175–94.

——, 'The union of 1603', in Roger A. Mason (ed.), *Scots and Britons: Scottish Political Thought and the Union of 1603* (Cambridge, 1994), pp. 17–40.

——, 'Ecclesiastical vitriol: the kirk, the puritans and the future king of England', in John Guy (ed.), *The Reign of Elizabeth I: Court and Culture in the Last Decade* (Cambridge, 1995), pp. 173–91.

——, 'O Brave New World? The union of England and Scotland in 1603', Joint British Academy/Royal Society of Edinburgh Special Lecture, 24 March 2003, British Academy Publications Online.

Yellowlees, Michael, *'So strange a monster as a Jesuite': The Society of Jesus in Sixteenth-Century Scotland* (Isle of Colonsay, 2003).

Younger, Neil, 'Securing the monarchical republic: the remaking of the lord lieutenancies in 1585', *Historical Research*, 84 (2010), 249–65.

Index

EU authorised representative for GPSR:
Easy Access System Europe, Mustamäe tee 50,
10621 Tallinn, Estonia
gpsr.requests@easproject.com

www.ingramcontent.com/pod-product-compliance
Ingram Content Group UK Ltd.
Pitfield, Milton Keynes, MK11 3LW, UK
UKHW041843150726

72141PUK00015B/133